PRISON CHEERLEADER

PRISON CHEERLEADER

How A Nice Jewish Girl Went Wrong
Doing Right

Arlene Peck

Copyright © 2009 by Arlene Peck.

ISBN: Hardcover 978-1-4363-4952-9
Softcover 978-1-4363-4951-2

All rights reserved. No part of this book may be reproduced or transmitted in any form or by any means, electronic or mechanical, including photocopying, recording, or by any information storage and retrieval system, without permission in writing from the copyright owner.

This is a work of fiction. Names, characters, places and incidents either are the product of the author's imagination or are used fictitiously, and any resemblance to any actual persons, living or dead, events, or locales is entirely coincidental.

This book was printed in the United States of America.

To order additional copies of this book, contact:
Xlibris Corporation
1-888-795-4274
www.Xlibris.com
Orders@Xlibris.com
46068

Contents

Foreword 7
Prologue 9
Preface 11

1	THE CASE OF THE MISSING TOMATO PLANTS 19
2	DAY OUT PROGRAM 40
3	MIKE THEVIS: PUBLIC ENEMY NUMBER ONE 47
4	BOBBY WILCOXSON: PRIDE OF THE F.B.I. 59
5	WILLIAM A.H. WILLIAMS: THE PATTY HEARST INFLUENCE LINGERS ON? 64
6	THE LADY OR THE TIGER? 77
7	THE WILSONS OR: BABY BROTHER AND THE BOSTON STRANGLER 100
8	PSYCHOLOGY, WITCHES AND ASTRAL PROJECTION 107
9	THE DAY THEY HAD OPEN HOUSE AT THE BIG HOUSE 122
10	THE DAY I WAS SET UP FOR THE FLIM FLAM 131
11	THE FRENCH CONNECTION WAS MORE THAN A MOVIE 137
12	THE NIGHT JULIAN BOND AND I BUSTED OUT OF PRISON 146
13	THE SHOCK OF RECOGNITION 165
14	THE ARCHBISHOP 173
15	THE INVESTIGATION 177
16	THE FOX PROTECTING THE HENHOUSE 188
17	THE TALK SHOW 198
18	NORMAN, THE BOMBER 206
19	STANLEY THE TOUCHER 216
20	I WAS A SPY FOR NATIONAL REPORTER 222
21	CONGRESSMEN HAVE FEELINGS, TOO! 229
22	ORGANIZED CRIME 232
23	THE THREAT ON MY LIFE 235

24	PRIME TIME: THE HIT MAN	253
25	THE FRENCH CONNECTION RETURNS	270
26	THE BUIIDING IS BAD!	279

Epilogue 289
Appendix I—The Letters 291
Appendix II—The Articles 308

Foreword

An aide de camp once asked Napoleon who he would get to guard the most vicious criminals in all of Europe at the new penal colony on Devils' Island. The Emperor is alleged to have responded: "Men more vicious than the criminals themselves."

The above response crystal clearly reflects the mental attitude that permeates the area of retributive Justice and, unfortunately, is not isolated to European countries. While it is true that the Atlanta Federal Penitentiary (the Big-A) cannot be compared to the nightmare existence that prevailed at Devils' Island, it is equally true that it does have many similarities. These similarities, however, have been somewhat mitigated by the concern of an amazing lady named Arlene Peck.

For more years than she would care to remember this dynamic lady has dedicated her time, energy, and money to creating what is now known as the Wednesday Evening Jewish Discussion Group—open to all men, regardless of their faith. Her efforts have become legendary throughout the Federal Bureau of Prisons and have been supported by a small but determined cadre of the local Jewish Community who have shown an unusually high degree of interest in their desire that the Jewish Discussion Group continue to function as a vehicle where the socially disenfranchised can gather and engage in intelligent and stimulating dialogues that cover the wide spectrum of everyday living. Inclusive are the insights given into Jewish history and religion, as well as an occasional glimpse into the penumbra area of the mystical Kabbalah as seen by our learned Rabbi guest speakers. To these beautiful human beings we, the outcasts of society, extend our heartfelt Shalom.

Readers who are not familiar with life behind the walls of the Big-A will find this book intriguing, fascinating and, hopefully, more than a little interesting. Those who are familiar will learn something new about their prior residence, which may have escaped their attention during the course of their stay.

Prison life is by its very nature an abnormal experience which compels the imprisoned to adopt abnormal standards in order to retain some semblance of sanity. In this artificially created environment, the weak and the strong tend to withdraw. Consequently, it becomes difficult for an outsider to penetrate the armor which we erect for our own self-preservation. For this very reason, it is a credit to Arlene Peck that throughout the many years of her program, she did manage to penetrate the hard exterior and get to the soft underbelly of us all. The rapidity of the prison population turnover afforded her the further benefit of exposure to a large segment of the men confined here. Admittedly, some of us initially attended the Jewish Discussion Group meetings solely to see the lovely ladies that Arlene Peck would invariably have among her guests. Being men deprived of female companionship we looked forward to speaking and sitting next to attractive members of the opposite sex. And the fact that most were pretty, intelligent, articulate and glamorous helped considerably. In any event, Arlene Peck's reputation, so to speak, became rapidly established amongst the prison population and her acceptance was a unique experience. Although she is an attractive and stunning woman she was considered by most of us as one of the guys, and nothing more. This is the highest tribute that she could receive from us.

The combination of Arlene Peck's exuberance and the natural reserve of the convicts stood in sharp contrast for a while. But her exuberance soon shattered the backbone of our reticence and the fondness grew rapidly. Thus, she has been able to write this book comprised as a series of vignettes based upon her personal experience over the years with the men in the Jewish Discussion Group. The book does not purport to deal with the complex problems facing the nation in the area of penology, but is instead a light and lively treatment of one woman's birds-eye view of a world reserved for men. What she saw and experienced in this world of varying perceptions we will leave to the readers' judgment. All that can be done has been done within the pages of this book and within the limitations of accessibility.

The Members of the Jewish Discussion Group.

Prologue

I wrote this in another life. In 1976, when I chaired the Jewish Discussion Group at the Atlanta Federal Penitentiary, I was a pot roast. That was before I discovered that I was chateaubriand.

I was married, my kids were in school, and I was 'looking for a cause.' When the offer came to be the only woman chairing a discussion group in that mysterious prison on the hill outside of Atlanta, I was definitely interested.

Had I known what I was getting myself into, I'm not sure I would have made the commitment. However, like a moth to a flame, I soon found myself 'hooked' by the intrigue and curiosity that I found on my weekly trips into 'the joint.'

Though just a small part in my book, looking back, I also realize that the guys in my group were among the nucleuses for the birth of the Muslim influence in our prison system. There were never more than a few Jewish inmates who came into the room that had been assigned to us. And those, I used to say, were products of mixed marriages. However, within a short time, many of the inmates who came into my group were wearing knitted caps and carrying the Koran. I didn't even know what a "Koran" was at the time. They told me that they belonged to a brotherhood called Nation of Islam. In those days, I was so naïve that I believed them to be a nice peaceful group. I felt that way because in those days, I had never even heard about Muslims. None of us had. In 1965, there were 6,000 Muslims in our country. However, these weren't "nice guys." the Atlanta Federal Penitentiary was a maximum security prison and these were the toughest men in the country. At the time, there were no Muslim Student Associations and most people were unaware of the Nation of Islam.

Looking back, I believe that this was one of the training camps for 'education' into this culture. These men, in the penal system, were learning about the Muslim culture and ensuing war. They were getting ready to spread the word when they were released. That was a period of incubation. And, like the rest of the country, then, and unfortunately now, I was oblivious to what was really happening. Islam literally had a captive audience of young black inmates. The chaplains had free reign to flow in and out of their "prayer sessions," teaching their version of Islam. And, when they were released, this growing group of radicals went out into the world spreading their doctrine.

Today, our prisons are doing the same, but their audience is growing by the thousands every month and it's being paid for by our tax dollars! And, during this time, the Saudis have invested our gas dollars to the tune of almost 100 billion dollars to bring down the government of America, via our own prison system!

As you continue to read, you will find yourself looking at an exposed Atlanta Federal Penitentiary not only for the corrupt business it really was, including the murders that took place there and the people that made it one of the most dangerous prison systems in our country and, eventually, led to the shutdown of the entire prison.

Preface

"Halt! Identify yourself and state your business." I looked around and noticed a little box on a stand near the front steps of the institution. From this box, a booming voice was issuing questions about the purpose of the visit and whom we were to see. Speaking to machines has always intimidated me and usually made me feel very insecure. It's difficult to feel that they really care about what you have to say. Meek I'm not, but at that moment I was. I felt stupid as hell standing on a foggy night on the front steps of the Penitentiary having a conversation with a faceless harsh voice coming from a box. Like an idiot, I stood there and tried to explain to the machine that we were visitors from the Bureau of Jewish Education and that was why we were trying to enter the institution.

For years I had driven past the Penitentiary without really paying attention. Oh, occasionally I'd tell my children, "See! That's where children who don't listen to their mothers end up!" It was just not the kind of place that I could visualize ever entering. When driving down Boulevard, one of the seamier streets in Atlanta, the Atlanta Federal Penitentiary, the massive city within a city, seems to rise like the Phoenix from the ashes. It sits on a hill, huge, grey and ominous. Driving into the entrance through big grey walls for the first time was an experience not soon to be forgotten. It was a foggy night. The atmosphere reminded me of a grim scene out of Edgar Allen Poe. Little bitty houses, spaced at regular intervals which were chiseled in granite are filled with tall guards with even taller guns. The effect is chilling.

If I'd only known what I was getting into when the call came in the winter of 1974 to be a volunteer for a program for Jewish prison inmates at the Atlanta Federal Penitentiary. The "Atlanta Arms" as it is lovingly referred to, is the graduate school of the penal system. No minor liquor store robberies or barroom brawls end up there. No sir. It is the biggie of them all. Visits into that place do not trigger the southern Jewish American Princess to become the Susan B. Anthony of the penal system.

In 1974, the initial request from the Bureau of Jewish Education was made to my husband to speak to the group. Occasionally, they would attempt to get a speaker from the outside community to visit and, when Howard was invited, it was as the master of the Jewish Masonic lodge. Since the Atlanta prison is a maximum security institution and highly restricted to outside involvement, my curiosity ran rampant and, he finally allowed me to tag along. The place held a perverse mysticism for me and this visit would be my ticket in to see what it was really like to visit a jail. It seemed almost inconceivable that Jewish inmates could be residing there. After all, our "chosen people" didn't commit crimes. Men that were incarcerated there just had to be the result of a mixed marriage. And of the few that did, what kind of men were they? What kind of crimes did they commit? I just had to know.

From the recording at the door, we were directed to another little booth stationed to the right of the front steps. A record was then played stating that visitors were not allowed to bring in contraband, whatever that was. After that we were allowed to proceed to the main door. With each hesitant step I made up the wide granite steps, thoughts began to enter my head as to the reasons why this could be a mistake.

Once inside, we were greeted by more guards and IRON BARS. To the left was a metal detector, just like at the airport, where a man was busy searching various visitor's bodies. Although this was the entrance room, the decor was lacking in cheerfulness and warmth as was furnished in 'early Howard Johnson' front desk. I will say one thing though, the marble floors were spotless. I wish I could get mine that clean. To the right of the entrance was a large bulletproof glass. Behind it was a switchboard with all kinds of phones and buttons. Although the halls were filled with activity, there was somehow a feeling of isolation and helplessness once I stepped inside the large main doors.

The left of the entrance waiting room was filled with sad eyed children with runny noses and sexy blondes in short skirts, popping gum and wearing K-Mart check-out hairdos. A buxom blonde was sitting next to me chewing a hang-nail and busily looking at pictures of Elvis in her worn out wallet. I wondered if the motorcycle parked at the front door belonged to her as she looked like the type of tough broad who not only didn't mind wearing a helmet, but could change the motorcycle's oil as well. Eventually, a guard who looked like an aging crew cut Marine, came to take us to the first gate. After checking over his list on the clip-board, he nodded to the guards behind the glass enclosure. Magically, the gate slid back, and before a chance for second thoughts, we were locked between two sets of iron bars. Within seconds, which felt like an eternity, another guard presented himself on the other side of the gate and the second ones slid back and we were allowed to enter. Men were peering at us from behind cell blocks and I was finding it difficult to act casual.

For some unexplainable reason I felt uncomfortable or rather embarrassed for them. There I was, watching them in their zoo-bars and all. And, yet, I felt an excitement of entering the unknown, and was finding the whole experience damn interesting. All along the walls were beautiful paintings that had been done by the prisoners. There were bright seas and landscapes that seemed so out of place in the surroundings. The new guard, who had been sent to escort us to the meeting room, could have passed as a twin for the aging marine that had escorted us in. His tie was knotted tightly and his eyes were mean. Because of my nervousness, I made a few half hearted attempts at conversation. His personality had as much charm as a letter from camp, and the remainder of the walk into the meeting room was made in silence. Finally, after climbing a flight of steps and being met by yet another sliding gate and guard, we were finally at the chapel-meeting room. There I met the men, who later were to be the beginning of 'Temple Yakkov' but were referred to by me as my 'Group'.

Curiosity had brought me there more than anything else. Howard's visit to talk to the inmates about the Masons was only my excuse to get inside the prison and see one for the first time. We sat in an empty room that echoed, while the men straggled by looking for a break in the boredom. They were really a motley crew. For a few awkward minutes we felt that 'Jack the Ripper' would come bursting in the door and use me as a hostage to break out of the joint. However, nothing so dramatic happened and eventually a half-dozen faces were sitting across from me. I was amazed; they looked just like real people: Far less menacing than those I had met recently at synagogue boards and other mixed gender meetings.

Howard told them about the Masons for a little while and when he had finished I looked at my watch and said to myself, "Oh God, now what? We still have two and a half hours to go." Apparently reading my thoughts, a dapper little man in the corner (who I was sure had to be in there for tax evasion), leaned towards me and said, "I know that I speak for the rest of the men when I say that you have no idea how much people like you coming in here are able to cheer us up. While you're here, maybe you'd like to hear a little bit about what we really need in here."

I wasn't sure I really wanted to know but to be polite I answered, "Well, sure, yeah, if you want . . ."

That's all it took. For the next two and a half hours all of them began to open up and tell us about the need for a regular educational program that would be geared along Jewish cultural lines. One would open up with, "Yeah, hey, what we need in here is people from the outside to come in and keep us abreast of the current events in general. Bring in people that know about the Mid-East situation and Israel and tell us what's going on out there."

Another chimed in, "Well, I was never too Jewish on the outside. What I'd really like is to have some rabbis or somebody come out here and teach me what a Jew really is. I never learned too much about Jewish holidays, ya know, customs, tradition, all that stuff."

Another beefy inmate, chewing on a nasty cigar, wearing a torn undershirt and chinos snickered, "He's right, we got the time, teach us. Frankly, I wouldn't mind learning what a beautiful girl looks like. Think you can get us a good looking teacher to teach us all this stuff?"

I didn't want to promise too much, especially since I wasn't sure the promises could be kept, but it was sort of touching. The feeling without exception was that these men wanted to feel that there was a link to a caring Jewish community outside.

As we were walking out, I looked at Howard and said, "Hey, what do you think? Let's go back again, huh?"

He looked at me incredulously and said, "God, why in the hell would you want to?"

"I don't know." I said, "I just kinda think that we're needed in there."

Howard shook his head and wagged a finger at me.

"Maybe you, not me. I'm out there breaking my back. Whoever's in there is probably in there for a good reason. They deserve whatever they get. The last thing I need on my agenda is to go out and visit the inmates. You want to go back? Great, but not with me."

We were half way home before I realized this time I hadn't noticed the men who were peering at us along the passage to the outside. I was too busy into my thoughts of the impressions with which I had left. Contrary to what my previously held beliefs might have been, the men were gentlemanly and so appreciative of the visit that we actually enjoyed the evening. We had a more captive audience.

Within a few weeks after the initial visit, the prison became my special project. The sponsor of the program, the 'Bureau of Jewish Education', promised me they'd notify the men or have the chaplain post up a notice in the bulletin that would be coming out the next week.

"Mrs. Peck, the authorities here have given us this room now from 6-9 p.m. every Wednesday. Before you came we had a little unofficial meeting here and the group decided to draft a charter. We chose a name. We're gonna be 'Temple Yakkov'. Is that OK with you? You gonna be able to come out here and handle this force?"

Well, I looked around at the expectant, hesitant faces that were sitting there and decided immediately, this is not the group that I wanted to get angry or disappoint. I was a little bit worried about this meeting every week business, but decided silently, "Oh what the hell." The commitment was made; now I had to see about doing something to follow through. I felt after even the first week that I wouldn't be able to handle it alone. I knew that the degree of success of the program would depend upon the kind of people I'd be able to bring. Who were they going to be? This was different from the Walt Disney life that I had led. Maybe its initial success was because it began as a cocktail party concept. I wanted 'good mixers' who would make the party interesting.

I have an old saying, "You don't know people until you carpool with them." This was doubly true with the prison program. It was difficult to find people to go into the prison with me. Most of the women I would ask had a far different attitude than the men. The men were for some reason resentful of the inmates. Either I'd be told, "Arlene, I'd like to help you out but I've got better things to do with, my time. I work all week trying to earn a living and I just can't see going into a prison on my free time to entertain a bunch of criminals."

Or sometimes I'd get, "Thanks for the invite but to tell you the truth I can't go into a place like that for six hours without getting claustrophobia. How do some of those guys stand it for years?"

Of those that agreed to come, some seemed to feel guilty enough to think that they wouldn't be let out when the evening was over. Worse than the fearful participants, were those who attended strictly for ego tripping purposes. The paths to presidencies of organizations are paved with names of those who list such 'good works' among their social volunteer causes. Then there are those who like to go to cocktail parties and add a little spice to their conversations by dropping the names of the bank robbers, mafia chieftains, and kidnappers who were suddenly their acquaintances. Rabbis would be brought in and usually I tried to throw in a couple of pretty girls to give the men something nice to look at. My circle of friends ranged from senators to talk-show hosts, so before long, experts from different, interesting professions were common visitors. As long as their attitudes were not ones of 'freak show' curiosity, guests were welcome. As word got around, and it did, among the inmates about the caliber of visitors, the number of men who attended weekly began to grow. The format remained informal, casual and usually we sat in a circle and 'rapped'. Everybody had a story, and these were incredible. Men that we had only known on the front pages became interesting and articulate individuals once we began to know them through the Wednesday evening discussion group.

Being basically such a law and order person, it took me a long time to realize just how needed the program was. In the beginning it might have been only to live a little vicariously through the lives of people whom I considered had led more exciting lives than I had at the time. My kids were small. The life revolving around me was little more than potty training and carpools. Organization meetings were beginning to bore the hell out of me. In fact, everything was. Suddenly, Wednesday evening became a world of excitement. It was nice, even, to meet people whose lives were even more boring than mine; who were not only interested in what I had to say, but in their own way, were living vicariously through the things I had to tell them about life on the 'outside'.

Looking back, I'm sure that my basic motives at first were little more than an attempt to spice up my conventional existence. If I had realized in the beginning how needed my program was, it probably would have been detrimental. Pressure was not something that I was seeking and had I felt them, they would have carried into the visits with the men. Somehow, it was a 'spontaneous element' that the men responded to. Whatever it was, 'clicked,' and as time passed, the men and their guests thrived on our 'Wonderful Wednesdays'. No, it was a kick, the whole idea of what I was doing delighted me for no other reason except that it was fun.

Time passed and I began to settle down. I began to notice that one of the reasons the men were responsive was not because they considered me a gorgeous, irresistible creature, but something was lacking in that place that a kind word seemed to help.

Things were going along fine at first. Prison authorities had no restrictions on the quality and number of guests. I merely had to bring a "Jewish program to the institution." Under the auspices of the Jewish Discussion Group, I brought in literature, prayer books, magazines, even Playboy slipped itself in. And surprisingly the men loved my Saks Fifth Avenue and Lord and Taylor catalogues which helped them catch up on the latest styles that were being worn on the outside. It was rarely the materials that I brought into the prison that was an issue, it was the speakers, such as Julian Bond. As more and more political and media people started to get on the visitor's list, there was a gradual, almost imperceptible change in the attitude of the warden and his personnel. It wasn't overt, but, there were subtle differences between me and the prison staff. It was as though I had come in a poor fourth in a Sarah Semitic contest and the anti-Semitic attitude was lurking. The priest, warden and his cohorts had a way of looking at me as though they were still in cahoots with the Gestapo and at any time would trigger a secret signal from Argentina and make them come after me with the dogs.

Neither the Bureau of Jewish Education nor myself were aware of the restrictions on women entering the institution. I really believe that it was months before anyone of authority realized that I was there and what I was supposed to be doing. Actually, I don't even think I knew why I was there and what I was supposed to be doing. Gradually I began to see the need for changes and much like a decorator looking at a room with an eye for making improvements, I began a campaign to change the Atlanta Prison System to be what I considered more compatible for everybody. Unfortunately, the men who ran the Atlanta Prison System did not agree.

By then, our program-making was too far entrenched into the lives of the men to make our removal a simple thing.

By the spring of 1975, when the numbers of Temple Yakkov began to reach between fifty and sixty men, efforts were being made by the prison officials to cut down the number. Restrictions were placed upon the number of guests whom we could bring in, their sex, and their ethnic background. For a while I was taking it personally that only my men were getting the special discrimination with these special restrictions. Nobody else had to go through this; not the Odd fellows, of which there were plenty, the Salvation Army or any of the other groups. Once, one of the guys laughed and said, "I really think they pulled a hell of a blunder when they let you in." He was probably right. I was more than likely a clerical mistake. Some nonentity along the way probably stamped the request that I chair a program and they didn't know how to get rid of me once they discovered that I might possibly be able to bring some real aggravation into their bland lives. To ban me initially, once I was entering the institution through the Bureau of Jewish Education, would be a direct insult to the Jewish community and they weren't ready for that.

In 1975, I was still new enough to the program to be extremely gullible and I entered the institution believing that we were all in 'prison reform' together. In fact, it took a long time to get to the point that I was even interested in what went on in the nation's prisons. Where I was coming from during this time were society parties and organization chairmanships. They had begun to bore the hell out of me and I was getting apprehensive that my life was turning into what I deplored in many of my friends. Life had to be more than lunch and tennis dates, watching your nails grow and extramarital affairs. The challenge was intriguing. I could be the first female into the institution with a regular program. And, if it happened along the way, the first female to bring in some needed changes into that place: to see that the men got what they had been guaranteed by law. But what they told me was that they were being deprived of was religious rights. Good, so much the better. I couldn't even explain to myself what made me take a position so alien to my image except that I saw myself sinking into times ahead of absolute boredom and heading a program at a maximum security federal prison would be anything but. The Atlanta Institution is the all-time biggie. It was the big daddy of the penal system. The maximum security prison of them all.

This was long before I saw how the prison system nourishes itself. The prison administration itself conquers the inmates by dividing them. Any program that unites or attempts to unite these men represents a real threat. Somewhere in the back of my head was the idea of being the 'number one' female to enter the place and make some changes. The idea appealed to me immensely to bug a few of the officials the men had been telling me were blatantly anti-Semitic. I had nothing to lose, so why not? Besides, I found it really gross that those who run the system don't want the men to have a unity, or a link with the outside world. They, for reasons that I still don't fully understand, would rather have the men fighting in the cell-block, rather than relating to each other and 'civilians', the 'civilians' from the outside, were dangerous to the"system". The public, the politicians and the media are specifically discouraged from entering because of administrative fear of discovery of the waste of tax dollars through corruption. But, this is hindsight. At the time it was difficult to understand any possible hassles could surface.

Chapter One

THE CASE OF THE MISSING TOMATO PLANTS

Taking any uncleared items into those big, gray walls is definitely taboo. I first discovered this early the following year, when I was called down to the warden's office. I had brought fresh-baked honey cakes for the guards at the entrance gate. When I was a girl, my mother used to tell me that if you go to someone's home to visit, you should take a little gift. With her words in mind, I took the guards some "home cooking" so that they would see what they were making the men in my 'Group' miss. (I'll admit, sometimes my logic leaves something to be desired.) The guards loved them, but such hostility from the warden. Such an angry voice on the phone, "Mrs. Peck, this is Warden Pagen I think that you had better come down here ... immediately, so that we might have a little discussion: It has come to my attention that you have been bribing certain guards."

"WH-AT"

"Yes, Mrs. Peck. It has come to my attention that you have been making efforts to familiarize yourself with certain guards and bribing them each week when you enter with various ethnic foods that you have attempted to bring into the institution. Mrs. Peck, do you realize that because of your actions, the prison could have had a break and it would have been your fault."

Somehow, the logic in this was nonexistent and I said as much.

"Mrs. Peck," he continued, "suppose the guards became used to the cakes and breads that you bring in?"

"So", I asked, "how bad could that be?"

He pondered this for a few seconds and then said, "Ah, but if they got used to it, and then one night someone else came up to the front desk with a cake, a cake laced with sleeping powder, and told the guards, 'Mrs. Peck sent this for you.' The men then proceed to eat it and fall asleep. The officers then would have the vital front doors unguarded, and a prison break could erupt."

I found it hard to believe that all this could happen from my honey cake. The strudel, but not the honey.

Taking anything into the 'granite city' is frowned upon. The officials look on everything as 'contraband', and often rightly so. People have been known to smuggle unbelievable things, from Hustler to metal files inside, in such innocent looking articles as cakes. Even a stick of gum is a danger because it can be used to screw up the locks. If arrangements are made ahead however, books and religious articles can be brought in.

Warden Pagen, the first of many officials with whom I was to lock horns, fit the image of a warden exactly. The man looked just like Broderick Crawford. The amazing thing about wardens in general is the fact that in order to be one, one has to have a high school education. That's it, a high school education. No background in social work, administrative training, nothing. He could have been a plumber before and still ended up a warden. In fact, I have yet to figure out what would make a man want to be even a prison guard. After all, it is a bit unusual. Perhaps the feeling of power? Could it have begun as a child when he placed his pet turtle in a box?

The Jewish inmates of the Atlanta Penitentiary, and most others around the nation only represent less than one percent of the inmate population. For the fifteen or twenty Jewish inmates that are there, the authorities feel that it doesn't pay for the prison system to maintain a resident rabbi. The Protestant Chaplain and the Catholic Priest act as the clearing house for the religious programs. I was starting to waver in my beliefs about law and order by the summer of 1975, but still very much of a novice concerning 'organized religion'. The inmates despised this priest and I discounted all their efforts to warn me that he was a snake. Possibly the biggest complaint against him was the fact that rather than being hired by the diocese, he is on the payroll of the Bureau of Prisons and considered very much of a 'hack'. It was possibly because of this that all of his 'good Catholics' were attending the Jewish group and it was quite embarrassing to him.

The first time that an actual set-up occurred was over the tomato plant incident. It was the end of the spring of 1975 when I received a call from a friend who worked in one of the local plant nurseries. He offered me, without charge, seventy tomato plants to take to the group. Now, at that price, if they never used them, it's still a bargain, so I called the priest and cleared them. His exact words were, "Fine, Mrs. Peck, you bring them on in and I'll carry them up for you."

Wednesday arrived, and I caravanned up there with three guards and a priest behind me. We had our arms loaded, carrying up seven trays of plants, and I delivered my presents to the group. What did I know? Nobody had ever told me that nothing like that had ever happened in a federal institution, so I failed to understand why the Warden was upset by my actions AGAIN. Although the men were delighted with my surprise, the warden was less than thrilled. About carpool time the next day, around 3:00 P.M., I received a call from Warden Pagen.

"Mrs. Peck This is WARDEN PAGEN. I want you to come up here immediately and pick up these plants that you brought into my institution. I will set up an appointment with you now and I wish to discuss with you your continuing actions about the Atlanta Federal Penitentiary."

The man sounded actually, hysterical. Now, I don't know what wardens have to do in mid-afternoon, but I looked over at the clock and saw that it was almost four o'clock and time for my kids to return home from school. Rather than fight the afternoon traffic, I said, "Oh, that's O.K. warden honey, you can have them and start a garden if you want."

With that his voice started to sound choked, "Mrs. Peck: What possessed you to bring tomato plants into a maximum security federal penitentiary?"

I told him, "Well, Warden, when I was a young girl, I was taken to see the movie, Bird Man of Alcatraz. It made a very big impression on me. I knew that you probably wouldn't allow me to bring in any pets but, maybe ya'll might allow a little plant? What could hurt?"

The man actually sputtered to me for five full minutes about what a 'double homosexual' he was (the Bird Man, not the Warden.) I still haven't figured that one out. Anyhow, he ended the conversation on a note of hostility, telling me that I was never to do anything like that again, and I was on borrowed time with my visits.

Hogan may have appeared to be hostile in his attitude to me, but this was the first realization that hit me that the men running our institutions were idiots, absolute idiots that have a 'God image' of themselves whereby they can summon anyone of their choosing by the mere snap of their fingers.

Looking on the brighter side, I thought the incident funny. 'I', a college graduate, had to contend with the mentality of a fourth grade drop out who could summon me at will, and I had to go. It was starting to get to me because somewhere in the recesses of my mind I was still thinking of myself as a taxpayer and the prison employees as 'civil servants' who's salary was paid by my taxes. I couldn't have been further wrong. They know, without a shadow of a doubt, that it is virtually impossible to fire any of the incompetents from their jobs.

Shortly after this 'incident', I went on a trip to the USSR. The purpose of the trip was to visit with the Soviet Dissidents. I wrote a series of articles on Russia relating how I smuggled prayer books and Jewish religious articles into the synagogues in Moscow and Leningrad.

Immediately after my return, I received a letter in the mail on very official stationary. It was from the warden's office, and the gist of which was that my presence was no longer welcome. Now this was a switch. Here's a place where everyone is fighting to get out and all of a sudden I find myself in the position where I'm having to fight my way in. It was an embarrassment to tell my children that mommy was barred from a prison. I called Georgia Congressman Elliot Levitas. Congressman Levitas contacted the Director of the Bureau of Prisons in Washington, Norman Carson. Magically, another letter of re-admittance arrived. Our friendly local warden never actually came out and said that I was a drug smuggler, but word came back to me that "Mrs. Peck was caught bringing plants into a Federal Prison." Now, I wouldn't know a marijuana plant if it were growing on my patio, but the warden had it sound as though I had been caught with my hands in the LSD jar. Considering I had three guards and a PRIEST, for heaven's sake, carrying up all those trays, I failed to see the logic about my smuggling. Why would I hide marijuana contraband in seventy tomato plants? After several letters back and forth to Congressman Levitas, the immediate confrontation was solved. Somehow, I believed it was because the "Big Warden in Washington" called down and asked Hogan, "What are you doing down in Georgia? Some little old lady down there is writing congressmen and senators about how our prison system is harassing free religion and especially Jewish programs." This is not the kind of image that they liked to portray to the public, and as a result I believe, it was with much reluctance that I was allowed back in. Warden Pagen, for sure, would never forget that I'd gone over his head. A few nights later I bumped into Warden Pagen at the entrance. He couldn't resist making a final comment about the Russian articles that were currently running in the paper.

"Why hello Mrs. Peck. I see that you seem to smuggle wherever you go? From your columns, it appears that you spent quite a bit of time doing some other smuggling during your trip to Russia".

Just as sweetly, I gave a big smile, and said, "Why Warden honey, do you mean to tell me that you are comparing the discrimination that I found against the Jews in the Soviet Union with the conditions that you have here at our local federal prison for our Jewish inmates?"

Broderick Crawford narrowed his eyes to slits and before he stalked off said, "No Mrs. Peck. That is not what I meant."

Our relationship did not go uphill from there. Three months of relative tranquility transpired. Once again, the men tried to warn me that this brief period was the "calm before the storm" and our guard should never be let down as to the real intentions concerning the Atlanta Prison officials and the continuation of our, by now, quite successful program.

The Passover Seder in early Spring is one holiday of the year that the group really looked forward to. Passover celebrates the sparing of the Hebrews in Egypt when God destroyed the first-born of the Egyptians. Passover lasts eight days; the dinner ceremony is held on the first two nights.

Our group was allowed one night. It's the one time of year that the group had a chance to show its appreciation to the outside people who had come in for weekly visits.

Now, I don't care if the inmate is locked up or not, there are certain privileges that I think everyone should be entitled to and religion is one of them. Every year, without fail, the administration would come up with a sudden crisis where for one reason or another, the men would not be able to have their yearly Seder. Passover of 1976 was approaching. The men were receiving indications from staff that the usual obstacles were going to be placed. Nothing specific, but little comments began to be dropped that budgets were tight. The group now numbered sixty-five men who regularly visited the Wednesday evening discussion and since only fifteen were actually Jewish, special meals could not be prepared for them. The messages were relayed back to me. As a result it was no surprise when a call came from the Asst. Warden's office that he and the prison priest would like to see me ... immediately! It was always immediately.

In a pouring rainstorm I drove down to the institution and arrived as scheduled. A guard ushered me into a little anteroom, where I was kept waiting for over an hour for Assistant Warden Watkowski and the priest. At last, they both came in looking very serious and after clearing their throats Assistant Warden Watkowski began to shuffle papers on his desk. I noticed his hands at that moment and saw that they were as soft as a baby's tushie and twice as pudgy. He struck me as a man who secretly wore black jockey-shorts and had a closet stocked with whips and chains. After a few minutes he stopped shuffling and began to tell me about the lack of budget for religious meals. They were not going to get away with what they were trying to pull! The men were guaranteed this meal in the Bureau of Prison's rulebook!

"Warden, if you have no budget for religious meals, then what about Christmas and Easter? I know that the men eat pretty well on those occasions, and I thought that those were religious holidays."

Without blinking, yet exchanging looks with the priest, the Assistant Warden leaned back in his chair, took off his horned-rimmed glasses in order to avoid looking at me and said, "Well, ahem, eh, Mrs. Peck, you see, those aren't religious meals, those are ... eh ... ah ... social holidays."

Now it was my turn. I took off my photo lens glasses so that I could give him the full benefit of my incredulous stare and said, "Father, surely I didn't hear right. Christmas and Easter are social holidays, and therefore the men are entitled to fancy dinners? But Passover Seder comes under this non-existent religious budget?

"That's right Mrs. Peck, so you see that's why we have to charge quite a bit of money to the men and the outside guests to cover the cost of this dinner."

"No, Mr. Watkowski, I don't see. All I see is that besides being contrary to the Bureau of Prisons Rules and Regulations book, it's a little strange that the authorities won't let me see the order for this 'new rule' from Washington in writing."

He pushed his thick glasses back up over his nose that was also pudgy and stiffly said, "Well, I'm sorry, that's just the way it is . . . rules are rules and I don't have the power to change them."

With those last words of wisdom, the meeting was over and I was escorted out. The men would ultimately be charged outrageous prices for the 'right' to have the dinner that was guaranteed to them, by law, to be without charge. Until then, I had been taking the little obstacles personally. This wasn't a personal matter against me. It concerned all the men in the group and the first in the growing list of discriminatory incidents that four years later culminated in a United States Senate crime investigation.

Despite the hassles of having it, the Passover Seder was really an all time unforgettable fun evening. The actual foods used in a Passover Seder are basic, but before the meal is served several symbolic foods are tasted, one of which consists of a roasted shank bone. This item serves to remind us of the sacrifices that were once made in the temple in Jerusalem on a number of holidays. There are matzos, which are unleavened bread to symbolize that the Jews had to leave Egypt in such a hurry that they could not even wait for the dough of their bread to rise. And lastly, some bitter herbs in the form of horse-radish, parsley and 'haroses', which was a mixture of apples, almonds and raisins finely chopped and flavored with cinnamon and wine. The non-Jewish cooks within the prison didn't have the slightest idea how to prepare these symbolic foods, so the priest called and asked me to make the 'haroses'. A little of this mixture goes a long way, and no more than a teaspoon is spread on the matzos. However, I counted on the priest not knowing any of this, nor about any of the ingredients used, especially that one soak apples in wine in large glass containers a week ahead of time. I fermented enough for six hundred instead of sixty-five; when it was time to bring it to the institution, the fumes would hit you ten feet away. I made the only 'haroses' that I have ever known that could actually be drunk.

Before heading over to the prison, a stop-over was made at the Atlanta Jewish Welfare office to pick up a few posters to brighten up the room because the prison dining room is very drab and tacky. That year I picked up fifty posters showing of hands that were clasped and wearing chains. On the caption, "Let our people go!", compliments of Soviet Jewry. The men loved the touches and thought the messages very profound! Since I had so much to transport, I'd try to get there a few minutes early in order to get help carrying everything from the car.

I arrived early and out of breath in the waiting room and grabbed a seat between a kid with a Mars Bar and a well-endowed woman clad in a Fredric's of Hollywood bra. Eventually, the rest of the guests arrived, and we were escorted down those long, marble, always clean floors to the end of the hall. On both sides were doors with bars where men were staring at us. Then a maze of hallways and doors led us to a separate building where we were going to have the meal.

The men were already there. I have noticed that the inmates were so grateful when given a chance to prove it. I wish my husband, just once, would push my chair in at home like they did at dinner.

After a lovely service, the men brought out the main meal. It always felt a little weird to see men who, at home, were big Mafia chieftains or whatever, now acting as waiters to the inmates and guests. During the dinner another myth about prison life was dispelled for me: the dinner was delicious! I'm like Will Rogers, I have never met a meal I didn't like, especially if I didn't have to cook it.

The burly man sitting next to me at the table was really very nice, only he looked as though a Mack truck had run over his face. His entire face was beaten up and bruised. I wanted to ask him what happened, but I thought better of it. One doesn't ask questions like that in such surroundings but I did ask why he was in there and was told, "They say I robbed 29 banks, but I was framed". It could happen? Later I found out that he had just had a face-lift a few days before. Through his puffy eyes he leaned forward and looked me in mine, "Yeah, my goil fren ain't gonna recognize me when I get outta here. I don't look nothin like the pictures I took when I came in. My whole profile is different now. What do ya think?"

I started to say thank God, as he didn't look too good at the moment. The men say you could die from lack of attention from a cold there, but face-lifts and hair transplants are plentiful. Imagine going into prison for twenty years and coming out looking younger than when you went in. I asked him to send me the surgeon's name.

My other dinner partner was a nice-looking guy in his thirties named Tony. Maybe nice-looking isn't the right term. He was sexy in a 1950's kind of way. Remember the type? With the duck-tail haircut that was encrusted with Vitalis with the black leather jacket with the collar up? He reminded me of one of the fellows who in fifteen seconds could unhook a girl's bra with one hand and never have her know, until it was too late. Today in our braless society he would probably be lost. He was the kind of guy of whom all mothers would say, "Don't let me ever catch you going out with that bum."

I asked how did he get to be Jewish with a name like Tony and he said, "Jeez, Italy is a country and Jewish is a religion. Don't you know nuttin?"

He gulped through his meal as though he expected that any moment someone would remove his plate. It was only when he seemed to be filled and had pushed the remainder of his food aside that he turned toward me and made any real attempt at conversation. He leaned back in his chair, nonchalantly crossed his arms while secretly watching to see if I had noticed that he was flexing his ample muscles. After he was sure that he had caught my attention, he slowly removed the toothpick from his mouth, and said, "You know, I don't really belong in here."

"Sure you don't."

"Naw, I ain't kidden, it was that broad that I was married to that pushed me in here. She couldn't have enough. Gimme, gimme, gimme. You married?"

"Very."

He switched the toothpick to the other side and gave me a well-practiced one-sided smile and said, "Yeah, all you married broads are alike. Slippin out on the old man when you think he ain't looking. My old lady used to sleep all morning, hit the cocktail lounges till dinner time, then run home so's I shouldn't find out about her screwing around."

I hated to disappoint him. For a moment I was tempted to say, "hooker" when he asked if I did any kind of outside the house work. Because of the wonderful relationship that Tony and his wife must have enjoyed, the man was convinced that all American womanhood did was sleep until noon, then have cocktail time until dinner, all the while waiting for her fingernails to grow. During those years, my kids were so young and life so regulated with children's activities that a trip to the bathroom was rarely alone. Good heavens! Where would I have found the time, opportunity, or energy if I had had the inclination?

When I told him my husband sold real estate, his ears picked up. He mentioned that he had a friend with a lot of Costa Rican money to invest. Actually, I think that's where he had hidden his loot.

My third dinner partner at the table was a very talented artist who reminded me of the Pillsbury Doughboy with the mumps. He was pale and white-looking from all that inside painting. The texture of his skin looked squishy. He wore his hair in the 'wet head' style, and he had a round little face that resembled an eager chipmunk. He looked like his name, Bertrand.

We had spoken before, during the discussion evenings. I remembered him as being absolutely bonkers about the Freemasons. When I mentioned to him that my husband had once been the 'Worshipful Grand Master', Bertrand began to send letters to him that were filled with strange Masonic talk. Each time that Howard would receive one of his letters he'd read it, re-read it and shake his head. Worshipful one or not, Howard did not understand one word that this guy wrote. Later, I was to realize that Bert wanted to be a Mason in the worst way. but because the Masons wouldn't allow a convicted felon to become a member, he made up his secret code and pretended that he was really in the lodge and knew all the secret language. Months after our dinner, I was in the Mason's Scottish Rite Hospital and, at several of the elevators noticed lovely landscapes with Bertrand's signature. He had donated them to the hospital. Besides being a strange individual, Bertrand really was sweet, and delighted in telling the story of his incarceration.

It seems he had ended up there thirteen years ago for 'borrowing' a military payroll. He'd never gotten around to returning it. Since he had a bit of time on his hands, he had decided to take up painting. He loved to discuss art and how he got away with his crimes, although not necessarily in that order. His luck was a little better than one of the other guys who managed to hide his haul, moments before he was caught. He thought he was home free, but while he was in prison serving his time, a high-rise office building was built on top of it.

Bertrand received his parole shortly after the Seder. Upon his release he found a lawyer and sued the military for back pay. Somehow, they had neglected to discharge him, and he won an Eighty-Seven Thousand Dollar judgment from the United States Government, compliments of our taxes. Not long after, Bert sent me a post card from some place in Tennessee, saying that he had married, had a successful art gallery and was making a fortune in antiques. Who says that crime doesn't pay?

I think my favorite part of the evening was when one of our local dentists, from the outside, sat down and looked over at his dinner partner, who happened to be Norman the Bomber. All through dinner he kept peering over at Norman with the 'Don't I know you from somewhere look?' All of a sudden the dentist choked, spilled his grape juice and cried out, "My God, no wonder you weren't at the class reunion."

In fact, it happens more often than not that the visitors know the visited. It proves a point about what a small world it is and "there, but for the grace of God go a lot of us." That evening, I had in the Group one doctor, a pharmacist, a psychotherapist, a manufacturer of corrugated boxes, and a porno king. These were the inmates, not the guests.

It was a lovely and enlightening Passover Seder. Rabbi Gils, who conducted the service, was a young articulate guy who was able to convey to everyone that there is a marvelous sense of the meaning to the Seder and to the Passover. Rabbi Gils left the men with the feeling that they had celebrated something that was religious, spiritual, and yet a physical freedom, something not too easily achieved in that place.

The notion of 'physical freedom' can lead to excesses. The evening of the prison Seder was the third night of the Passover holiday. Passover Seders are traditionally given only on the first two nights: but, the men in 'the joint' plan them on a third night to assure the attendance of guests, who would otherwise be home with their families.

But missing from the Group that evening was Harry Swinger, one of the all-time greats. It was Harry's absence that led to an incident to which I lovingly call the 'Blessings Come in Many Ways Afternoon.'

Now and then a noticeably younger man comes into the group, causing me to wonder what such a young-looking person could have done to warrant imprisonment in a maximum security facility.

Harry Swinger probably sauntered into the 'Group' because someone surely told him that women came into the discussions. He always managed to sit himself down next to whichever female I brought in that night.

Harry was the type who would do well in the single's bars. He always looked like the kind that you'd see selling used cars on southern television stations. He was tall, nicely built, wore his hair short and curly, and he wore metal-framed glasses when he thought no one was watching. He also wore his prison garb with style and it was obvious he belonged in tight Qiana shirts cut down to the navel showing off his hairy chest, with enough heavy chains around his neck to endanger him with electrocution during a thunder storm. He was prone to telling every female that I brought in, "Not only are you beautiful, but you're different from the others that Arlene brings in here. You have soul. Where others are lacking in the substance, you possess."

He was adorable, except that his nose was bent to one side from a fight in years past. Even that added to his considerable charm. I could easily picture him as a lover instead of a fighter.

Somehow, he did manage to shoot himself in the finger and needed a new plastic knuckle. That's how I was able to find out through him that God works in mysterious ways in carrying out her blessings.

My family had just sat down to dinner preparing to finish up the Passover leftovers when the phone rang. It was Harry calling from the hospital. Amazingly, he had managed to have himself put into a private hospital instead of the prison hospital. He was there with around the clock guards, and I found out later, he was not allowed to have visitors. This didn't stop Harry.

"Hello, Arlene? Hey Babe . . . It's me, Harry, Harry Swinger."

I knew the cellblocks weren't equipped with phones, nor was Harry up for parole anytime soon. I wondered how he had managed to call me, but Harry cleared up the question when he continued with, "I'm in the hospital, all alone, and on the Passover holiday with no one to care or come to visit me, except the uncaring guard stationed outside the door. Do you think that you could arrange for a visit? Please?"

His voice had a lost, forlorn sound on the phone. Now how, especially on a Jewish holiday, could I turn down a plea like that? Bright and early the next morning, I raped all of my azalea bushes and filled the station wagon with flowers. I packed him a lunch of our entire leftover Seder dinner and headed for the hospital.

Everyone knows that chicken soup is the Jewish answer for Penicillin and the cure for everything from failing eyesight to hemorrhoids, so I brought him flowers, chicken soup, and other bits of soul food. There was enough in that car to feed starving Europe for a week when the great flood comes. After all, what more could a young good-looking guy who has been incarcerated for twenty-three months want, right? That's what I thought, anyway, until I asked, "Poor thing! Is there anything that I might bring you or do for you that might make your stay in the hospital more bearable?"

I was thinking in the realm of fluffing up his pillows, bringing in some C-rated books, or better yet, Biblical matter. Instead, Harry looked over at me with his mod glasses, pushed aside his chicken soup and beamed, "Well, as a matter of fact, there is."

He motioned me over to his bedside and in a faint whisper he looked up at me with pleading eyes and said, "Do you think you could have a piece of ass sent in to me?"

"Harry, you want, I should bring you up a piece of what?"

"Well, you know, like, get me a hooker in here."

"Harry, I have to tell you, in the Walt Disney circuit that I travel, I don't maintain the number of a hooker in my address book."

"Well, you asked, I mean, chicken soup and all that is nice, but . . ." as his voice trailed off.

"Listen Arlene, I really appreciate all you've done for me. You've really been nice n' all that, visiting and all but, if you really want to do a 'mitzvoth' (blessing) then have I got one for you."

Now, his request didn't seem all that illogical and I found myself thinking, "What am I getting myself into?" Harry continued with his lost little boy look. He motioned me close and whispered, "What harm could it do? I'm not asking you to cash one of my bad checks. I just want you to send someone over from the local massage parlor."

Here he has three Federal guards alternating outside his door, and he's making plans to have a woman sent in; just like a pizza! I told Harry that it wasn't a service of the Bureau of Jewish Education, as we didn't sponsor that kind of "education" and I left.

As I was leaving the hospital, I passed the front desk to check in on another patient that I knew in the hospital. The lady at the information desk was sort of attractive in a bland, hair-tied-at-the-nape-of-the-neck way, and she looked as though she'd always worn heavy tweeds and never had the need to perspire. We began talking and I ended up telling her, "It really is such a shame, a nice boy like that having to spend his religious holiday all alone."

I neglected to mention the round-the-clock guards. In her best southern charm accent she gushed, "Well honey, that sure is a shame. I know how lonely it is being in a hospital with no family to mention. I'll tell you what, honey, as soon as I get off work here at this desk, I'll take a ride up that little ol' elevator and stop by his room and tell him you sent me. Reckon he'll like that little ol' surprise?"

I was half-way home before I realized what I had done. If she'd gone into his room and said, "Arlene sent me", Harry might have thought, "What about that? She really sent someone' and then acted accordingly. I worried about his ending up with other charges along with "bad check", namely "rape". When I returned home I was having second thoughts, so I called a young, swinger cousin of mine and mentioned Harry's problem to him. Somehow, I found myself relating Harry's request as though it were coming from me.

"Well Joey, you see, chicken soup is a cure for a lot of ills, but it just can't cure everything. Think about it, you're both the same age. How would you feel if you were behind bars for almost two years with the prospect of many more to come before you saw a female up close again?"

Somehow, young boys under twenty-five can understand and feel compassion for that situation. They still think with their glands and their crotches instead of their minds. Rarely can they reason with a hard-on. Cousin Joey thought for a few minutes about who he knew at the local bath house, made a crass joke about my going into procurement, and said he'd get back to me.

The next day I took time out from my usual life of excitement, broke an appointment with the gynecologist, and decided to make a fast visit back to the hospital with a friend of mine, Shirley.

Shirley traveled the jet set, was quick with the quips, and became involved in the program initially for kicks. She had a great body, and since she had made a visit to the local plastic man for a few nips, tucks and the whole damn face lift, didn't look her forty years. This drastic change had transpired her, because she had found a 'friend', years her junior, and decided, "You only go through life once, so do it with gusto." The secret was not letting her husband know who Gusto was.

It was with reluctance that she agreed to visit the prison. Her beat was more Sacks and Neiman Marcus. I convinced her that it would be the highlight of her week and, with a little trepidation, she made that first visit. Within a short time, she became a regular. Eventually her attitude changed when she became aware of the injustice that she had seen within the system.

The little excursion into the hospital appealed to her also, as it was against the 'rules' and we were both a little bit jaded from our experience with prison reform or, the lack thereof. We had seen the administration set up some really sick situations to encourage homosexuality, so when Harry's proposal came, it seemed logical that we do whatever we could to fight what we considered the evil forces from within. Incidentally, Shirley is a school teacher. It's really very paradoxical as her image is Gucci-Pucci, but somehow, during her college years, she felt the call to teach and somehow became a very good one. A little off-beat maybe, but progressive. However, what she learned that afternoon she can't teach to her class, no matter how progressive.

It was lunchtime when we arrived. Before we entered the room we heard squeals of laughter emitting from his room, sounding something like cocktail hour at Doctor's Memorial. We walked in and saw Harry sitting up on three pillows, and eating a meal that looked as though he had checked off two of everything on the menu. A bottle of Chevis Regal was on the dresser. Two nurses walked out laughing when we walked in. The "Atlanta Arms" as we fondly dubbed the "Atlanta Pen", was never like this. He waved us in with a chicken leg, mumbled an introduction of sorts to his guard, who was deep in the depths of "culture". The guard was reading a literary book entitled, "Goldstein and the Black Junkie."

We had a nice visit for about ten minutes, when the phone rang. I don't believe inmates were allowed phone calls but obviously Harry had arranged everything. The call was for me. It was my concerned Cousin Joey on the phone, ready to do his good deed, and letting us know that was on the way:

"Remember that little problem you discussed with me earlier Arlene? Well, I'm down in the lobby with a friend, a very good 'friend,' and we want to come up. I called my local bath house, and I've made arrangements for house calls, or in this case, hospital visits. I never promised you a rose garden, but how about curb service."

Harry meanwhile, was lying there, no longer forlorn, but wearing a grin that told it all. The guard coughed discreetly, and Shirley took over. Friend Shirley is very Gucci-Pucci and has not made a bed in years because of her life style of maid service. Shirley said, "My God, it's like a pig pen in here. Don't they ever send anyone in here to clean up?" She scurried around the room picking up papers and obscene magazines. I know obscenity is only in the eyes of the beholder, but I beheld and they were obscene. Frankly, I was more concerned with the friendly guard, but he just nodded his head knowingly. I assumed that Harry had taken care of him.

Harry's room was situated between the elevator and the visiting room. Harry ushered everyone out of the room, into the visiting room, including the guard. A minute later the elevator doors opened and Cousin Joey entered the hospital to see the patient, with a friend, of course. From the fast glimpse that I had of her before they entered Harry's room, I learned that one cannot always tell character from appearances. She looked just like someone's daughter. Someone's nice daughter with a slight build, small features, classic almost, wearing jeans over a cute little tushie and I swear, her hair was tied up in pony tails. She also had a loose top and very little, if any make-up. She looked as though she'd been raised on country sunshine.

Now I know what my mother meant when she said you didn't have to smoke or drink to be a 'bad girl'. A few minutes later, Cousin Joey walked out of the room alone, and we all sat down in the waiting room. Wait, we did, for what seemed to be hours and hours. I'm sure that to Alfonso the guard it seemed even longer. He began to get very nervous after ten minutes and absolutely frantic after twenty. Beads of sweat began to break out on his upper lip, which incidentally was big enough so that he might suck an orange from across the room. He sat by me nervously, flicking his afro with a pink pick and every few minutes his expressive eyes would dart over in the direction of the clock, the clock that refused to move. I tried to make him feel better and said;

"Listen, give the guy a break After all, how long could it (whatever it was) take? Harry's been in jail so long that I'm sure that any minute his new friend will come out."

I don't think my musing helped him much. The guard seemed depressed and finally threw down his book and began pacing the waiting room.

"I knew it, I knew it. I never should have let him talk me into going along with this. I know it, somebody's gonna catch him any minute and my ass is going to be on the line."

Cousin Joey sat there with a knowing look on his face. Shirley suddenly became busy rearranging her hair and the orderly came by banging mops. I know they all do that intentionally, bang things in hospitals, usually at 5 A.M. It was just part of the job. I jumped up and intercepted him outside of the door. As casually as I could ask anything at this point, I said, "Hi guy, where you going?"

He looked at me with those dull orderly eyes and said, "I done come for the tray."

The guard choked on his Fritos and with quick thinking I told the orderly, "You're too late, they done come and picked up the tray".

The last we saw of him, he was walking down the hall mumbling to himself, "Ain't nobody supposed to get that tray but me."

Minutes passed, but they were tranquil until two nurses approached the room, like bookends, giggling in such a way that I wondered what usually transpired in there with his nurses. Before they had a chance to push open the door I stopped them and whispered, "Puh-lease you have got to be quiet! The patient in room 102 is very ill and cannot be disturbed as the priest is with him now. We're his relatives and waiting for the counseling session to be over."

Since Alfonso was black, I wasn't sure that we could pass him off as a relative, but the nurses didn't question and said they'd be back later, after the counseling session with the priest. Heaven forbid they should know that a nice Jewish boy was in there doing God knows what. At least it wasn't a complete lie, since I firmly believed that some kind of counseling session was going on.

As hospital time passed, and in this case it was slowly, I became somewhat annoyed.

"C'mon Shirl, let's go. I've got to go to the beauty parlor before I miss my appointment."

Shirley, during this time, gave every indication that she was glued to the seat.

"If you think I'm leaving now and missing the final outcome you're mistaken."

In an effort to shame her, I said, "Shame on you. What are you doing? What are you, some sort of a voyeur? Listen, if you leave now and take me to my appointment, I'll see that notes are taken to let you know what all has transpired. I'll even report back to you later when Harry calls. OK?"

She wasn't buying it, and buried herself even deeper in the beat-up vinyl couch in the waiting room.

"Hell no, I won't go." "I might miss something."

I looked over for encouragement from Cousin Joey but he seemed to be busy ignoring me and slouching in those terrible hospital chairs. Guard Alfonso was slowly developing a stutter. Finally, after an hour and forty-five minutes, the door opened and 'Little Miss Benevolent Heart' came out smiling. She hobbled, yes hobbled, to the elevator and rode down with Cousin Joey, who by now also had that gleam in his eye. Alfonso, Shirley, and I leaped toward the door, and Harry looked as though he were in need of a priest for real. From the expression he wore, the final breath would be in bliss. I'm not sure exactly how payment was arranged, but I do hope she hadn't taken a check.

His mother obviously raised Harry right, because three days later I received a thank-you note in the mail. In part, this letter said, "Thank you for making my stay in the hospital such a memorable one. It was one that I shall never forget. Nor will the men in the 'Group' with whom I've shared my experience." My husband wasn't impressed with the kindness that was shown through my 'arrangements' that were making me a legend within the institution.

It was also those types of 'arrangements' that were responsible for the men in my group accepting me as 'one of the guys,' and for the prison staff, although they couldn't prove anything against me, keeping a very watchful eye. As I said before, that was the day that I learned that blessings come in many ways.

The problems of Harry Swinger were of such a nature that we didn't really expect their solutions to be provided by the officials of the prison system. They were more in the realm of the lustful, physical unfortunates that the Bureau of Prison doctors couldn't cure. Our nation's prisons house all sorts of nutsy-type criminals. Surely prisons, and especially federal prisons, had counselors available who were trained in social work and doctors who were trained in psychology. Makes sense, right? Nope. You would not believe the sick souls roaming around our institutions with virtually no care. These are the same ones who immediately return once they are released and the circle begins again. The distressing realization of this situation, as a taxpayer, is that it hits all of us in our pocketbooks. Louie was a beautiful example of what's wrong with the way it is.

Louie walked into a meeting one night and we were introduced. He sporadically appeared and stood on the sidelines. I didn't know anything about him, but within a week or so, he made it a point to come up to me and tell me his story.

I was to find him a paradox because he was one of the few that I was to meet through the years who was knowledgeable and concerned with Judaism. He was also able to become one of the first of the men to give me a twinge somewhere in my subconscious. Maybe the prison system is not what I had thought it to be. Eventually, Louie was the catalyst who brought home the distressing realization of the mess that defines our prison system, and how as taxpayers hit us in our pocketbooks.

Louie loved cars. In fact, it was Louie's intense love of cars that resulted in his being where he was. Louie was the tennis pro of the prison, and he looked the part. All summer long he wore his tennis shorts and, as it got colder, his warm-up suit. Louie wore his hair cut very short. He had a wiry body and a thin, angular face with a bushy moustache, and his eyes were always moving.

His attendance was sporadic. Weeks would go by and we wouldn't see him. When he would appear sporadically and stand on the side lines. Later I was told that he came so seldom because the meetings reminded him of what he was missing and depressed him. Other than being in top shape physically and telling everyone within earshot everything they never wanted to know about tennis, he was super knowledgeable on one other topic. He was an unbelievable authority on the Bible, and particularly rabbinical studies.

It came as a surprise to find out that he was one of the members that was Jewish, mainly because he had a couple of ugly tattoos and that is really so un-Jewish! When I told him that, Louie just laughed and said, "That's OK, I'll just have the tattoo's cut off and be buried in a goyish cemetery."

"But why do I see so many men in here with them?"

Louie twitched his moustache, ran his hand across the back of his neck in a massaging motion while he thought and finally said, "Well, I suppose the only way that we can be different in here is by making ourselves individual. You know, wear our hair long, short, tattoos', anything to keep from being a number."

"Yeah, I suppose you're right, this place doesn't offer too much color, but, all these men that I see walking around in here had them before they came didn't they? There's no way to get a tattoo inside the prison, is there?"

Louie was beginning to enjoy the attention that his tattoo was attracting by our conversation. Patiently he began to explain to me, "Arlene, you can get anything you want in here, including tattoos. Ya see, despite the fact that special equipment like that isn't allowed in here there is a way to use a cassette machine. You put a little ink in it and wa-la, a tattoo!"

I found the ingenuity commendable and told him so, "Aw, that's nothing, we have everything except broads in here. Home brew, there's a million ways to make it. It's pruno, fermented fruits, tomato puree. Drink it and you might lose your voice for a few days, but it works."

Louie was a perfect example of the lost souls who roam the less than hallowed halls of the institution in dire need of mental help, but who never receive any. Although Louie was a criminal (a definite criminal type), he also was a guy who needed help a lot of it.

Over a period of several years, Louie would go out and find a car to steal. A red car, a red Camaro to be exact. He would then proceed to drive the said car over a state line, find a policeman, turn himself in and go directly to jail. That's just not normal. Much about Louie was abnormal. The prison officials however, didn't think that actions like those were in need of analysis. Somewhere budgets are allotted within our government bureaucracy for psychiatrists to work with men like these, but they were never much in evidence during my years there. In all the times that Louie was in various prisons, no one asked or wondered why.

Louie would do all sorts of rebellious things, like tell the guards to go to hell. He would refuse to shave. Once I asked him, "Why do you seem to go out of your way here to make your life difficult?" He leaned back, twirled his tennis racket and gave me a thoughtful sardonic smile, "Well, ya just gotta do what you believe in . . ."

In a place like that, such behavior is not wise. Louie found out the hard way. For his antics, he ended up in the hole-solitary confinement. Each time I would go in to the meeting, I would ask, "Where's Louie?" and would receive the answer, "In the hole."

I would have made the effort to visit him, but the prison has another rule, that one cannot visit individuals and still be a part of a program. It's either one or the other. Although I have rarely agreed with the officials, this is a rule that makes sense. Believe it or not, it is very easy for romances to start from programs such as this, and the warden's office frowns on this practice. I suppose the women's husbands do, also. I personally liked the rule because I just didn't have the time to make extra visits into that place, and I liked saying, "I couldn't" better than, "I wouldn't." I had enough on my hands organizing a program each Wednesday evening with seven or eight interesting people in tow.

So, although personal visits were out, I would still call and inquire to see whether Louie was still in solitary, and if and when he was going to get out. Each time I would receive the same answer from Warden Pagen, "Mrs. Peck, the man is in there on a voluntary basis and can leave anytime he wishes."

Sometimes people have themselves put in protective custody, so although the statements of the warden didn't ring quite true, I let it ride. About six months later, word was relayed to me via the grapevine that Louie was in the hole and had to see me. He sounded quite anxious that I visit him and that I bring a rabbi and a prayer book. Now, that sounded pretty urgent to me, so I called the warden.

"Hello? Warden Pagen, Arlene Peck . . ."

The response was an icy, "Yes?"

"Well, I would like to ask a favor . . . hello? Hello? Are you still there Warden Pagen ?"

After a long pause, "Yes, Mrs. Peck?"

"Well, Warden Pagen, although I know personal visits are not allowed to the inmates when one is a participant of a program, I have received what sounds to be a pretty urgent request to send help in to Lou Almark."

After a little barely audible sigh, "Mrs. Peck, you know the rules, and though you continue to disregard them, they must be abided by."

"Well, yes I know, visits aren't allowed and usually with good reason, but this man is obviously calling for help. From what I know about his past history, he needs all the help that he can get. Would it be possible to make a onetime visit with a rabbi and a prayer book? Let's just see if we can set up some kind of program, a religious program, and do what we can to help."

"Now Mrs. Peck, you know the rules, why you persist in breaking them is beyond me, but no, you may not visit Lou Almark, and no, I will not allow it."

So much for cooperation. It was an answer that was expected, but at least we tried. It was one thing to turn down our request, but quite another to send one of the guards down to Louie in the solitary confinement area and kid him and ridicule the man with, "'You won't get anything but grief from trying to bring in outside agitators', and the warden said that, 'Hell will freeze over before he'd let any of them in with anything to see you'".

About ten months after all this began, I got a call from Louie. The kids had just left for school, the house looked like the Egyptian tombs, the dishes were piled high in the sink, and then Louie called. At first it was difficult to hear him as he almost spoke in a whisper; for a moment I thought I was getting an obscene phone call. Finally, I was able to make out, "Arlene? psssst, Arlene,? it's me."

"It's me who?"

"You know, Louie,"

"Louie from the prison?"

"Yeah, I got out and need someone to talk to. I'm at the pancake house, will ya come?"

He was out! Since this was the first time in a year I had heard from the guy, I left the dishes where they were and drove over. I was also dying of curiosity since for all practical purposes he had dropped out of sight. He was standing apprehensively outside the restaurant in his new leisure suit and J.C. Penny turtleneck sweater, holding a duffle bag resembling an older version of a 'send this boy to camp' advertisement. He patiently waited while I searched for a parking spot for my ancient automobile. He didn't really speak until we were seated. Louie nervously looked over his shoulder. When he was satisfied we weren't being watched, he nodded his head and leaned over and whispered, "I wanted to make sure we weren't followed."

I ignored the cloak and dagger aspects and told him that I was delighted with the nice surprise that he was out.

"Louie, what happened? How did you arrange it?"

He shook his head, looking genuinely puzzled and said, "I'll be damned if I know."

He then spent the next hour relating to me how they opened the doors for him at three o'clock in the morning and said, "GO."

Now, prison procedure doesn't work that way. Everything about his release seemed irregular. But then again, the whole system suffers from 'irregularity.' The men always said that they had to go before a parole board and if they passed that test, then the arrangements were begun to set the process in motion whereby they were to be released. Nothing with Louie went the way it was supposed to go, but at the time, his release was such a blessing that neither Louie nor I wanted to pursue the matter. Together, we decided that the best plan of action for the moment was to use the bus fare that he had been given and go back to Miami, to his mother. Most of all I told him, stay away from red cars, especially Camaros.

The next morning I sent the kids off to school, took a minute to sit down and have a cup of coffee and read the last day's paper. The first thing that caught my eye was an article on the front page about an inmate of the Atlanta Penitentiary's being kept, 'accidentally' a year and three days too long. The inmate, according to the article, was my pal Louie. It stated that Louie had been kept longer past his sentence than any other inmate in the history of the Federal prison system. According to Warden Pagen and various prison officials, Louie's records had been lost and that was how this horrendous 'accident' happened. THEY LOST HIM? I knew nothing could be further from the truth, since I personally had been keeping the warden and the same various prison officials informed of his whereabouts each time I called to inquire about why they kept a man in the hole so long.

I mentioned this fact to a friend of mine who worked for the Atlanta Journal. A few hours later he called back to say that his newspaper offered to fly me down to see Louie in Miami. He had been tracked down at his mother's and the Journal wanted an exclusive interview with him. I was the only person with whom Louie would speak. Later in the day, another call came. This time it was from the Congressman Andrew Young's office.

"Mrs. Peck?"

"Yes?

"This is Congressman Andrew Young's office calling. We've had some inquiries from the justice department about a certain Louis Almark? We believe that you're acquainted with him?"

"I sure am."

"Well, we were wondering if you could tell us if you know of his whereabouts? It seems his case has taken on some very unusual overtones and we would like to look into his case more thoroughly."

"Well, I do know where I can reach him on the phone. If he would like to speak with you I'll put him in touch."

Although we had done nothing wrong, the whole issue was now getting pretty heavy. Why was the Justice Department getting involved? What did Congressman Andrew Young want out of this? Nothing made too much sense at this point. And, on top of everything else, the newspaper was still asking me to get in touch with him so that they could get an interview. A trip to Miami at newspaper's expense was tempting but I finally made the big decision not to go. Instead, I called down to Miami and reached his mother. Louie was sleeping, but his mother and I were able to have a few moments of conversation, despite the fact that she was so distress she was barely able to speak.

"Oh! It's just terrible! I can't walk out the front door without some newspaper person trying to knock me down. The questions they ask are just terrible. I am just so embarrassed in front of the neighbors. No one where I lived knew where Louis was and now the whole world does. I just don't know who to trust, or what to do about this whole situation. Imagine keeping my son in that horrible place a whole year past his sentence."

She began to choke up and it became difficult to speak with her. My parting words were, "Well, don't make any rash decisions and get yourself a good lawyer who doesn't want to become a partner with you. Good luck dear."

Nothing appeared in the papers again, nor did we hear the final results of Louis Almark. After the commotion and turmoil died down and they had some time to think, they would have been damn fools if they didn't find a good lawyer and sue the hell out of everybody. Except, the 'everybody' who probably footed the bill for this little 'accident' of the Bureau of Prisons was us, the taxpayers.

It cost twenty-four thousand dollars a year to keep a man in prison. Add this to the amount Louie should have, and probably had, receive from our government in his lawsuit, a person could send three children through college, dental and law school, and still have enough to pay off his mortgage. As taxpayers, we all pay for it.

Not long after, the Atlanta newspapers ran a couple of articles on how Warden Pagen left the prison to retire, with a FULL PENSION, and how the prison guards gave him a party to celebrate his wonderful years that were dedicated to public service.

Arlene Peck with Cong Elliott Levitas
June 1976
Meeting about the Prison

Chapter Two

DAY OUT PROGRAM

The Atlanta Federal Pen is a maximum security prison. The men in the prison are older and more established in their specialty of crime. The average age is over forty, and here one rarely finds the petty burglar or impulsive criminal. These are men who are in there for bigger, federal crimes; robbing banks, extortion, etc. As I said earlier, it wasn't very Jewish to be part of that place. Even though at the beginning I was kidding when I said they had to be products of a mixed marriage, I wasn't far from wrong. At any given time there were never more than 14 to 20 Jewish inmates in my group. Even among those I had my doubts about how devout they were before they entered. Although I never actually had a list of their offenses, I know that most were in there for non-violent crimes. A few were in there for securities violation, and a lot of them were in for drugs, conspiracy, forgery and inter-state robbery. First time criminals did not end up there.

It took me a long time to realize how unique my program was, since females are not allowed to head discussion groups in any federal prison in the country. I found it hard to believe that nowhere but Atlanta was there such a program as ours. As time passed, I would meet inmates from other institutions around the country and ask how the outside programs were where they came from. If there was a program at all, it was the Salvation Army or the Odd Fellows. The NAACP was big everywhere. In those days, no one had heard of the Nation of Islam. It was, I believe, in it's formation period.

But our Wednesday-night program was one of a kind. Moreover, we were able to arrange a 'day out' program. I was only able to arrange it a few times, but the men involved probably relived their days out for months after their return. I'm not exactly sure how it happened, but I believe the priest who was there at the time was sending out feelers to the warden because the priest wanted to take a few men out of the prison to visit the Monastery near Atlanta. I jumped on the fact that it would be discrimination if we weren't allowed to go on a Jewish Journey the same as the Catholics. A good offense is to put them on defense. Rather than risk making waves

40

in the Jewish community, someone in the administration decided to OK a day out for the Jewish men who were closest to their parole.

The first to be cleared was Al Cohen, a small time criminal. Hal was a hometown Jewish boy whose mother was a lawyer. He was her biggest client, and most of her efforts went to keep him out of jail. His life style was typical of nice, southern Jewish boys. Hal was a cowboy at heart. He liked pot, wild women and communes.

When I first met Hal, he looked like an aging hippie. He wore granny glasses and all the other trimmings of so-called 'free spirits'. No one told him what he thought was 'with it,' wasn't anymore. I don't think I ever saw him on a Wednesday evening when he wasn't wearing a dirty torn undershirt with his belly, which was considerable, protruding from his pants. His pants were usually too short, and his white government-issue socks were inevitably down. Add to this a sandpaper personality with a voice to match and an ever-present cigar and that was Al Cohen. He was basically a pretty nice person, but not exactly what one would call a born winner. He was living proof that nice guys finish last.

One night, one of the guys saw me talking to Hal and came over later to discuss him. They did that a lot, bad mouth each other. Anyhow, this time it was charming Marvin who came over, "That Hal's something, isn't he?"

"Yeah, adorable. To know him is to love him.

Actually, I really do appreciate him, sort of. He's so . . . basic!"

A little disdainfully he continued, "You know what he's in here for don't you?"

"Marijuana isn't it?"

"Ummmm. Hal's really a farmer at heart, except his crop was grass. When they grow that stuff out west, they plant corn all around it to hide the illegal 'crop' in the middle. Hal would plant his garden somewhere in Kansas, make arrangements to have it cultivated, and return home. A few months later he would go back in a panel pickup truck and have his product cut, cured, packaged, and sold on the open market."

Marvin's intentions were probably meant to shock, but I found it kind of funny and laughed, "Doesn't the government frown on that type of transaction?"

"This is where the good part about a woman doing him in begins."

"Marvin, I can't see Hal as a lover who got turned in by a woman scorned."

"He wasn't. This guy was such a schmuck that he picked a girl who was a police informer to set up light housekeeping with. She turned him in."

Like I said, not exactly a born winner. At least his attitude was good. Hal once told me that he lived by the creed, "If you can't do time, don't mess with crime."

When Hal first met me, he laughed and said, "I hope you bring in some nice, good-looking broads into this joint. I mean, I like the culture program and religious discussions and all that, but I wouldn't be adverse to getting my culture from good-looking broads."

By the time we met he had already served a couple of years and was few months short of his release. He was the first to be cleared by the warden's office to attend our Jewish holiday.

Hymie Dusman was the next to be cleared for a 'day out.' He came from another era. He was the Jewish version of a dignified 'Godfather.' He was what he was. By that, I mean he was a man who disapproved of immoral people but condoned crimes that were for business only. If the respect shown to him in our meeting room was any indication of how he was treated down in the cell block, then the man never had to lift a finger for anything the entire time he was doing time.

At the time I met him, I was told that Hymie was in poor health and that he was younger than he looked. He was in his early sixties, but he looked much older. His face was drawn and his color pale, but his eyes were strong. When he walked into the room, half a dozen of the men would jump up to give him a chair. When he spoke, NO ONE interrupted him. Although he was slight and small in stature, you almost felt as though 'Big Daddy' had walked into the room. Later I was to discover that he was a close business associate of the infamous Meyer Lansky and their relationship went back to the 'early days'. He lived by the code of the true criminal. Hymie could not condone 'stoolies,' nor would he approve of drug traffic. Drugs to him was not a 'clean' business like gambling or prostitution.

It was around the time of the first Passover Seder that we first met. The dinner was coming up. As a 'special' surprise I almost went blind crocheting personalized yarmulkas (head covering) for the men to wear that evening. The group those days was fairly small and numbered only around twenty-five. The Wednesday before the Seder, during the 'rap session,' I brought out the box that was filled with the yarmulka's. They got a kick out of the idea and as each one went to the front of the room to pick out the one they wanted, they were given orders to take ONE. When it was Hymie's turn, he took three (for the gang in the cell) and I rapped him on the knuckles with a magazine with the admonition . . . "ONE!" The room stilled instantly. Mr. Susman was not to be spoken to in such a disrespectful way, but what did I know? Fortunately for me he saw the humor in the situation, laughed and broke the ice. Once he laughed, it was O.K for the rest of the guys, but the message was definitely clear.

His home was in Miami, but I understood that he met and married his wife in Cuba. That was in the days of Batista, when Hymie was running the gambling operations and before he had to flee from the Castro regime.

According to rumor, one of the charges against him was smuggling a plane load of arms that had been stolen from a United States Armory in Ohio. The weapons were brought down to fight Castro. It was not in the best interest of the 'mob' if he were to come to power. Well he did and Hymie eventually ended up at the Atlanta Pen. Prisons keep a separate list of 'organized-crime inmates' and I was sure Hymie was high on their list and would be the last to be let out. That's why I was surprised to find out he was the next to be cleared by the warden and priest for the 'day out' program.

Marvin Spatz was the last of my guests of the afternoon. He would have been an asset to any cocktail party. He was witty, personable, bright and all 'con.' If I had not known that this was a maximum security prison and most of the men were there for previous offenses, I might have believed him when he said he had never been in trouble before. The man was all charm. He hadn't however, been able to charm the men who lived around him. Personally, I found him suave, and if he had only been a foot or so taller, very attractive. Whatever his crime, I was sure it had to have been non-violent. The man was definitely a smoothie and a big spender. According to his wife, with whom I was later to speak, he was also a non-supporter. He told me that he was a manufacturer of corrugated boxes. I found out that he was half right. His brother was a manufacturer of corrugated boxes.

Knowing how the prison officials felt about me, I didn't want to push my or my prisoners luck by being the one to pick them up. It was arranged through the priest to have the men driven by a guard that the men themselves paid for, to accompany them to our synagogue. I would pick them up from there. Friend Shirley and I met them and had the guard drive them over to my home, where the table was laden with Jewish soul food. Hal took a look and said, "Oh, my God, blintzes, lox spread, bagels, cream cheese, kugel, do you realize that there are men in the 'joint' that would kill for less than this?"

From what I had seen, there were guys in there who would kill for a pack of cigarettes but, why alarm the man? After all, he still had to live there.

While Hal sat down to inhale about six dollars of lox spread, Marvin flashed a big smile at everyone, threw a wink at me and said, "Where's your phone, sweetheart? I gotta make a couple of important long-distance phone calls, collect of course."

When the bill came, we found out differently.

Mr. Susman made a string of phone calls, and we all sat down for breakfast. Hal looked up from his gorging, and said;

"Well, maybe I could make room for a little more."

He looked over at Horace the guard and laughed, "Hey, buddy, don't they feed you this kinda good food in South Georgia? See that stuff in the center, it's gefilte fish. One taste and you'll never go back to ham hocks! Har, har."

Horace was a nice enough guy, but from the expression on his face, I could tell that this was not his type of brunch. He was a mayonnaise on white bread with corned beef type. As soon as the dishes were cleared away, I said, "OK, guys, let's go and get our Jewish culture."

Before the prison officials gave consent for the trip, I had to submit a list of places I expected to take them. Hurriedly, we covered the synagogues, Hebrew Day Schools and, Israel Bond office. At each stop we would make sure to have our picture taken, in front of the place, just in case proof were needed that we really went. It was a marvelous idea, except no one remembered to take the lens cover off.

Lunch was at a local deli, where we all loaded up on corned beef, pastrami and kosher pickles. Horace ordered his with mayonnaise. For the rest, it was just as important that their stomachs also have some Jewish input.

My husband, who had been skeptical of the whole 'day out,' didn't believe me when I asked him if he would like to spend the day with Shirley, the guard, and a few of my 'friends' who were leaving the prison for the day. He gave me a long look as though I needed help.

"Where are you and your inmate friends going to have this little lunch, in the guard tower?"

Howard was still laughing to himself at his dumb little joke when he gathered up his jacket and left for the office. I knew that he would never believe that I had arranged such a day if I didn't show him. So, with that in mind, I suggested to everyone that after lunch we should all go to the Regency Hotel for cocktails. The location was made even more desirable because it was right next to Howard's office.

The Regency Hotel is a member of the Hyatt chain and was constructed with all glass elevators and impressive architecture. The average tourist walks inside the lobby and cranes their neck for a better view. After the three desperados, Shirley, the federal prison guard and I ordered cocktails. I casually excused myself and phoned my disbelieving husband. He came to the phone to hear me say, "Hi there, It's me . . ."

"Me who?"

"The sex symbol that you live with. I'm next door at the Regency and thought you'd come over and join me for a drink."

"Join you for a what? You don't drink."

"Well, I do now, and if you don't want to see me smashed all by myself, you ought to come over and join me."

I knew this was enough to arouse his curiosity, since in my day of carpools; orthodontists and brownie baking, mid-afternoon cocktails did not comprise my typical day. I'm simply no drinker. Before he had a chance to ask me any questions, I hung up the phone and joined my group back at the bar.

It wasn't long before my skeptic husband entered the dimly lit bar. He walked into the room, eyes squinting, coat slung over his shoulder, exhibiting an attitude of absolute mistrust.

"I don't believe it! You actually pulled it off. How you arranged it I don't know, but I gotta admit, you did it! Three, count them, three and the damned federal guards thrown in for good measure."

Hal, who until now was distracted watching the tush of the barmaid, looked up, saw Howard and in the process of knocking over a chair, held up a scotch and let out a yell like a fog horn.

"Hey, Pal, here we are. We've got your wife captive, har, har, har. Think we can take her back to the 'joint' as a hostage with us?"

Actually, despite his basic disapproval, Howard showed a sense of humor and even went so far as to join us for the mid-afternoon refreshments. Only once did he say, "Well, we people who have to work for a living have to leave you nice people and go back to work."

It was just as well, as the next stop that we had on our agenda was pool-hopping at a friend's plush house.

We arrived for 'cocktail time', and our gracious and well-endowed hostess greeted us at the door wearing a miniscule, yellow, polka-dot bikini. Sandi was a Yankee who passed for a California girl. Long slim legs, usually tanned, connected to a body that made Hal's glasses fog up and his hand freeze midway as he was removing his Camel. He was definitely a 'camels' type. Hymie and Marvin noticed her attire, or lack thereof, but a bit more discreetly than Hal. After the introduction we received, I was awfully glad to see that Sexy Sandi's husband Sol was there also. It was nice to notice that he wasn't wearing a bikini.

We entered in a group and were ushered through the foyer into a California style den. Once again we were offered drinks and our choice of bathing suits for a dip in the pool. Sol had a full selection of suits for the men but Shirley and I had a choice of skimpy or less than skimpy. Since there wasn't one of my usual neck-to-knee bathing suits available, I chose pool-watching.

Everyone was enjoying himself tremendously. The three inmates were able to handle the opulence; but the guard, Horace Hillbilly, was not used to this grandeur. It was as if it were he who hadn't been around women instead of my afternoon guests, by the way he was ogling Sandi. Between dips in the pool, Sandi sauntered by with a tray of hors d'oeuvres;

"I just thought if you fellows might want a little something to eat, so I thought I'd bring you a little snack here by the pool."

The others kept their cool, which was I'm sure difficult enough to do after a leading comment such as that. Hal slid into the pool with an expression on his face as though he had died and gone to heaven. Horace was blissfully floating around the pool while the basics of a good party were beginning. It was too good an opportunity to let pass. I grabbed a camera, remembered to remove the lens cap this time, and walked over to where the guard was frolicking in the pool with my bikini-clad friends with a martini in his hand. I looked over and said, "Smile Sweetie, you're on Candid Camera."

"Hey, don't do that, I'm on duty. You wouldn't want me to get in trouble would you?"

Of course I didn't. I just wanted a few good compromising shots that he wouldn't want the warden or any officials to see. Horace was really a nice man, but, at this point I had become so suspicious of the motives of anyone involved within the walls of the Atlanta Penitentiary that my motives were now devious. I just figured that such pictures would be extra insurance if Horace ever tried to give the men a hard time when they returned. Sometimes you have to fight corruption with a little corruption of your own.

Like any Cinderella story, we knew we had to get the men back before curfew, in this case, 9 P.M. Night was quickly upon us and we really had to fly. Instead of a magic castle inhabited by a god fairy, we faced the reality of the 'wicked witch', waiting at the guard tower.

I don't believe that ever before in the history of Federal Prisons had a stranger group spent an afternoon at 'liberty'.

Chapter Three

MIKE THEVIS: PUBLIC ENEMY NUMBER ONE

The 'Day Out' activity was a real coup. The following week my program had doubled the number of participants. Many newcomers came to see the 'broad' who had actually managed this incredible feat. Word had spread that Wednesday night was a happening night. I was astounded to find myself becoming involved with people I had seen only on TV specials, nights that I looked like the 'Hit Parade of the Post Office Top 40'.

Certainly, one of the more stellar personalities was America's porno king, Mike Thevis. Long before Mike Thevis was moved up on the top ten list to number one of the FBI's most wanted, he was a regular member of the Group. I probably wouldn't have noticed him, except he was so famous. The men immediately pointed out Mike to me. And truthfully, the infamous have always fascinated me more than the famous, so I took special note. Besides, it was the presence that either as a result of his fame and notoriety or in spite of it surrounded Mike like an aura. You just knew he was there, not good looking, pleasant maybe, but yet you noticed him. Once I noticed him, I made it a point to know him. I wanted to know what made the man tick. It wasn't out of a need or knowledge that one day I'd be writing about him. No, it was like meeting a living legend. There was no way that the man could have had all the women he was supposed to have had or committed the crimes that he was rumored to have done without being burned out years before. I wanted to know why he was drawn into our Wednesday evening discussion group. He was Greek, and therefore not Jewish, but he became enthusiastic about our discussions. He once told me he felt that the 'Group' offered the one chance he had during the week to stimulate his mind.

That day, my feelings were mixed as to the guilt or innocence of the man because of the charges against him: murder, extortion, arson, and conspiracy. And, if true, probably the closest thing Atlanta had ever had to a Godfather. But, looking back in the winter of 1976 when his pornography empire was a constant headline, I was comparing him and his crime to the persecution of Lenny Bruce. He had already earned his reputation locally, but his incarceration escalated his repute to a national scale. Thevis was now

47

the porno king of the country. He was much like another Greek, Onassis, who began with nothing and ended up with an empire. Except the roads he chose were different.

He owned it all in 'adult books and magazines,' everything but the trees. He owned the paper company that was selling the paper, the printing companies that were printing the magazines, the publishing company, and the national and local distribution. Along with this, Mike owned some 200 retail stores that were in turn, selling his products at an incredible rate.

He skimmed hundreds of thousands of tax-free dollars out of the multi-million dollar business over the years. This massive operation continued after he went to prison in 1975, and even after he escaped from jail on April 28th, 1978. Mike, on one occasion told me, "I believe that it's not going to just happen. You have to make it happen. Whatever I got, nobody gave it to me. My family was Greek immigrants from Greece that didn't have two nickels to rub together."

He paused to place his next words, "When the rest of the kids would be playing or going out for the team, I'd be working my butt off."

I believed him, as Mike had an intensity about him that led me to believe that even in prison he went about his duties with the zeal of a still-powerful executive. (Which, in fact, he still is.) Later, he was to give an interview to one of the Atlanta papers wherein he was quoted, "Hell, I can remember when I married my wife Joan, in 1948. It was near Christmas time and we were living in some little apartment right behind the Atlanta Penitentiary. I can remember sitting down on the curb and crying because it was so cold and the motor had-frozen and I couldn't get to my job. I didn't have enough money for antifreeze. I was in the habit of coming home at night and draining the water from my radiator and then putting it back into the car in the morning. Well, that morning it was so cold I knew the engine would freeze up before I could get three blocks down the road. I was a kid, and I sat down and literally started crying. Times haven't always been nice, is what I'm saying."

Mike started his own empire and built it as a very legitimate business man. He began with a three-stand shoeshine and newsstand but was determined to be a millionaire by the time he was thirty. By the early 1960's Mike was on his way. His family had grown to five children and he was adamant that they should have the things he never did.

Whatever the location of his stores, which by now were located in Jacksonville and Tampa, Fla., Memphis, Tenn. and Biloxi, Miss, there was a peculiar pattern to the sales and he enjoyed telling people, "There I was doing inventory one day, and I noticed that 90 percent of my profits were coming from 10 percent of my inventory: girlie magazines."

Thevis branched out into publishing and after his first publishing efforts, a book on Vietnam, a religious study, and a book of maps failed miserably, he turned his attention to the more lucrative aspects. He then printed a book that listed the location of all the nudist colonies in America. Later Mike was to recall, "It musta sold a zillion copies and didn't even have any pictures, either."

That was when he made the decision to remove all the non-adult literature from his stands and stock the soft-core magazine like Playboy, Dude and Gent. Surprisingly, one of his earliest arrests was for selling Playboy. Gradually, as the courts, during the 1960's liberalized the definition of obscenity, the girlie magazines were removed for the strictly adult reading. From that he progressed to hard-core fantasies, to raunchy, full-color genitalia. During this prosperous time, Mike Thevis began to open new bookstores and theaters around the country under his Atlanta based holding company, Global Industries. Next, came companies to distribute magazines, films, and other sex-oriented products to others. Business was booming and the American public was buying.

His organization, which by now was considerable, extended as far as Alaska. Eventually, there were eight wholesale operations around the country. Mike ran a tight organization and his workers were given regular lie-detector tests to find out if they were stealing. Surprisingly, there was an enforced rule against affairs among employees which somehow did not apply to the boss. By this time, he began his long, open relationship with Patricia McLean, who had come to work for him at the age of 20. His double morality code did not only extend to his employees, but, the strict standard that Mike had set up for his employees extended into the Thevis home. No racy magazines, not even Playboy, were allowed for fear the children might see them.

The public clamored for what Thevis had to sell and as big as his organization was, it still had yet to grow. This was because of a simple little machine that would make him his fortune. This was the peep-show machine.

The modern peepshow machine originally had colorful red balloons painted on its side and was designed to show Mickey Mouse films to children in shopping centers and amusement parks. It was a large, box-like device with a small glass window into which the child could 'peep' to view a short segment of cartoon. For a few minutes, the child could see a show by paying only a nickel or dime.

Mike found a better, more lucrative use for these machines. The price was no longer to be pennies for cartoons but quarters for bare-chested women dancing suggestively. The viewers of these shows would continue to place quarters in the slot until they had paid $12 for a 12 minute episode. Mike had an eye for what the public wanted and although the 1970's approached and rubber sex organs were making their way onto the stands of Thevis 'adult' bookstores, it was the peep-show machine that was the catalysis to trigger him nationally as 'King of the Porno'. He devised a method for collections whereby he could operate these machines thousands of miles away, and all that had to be done was once in awhile take a meter reading and see if the money that had been delivered to him was correct. The machines had been made secure and foolproof in the method of collections and the money began to roll in. To insure that this situation would continue, Mike insisted on never selling but instead leasing the machines to thousands of stores around the country and always keeping half the proceeds from these machines for himself.

Later, after he had been arrested and incarcerated in the Atlanta Penitentiary, he told a reporter, "I began to manufacture 50 machines a week. The country at that time was so wide-open; it was like opening the west. We couldn't make enough machines to satisfy all the demand. At the peak I had about 4,000 machines. A good machine could produce $125 a week, gross, to be split between the operator and myself."

Potentially, that brought in an income of around $25 million a year, much of it hidden in cash profits from the Internal Revenue Service. Although he reportedly paid taxes on an income of about $1 million dollars his style was flamboyant, and his enemies many. Thus far he had managed to stay out of prison, although he had racked up over 100 arrests for distribution of pornography. In 1977, a federal grand jury convened in Atlanta to hear evidence on crimes attributed to Thevis other than pornography. That's when the downfall of Mike Thevis began to gain momentum. As early as 1973, a near fatal motorcycle accident brought him to the brink of death. A speeding car forced the motorcycle that Mike was riding off the road and down a 50-foot embankment near the Chattahoochee River inflicting massive internal injuries. His health never fully regained and his luck was beginning to waiver. In 1975, a couple of his many obscenity-distribution arrests were pushed through and he had to go to jail. It was during that time that we first met.

I was disappointed in our first meeting. I had almost expected him to arrive with arms laden with dirty pictures and phallic symbols. Somehow I felt his appearance should have been seedier. True, within those prison walls I knew he couldn't wear black shirts with white ties but at least a man with his background should have had heavy eyebrows, maybe a gold tooth or two and a pock-marked face. It would have been wonderful if his nose had been broken and along his cheek ran a long knife scar. However, the man had none of these marvelous characteristics.

He came into the meeting room walking heavily, with a cane. His limp was the result of the motorcycle accident, and for awhile, many thought he would be permanently paralyzed. Mike had made a remarkable recovery, yet his condition might have further improved had there not been a battle-of-wills between the prison officials and him. The administration at the Atlanta Prison was determined that he use their doctors, and he was equally adamant that he use his own specialist. I remember his coming in, obviously in pain from his back injury, and saying to me, "With all my money I can't save the government any. I want, and need that back operation terribly. I want to bring in my own specialist, with everything to be paid for by me, and they want me to use the prison butchers. I'll be damned if I'll let them come after me with a knife."

As I found out a couple of years later when I triggered off the Senate Investigation into the Atlanta Prison by bringing in Julian Bond as the speaker, Mike was right. There were many horror stories to be told about the prison doctors. As for Mike and his justifiable fear of prison surgeons, nothing had been done to help his back. A few of the times that we spoke about his back condition, Mike seemed depressed about this situation.

He came into the meeting, sat down heavily, and placed his cane carefully between his legs. He had just been told that he was going to be transferred and it visibly depressed him. Toward the end of the meeting I was able to sit by him for a few minutes and we had a chance to speak. I enjoyed speaking with him as there was something almost charismatic about him. Possibly from reputation, or charm, Mike would lend an excitement when he entered the room. He looked like the middle-class executive, exactly what he was on a grand scale before he entered the penitentiary. His Greek heritage showed in his piercing dark eyes that crinkled around the edges. Within them seemed to lurk a little bit of devil glint. The last time I saw him he was sporting a well-cared for Van Dyke. It was rumored that Thevis had a hypnotic effect on people that worked for him and elicited loyalty from his employees. Whatever the reason, people were drawn to him. Toward the end of our last meeting, he mentioned that he would probably not be able to see me again at the meetings. I was sorry to hear that and asked him, "Mike, how do you know that you're going to be moved?" He shook his head and said, "I know. The word was passed on to me, and although this isn't the first time, this time it hurts. See, they can't make it easy for me. My family is here, it's convenient for them to come see me, instead of taking out of town trips. I have five kids you know, each six years apart from the next. Anyhow, with them in school and all, it's not easy for them to get away. This way, I get to see them once in a while."

There wasn't much that I could answer to this, so I just gave a willing ear and told him that I hoped that it wouldn't happen. Maybe he'd be able to serve out his sentence in Atlanta.

He was right, however. The next time I was there, I noticed that Mike wasn't in his usual seat, and I inquired as to his whereabouts. He had been transferred. Whether justified or not, he carried an aura of paranoia. People were out to get him. His having a couple of bodyguards might have added to that image too.

Once, I asked Thevis why he felt the need for a bodyguard and he laughed and said, "Do you realize how many people here try and hit me for extortion? Arlene, you've got the cream of the crop in your 'Group'. But, not everyone here is as nice as you'd like to have them. This place is the pits, from the guards on down. I've got guys trying to put the bite on me."

He nodded over to his right at his friend, who looked as though he had been lifting weights since the crib and continued, "Sean, my Irish friend here, is just around to give a little added protection and to see that my back which is put together with pins and spit, doesn't have any bad accidents while here. Right Sean?" Sean didn't say too much. He just sat there looking like wall to wall muscle. He had a slight satisfied smile that revealed a big gold tooth right in the middle of his mouth. I found it very distracting the way he just sat there sucking the air through his teeth and giving out a low hissing sound.

Mike, that particular evening, looked weary and full of prison fatigue. His attitude and nature is not to give up, but that night, he was not only pensive, but tired. "Arlene, I wish to hell I knew whom I offended a couple of years ago, so I could apologize now and have a chance at getting out. Ya know, when I ran an empire of over five hundred employees, I wouldn't have some of the guys here flush my toilet. They've gotten me so institutionalized that I'm now walking around saying, "Yes, boss" to them."

As I became familiar with Mike and his situation, I had to agree that someone didn't like him. This was in 1977, before so many changes and events took place that were to make me draw back and realize that maybe those that were out to get him had good reason. During this time, I had just finished reading the life story of Lenny Bruce, so my attitude was one of sympathy. I felt then, that if Thevis had committed terrible crimes, he should have been tried, convicted and put into prison. The charges were comparable in my mind to Lenny Bruce in that the time he was serving was for pornography-related crimes. I thought that everyone connected with the way he made his living were tacky and sick, but Mike didn't force anyone to buy what he was selling and his fortune was made from a willing public. Whatever the reason people would frequent his adult bookstores, Mike wasn't standing there with a gun. There is also a grain of truth that his millions of dollars gained yearly with a business staff of hundreds might really grate on the ego of an $1000 year government employee. He remarked ironically once to me, "Wardens and guards I think, come down harder on people like me because of their own miserable lives. They leave dull, bland, boring wives and watch me have women in to visit whose perfume they could never even afford to buy. They resent my high priced lawyers. They resent efforts that are being made by others in the prison to see that I live in relative comfort."

To people who are imprisoned, guards, wardens, and even prison chaplains, represent power. I saw a lot of losers on the other side of the bars during my years of weekly visits. The men who always seemed to go into this field were not the dedicated social workers or educated administrators I somehow expected. Usually, I found them to be the type who back in high school, if they went that far, could never make the football team, honor society or girl of real class. I thought Thevis, and those like him, had too much for those who had so little.

The mafia has long known that the American public does not like flagrancy in crime. Thevis' personality was such that he was not able to live understated. He had to draw attention to his success and 'style' and live by the code, "If ya' got it, flaunt it." Mike was proud of himself, proud of how he had risen in the world and this possibly contributed to his downfall. When the Reader's Digest wrote an article about him titled the King of Smut, Mike liked showing it around. "Just make sure you spell the name right."

Years after he had become a household word, a former associate of his would comment, "There are other people in the country as big in pornography as he is. But, nobody's heard of them because they don't go around telling everyone how big they are."

True, the charges, if proven against him, were deplorable. How did he rise to the top of the FBI's 10 most wanted list? Why? I've seen dozens of men throughout my years of involvement within that institution who had killed, personally, many men who had never received the notoriety that Mike achieved. Gary Bowdach, whom I will write about later, is walking free today. He was a convicted 'hit man' who cold-bloodedly murdered many. What makes the difference in Mike's case? Certainly, a goodly part was caused by his flamboyant style. Or, as he claims, "The victim of government on a morality binge." By the time he was convicted on three counts of interstate transportation of obscene materials, Mike Thevis had become so distrustful of his associates that he had a tap placed on the telephone of his closest aide. He even had a meeting called when he learned his workers were abusing his watts line for personal calls and warned the employees that the lines would be tapped. When the employees simply switched to making their long-distance calls on the local lines, he began selecting a 'phone of the day' to be monitored. By doing it that way, no one could ever figure out which phone was being tapped. The men closest to him began to turn on him and give testimony against him to the government. One of these was Roger Dean Underhill, who was to become the chief witness against Mike. He later was mysteriously murdered. According to friends of mine who were once close to Underhill, Roger had the coldest, meanest S.O.B. eyes you ever saw. They were like ice. Icy eyes that made you believe that he would kill his own mother. He was mean as hell and yet, something about him was fascinating. Somehow, you wanted him to notice you. He had an ex-beauty queen wife that was really a nice girl, but she always seemed scared to death of him. Before his death, Underhill told his story of involvement in murders he had done for Mike Thevis to the FBI. Agents gave him a lie-detector test on his story and, he passed. In vivid detail, Underhill described being the middleman in the murder of James Mayes Jr., who had once worked for Thevis, then went into the peep-show business himself, with Underhill as a partner.

Kenneth 'Jap' Hannah was another unsolved mystery. Hannah was shot three times in the heart and once in the face with a .38-caliber pistol. His late model, gold colored Cadillac was checked into the parking lot at Hartsfield International Airport at 10:03 a.m. on Nov. 13th 1970. This was an hour and 20 minutes after he visited Thevis in his Marietta Street Northwest office. Three days later, Mr. Hannah's body was discovered by the authorities in the trunk of his Cadillac, still parked at the airport. Over the years, Thevis steadfastly denied any knowledge of 'Jap' Hannah's death. Underhill's part in all of this could never be fully explained. He died before he had a chance to testify before the jury.

He was killed during the period of time that Thevis was free. Underhill was ambushed while showing a piece of his North Atlanta property on the Chattahoochee River to a potential investor. The potential investor, Isaac Galanti, was also killed. He happened to be a neighbor of mine, and a truly fine man who just happened to be in the wrong place, at the wrong time. That was his guilt. No one has yet been charged in the Underhill and Galanti deaths, but both Thevis and his attorneys have predicted he will be indicted in the case. Mike Thevis had denied, however, that he had anything to do with the killings. A year ago, when we were friends, I would have believed him. Now, too much evidence pointed to killings and sudden deaths of people that were detrimental to him. When we last spoke, things looked bad for him, but not nearly like they had at that later time.

Leon Walters, the number 2 man behind Underhill, was a key figure against Thevis in the government's case against him totaling 114 racketeering charges, including murder, arson, extortion, mail fraud and obstruction of justice. According to Mr. Walters, "Mike Thevis is not the brilliant businessman who built an 100 million dollar empire by outsmarting his competition. Mike never had an original idea; he simply used other people's work."

Walters had been pictured as a man jealous of Mike's accomplishments and who often had to show off what he felt was his intricate part in the organization to others. According to him in a press report, "When Mike started a new enterprise he started at the bottom, picking peoples brains, and then discarding them. Then he went to the next level and picked their brains before discarding them."

Eventually, Walters became president of the Thevis companies but was fired by Mike before he went to prison in December of 1974. In May 1977, an attempt was made on Walter's life while he was watching television. He heard someone tapping on his bathroom window. When he went to investigate he saw a hand holding a 9mm pistol come through the window and begin firing. They missed and now Walters is a key witness against Thevis. Walters once made the comment that, "Mike never believed in sharing the bounty with those who helped him make it. He always gave it to those that didn't deserve it. After all, I was the go-between that paid off all his ladies."

Which brought me to my next question, what about his ladies? Even his enemies admitted that Mike had a hypnotic effect on the people who worked for him. Did this same relationship carry on into his involvement with women? Patricia McLean, an attractive, one-time waitress who rose in the ranks to become the President of Global Enterprises, a holding company corporation that once controlled some of the Thevis pornography operations, was a slim 29 year old that had power of attorney for Thevis, which gave her control of holdings estimated at between 1 and 12 million. Global Enterprises is a subsidiary of Fidelity Equipment Leasing Corp. which was supposedly sold to Laverne Bowden, Thevis' former personal secretary, for some $12 million in 1974. The Thevis organization tentacles were far-reaching and have long been considered a model corporation maze, with a series of interlocking companies held by holding companies. There is also an equally intricate series of interlocking law organizations which may employ as many as thirty or forty lawyer's, altogether.

Ms. McLean had been accused by the government of knowing about, if not participating in, Thevis' escape plans when he walked out of the Floyd County Jail in New Albany, Indiana, on April 28th 1978. According to testimony, even sexual visits were arranged for Mike with Patricia McLean. She was also the last person to see him before he made the escape that touched off a nationwide manhunt that was reminiscent of the Patty Hearst search. Mike walked through an unlocked door that had been propped open by a soft drink can and walked away without a trace. The intense search for him finally culminated when he was apprehended with yet another woman, Jeanette Evans, six months later in Bloomfield, Connecticut.

Miss Evans and Thevis were at a Suburban Hartford Bank in November of 1978 attempting to withdraw a large amount of money, when officials became suspicious. The authorities learned of Thevis' identity after hours of questioning and checking records. Jeanette Evans, a successful Marietta, Georgia real estate agent was arrested with Thevis and charged with harboring a fugitive. Found in Thevis' car was an estimated one million dollars in diamonds and $562,000 in cash. This led the FBI to search several bank safety deposit boxes apparently rented by Thevis under different names. Caught also in this web of criminal charges was Ms. Evans's cousin, Bart Hood, a mild mannered assistant police chief of Summerville, South Carolina. When this once respectable family learned of Jeanette's involvement with Mike, they said, "The only sin she's committed is loving him. We still love Jeanette and will do everything we can do to help her. We pray that what will come of this is that she will be led to the Lord. We advised her over and over to leave him alone. We're Christians, and he's everything our family hates. I guess she loved him in spite of all she could do. This is the worst thing that's ever happened in our family."

The answer to possibly one of the biggest questions has not been answered since Mike was apprehended. With all the money he had stashed away and the connections that he undoubtedly had to help him flee the country, why didn't he? Few people who escape have the opportunity of funds that were available to him. They usually get caught trying to rob a store for get-away money or someone turns them in. Mike didn't have that problem. Like Judge Crator years later, people thought he'd be speculated upon as to the disappearance.

Each time I read a new headline about the murders that he was supposed to have engineered, I remembered that last evening I saw Mike.

He had come into the Group, mainly to say good-bye. As he predicted, he was being transferred. Somehow, during our conversation, I casually mentioned that I was on the program committee for my synagogues bazaar, and that the sisterhood was trying to find some sort of entertainment for the children during the carnival. With a perfectly straight face Mike said, "Why don't you let me send you out some movies?"

I liked his sense of humor! The sisterhood would have died if they had known who and where the movies were coming from, but I had no intention of telling them. With all the casualness I could muster, I asked, "What kind of movies did you have in mind?"

Just as casually, Mike leaned back on his cane, scratched his Van Dyke, looked up at me with an absolutely evil glint in his eye and said, "Lassie, Come Home!"

It was then I realized it's not always what you say, but how you say it. I almost asked Mike if Lassie was wearing dark glasses and black socks.

We made arrangements to pick up the movie from Thevis' home, which to the outside observer closely resembled the Taj Mahal. What a home!

Since his incarceration, it had been placed on the market, but with a selling price of two million dollars it had found few takers. Eventually it was to be sold for a courthouse step sale for $12,000, minus loans of course. It sat surrounded by elegant grounds and a pond stocked with swans. The first thing one noted on approaching the house was the massive wrought iron gates and fences. Much like the prison, there was a little box you spoke into in order to enter the grounds. I nervously shouted into the thing while friend Shirley, who had accompanied me, waited in the car.

We almost expected someone to jump from behind a tree and holler, "RAID". Instead, a courteous voice announced that Mr. Thevis had said that we were expected and that we could enter. The heavy doors on the right of the driveway must have cost a quarter of a million dollars, and they were just for the caretaker's house. The drive was long and the property was covered by a blaze of azalea bushes that cost over $30,000 to install. A little further up the drive was the house. Shirley looked over to me and said, "It's a good thing that we drove my Bentley today instead of that tacky orange thing you call a car, if only to impress the houseman, Leo."

I was busy noticing the outside decorations.

"Ummm, did you notice that statue near the gate of a snarling lion and a cute little gargoyle further up?"

"Uh huh. The resemblance to the warden and his assistant is uncanny. Mike had told me that Leo, the houseman would be expecting us. Somehow, we weren't expecting him. He was adorable. He reminded me of a short King Kong in Western cowboy boots. He would have been bald except his thin black hair was carefully streaked across his scalp to give the appearance of fullness. He looked as though he was in the habit of changing the oil in his hair every 50,000 miles. He was dressed in chinos and a white tea shirt stretched tightly across his muscular body. As Leo held the door of the Bentley open for Shirley, I noticed that his hands bore the scars of many battles. Shirley, on the other hand, was busily memorizing everything of value about the house. The foyer in itself was an excursion. A tour of that place could have easily taken over an hour. The entire ceiling and wall panels were painted by an artist Mike had imported from Europe. Rumor had it that he was paid a hundred thousand dollars to paint the mural. Each scene was created from a story in Greek Mythology. It was reminiscent of a Greek Sistine Chapel. Fittingly, the story of Leda and her swan were created in living color. Shirley pinched me and I thought she had drawn blood.

"Psst. Look at this den. Did you ever see anything so big in your life? What's in that corner?"

She peered for a moment and then exclaimed, "Good God! Sitting on that inlaid table is an entire city carved in ivory; the thing must have cost a fortune!"

We were dying to see the bathrooms because we had heard that there were even musical bidets. (Now, that's class!) Until then I had always thought that class was not having to pull in chairs from the kitchen when you're serving dinner in the dining room, but G-d, a musical bidet. Fortunately, Shirley has a kidney condition, and as soon as we entered she asked Adorable Leo if he would be so kind to show her to the bathroom. He did, but he escorted us to the maid's quarters. The maid unfortunately, didn't have a bidet.

I don't know who cleaned that house, but the cost of the upkeep of the grounds alone could have fed a starving country in Europe for a year. As we walked around the lush grounds and wandered through the vast rooms that were loaded with elegant furniture and original paintings, I thought of the conditions that Mike is now living under. The adjustment must have been tremendous. Walking around the opulence of his home, it was easy to understand what Mike meant about being 'institutionalized'. The Atlanta Arms, with all it offered, didn't have what he must have been sorely missing. Mike had gone from rags to riches and back to rags, at least in living style.

Our exit was uneventful, as were walking back toward the car, I noticed a beautiful little boy of around three years old peeking from behind the maid's dress. Leo mentioned that it was Mike's youngest son, Jason. As we drove away, there was with a feeling that the FBI were probably peeking at us from somewhere also.

The sisterhood appreciated the film. They almost suffered mass apoplexy when it was brought up at the board meeting that they should address the 'thank-you' note, "in care of Mike Thevis, U.S. Prison".

Chapter Four

BOBBY WILCOXSON: PRIDE OF THE F.B.I.

Looking back, it was obvious from the very beginning that the prison officials liked little about Arlene Peck. Not that I blamed them much sometimes, I did have an urge to drive them crazy. Anyway, the warden still hadn't forgiven me after the incident of the tomato plants and the fact that I'd gone over his head and came back in, via my congressman. I'm sure word had traveled back over the hooker in the Harry Swinger hospital incident and the questions that rose concerning Louis Almark were also certainly not appreciated. Personally, I could never see the logic of them holding a grudge, but then, I found prisons terribly illogical anyway. Many of the inmates inside the institution cared about nothing. Nor did they have a sense of logic. The attitude of many was, "Well, I was in the liquor store robbing it, and had everything under control, and if the cop didn't come in, then I wouldn't have had to kill him . . ."

The men who ran the prison seemed to function with the same illogical behavior. My own behavior was surely turning illogical also. At that point, I was beginning to think that the outlaws made more sense than the ones running the place. Now, that's certainly illogical; especially for a Jewish American Princess from the South, with a very law and order attitude, who initially had entered the place for a lark.

One of the weekly regulars was a sweet looking little elderly man. He was a cowboy from California and his skin was leathery, as though he'd been riding on the range for years. His face was gaunt and it was difficult to see his eyes because of the thick glasses he wore. Every time we spoke, he put his face right up to mine. This worried me about his intentions, until I found out that the man, who wore thick glasses, also had one glass eye. This gave him a look of sheer intensity.

The rest of the inmates didn't seem to like him very much. They all thought he was a snitch. I never really believed the rumors about his turning his friends in; however, some of the men eventually did. Just like in one of those television prison shower scenes, someone zapped him with a knife and left him there for dead. When the priest went to give the Last Rites, my friend Bobby said;

"Hell, get me Mrs. Peck."

"But Bobby, my son, you know not what you say. You are a Catholic and I am a Priest. Mrs. Peck can do nothing for you now."

"The hell I'm a Catholic and she can do a hell of a lot more than you can. If I'm gonna die, then I don't want it to be with you. Now get me Mrs. Peck"

Well, the Priest relayed the message, which unfortunately was delivered during a PTA meeting at my children's school at 'The Hebrew Academy.' The only reason I can remember it so clearly was that it struck me as funny because I was in the middle of hearing a speech from the Rabbi when I had to leave because of an emergency call from a priest. He was abrupt, but compelled to do his duty by giving me a re-run of his conversation from the 'deathbed'. The Good Father's voice was oozing with sarcasm when he said with petulance, "Uh yes, Mrs. Peck, this is the priest at the hospital, and I'm just calling you because I've had a request from Bobby Wilcoxson. The man is bad off, almost on his deathbed, and he doesn't seem to want my help, or guidance. God rest his soul, I doubt if there is anything you can do, but I did tell Bobby that I would call you and relay the message for whatever good it will do. He wants to know if you will come to the hospital."

"Well, sure I'll be there just as soon as I can grab my coat and get out of here."

I hung up the phone thinking, "Oh, that poor son of a bitch. The man gets stabbed and I'm the only one that he can think of to call for help. For some reason that's really pitiful. In the whole damn world, I'm the only one that he can call to play his farewell scene."

I drove to the hospital experiencing mixed emotions. On one hand I felt almost a duty calls sensation which in a perverse way was exhilarating and on the other hand scared as hell. I had never seen anyone die before and I wasn't looking forward to the experience. The last thing on my mind were the hassles once I got there. The priest was obviously not delighted to see me. "Uh oh," I thought as I passed by him in the hall. First, the Warden hates me because of the tomato plants, then the Assistant Warden Watkowski because of my pushing through the Passover Seder and my latest campaign for kosher food into the institution, and now I'm starting with the priest. I was 'horning' into his territory. Too many of the Catholics were showing an interest in the Jewish Program. It went against his very nature that a Jewish woman should have been called in, when by rights, it should have been him giving the 'last rites.' This was his area of expertise and he alone should be in charge. He did not greet me warmly when I arrived at Grady Hospital. Outside the hospital room of Bobby Wilcoxson, was a guard with a head like a buffalo. Usually a guard would be stationed so as to see that Bobby didn't escape but in this case he was there to make sure that someone didn't come back and finish the job that had been started with the original murder attempt. Even if the door had been left open, the man couldn't have crawled out the door as he had been cut apart. He was almost a living hysterectomy. As I tried blithely to enter the hospital room, Old Buffalo Head firmly stated with all the warmth of 'Bluebeard','"No one's allowed in here, except the doctors and the priest to see the inmates. You ain't gonna get in so you's best go on home."

If I were to be forbidden entry to see Bobby, why was I called at all? Rather than stay and make a scene I decided to return quietly home and send a bouquet of flowers. Everything in prison is a black and white world. There are no colors in prisons. No fragrant smells of flowers or soft lilting laughter of babies or sounds of children running. People who run in prisons get shot. As soon as Bobby was fit, he wrote me a beautiful letter saying that it had been twelve years since he had been that close to a flower. He spent two whole pages describing the joy he felt in the hospital at smelling the flowers, at feeling their texture and, of all the vivid colors.

Every time I would see Bobby, he would tell me what a dangerous man he was. He looked as old as incest, with leathery skin, and such a "grandfather" type that I could never believe he had robbed all the banks attributed to him and caused all the chaos he claimed. I should have believed him when he told me that his crimes had been the basis of many of the Detective Marlow novels. He didn't lie. His partner, Albert Frederick Nussbaum began to write, himself, while in prison and had gone on to quite a lucrative career as an author.

Before my book went into publication I tried to have each man about whom I had written of read what was said about them. I wanted to see if there were any suggestions or corrections. Possibly, information could have been made more factual. Bobby was quite proud of his former partner's success and offered to have Mr. Nussbaum read and critique my material before it was printed. According to Bobby,"Arlene, if you would like me to, I will contact my partner in crime, who has been out since 1976, and have him read your book even before it is finished. Al is revered for his book reviews and he is considered an authority on any writing about prisons, crime and criminal writers. His book reviews on Judge Frankels, U.S. District Court, New York, got a full page in May Issue of Harper Magazine. That's how he's earning his living now."

It's too bad we never met, as with a success story such as that, you gotta admire the guy. Actually, it illustrates very well what could possibly be the story of so many of the men in the Atlanta Penitentiary. Most of the inmates in these federal institutions are exceptionally bright and the traits that are devious could be channeled creatively down an honest path.

Bobby didn't lie when he boasted how he had gone down in the annals of crime history as someone who was a living legend. In the winter of 1977, my husband and I took the kids on a belated bicentennial tour of Washington. On one particular morning, it was raining like the Armageddon, and we took refuge in the FBI building. There was already a large group to go in, and we joined a tour of about thirty others who were just preparing to go down the corridor with a young Efrem Zimbalist-looking agent who was assigned to them. It was positively vile that the man was so clean cut and wholesome looking. He looked as though he had a closet full of three-piece double-knit suits in different colors for each night of the week. His favorite drink was probably one-half Scotch and one-half Polyester. We looked as though we had just walked out of the rain and he had an air about him of just having emerged from the shower.

Since we joined the tour late, we would have preferred to stay unnoticed. Everything went normally for the first 20 or 30 minutes, and we were finding his talk fascinating. Eventually, the agent stopped so that we might see a special display of the FBI's most famous cases that were posted around the room. Rows upon rows of pictures from the annals of the FBI fugitives were put on display. Everyone was crowding around the pictures for a glimpse of this gallery of notorious criminals. Occasionally, the agent would stop in front of one of the panels and give a little schpiel about 'rogue' and his offense.

All along the walls the pictures were complete with diagrams of the banks that were robbed and pictures of the men who, according to the FBI were the all-time masters of disguise. While he was talking about the dangerous criminals, Bobby Wilcoxson and his partner, Albert Nussbaum, I noticed something was familiar about one of them. I didn't give it too much thought, as I have a tendency to think that of eight out of ten people I meet are familiar.

All of a sudden, my son ran up to the picture, took a long, careful look and gave a cry like a fog horn, "Look, Daddy, there's Mommy's friend, Bobby, the bank robber!"

The entire room full of tourists turned to look at me, filled with curiosity. Efrem, the FBI agent who was standing to the side, eyed me suspiciously. Undoubtedly, after the commotion we caused, there was a dossier on Mrs. Peck located in the FBI files. My son provided a real clincher when he returned home from school one day with a book that he had checked out of the school library. The title of the book was, "The FBI's Most Famous Cases," with a foreword by J. Edgar Hoover. In part it read:

"On December 15th, 1961, while Albert Frederick Nussbaum sat in a car outside, Bobby Wilcoxson entered the LaFayette National Bank in Brooklyn, New York. Wilcoxson armed with a submachine gun shouted,

'This is a robbery!' He walked over to the bank guard and fired four shots which left the guard dead on the floor."

It further described how, unknown to the robbers, a bank customer escaped unnoticed and alerted the police. A police officer, having arrived at the bank saw Wilcoxson and opened fire. My 'kindly' grandfather fired a burst of bullets that sent the officer spinning out the door and onto the sidewalk. This robbery was one of the many that were pulled off by this busy twosome.

The FBI then launched an intense investigation that lasted two years. By the time Nussbaum and Wilcoxson were finally caught, they had accumulated an arsenal of weapons, robbed at least eight banks, and terrorized the nation's capital with a series of bombing incidents and bomb threats. A few of their 'minor' charges were violation of the Federal Extortion Statute; the transporting of stolen cars interstate and passing stolen checks. They committed several burglaries and violated the Federal and National Firearms Acts. The part that really blew my mind was the statement that they violated the White Slave Traffic law. I found it incredible that this sweet little man that I had come to know even knew what that was. He just didn't seem the type.

I read on and learned that;

"The FBI learned through an accomplice that Wilcoxson's partner, Nussbaum, had accumulated a large number of firearms on a farm in a rural area not far from Buffalo, New York."

In late February, 1962, FBI Agents found this arsenal, and according to them, it was unequalled in the annals of crime.

"The farm where Nussbaum and Wilcoxson practiced shooting was also located. Agents dug bullets out of trees and later recovered cartridge cases from the ground. These were found by the FBI laboratory to have been fired from the same gun used to kill the bank guard."

From there the investigation continued to even spread further. The entire country's law enforcement staff searched for these men.

Finally, during the summer of 1962, Bobby blundered during a robbery. Nussbaum was unable to function without Bobby, and finally 'snitched' on his former friend and partner, Wilcoxson. He reported to the FBI where Bobby might be found and that was the beginning of the end. The FBI surrounded Bobby's house and without a single shot being fired, the FBI closed the career of the most dangerous fugitives since the gangster era of the 1930's.

I brought Bobby in a copy of the FBI's most wanted book to see what his reaction might be. More than anything, I think it was one of pride. He turned the pages of 'his story', peered at me through those thick glasses and said, "Hmm, I told you so."

Chapter Five

WILLIAM A.H. WILLIAMS:
THE PATTY HEARST INFLUENCE LINGERS ON?

If the question is,"What's a nice Jewish girl going in a place like that?" then a version of it goes double for whom I intend to talk about next. Usually, familiarity breeds contempt, but in the case of the guys in my'Group', with many I've been able to maintain a closeness. As the years rolled by, they served their time, made parole, and we'd still manage to keep in touch. Sometimes the guys would call just to let me know they were passing through town. There are times when my house served as a'half-way house' for families or inmates who've left the'fold', but wanted to talk. However, by the very nature of the situation much of my relationships with the men had been transitory. For whatever reason; transfer, lack of continued interest, release, the men eventually moved on and contact was lost.

Volunteers going into prisons learn in the very beginning that if they are to be successful in their endeavors, preconceived notions about inmates and their crimes should not be allowed to enter the program or the minds of those conducting it. The goal of our Jewish discussion group was to be a learning experience for the men and our message was not one of conversion, or even repenting. We only wanted to give a link to the outside Jewish community and to educate, in whatever way we could, men who had little or no knowledge of our religion. Most of the time, I had no former knowledge of the inmate or the cause of his incarceration so our relationships were able to stand on their own. William A.H. Williams was to be the exception. I knew who he was, what he had done and before I even met the man I couldn't stand him. He was a notorious anti-Semite and his views of the Jewish people were well known. At the time of his capture, much news coverage was given to the fact that his car was covered with hate stickers."Oil yes, Jews No, burn Jews . . . not oil . . ."He had been quite vocal. Despite all my liberal intentions, it was with actual dismay that I saw him walk into the Wednesday evening discussion group. Williams waited until the meeting was over and then with a big smile walked over to introduce himself. With each step that he took toward me, I sat there thinking,"Oh God. What in the world is this man doing in the Jewish Discussion group? Maybe he wanted to go to a Ku Klux Klan meeting and walked in here by mistake. Oh God, he's coming over to talk to me. What in the hell am I gonna say to him?"

It was inconceivable that I would have any rapport with a man who held his anti-Jewish views. Everything about him was repugnant to me. I was determined to dislike him, just as I hated everything which he stood for. I looked up and he was standing there holding out his hand and saying with much self-importance, "Hello, I'm William Williams, William A.H. Williams."

Well, my G-d. With his name and picture being plastered all over the newspaper, I had to know who he was. Everyone knew who he was. However, I'd be damned if I'd let him know, that with his chubby body and handlebar moustache, he would be recognized anywhere, so I replied, "Nice to meet you, I'm Arlene Peck."

A little taken aback, he answered me, "I don't think you understand, I'm William A.H. Williams."

Just as sweetly, I replied, "I'm Arlene G. Peck."

Somehow, that really got his attention. That was not the reaction this 'outlaw' wanted or needed. As far as my attention, it was difficult to even concentrate on what the man was saying. All I could think of was, I don't want to be friends with a disciple of that Nazi, J.B. Stoner. It was difficult to even give the appearance of politeness. Actually, I remember very little of what he had to say during that first introduction. I kept thinking, he doesn't look very much like the criminal type. If he didn't have that big handlebar moustache he would look very much like those men with beer bellies who hang around with Billy Carter and the good ole boys. Actually, without too much difficulty, I could visualize him driving a pickup while chewing on a toothpick and holding a can of Budweiser. I knew he had to be crazy.

In 1976, Williams had kidnapped the editor of the Atlanta Constitution, Reg Murphy. At the time, everything Williams did or said was news. And true, at the time of our meeting, enough time had elapsed so that people didn't read about him daily, he was still news. I was finding it extremely difficult to concentrate on hating a man who at first glance resembles Yogi Bear. When arrested, he was overweight, and despite his large frame, (he was at least 6 foot 2 or 3) weighed well over 200 pounds. Back in 1976, when we began our strange relationship, Bill was still a product of the old south. I am sure that he was the type that would stand up and give little old ladies a seat on the bus or say, "Yes Ma'am" to anyone over thirty. As the months passed and he became a regular in the group, I had the chance to study him more closely. Often he was dressed in blue sneakers, short white socks, yellow polyester Bermuda shorts, and a tee shirt. His hands were large and his fingernails were always cut short and very clean. His hair was a cross between wet-head and early 1955. As I began to know this man and his story, I couldn't help but find it fascinating. I often wondered how an anti-Semite or a Hitler or a J.B. Stoner was made. Well, from Bill and his past history and background, I began to find out. When he first began coming to Wednesday evening discussion group he was tense and would sit off to one side, withdrawn from the rest of the men. His arms were usually folded tightly across his chest, and his eyes were constantly darting around. It was as though he expected the men to retaliate for the many injustices he had done while a member of his church and JB Stoner's Nazi organization. It took me a few weeks, but I finally got the nerve to ask him, "Hey Bill, c'mon, tell the truth. You were looking for a meeting for the Ku Klux Klan the night you came in here, right?"

Bill looked a little uncomfortable until he realized I'd meant it in a kidding way, and then he said, "Well, as a matter of fact, I entered the enemy camp as a diversion from boredom. But ya know something, Arlene?"

"No, what?"

"I came, in truth, from boredom, but something about these meetings has been changing me."

"Yeah, in what way?"

"Oh, I don't know. I guess I've been able to change a lot of stereotype ideas I'd had earlier."

It wasn't hard to imagine from his recent past what they were, but I asked anyways, "Yeah? Like what kind of ideas?"

Bill was starting to look a little bit uncomfortable, so I decided not to pursue it too much. He kind of shifted in his chair and said, "Oh, I don't know, I'm kind of getting an understanding now of people I've been raised to despise. In fact, of late, I'm starting to feel guilty about being accepted by people who I once hated during my association with J.B. Stoner."

The change was beginning to happen in me also. I was finding it more and more difficult to dislike this man. By the latter part of 1975 we had the beginning of what was to turn into a special relationship. Bill was an individual with serious problems. In straight body language, he did not fit and I wondered why he was really there. And speaking of his body, he was very muscular. However, I didn't think that he would ever search out any type of physical confrontation. He had been very, very careful not to let himself get into trouble with either the officials or the inmates. He was a loner. But as a result of the program, Bill became friendly with a Jewish inmate within the institution. The man, Norman 'The Bomber,' was able to leave a lasting impression upon Bill. Because of this friendship, Bill gradually began to have an understanding of the people he'd been raised to despise. Once, with actual wonder in his voice, Bill commented, "Man, I still can't get over the forgiving attitude of these Jews. They've got good reason to hate me, and yet, when I come into the discussions, everybody is so nice, and they know who I am."

And Norman, who is Jewish, would tell him, "You don't always have to get even when you get mad, we may have a reason to hate you but we don't have the right. We cannot be Jewish and hate you at the same time."

As Bill came to know the group and Norman, he began to realize that we stress education, not conversion. Gradually, he began to take college classes that were offered to the inmates. Even though his self-image was nil, he surprised himself by ending up on the dean's list, time and time again. Eventually, he went for a master's degree and consistently stayed at the top of the class. This, from a 10th grade drop-out with a redneck background. Although his attendance now seemed natural, I realized that William Williams' becoming a part of the Jewish group was a paradox. Everything he had been taught concerning Jews and their situation had been distorted hate propaganda. Something about his whole story made one want to find out more than he was willing to tell. I became a link to Bill and to the questions that he was having concerning religion and people that he had learned to hate. Actually, my first thought of writing a novel was planted by Bill. I had long been writing a weekly column in a National Jewish newspaper, The Jewish Post and Opinion, which the group had a subscription to. Bill became an avid fan of the column, and as a result he approached me one night with the request that I write his story. I laughed and said, "Bill, that's very flattering and very sweet of you but I know nothing about writing books. It's just not my bag."

It was one of the few times I ever saw him look intense, and he said, "Arlene, there are very few people in this world I trust. You're one of them. I haven't given an interview in three years. I've got a story that should be told and I want you to be the one to write it."

I didn't want to disappoint the man, but I finally had to say, "Listen Bill, I just don't know anything about writing books. I know even less about your story, how am I going to write about you when I know very little about you?"

He thought about that for a few moments and he said, "Hey listen, don't give that a thought. I'll see you know all about me. How's that? I'm going to send you a copy of my psychiatric report in the next day's mail. You'll really get an earful. Tell me if you don't think it's worth a book then."

Within a few days, a large envelope arrived at my house, jammed with papers and clippings and Bill's psychiatric report. Actually, much of it confirmed a lot of what I already knew. William A.H. Williams felt that nothing he ever did ever went right.

He was the youngest of four sons of a retired civil service fire chief. His father taught him at an early age that he was nothing and that to show a kindness was a sign of weakness. I had read his psychiatric report and it was a horror story of sadistic parents and uncaring family but I wanted to hear him say it. As our conversations began to go deeper, I asked Bill once, "What about your childhood?"

"If you think I was abused, you ain't seen nothing till you see the old man beat J.D. J.D was the oldest brother, and spent a lot of time in the state mental hospitals. Maybe, because of this he got even worse treatment than the rest of us."

Bill wanted to drop the subject but I pressed further and he finally continued with;

"Well, I've seen some pretty sad situations where the old man would beat him until he was tired, and then he would rest a few minutes and start beating him again. This happened to all of us, but J.D. I think got the worst of it.

Once, after hearing the story of J.D., I wondered what eventually happened to him. When Bill was asked, a pained look came over his face and he seemed to hesitate for a couple of extra seconds, then it came pouring out in a rush.

"Yeah, OK, I'll give you an example of the kind of proud father that I was blessed with. In December of 1972, my oldest brother J.D. was involved in a very serious automobile wreck in which he was just absolutely crushed from head to foot. J.D. stayed in an intensive care unit at Kennestone Hospital for 21 days and had died clinically twice. In that period, he begged to have his father to come to see him, but the old man wouldn't go. He hated J.D. and kept telling us that the best thing that could happen for him was for J.D to die. J.D. was finally released from the hospital and had nowhere to go."

"Bill? What do you mean he had nowhere to go? How about your house? Your parents?"

Emphatically, he shook his head:

"I mean he had nowhere to go. I was in Florida at the time that I heard that he was released from the hospital, I was furious. The old man had a 5 bedroom house and plenty of room to spare, and he refused to let my brother come home. Some friends took him in and a week later he died."

The question arose in my mind, what about the rest of his family? Why didn't he come in from Florida to handle the situation, where were his brothers or their families, but it was obvious that the subject was painful to him. But, he wanted it out.

"Here you have a son calling for his father to come to see him before he died, and the father wishing that the son would die. I want that S.O.B. to be known. I want that to be in the book if nothing else gets in there."

Later, I wondered how the hospital had even let J.D. out in the condition he had been in.

Bill grew up feeling worthless in everybody's eyes. And, although he was never given love or attention at home, his family certainly managed to find the time to instill hate. I remember Bill once telling me, "Momma never gave me attention, or anything else for that matter, not even a childhood. The only thing that she ever gave was that damn Noonday Baptist Church where they dragged us every damn Sunday and Wednesday night. Looking back, the only thing I can remember learning about was the 'Jewish Conspiracy', and that behind every rock was a few waiting to take over the country."

His voice trailed off . . .

"Oh yeah, they taught that good . . ."

When Bill was sixteen, while singing in the church choir, his father noticed that Bill had an erection, and running across the room, forcibly removed him from the choir and beat the living hell out of him. Then, he made Bill return to the room and apologize to the congregation. Talk about sick. It was over a year before he would return to church.

When Bill and I discussed this part in the book, he was insistent that I remove all references to the things that his father did. He felt a shame that was misplaced and I hoped that by this time Bill realized that it was the best example that could be given to show what he had to overcome and how far he had progressed.

Bill saw his father as a monster, complete with horns, daggers, tail, and holding clubs with blood dripping from them. Nice huh? His mother, according to him, was so afraid of his father that she would stand and wring her hands while Bill was getting, along with his brothers, his regular beatings.

He drew his mother as a small dumpy woman, with no eyes, hands, ears or mouth. She finally told him to leave when he was still a teenager to avoid being beaten to death by his "Good Christian" father.

Only once did we really have the few minutes extra after the meeting to discuss his father. All I had to do was mention the man and Bill was like a volcano. As the subject of his father was brought up, Bill's expressive eyes would turn immediately sad and he said, "What a mean SOB he was. God almighty, how old do you have to be till the hurt goes away? Or does it ever? After the life I've led, these walls aren't too much different from the walls of hate and isolation I've had the better part of my life."

The conversation was too heavy for me in a crowded room so I glazed over his comment with, "Aw, c'mon, at least when you were outside you could go elsewhere if you didn't like where you were. Here you've got bars, or have you noticed?"

Bill just sat there looking at me with his soulful brown eyes and said, "That's where you're wrong. My whole life has been a prison. Talking to 'him' was like talking to a wall, only his wall would beat you till you were bloody. Nothing, less than nothing, was what he made me feel like."

He squeezed his eyes shut and seemed to go off into the recesses of his own mind. After a moment, Bill looked past me and continued with, "He'd take the switch to me till I couldn't take it anymore. I'd take off and the police would get me every time. I'd try to tell 'em why I left, but they didn't care, nobody did. They'd take me back to that hell hole. Daddy would be the picture of the concerned father over his runaway son, and the minute the cops would walk out the 'old man' would make me strip naked and beat me until I was covered with blood. He'd beat me with his fist and only when he saw I was past feeling, only then did he let go. God I wanted to kill him. Tried to too. Only the good die young and nothing I did ever seemed to work."

Bill ran his hand across his eyes to hold back the tears. Without even realizing it, his body gave an involuntary shake as he remembered.

"Once I took the nuts off the left front tire of our car and my father had a wreck . . . he never knew who did it. I wanted to tell him, let him know how much I hated him, but damn, even then I was a failure."

Shortly after I read the report, I saw Bill and I was dying to speak with him. Most of its contents were about his bizarre behavior and it became easier to understand him when I read about his relationship with his family, or rather his lack of one. Usually, I tried not to sit next to someone who had become 'special' to me as the men were so damn observant that before you knew it, they thought you were up to something, and it was important to keep up the 'group concept'. Instead of risking another call into the warden's office because of any special friendships I might have made with an inmate, I made a list of questions, and within the week, his answers were mailed in. One of them concerned one of Bill's older twin brothers, Ronny.

"I wasn't the only one to get the beatings. One day I remember, the 'old man' had his knees pinned against Ronny's shoulders, and was systematically beating him with his fist. I honestly thought Ronny was going to be killed. I ran into the 'old man's' room and started looking for the .22 pistol. Had I found it, I would have put a stop to all that bullshit that we had to suffer at the hands of that maniac."

As early as possible, Bill and his brothers joined the Georgia National Guard. He was sixteen and his brother seventeen. They eventually planned to join the navy.

For a couple of years he wandered around. In the Navy, the violence building in him finally erupted. Bill almost beat a guy to death whom he mistakenly thought was about to hurt a sleeping friend. He beat the man so ferociously that until this day, the victim still has not recovered. That incident shook Bill so, that he has not drunk or fought since. He was finally given a medical discharge. In view of his basic prejudice, it was ironic that the man he had defended was black.

With this bizarre background, William entered the organization of J.B. Stoner. Stoner is a pathetic little creature. He is crippled physically, from polio, but it's his soul that makes one's skin crawl. Stoner is also presently under investigation for a bombing in Alabama several years ago where four black children were killed. He is the president of a hate organization called the National Socialist Party, headquartered in Atlanta, and from time to time, runs for public office. Frighteningly enough, the last time he ran for governor, Stoner received almost 80,000 votes in the State of Georgia. Stoner cultivates individuals like William as followers for his hate organization. With Stoner, Williams could be an important person. He was also a willing pupil and soon became front man for Stoner's hate rallies.

During our time together, Williams came into possession of the 'papers' that would change his life. According to Bill;

"It was an entire filing cabinet of documents that had been stolen from the F.B.I., that told of scandals, payoffs and kick-backs from several of our U.S. senators and congressmen that have been suppressed."

Bill never made these papers public. They were supposed to be buried in a dead wall somewhere that only Bill knows. I am certain they exist for Williams knew too many details that he could never have known otherwise. He spoke in detail of the Senator Herman Talmadge's land and stock deals two years before any of them came to light. In fact, I even went as far as meeting with the Jack Anderson machine in Washington, and for a couple of weeks, letters and phone calls were going back and forth furiously. They wanted the 'papers,' but I didn't have them to give.

These exposed papers served as the catalyst in Bill's incoherent and scattered mind when he kidnapped Reg Murphy in 1971. According to letters written by Bill, he states, "In order for me to make any sense out of what was going on at the time, I must confess that William A.H. Williams was two people. The first entity being me, William A.H. Williams, the second entity being Colonel William A.H. Williams, American Revolutionary Army."

Bill continued in his letter, "Sometime in the Month of December, 1974, Col. Williams took complete control of 'my' action. I could only stand by and watch the catastrophe takes place. It's as if the kidnapping had been planned a long, long time ago, and was waiting to take place. There was really no plan involved. It was a spontaneous and impromptu reaction."

The amazing part about all the revelations that Bill made to me in his letters were the in-depth, self-analysis that he had to make in order to answer any questions concerning the kidnapping. One of these letters answered: "I felt that I was somehow divinely led. The divine revelation bit may sound foolish; however, when you can see where I was coming from you'll see the divine revelation is not far fetched. I'm coming around to a broader sense of reality, but it's been a tough up hill battle."

It wasn't too big a surprise to find out that Bill was now majoring in psychology in college. He strongly believed that, "education has been the magic key to my whole thought system."This has come, surprisingly enough, through our prison system.

Although it doesn't make sense, it was probably true that at the time of the kidnapping, Bill was so intoxicated with his momentary power that nothing he did made any sense.

According to Bill, "First you must understand that I never considered that Mr. Murphy was ever kidnapped. In my view of things at the time, I felt that my action toward Murphy was no different than the action of a Patrick Henry or a Thomas Jefferson. I had at the time, F.B.I field reports of criminal activities of certain U.S. senators and U.S. reps. These papers are not figments of my imagination in that Murphy admitted during the first trial (1971) that he had read a portion of them. I quite frankly wanted Murphy to (as a condition of his release) publish these documents. This was the sole intent of the 'arrest' of Mr. Murphy by the revolutionary army."

Bill neglected to say that the only member of this 'army' was William A.M. Williams.

"Secondly, you must understand where I was coming from mentally. Frankly, at the time of the 'arrest' I felt that it had to be done. I considered myself a PROPHET OF GOD. That state of mind does not exist in me today, but it must be considered in the overall picture, in that this knowing made everything right."

According to Williams and substantiated by his court appointed psychiatrist, Bill had no intention of harming the Constitution Editor that evening. He honestly believed that he wouldn't be able to go to a man like Reg Murphy and just tell him the facts. Admittedly, it was a little drastic to abduct Murphy from his home. It was even a little more drastic to put the man in the trunk of his car while Bill decided what to do with him. But, his intentions were for a 'cause' rather than the $700,000 ransom. At the time of the kidnapping the thoughts of the night and the reality of the day seemed to blend into each other and it was hard to separate what was real and what he wanted it to be. If he exposed the truth as he knew it, he would be ridiculed by others as he had once been by his father.

It has been many months since we'd discussed this topic but, in 1977-78, the Atlanta Federal Penitentiary had a rash of eleven murders within a year. Bill and I had a lengthy discussion that was hard to forget. It was as I was gathering up my shopping bag full of magazines and old junk mail from home when Bill approached me. The guard had come to tell the six guests who had come in for the evening that it was time to leave and behind him I saw another inmate casually stroll past and glance in. It was Bill.

"Hey, little sister! You been reading the papers?"

"Sure."

"Well, in case you don't see me next time you come in; you'll know 'they' got me."

That was sort of an alarming statement to make and he said so,"Well, Arlene, with all the murders that have happened here the past month it's hard to shake the feeling that I could be next."

I knew he was pretty much able to take care of himself so I tried to make a joke out of it and laughed,"Bill, who's gonna want a big teddy bear like you?"

"Oh, I'm not worried about the men in here, uh-uh. Rather, it's a feeling I get that if I ever did get a 'hit' it would come from somebody sent by the FBI rather than another inmate."

By now, he looked embarrassed that he had even brought the subject up and still he wanted to tell someone on the outside his feelings, maybe as sort of a cushion, in case anything actually did happen.

"Don't forget that I still have the 'papers' that 'they' didn't want the American people to see."

Today, I'm not a believer that I once was, not just with Williams, but everyone. But, how do you explain all the detailed stories that he had to tell about Herman Talmadge's financial affairs that have since come to light?

Whatever the reason, the kidnapping was real and his problems with his marriage during that time were real, also. Pressures had been building up in him and Bill's marriage was hitting the skids fast. Things had changed drastically since the early romantic days. Years before the kidnapping Bill had married a waitress named Betty. Their courting started in a waffle house, not exactly a classy beginning, but, considering the ending they had, it was fitting. She was a bootlegger's daughter from Viper, Kentucky. Her involvement in the kidnapping was the most 'togetherness' they had had in a long time. At the time of the trial, Bill had successfully kept Betty out of it. But, after it was all over, he admitted that she was in on everything. Once I asked Bill if he had ever mentioned Murphy to his wife earlier.

"Hell yes, I mentioned Murphy to her. As a matter of fact she was standing by my side when I called Murphy on the phone to make the appointment with him. She knew what was going on, and yes, I received a great deal of encouragement from her."

His method of kidnapping this famous figure read like a scene from fiction. Everything that a kidnapper could do to screw up his escape and make sure that he was caught, Bill did. Of course it wasn't too bright of Murphy to go alone in the car, willingly, with this 'nut' Colonel Williams. The 'Colonel' lured Murphy by telling him on the phone that he was a wealthy man who wanted to give three hundred thousand gallons of oil to someone worthy, and he wanted Murphy to be the go-between.

"Somehow, we set up an appointment to meet at his house to discuss our business deal. I remember crying most of that day. I do remember being at Murphy's house, but I don't recall the drive from my house to his. What is the most outstanding event in my mind during those days is, that I had no choice. I simply could not stop myself. It didn't matter to me if what I was going to do was right or wrong, the fact is, I was going to do it, and noting could stop me!"

Now, the part about the 'papers' comes into sequence.

"After Murphy had read the papers, and we had talked at length about politics and, after he agreed to publish these papers; at that moment that he agreed to print those FBI documents, the kidnapping for all intents and purpose was over. Murphy informed me that no one would believe that he had been kidnapped unless he was held for ransom. I swear before G-d, that it was never my intention to hold Murphy for ransom. Murphy had to guide my every move concerning ransom."

Knowing how William's mind worked during this time, it was almost anticlimactic once he possessed Murphy. He had a fantasy that he was leading the American people to the 'truth,' but things always got fuzzy at this point and Bill was never quite sure of what he wanted to say. At the trial, the papers were mentioned, but never fully. Much of the actual events never came out. For three years, Bill never spoke to anyone or revealed his feelings until he asked me to write his book. He had, and I say 'had', because I think he has changed a lot in the past few years, a complete mistrust of everyone, especially the media. He felt that Reg Murphy realized that he had a nut on his hands, but a harmless nut that he would be able to handle easily. Bill came out of the entire situation feeling like the real victim. Reg was able to get front page headlines for weeks as a result of the abduction and finally ended up working for the Hearst organization in San Francisco. The best that Williams got out of it was forty years in the Atlanta Penitentiary.

No, I take that back. When he came into prison he fantasized a great deal and could not distinguish between his imagination and what was really going on. The difference between him and the other inmates in that respect is so many of the men leave, after years of incarceration with those traits. Upon entering those prison walls he was a 10th grade drop-out. As time passed, he embarked on a self-help program for mental and physical well-being. First the handlebar moustache came off, followed by pounds and pounds of weight. Most important, the man discovered that he had a mind, contrary to what he was taught, and a good one at that. His formative years were fought with hate and violence. His soul was a sensitive one and the pressures were much too deep. The man cracked. The system during those days did not go deep enough into a case like this to understand the reasons why. Any crime, especially a kidnapping is difficult for the normal and average mind to comprehend, but they happen, and Bill's story could be behind many of them. It gave Bill a chance to realize his potential. He fortunately used that time to realize his capabilities. He also developed confidence in people. Because of the education he received and all the genuine care he had gotten from volunteers, he was able to realize that everyone is not the enemy.

His wife had her problems also. At 19 she and Bill were divorced. Eventually, she made the front pages for setting some guy up in a hotel room, complete with pictures and everything. Instead of paying off the blackmail, the man went to the police and she is now serving time in a women's prison. She and Bill are now divorced. In all probability, with her hillbilly background and his improved education, they would never have been able to relate to one another again. They have little in common anymore, except maybe prison. And, the children. He missed them very much.

And, Murphy, what was his story in the kidnapping? He told me of a garishly dressed man in a maroon cowboy hat, green nylon windbreaker and maroon pants coming to his door. His story coincided about the lure of 300,000 gallons of oil that 'Lamont Woods' wanted to give to a charity recommended by Murphy. A few minutes after Murphy went with his abductor in a car, Williams began to ramble on about the Jewish domination of newspapers, corporations and governments. His next comment was,"Mr. Murphy, you have been kidnapped. We're going to straighten out this damn country. We're going to stop these lying, liberal news media."

Bill rattled on about the American Revolutionary Army, "It had 223 members and six colonels. I command the American Eagle Division located in the Southeast. The Northeastern section is called the American Falcon. I can't tell you more details now, but I will later."

All through Reg Murphy's testimony, his recollections were much the same as Williams but when you speak to both, the interpretations were much different. When Bill was asked the question,"who felt the most fear, you or Murphy?" he answered with,"A man that feels true fear will at any occasion try to get away from immediate danger. Murphy had ample opportunity to escape from any fear he might have had."

He continued with,"For instance, when I would stop and make a phone call, I would park just as far as possible from the pay phone in order to give him a chance to leave. The following morning when I ordered a large breakfast for the both of us, I went out to pick it up. I stayed away for over 45 minutes with Murphy alone in the hotel room, with a phone. Why didn't he call for help? He was free to do as he pleased. While I was away, he took a shower, brushed his teeth, etc. but he wouldn't shave. Can you figure out why he wouldn't shave? It wouldn't have looked very good on T.V. if he were clean shaven. Once I left Murphy in the back seat of the car sitting up. The windows were down and he was in very close range of the gas attendant.

He made no effort to communicate in any way to the attendant about who he was or anything, even though he did hold the attendant in conversation. I don't know what he said, but it sure wasn't,"HELP". There were numerous times that Murphy could have simply walked away, but no such luck. I was stuck with a person who knew that he was in safe hands and that he would be able to capitalize on the sickness of a human."

Now, the same situation as seen through the eyes of the kidnapped:

"The Colonel was in a good mood. He allowed me to shower, He gave me a pair of his fresh socks. We had eggs, hash browns, bacon and toast. He had milk and I had coffee, and he went to the restaurant to pick it up. It was the first food I had eaten since Wednesday, and the last I would eat until the terrible ordeal was over."

Nowhere in either version was there mention of Murphy attempting to get help. Williams question was a good one. Why didn't Murphy attempt to cry out, or leave when Williams was otherwise occupied? Murphy mentions the $700,000 but not as being his brainstorm as Williams insists. Nowhere in the newspapers when Reg Murphy was giving 'his story' did he mention the 'papers' that were supposed to be the cause of the whole macabre incident. Did Murphy see them? Again, if they didn't exist, how did Williams know so much about scandals that have come to light? Most of all, could any of us have withstood the pressures of the mind that were a way of life for him? According to Williams as he reflected on this situation a few years after his arrest in 1971 when I asked him about how he felt his mental health was at this point:

"I honestly feel that Murphy is probably a lot sicker, mentally, now than I was back in 1974. Murphy needs help. There is no doubt that he lied on numerous occasions when he simply didn't have to. But now, we get back to the F.B.I. Had Murphy simply told the truth about me, and my mental condition, and the way he was treated, I feel that instead of being sentenced to 40 years, I would have probably been sent to a mental hospital. Dr. Askren, (the court appointed psychiatrist) felt I should have been sent to psychotherapy treatment. However, because of the F.B.I papers, this just couldn't be allowed."

"Bill, do you really believe all that?"

"You're damn right. That's why all the cover up. That's why I'm supposed to be a terrible kidnapper with only thoughts of getting a lot of money, instead of a mentally sick citizen in need of a lot of help and understanding."

He told me this in 1977 and other than the initial interview with the court doctor, the man had yet to be allowed to see a psychologist for years to come and why? There was a time that I never would have even figured I'd be able to even tolerate the man, and today I have a lot of respect for his ambition and how far he's come and we've ended up having a very special friendship that continues to this day.

Chapter Six

THE LADY OR THE TIGER?

As 1977 rolled around, I was beginning to worry that I was relating more psychopaths living in the institution than the ones running it. I had become involved with a multitude of psychotics, psychopaths, neurotics involved in situations that I'm still not sure were fact or fiction. It would have been easier if I had just taken my guests in each week, present religious oriented programs and not become involved with them, but that just would not have been as half as much fun. Usually, the personal and emotional problems that the men brought with them were right up front, and it wasn't too difficult to see who the real crazies were. Occasionally, I'd come across one of the men who would really have me spinning my wheels. Bud Culligan was one of them.

The men in my 'Group' were definitely unique, but of all of them, Roland B. Culligan was the topper. I noticed him immediately, mainly because he didn't have any visible tattoos and in no way did he fit the criminal stereotype. He had the word 'executive' written all over him.

Bud was tall, thin and had a very military bearing. There was just a trace of that shark-like image that is found in top military men, major mafia bosses and the very beautiful people of the jet-set crowd. His carriage was that of one who had achieved power and had exercised it over a long period of time. His hair was grey at the temples, and if it were not for the setting, it was easy to visualize 'Bud' as a successful stock broker. My intuition was right when it told me that he was not the regular run of the mill bank robber.

One time when I told him of my impression, he sat back and looked at me through those crisp, cold blue eyes, took a puff on his pipe and said, "I'm not what I seem." Even his khaki uniform had a tweed look to it.

About the second or third month he had been coming into the 'Group', events were to take place that verified his words. He wasn't what he seemed.

It was a big prison rule; no one can carry anything into a maximum security federal prison. But, every Wednesday, year in and year out, I would enter the institution loaded down with all kinds of junk mail, magazines and stacks of Jewish newspapers in case the group wanted something to read. I think I hoped secretly I'd get lucky and someone would want to search me. Anyhow, one particular evening, as I was gathering up my paraphernalia, Bud came up to me and said, "I've decided to trust someone on the outside, and it looks like you're it."

He then looked over his shoulder to make sure that we weren't being overheard and continued in a conspiring voice, "Arlene, in the next few days you are going to receive a package in the mail which will explain further who I really am. Read it over carefully and we will discuss the contents on your next visit. Under no circumstances are you to discuss with anyone what you are to read."

Comments such as that have an ominous thread, and for the next few days I waited with 'bated breath'. Sure enough, a package was delivered to my house. I could have gotten a hernia lifting it. After wading through the material it became obvious that the 'heaviness' applied more to the content than to the bulk.

For the next two hours, I sat down to read some really scary stuff. According to the story, my 'new' friend, Bud, had been a secret agent and 'hit man' in the CIA for over twenty-five years. His 'cover' had been to work as an Eastern Airlines pilot. I knew it! That's exactly what he looked like, an airline pilot. All of a sudden everything fell into place. Those crisp eyes with the sun lines, the pipe he smoked, even his name, BUD. They all look like middle-aged John Denvers, but taller.

The files were incredible. It was difficult to believe the names of the people that guy was supposed to have 'removed' from society, all under the auspices of the United States Government, names like Dag Hammarskjold, Trujillo, King Farouk, Nasser and more. What's more, he even went into detail how, what, when, where, why and whom these people were with when it happened. The descriptions were so vivid that when he spoke of these people who were pages out of our history, it all sounded very real. When he described how Farouk died, he went into detail. His files had whole pages relating how Dag Hammarskjold was 'murdered' by the CIA through him. In part, he wrote:

"The executive action involving Hammarskjold was a bad one. I did not want the job. Dammit, I did not want the job. The airplane, P-38, was purchased in Houston in 1960, shipped to Tripoli, Libya, assembled, and test flown by American Oil associate of Don Aulbrou. Don had been with me in '52, on the Point 1 program. I intercepted 'D'. His trip at Ndola, No. Rhodesia (now Zaire), flew to Ndola, shot the airplane, it crashed, and I flew back the same way. Gen Shmen Khan-Libyan was my contact in Tripoli. Khan sold the P-38 to someone in Beirut, Leb. That was his pay."

Later in his particular letter to his lawyer he writes, "I know it's necessary, but I dislike this very much. I hope with all my heart this is enough to get me home. Then you can have the whole nasty thing in your lap. I say nasty—I went to confession after Nasser, and I swore I would never again do this work. And I never will."

It's not easy to clean commodes and cook suppers after reading information that could shake the country. I wondered if the prison officials knew any of the bizarre story that I had been told. In fact, did anyone know? A little twinge of apprehension told me that the less the men or the officials knew about my contact with Mr. Culligan the better I would be. Since there were so many of them and so few of us outside guests, usually ranging from eight to ten, it was difficult to keep any private conversations with the few men you were able to speak with, from the other men, and one had to be so careful not to show too much friendliness to one specific inmate, so that the rest would not become resentful or jealous and report it to the officials. My situation with the prison officials, which was precarious to begin with, made it necessary that each visit into the institution literally became a war of nerves, my nerves to see that they didn't find out what Mrs. Peck was up to again.

Within a few days of the initial correspondence, the phone rang and a friend of Bud's, Chris, was calling to establish himself as my 'contact'. I didn't have long to wait to find out.

"Hello? Arlene?"

"Yes?"

"My name is Chris, I have been contacted by a mutual friend and told that you can be trusted. I can't speak over the phone because it might be tapped. However, in a few days you will be receiving a package and contacted further, after you have had a chance to go over it . . . click."

My hand froze on the phone and I desperately wanted to call the man back and say "Hell no, I can't be trusted. I don't know what you're talking about and further more, I don't want to know what you're talking about. I'm a yenta. I tell everybody everything."

Instead, a few days later my contact, Chris, sent me some tapes and correspondence. In the tapes there was more 'scary stuff' that made me feel as though I were becoming a security risk just by hearing them. Mostly it was conversations from Bud's wife describing what living a life in the CIA was like. One thing I never realized was that the CIA, otherwise known as the 'Company,' employees have rank, just like in the army. My particular agent, Bud, was a Brigadier General, or so he said in his papers. Bud's wife, Sara, said that wherever they go is noted, and their family is under surveillance at all times. By the time I finished sifting through all this incredible information I was looking over my shoulder.

Why me? I didn't want to be trusted. Friends would tell me about affairs they were having and even that was too much of a burden. I had terrible visions of irate husbands calling me and demanding to know if their wives had really spent the evening with me instead of their suspected lover. Nothing of my nature suggested I could be trusted, and there I was reading reams of information that were supposedly labeled 'Top Secret'.

For the next few days I pondered on how and what to do with all this 'data'. Should I go to the authorities with this strange story? And if so, which authorities? It was all so dramatic, reeking with intrigue and conspiracy, accusatory and tantalizing, yet vague, elusive, perhaps even illusory. Along with its cry-wolf quality, it could mean anything, or nothing. On the third day I decided to go to Georgia Congressman Levitas and throw the whole thing in his lap, let him dismiss the whole thing as a sick hoax, and go on my way. But, by then I was hooked on this whole intriguing situation and decided to follow it up a little more.

My congressman had a hell of a nerve leaving for Washington the day before I arrived, so I settled on his secretary, Mary Ann, on whom to dump all this information. Rather than laugh the whole crazy story off, she too became interested in separating fact from fiction. I dubbed her 'Secret Agent Matzoh-Ball' and left what papers I had so that she might read them overnight.

She had been working for the congressman for many years and her reputation was one of being a political pundit of hell in the world of politics. She certainly couldn't fit the image of a congressman's 'swinger' office aide who neither typed nor answered the telephone, made popular by Elizabeth Ray. She was short, slightly chubby, and even a grandmother. Most of all, the woman was smart. That's why I had such a jolt when she too, seemed to believe the story.

The following Wednesday, as I was leaving to take my regular group to the prison, I received a call from Mary Ann;

"Arlene, think you could get me into your prison group tonight? There are a few things about this story that don't make sense and I want to check them out."

She seemed to sense my bewildered attitude because she laughed, and in her direct, no nonsense voice continued, "O.K. I want to find out why a man, who received a less than honorable discharge, as he is supposed to, is hired as a pilot for Eastern Airlines. I also want to know why a man who is fired from Eastern Airlines, then sent to prison for bad checks is hired as a pilot for another CAB regulated airline. According to this man's records, that's exactly what happened."

She paused to light up one of her non-stop cigarettes, blew out the smoke and said, "Arlene, things like that just don't happen, someone makes them happen. And, if that's the case, I want to know who made them happen, and why."

I told her that I'd make the arrangements about getting her name added to the list and she closed the conversation with, "Good. Be ready at five o'clock and I'll pick you up when I leave the office."

After we arrived at the prison, we were escorted to the meeting room. Bud was sitting in the corner puffing on his pipe and easy to spot. All that was lacking were the suede patches on his prison garb. Mary Ann sat pensively next to him, occasionally nodding her head at something Bud had to say, and now and then she would make notes in a pad she had taken out of her purse. Meanwhile, I was nervously trying to carry on conversations with the other men and not do anything that would arouse their curiosity. Briefly, the three of us were able to speak alone for a few minutes, and Mary Ann left the penitentiary with the same impression that I had received a couple of weeks earlier. As she dropped me off at my house, Mary Ann laughed. At the moment she looked a little like a sly elf when she said;

"O.K. Agent Chicken Soup, I think there is something to this story. The pieces to the puzzle just don't fit into place like they should. Something about his story intrigues me. Come on in to the congressman's office tomorrow and start making calls on the Watts line to check out the facts."

I loved it. Even she, who by the position she held, represented Washington and congress and everything glamorous, felt it was time to start worrying that some of his story could be true. All of this cloak and dagger game was becoming very exciting.

Bright and early the next morning I headed for Congressman Levitas' office. However, it was not before I received a special delivery package in the mail with more claims of involvements and crimes committed by the CIA. 'buddy'. If Bud Culligan had done half of what he claimed, no, one-tenth, then 'they' could sentence him to thousands of years. Part of the papers that the 'contact' from Florida sent were copies of a lawsuit that Bud had pending against Stanfield Turner, the head of the CIA and the United States of America, for violation of his civil rights. What I couldn't figure out was why there would be a suit against the head of the CIA if Bud had no knowledge of Turner or the Agency. The plot was definitely beginning to thicken.

The air was electric when I entered the congressman's office. Everyone was rushing busily around doing whatever the congressman's staff does. To the right of the reception room was Mary Ann's office. I found her buried behind her desk which was piled with stacks of paper. She was sitting carrying on a conversation, while the lights were lit up on the hold phone buttons. Never breaking stride, she rummaged through the piles of paper, which to the outside observer looked as though a herd of elephants had set up camp, and finally came up with a memo pad. With her free hand, Mary Ann wrote out a note explaining how to call out on a Watts line and motioned me into an empty office to use the phone.

The desk was messy, but large enough to put down all million and one papers that I had brought along. It wasn't until a few minutes had passed that the realization hit. The empty office I was in was the congressman's private office. No wonder everything looked so neat. I was sitting at Congressman Levitas' private desk, speaking on his private telephone, making calls to check out a story that was bigger than Watergate. He probably would have had a stroke if he had seen me, but I thought it was great! It was kind of titillating, acting as if it were an everyday occurrence that I was able to prop my feet up on the desk of a United States Congressman and get to work. I think if anyone had walked in during that time, I would have jumped through the ceiling. I was never able to shake the feeling that 'Big Brother' was watching me for having the nerve to do what I was doing.

Among the reams of papers that had been sent, via Chris, there were many names that, if possible, I intended to contact and find out what they thought of the story. The first name on the list was Eric Fettman of the New York Post. His New York office relayed the message to the operator that Fettman had been transferred to California but was now on vacation. The next three people I tried to reach weren't home either. Great! My one chance to use a Watts line and no one stayed home to receive the call. Unfortunately, I take things like that personally, and I was beginning to think everyone was avoiding me when I decided to call Sara, Bud's wife, and find out what she was like and what she thought about this situation.

Sara answered on the first ring and sounded delighted to hear from me. Although she had been expecting a call from me, she warned me about talking to her over the phone. In a slightly southern voice, she said, "You must be very careful of what you say or any name you mention, as the phone is definitely tapped."

It's difficult to continue your train of thought in a conversation when a comment such as that is made but I made a stab at it.

"Who do you think is tapping your phone?"

"Oh the 'company' naturally. They monitor everything I have to say and are always watching the house to see where we go or whom I have contact with."

Now I was beginning to wonder if I had two loonies on my hands. The whole damn 'adventure' was beginning to take on an unreal quality. And yet, could someone else be really listening to our conversation? Plunging ahead, I told her that I was trying to help her husband which she already seemed to be aware of through the mysterious Chris. We finished our lengthy conversation with, "Well Sara. No one seems to be home to answer the calls that could verify any of the stories that your husband has written."

"Have you spoken to Jim Willworth from TIME Magazine, or Jorge Hyatt?"

"No, should I?"

"Well yes. I think you should get in touch with them. Jorge Hyatt is on the staff of Yale Law School and these people can tell you quite a bit."

Briefly, I wondered why she could mention names on the phone and I couldn't. I told her I'd check with them and get back to her.

By the time the call was placed to Mr. Hyatt, paranoia was setting in and I began to wonder if even my congressman's phone was bugged, but decided, what the hell! Also, there was safety in numbers and I intended to tell the world. Eventually, Mr. Hyatt came on the line, and he didn't sound very 'Yale', mainly because he had previously come from Cuba.

Hyatt seemed surprised to hear from me, but he was charming and said, "Oh, yes, sure. I know Bud Culligan. He wrote to me from prison when he was in Leavenworth. Actually, he wrote to Yale Law School to see if we might be able to help him with his legal problems. The letter was then forwarded to me."

I thought it strange that an inmate from a federal prison would write to them and I asked if he thought it were a bit unusual?

Jorge paused for a few seconds as though considering the question and answered, "Yeah, I suppose it could be considered pretty unusual."

"Why Yale, I don't know. I suppose it's because we involve ourselves with situations that are considered 'untouchable' elsewhere. Anyhow, I became so immersed in this case that for a while I cornered people like wild animals. I mean this case became almost an obsession with me."

It is also beginning to get to me and the more Hyatt and I spoke, the more our feelings on the case coincided. By now we were on a first name basis and he told me, "Arlene, things just didn't check out the way they were supposed to with this case. We tried to check it out with the Senate Sub-committee and finally went to Senator Church. No one would verify if he believed this story."

I remembered what Mary Ann had said about his CAB regulated job with the airlines and inquired if in his travels, he had spoken to anyone that Bud had worked for.

"Believe me, I talked to everybody. I spoke to the chief investigator for Eastern Airlines and he remembered Bud's working for them. I personally feel that at some point Bud worked for the CIA."

It was the same conclusion that I had come to.

"You feel that also?"

"Well, maybe not as the top agent and hit man as he claims, but somehow in a private capacity for someone who was on the CIA payroll. I do know that at one point the Central Intelligence Committee received an official memo from the Senate Select Committee on this matter. I know that they looked into it and asked the CIA about Bud. I was never given any kind of answer, but I am sure that our phone was bugged after that."

The difficult thing to explain was how and why the Senate Sub-committee would go to the CIA and ask such a dumb question in the first place. Asking a question like, "Is Mr. Culligan really a top official in the CIA and did he really murder several world leaders for your agency?" is like asking the fox if he ate the chickens. Did they really expect a truthful answer?

Yale did believe the story enough to arrange to have the Senate Committee speak to Culligan while he was in prison. What was discussed, I never learned. The whole case was so paradoxical. So many things that he claimed had to be lies. They just had to! Hyatt even told me that he contacted Gordon Liddy when he was in prison, and Liddy had never heard of Bud. Yale people flew out to Leavenworth and interviewed people in the federal prison. They wanted to get a biographical profile on Mr. Culligan. They interviewed men who had roomed with him and asked what kind of books he read. He read a lot of spy novels, but particularly CIA agent Marcletti's book.

Fatigue was setting in from staying so long in Congressman Levita's chair, but I wasn't about to quit when I was ahead. We began to go down the list of political murders Bud was supposed to have committed. When I got to Rafael Trujillo, Hyatt interrupted in an excited voice and said, "Hey, wait a minute! See! There's a lie right there!"

"Why?"

"Because I interviewed the guy who pulled the trigger. A group of people bumped Trujillo on a highway on the way out of town. The man is now a high official in the Dominican Republic."

About this time, the thing that impressed me the most was that a lot of very important people sure had gone to a lot of trouble and expense for a man who was a hoax! They went along with him until he refused to let them have possession of the journal that he was supposed to have hidden. According to Bud, this journal was the only thing that he still had possession of and it was keeping him alive. It was supposed to contain detailed proof of the inner workings of the CIA for the twenty-odd years that he allegedly served with them. All he was supposed to have now were the copies as the 'company' had managed to gain control of the original journal. Yale University considered this an important point. Later I found out why. Hyatt casually let Yale University's interest drop.

"Don't you see, Arlene? Bud could have written this journal that he speaks about at any time. But, and this is a big 'but', if it were the original, then Yale has a machine that is able to tell to the minute how old the document is."

Now things were falling into place as to his interest.

"Oh, so when Bud speaks of things like the Kennedys and events that were to take place and if he wrote them down before they actually happened, then the rest of what he says could be true."

Static interrupted our phone for a minute and then Jorge Hyatt laughed.

"I wonder now that you're involved, as I once was, how safe is your phone? You realize of course that this elusive journal is supposed to name names and contain messages and pilots logs that were kept from these missions."

While hearing all of this, I was thinking, what if Culligan really does send me to pick up this damning and dangerous information? How am I going to being a courier for papers that could shake the country? Did James Bond ever have to put up with this kind of inconvenience?"

We ended our call on a cordial note, with Yale's offering to fly me to pick up the papers and referring me to Jim Willworth from TIME Magazine. From what I could gather, Mr. Willworth came into the picture when the Senate Committee was giving Yale a hard time. They wanted someone of stature from TIME Magazine to be able to inquire why there wasn't any progress being made. One specific question Yale had was why the armed forces denied that Bud was actually in the service, although Jorge Hyatt had somehow gotten hold of his class picture. Why would the military lie? With this question and a dozen more questions in mind I placed my next call to Jim Willworth of TIME.

As soon as I said why I called, he said, in a deep radio announcer voice, "He's got you hooked now too, huh?"

At this point I really wasn't sure what I was but I said;

"Well, I don't know what to believe. What can you tell me that might help me in solving the saga and mystery of Roland B. Culligan?"

"Well, I got into it years ago. I became involved because of a request from Yale Law School. Well, I even went to Miami to check him out."

Jim seemed to think during this point in time that the man was a fraud, but he couldn't be absolutely sure. We all seemed to have that little twinge of doubt. He related to me the lies that he had caught Bud in, but there was always the off chance that he might have been telling the truth on something else.

One story that Jim told me was noteworthy;

"Bud was supposedly in Saigon to pull off a hit. By sheer chance I had recently done an assignment there and one of the really unforgettable things in that city is Timconut Airbase. I figured if our 'friend' Culligan had really been there, he had to have seen this airport and would be able to describe it for me. Well, he couldn't and he didn't. A couple of days later I received in the mail a letter describing the airport and surrounding countryside; but at the time I needed it to convince me, he couldn't do it. Personally, I think the guy does a tremendous amount of research and searches out the little known or rarely published tidbits that give his story some sort of credibility. He'll give a pattern of stories on what he's learned from these tidbits."

I asked Jim if he had ever talked to any of Bud's family, and he said that Bud had been disowned by them years ago. According to the personnel report from Eastern Airlines, there was a brother of Bud's also working at Eastern Airlines as a pilot. When I had the chance to go through the criminal record later, I noticed that in 1912, Bud was arrested for impersonating an officer. The strange twist to this incident was that he was in his brother's uniform, his twin brother. Yet, when confronted with the question of his brothers, he told me he had a sister, no brother.

Later on in the conversation, Jim Willworth asked if I had spoken to Bud's wife or heard the story of how Bud and Sara were attacked by a foreign agent on their honeymoon. This was one I had missed, so I said, "No, tell me."

Jim went on to relate, "Well his wife, Sara, seems as though she's normal enough. Jorge Hyatt and I flew down to Palm Beach to interview her. We taped almost twenty hours trying to break her story and couldn't shake her. One story they both tell happened six or seven years ago while they were on their honeymoon.

"Yeah, they were on the patio of their motel, and Bud recognized a foreign agent coming toward him with his gun drawn. Bud wrestled him and the gun to the floor, managed to tie him up and escaped. She swears that this really happened."

I interrupted with, "Yeah, well, how do you explain something like that?"

Jim continued, "I have no doubt that it probably did happen, except the difference is in the interpretation. I personally think that it was the house detective or someone from the bunko squad coming to get him for something that he did that she didn't know about."

I pushed further with, "What do you think? Could she have deluded herself into believing that all these things really happened? What's the old saying, 'Love is blind'?"

He paused for a moment as though weighing his answer and said, "I don't know. I flew down there to Palm Beach where she lived and spent several days checking him and his story out. We tried to shake her story of seeing and living all these things. I've got to admit that at no time did she falter in her story. Hell, I checked out their neighbors and even the family doctor."

While Jim was speaking, I reflected on what he was saying and what my experience with Bud had been. True, I hadn't spent thousands of dollars like these men and magazines had done, however, I had already invested lots of hours trying to check out all the angles of his story and it didn't always check out. For instance, Bud once mentioned that he had had a big estate in Palm Beach. When ownership of this estate was traced back, it turned out to be a sleazy apartment on the beach where he had probably lived. When Bud was confronted with this, his story was vague.

We spoke for a few more minutes and ended the conversation on the note that TIME Magazine and Jim both thought that the man was a hoax.

However, his parting words were, "If Bud should entrust you with the knowledge of where this journal is, maybe something could be arranged to fly you to the city where these papers are and maybe I or the magazine could arrange to see that you were escorted to pick them up?"

If the man was a hoax, then why go to all that trouble to fly me anywhere. At that point in time, I wasn't able to go anywhere to pick up anything until I had a chance to think it over and to speak with Bud at the prison.

Jim didn't feel that Bud would be prone to having any more dealings with him or Jorge.

"There came a time when I just wouldn't go along anymore, at least until I had the journal in my hands. Bud now feels that I betrayed him when I refused to do anything more without the journal in my hands. It ended when I still wasn't sure, but couldn't afford to spend any more time with him, unless I had results."

Even though I was starting to feel guilty spending the entire day with my feet propped up on Elliott's desk, I decided to make one more call to Bud's wife, Sara. She answered on the first ring and sounded more South Georgia than international spy wife.

"Hi, Sara, this is Arlene Peck again. I'm just calling to let you know that I've had a busy day. I've been tracking down all the names that have been involved with Bud and his story of his years with the CIA. It seems as though a lot of pretty important people have been flying around the country checking out his story."

Her voice took on a noticeably colder tone, "Oh? And, did any of these men that you contacted offer to be of any help?"

"Well, I was brought up current by the two men that you told me to contact earlier, Willworth from TIME, and Jorge Hyatt. But they, from what I gather, didn't have a very satisfying experience from their involvement into the matter."

Even though she had mentioned their names earlier and suggested that I speak with them, Sara now seemed upset. She almost shouted into the phone, "Don't be all impressed by their important positions; they are not to be trusted."

It was difficult to understand how the woman could be upset that I had gotten in touch with her contacts, men with impressive credentials. When I commented that TIME Magazine and Yale University are important, she shot back, "Well, they may be important but they are not to be trusted. Bud and I feel that Jorge Hyatt and Yale have been told to back off by the 'company' and that TIME is an extension and really only a front for the CIA."

"WH-AT?"

"And, furthermore Mrs. Peck, I don't think that my husband would agree to having either of these men go with you to pick up the journal. That is, if he would agree at all to have it picked up by anyone. I'd really rather not talk on the phone anymore because anything I say is being tapped and I think it best we don't discuss anything more over the telephone."

Then came the topper. As I was walking out of the congressman's office, Mary Ann motioned me into her very messy office and asked how I made out. Still stunned by Mrs. Culligan's comments I relayed parts of our discussion and finished with, "And, do you really want to hear something funny? His wife doesn't want me to talk to TIME because she thinks it is connected with the CIA. Isn't that ridiculous?"

Rather than laugh like I expected, Mary Ann was busy drawing circles on an official looking paper that someone had spilled coffee on. She gave me a long thoughtful look. She finally said, "Arlene, sweetie I don't want to unduly alarm you, but it's long been known in journalistic circles that TIME Magazine could very well be a CIA cover. Maybe if this thing goes any further, you ought to leave word with our office about what your itinerary will be and how you can be reached. In fact, you might even want to call in."

She saw my look of sheer terror and laughed, "Oh, don't worry, it's nothing serious. It's just in case anything should happen, and then we would want to know where to start the Arlene Peck Memorial Fund to investigate CIA activities."

VERY FUNNY!

I doubted that my congressman would ever know that I even went to his office, much less spent half the days on his Watts line. However, a week or so later, my neighbor attended a dinner at which Congressman Levitas was a guest speaker. She went up to him at the end of the evening and introduced herself and told him that I had been borrowing her xerox machine to send him letters. Elliott lifted his eyebrows, gave a slow smile and said, "Oh yes, Arlene Peck, my favorite constituent. We're thinking of putting an extra line in the office for her."

On the drive home I kept thinking of the crazy afternoon that had transpired. It was far from over yet. As I pulled into the driveway, the mailman was just pulling up in his truck to deliver the mail. Among the usual garbage, there was a letter from Bud. After I finished reading it, I didn't know whether to laugh or cry because it was so hokey or, because the whole thing was getting so scary. In part, the letter read;

"The important message of this letter is to make you aware of the danger you are now capable of exposing yourself to. My intent here is not to frighten, but to caution. The men responsible for Dallas are still alive and well. And, as Yale and TIME told you, if only twenty percent of my allegations are true, you have a tiger by the tail."

There were some more instructions, most of which I didn't understand. Part of them was in the form of directions. There were special words that

I would have to say to people, and they, in turn would tell me how to contact other people who had the journal. I was fast reaching the point that I wasn't even sure I wanted to know where anything was. I am also a very inquisitive person by nature and so I knew that I couldn't let anything drop at this point. I had to follow through. Bud had, moreover, closed the letter with the caution.

"I keep reminding you that this is a deadly game of human chess you are playing. If you really believe that I am lying, STOP NOW!"

It was too late for that now. After the postman left my place, he delivered a letter to my neighbor, who in turn, came over to my house. He handed me a large letter from my 'original contact', Chris, who had fallen into this same situation months ago and had spent many hours and a lot of money trying to help Bud. Chris believed in Bud's story and the enormous power of the CIA and wanted to have his own part in exposing it. The man had gone to much trouble in acquiring an Atlanta street directory and writing to my neighbor asking him to hand-deliver the enclosed letter to Mrs. Peck. Chris wrote him that he didn't want Mr. Peck to see it. I thought, "Good God," now my neighbor thinks I'm having an affair with someone in Florida!" I didn't know whether to be flattered, or think things had gone far enough.

My neighbor left after giving me what I swear was a leer. I started to explain to him that the letter was delivered to him because there was a strong belief that my mail was being watched by the CIA. but I figured he wouldn't believe that either. So, I let him go and thought, "He'll be sorry. They'll all be sorry when I'm a guest on the TODAY Show for breaking a case bigger than Watergate!" I was already upset at the strange looks that my friends were beginning to give me when I mentioned a little of what I had become involved in.

By that evening, my phone was ringing off the hook. Chris was calling from Florida to see if Bud had sent any directions for him. Jim Willworth called to make arrangements to have me taken to where the journal was so that we might be able to settle this whole mess. After all that I had been told about TIME, I didn't want to hear or see that magazine even in a dentist's office, so I asked Jim to call me back after I had at least talked to Bud again and we'd go from there. And, last but not least, Jorge Hyatt was back with a list of comments I would make on his behalf the next time I got into the prison.

Jorge had really been deeply into this case until he called Bud's bluff and said the same as the others. Unless he had the journal, he couldn't go further. That's when, according to Jorge and Yale Law School, Bud backed out. Jorge felt that you could have all the rifles, but without the ammunition you had nothing. You needed bullets. That is what the journal was. When I spoke to Bud earlier in the week, he told me that he never gave the papers to either of these men because he didn't trust them or the people that they worked for. I didn't know whom to believe.

During the last conversation I had with Jorge, he said, "Yale and I have put in thousands, literally thousands of hours of investigation, and, although we believe that Bud exaggerated a lot, some of it might possibly be true."

"Jorge, what do you think of all the killing and assassination parts of his story? Do you really think that he could have done them?"

"Well, that's hard to tell. It's quite possible that he could be a hired killer. I don't think that the CIA would have a hired killer on the actual payroll, but it's very possible that he worked within the CIA system, much in the same capacity as an FBI informer. They are never actually employed but are paid on a fringe basis within the organization. The CIA, it seems, has unlimited funds to hire killers with adventure in their blood."

The next morning I headed for Congressman Levitas' office with a fresh list of names that I hadn't reached yet. When I arrived at the office however, I found the staff an utter beehive of activity. 'The King' was in town from Washington and in his office. Rather than tell the congressman to remove himself from 'my desk', I decided to return home and read through some of the documents that had been delivered by various methods over the past few days.

Going through Culligan's papers, one really startling tidbit caught my eye; he went into a complete and detailed description of how he murdered King Farouk. In part it read;

Dated 3-18-65 Rome, Italy, King Farouk picked up his mistress Anna Maria Gattiat her apartment at 8 La Viole Ostince around 11:00 P.M. They went straight to the Isle de France for supper, arriving around midnight. King Farouk ordered a huge leg of lamb and consumed over a gallon of soda water with coke. King Farouk was injected with a fatal drug at 12:59 A.M. This was done by the waiter, Elio Piermattel, who was Mr. Culligan's confidant in this EA. Due to King Farouk's enormous size; Mr. Culligan miscalculated the size of dosage necessary to bring immediate death. King Farouk was taken by ambulance to San Camillo hospital where he died at 2:05 A.M. The doctor in attendance was Dr. Nicola Wassa."

Was this true? Were these details accurate? I sat there in my den thinking to myself that if I tried to tell my friends this weird story, they would have carted me off to the funny-farm. And yet, this man wrote in such detail that it just had to be true.

By the time I had finished going through all the papers again, it was almost one o'clock in the morning. I was still too excited to sleep, so I went into the bedroom, woke up my husband, and said, "Howard, I just finished reading the confession of the man who killed Nasser, King Farouk and just about everyone important who has been assassinated in this country for the past three decades. Isn't that exciting?"

He rolled over, mumbled something profane, placed his arm across his eyes and said;

"You woke me up just to tell me that. I think you've flipped, now will you please turn out the light and go to bed."

Now, if my own husband had that kind of reaction, how was I to tell the world what I knew? Besides, did I really want to tell the world? Yes! If any of this were true, and look at all the important people who had been involved before me and believed it, I did not want it to be my secret. Was my husband right, that I was making a damn fool of myself, getting involved in the whole thing in the first place? Probably so, but it had been kind of fun around the house those past few days with the phone ringing off the hook and all those people waiting for me to lead them to the journal.

In one of the letters Bud had written to me, he commented, "I have asked you to contact a 'gutsy' newsperson. I need someone who will go to bat for me. I will provide the last copy of my journal if I feel the person will help. In fact, I almost asked you to bring the journal to Judge Young in Orlando. I did not ask you, because I don't have the right to involve you in such a seamy business. Perhaps I have gone too far already in asking you to first, believe in me, and second, to help me."

The next morning I was delighted to learn that Levitas had returned to Washington, the office was calmer and once again, I had my Watts line and desk to myself. My first call was to Judge Young in Orlando, Florida who was a presiding judge in the suit that Bud had pending against Admiral Stanfield Turner, Director of the Central Intelligence Agency, and the United States of America. Again, heavy questions. If the man were lying, why would Bud be suing the head of the CIA? Just to check it out, a call was made from the congressman's office. No one but his secretary would speak to me and she said that Judge Young would be forbidden by the court from speaking as he had a case pending concerning Mr. Culligan.

So trying to get a federal judge to speak about things he wasn't supposed to, is a "No-No." I told the nice lady goodbye and sighed with relief, federal offenses I didn't need.

The next person on my list was Paul Comerford. From what I had been told by Sara Culligan, he was a reporter on the National Enquirer and had been very helpful with her problems. I called him in Florida and caught rum in the midst of a move to South Carolina. The reaction I received from his was much the same as I had gotten from everyone else. The difference was that he still had the trust of the Culligans and they didn't feel that he had been 'gotten' to by the CIA.

Paul was now working free lance; however, at the time he became involved, he had been working as a reporter for the National Enquirer newspaper. He had also dropped his investigation when it came time to see this journal and Bud Culligan would not, or could not, deliver it. Again I found myself saying;

"Paul, I know that you, like those before you, were completely wrapped up in this 'case' and disappointed when Bud didn't come through with the proof, but really, this time it might be different."

"Things would be different now?"

"Well, this time Bud wants to release the information and he is becoming more and more concerned about how long he'll have to stay in prison and what might happen to him while he's there. Anyway, there is more than an even chance this time that he means it. Are you still interested?"

An edge of excitement crept into his voice and he said, "Hell yes, I'm still interested. Hey listen, why don't you wait right where you are now and I'm going to call the editor of the Enquirer and see how they feel about me getting involved with this again, at their expense. O.K?"

Within a short time, it was Paul calling again, "Arlene, I called the editor and would you be willing to fly with me, all expenses, and hotel, food the works, paid, to go and get this journal? I spent a lot of time on this investment and although I'm at the point where I don't believe a damn thing, I'd sure like to finally get this settled one way or another. At one point, Culligan had me flying all over the damn country interviewing people in his behalf."

Rather than give him an answer, I said I'd have to let him know after I spoke to Bud. I would be going into the prison the next evening.

I checked out with the congressman's staff, who at this point didn't quite know what to make of me, and I headed for home. Halfway there, I made a little detour to the offices of UPI and stopped to see a friend of mine, Jim East, who is now the Southern Director of United Press International. He listened to my story of assassinations and foreign espionage, and from his expression, it was obvious that he thought I had lost my mind. He was sweet enough to make up a contract to be submitted to the Enquirer to protect my 'scoop.' In this agreement, the National Enquirer was to agree to pay all expenses and pay me ten cents per word for every word they wrote on this subject until 1987. I was to receive all books, files, recordings or television rights with regard to Mr. Culligan. And last, but not least, I wasn't to be held responsible for any litigation which may arise from publication of any information of Mr. Culligan and his alleged involvement.

Damn! All the danger was starting to be fun! Armed with all of this, I returned home.

Shortly after dinner, Jim Willworth called. Casually, I broached the topic of his magazine and their CIA involvement. He chuckled and said;

"Me? Involved with the CIA?"

"No, your magazine."

There was a slight pause and then, "Well, I suppose it's possible, but not in recent years. Certainly I'm not connected with them anyway. I didn't think that Bud would trust me when I heard you mention our working together, but I figured I'd give it a try."

More pause then.

"Well, what will you be doing now? You're not going to drop it, now that you're hooked, are you?"

I casually mentioned that I might be working with the National Enquirer and the silence was deafening.

"My God, you're not planning on doing anything with that rag are you? They write articles that are titled, 'I Threw My Child in a Pot of Boiling Rattlesnakes'."

That summed up his feelings on the National Enquirer, although he eventually did grudgingly admit that they had improved somewhat in recent years and now liked to write about scandals in government. We spoke a few more minutes, and before hanging up, his voice took on a more serious tone and he left me with points to ponder.

"Remember Arlene, this could be a trap either way."

"Huh? How?"

"Well, Bud was out of jail a few months, remember?"

"So?"

"Well, what was stopping him while he was out from flying to wherever he's told you this 'supposed' journal hidden? Even if it does exist, he could have written and hidden it long after the fact. That's why you need Jorge Hyatt and Yale Law School. The machine they have could tell you to the minute if all this was fact or fiction. While he was out, why didn't he go after this journal and pick it up himself?"

It was a good point. When I asked Bud the same question, later he told me that he was being followed during the short time he was out.

I agreed that I would get back in touch with Jim after another conversation with Bud. Now, it was my turn to wait with nervous nerves until I went into the prison and saw Bud, so that I might get the instructions on how to pick up this elusive journal. Finally, Wednesday evening arrived.

The last forty-five minutes of the meetings were always 'social', when we didn't discuss anything special and usually broke into little individual groups. It was extremely difficult to have private conversations because there were always informants. The Catholic Priest had people attend the meetings for the express purpose of keeping an eye on everyone so that they could report back to him. He was constantly on the lookout for minor infractions that he might be able to blow up into something to discredit me or the program. As difficult as it was, Bud was able to save a seat for me next to him, and I was able to have a few minutes to speak with him alone.

Bud was sitting with his usual aura of calm and smoking serenely his inevitable pipe and looking so normal. It was just so damn hard to distrust someone who looked like he did. I told him all that had transpired on his behalf during my busy week. He became visibly upset when I mentioned that I had spoken with Willworth and Hyatt. His calm was gone and his eyes had gotten a look in them that was frightening and he moved his head closer to me and in an intense voice said, "Why? WHY did you contact them? What possessed you to get in touch with those two, me? Of all people, why them?"

Defensively I said, "If you'll remember, your friend and my mysterious 'contact' from Florida, Chris, who sent me a ton of your papers, told me to do what I could do in tracking down anyone that could help in your crazy situation. Well, among the hours of files that I had to wade through, you had their names and numbers as being involved with you."

Until then, it was virtually impossible to have the image that the man was anything but a dignified executive, but suddenly, his eyes became colder and considerably smaller. He nodded his head while I spoke, but his mind was on something else. Finally, his eyes moved to slits and emphatically he said, "Under no circumstances are you to speak with them again. Now, the pick-up of the Journal will be from Chicago. You will get further instructions, but the pick-up will be from there."

I must have looked startled because his face softened.

"Are you concerned about the danger you are now facing, that you are probably being followed and your phone is now bugged?"

That wasn't it at all. How could I tell him that I had been hoping he had put the journal in some fun place like Acapulco or Palm Springs? It was just my kind of luck that I would end up in Chicago in the winter. Now, all I had to do was go home and convince my husband that I had to go on a mission for my government and find some strange man in Chicago. I had the feeling that it wasn't going to be easy. Howard had long ago lost his sense of humor when it came to my prison 'involvement.' The guard was peering in the door, getting ready to notify the guests that the meeting was about to break up, and hurriedly, Bud scribbled on a piece of paper the place and name of the man in Chicago. I looked at the slip of paper, back at Bud and said, "That's it?"

Bud shook his head and said, "No. The man is now in extreme danger and could lose his life if you mishandle this.

Great. Just the kind of guilt that I needed to be laid on me. People will die if I screw up this mission. Bud then gave me a whole involved message that was to be relayed to the party in Chicago. This new contact was on the staff of one of the institutions of higher learning there. After I reached him and relayed Bud's crazy message, I was to receive another phone number from the man who actually had the journal in his possession. Bud gave me that man's name also, but I had to call the first one so that he might relay the message. The complexity was starting to get to me, but it was too late to stop now. I didn't hear too much of the rest of the meeting, as Bud had gotten my adrenalin going with all these tales of intrigue. I promised to get in touch with Bud and let him know when I was leaving for Chicago with Paul, the reporter from the Enquirer.

At the crack of dawn the next morning I headed for my neighbor June's house to use her phone. The phone at my house was making strange clicking noises and I really thought that it was bugged. After spending the next hour trying to trace my mysterious contact, I began to believe the man did not exist. The University existed, but no one had ever heard of my man. No stone was left unturned. Calls were made into the Dean's office, personnel records office, everywhere. If this person existed at all, he was nowhere to be found. I began to get my first real twinges of, I'VE BEEN HAD. Finally, I gave up and called my Enquirer friend in Carolina and turned the same names over to him. If these people did exist, and there was beginning to be strong doubt, then maybe Comerford could succeed where I had failed. Paul and I hung up with plans to talk later and check if he had made better progress than I.

Sometime that afternoon, Eric Fettman of the NY Post called back and apologized for not returning my call from the previous week. He had been out of town and had just received my message. Once again, I found myself telling someone of importance the story and asked him what he knew about our 'mutual friend,' Bud Culligan.

Fettman also had quite a story to tell about his involvement with Bud. Like others before him, he had spent much money checking out Bud's story. Mr. Fettman told me what I had heard before and then some. He too, found this an intriguing story. But, when something failed to check out the way Bud felt that it should, then Bud's stock answer would be that the people involved had either been part of the CIA or were bought off by them.

Fettman was happy to discuss how he had gotten involved with Bud. It was much the same way that I had. The man from Florida, the one who sent all the mysterious packages, contacted Fettman for help with Bud's case. About this time I began to think Chris was a nut for having the faith he had in a man who didn't deserve it. This was further strengthened when Fettman casually dropped the fact that when Bud Culligan was out of jail, he left a string of bad checks to a lot of people, including Chris. Fettman also commented on the fact that Chris's wife was thoroughly disgusted with her husband for having this blind faith in Culligan; she herself didn't think Bud was anything but a con man.

Fettman had gone to interview Bud and those associated with the case; but when it came down to getting the journal or coming up with some definite proof, Bud always had a reason why he couldn't give him the journal. The last time they had spoken, Bud had promised to have it sent to a special courier. A few days later, when Fettman hadn't receive anything; he called Culligan again and asked what had happened? Bud asked him to wait a few hours and he would find out what happened. Eventually, he called back and said that the man who was to send the journal had been bought off by the CIA for ten million dollars. He had only one journal left and he was afraid to take a chance on it's getting taken by the CIA.

One of the things that most convinced Fettman that Bud Culligan and his whole story was a farce was the name of Victor Marchetti. Marchetti, a one time CIA agent, had written several books on this organization. Bud claimed to have known and worked with this man yet, when Fettman spoke to Marchetti and asked what Bud's relationship was with him, Marchetti disclaimed ever hearing of the man.

One interesting letter that had been mixed among the others and sent via Chris, was one that claimed knowledge of the Kennedy assassination; the who, what, where, etc. He said that his journal would prove that Oswald did not work alone. Fettman told me that one time, he went through the back clippings of the Kennedy assassination and took out several names to confront Bud with. Bud was unable to identify any of the names. He was only able to discuss the names that had already been in the news. Still, the nagging thought kept making me wonder why this man, like the others, had spent so much time and money on someone that they felt was a hoax?

As far as the invisible Chris, I had begun to believe that he was as nutty as the man he championed. Chris was like an alter-ego in his defense of his friend Bud. It was a case of Cervantes tagging along after Don Quixote. No matter how the facts proved Bud wrong, Chris had to defend his friend.

Chris continued to call me daily to see if I had heard anything. Finally, I said, "Did it ever occur to you, that you might be living vicariously through Bud?"

His voice quivered as he answered, "No, it hasn't . . . wha . . . what do you mean by that?"

From his tone, I could tell that these comments were making me turn into the 'enemy', but I didn't care.

"Exactly what it sounds like. Did it ever occur to you that Bud's whole story could be a joke and maybe your trust could be better placed elsewhere?"

His silence said that he wasn't happy to hear these things and I even went further and said, "Dammit Chris. I'm certainly not a spy, nor do I even know anybody who is. No one has bought me off, nor has anyone intimidated me as you say the others were. Why in God's name did Bud back off when it once again came to the point of proving his story by coming up with what he doesn't have. I don't believe the damn thing exists anymore, if it ever did. How do you even believe the man is telling the truth, especially since he walked out, owing you four or five hundred dollars?"

I broke off the conversation when Chris gave me the answer that at the time seemed incredibly stupid.

"Maybe all these people have gone underground because the company received word first that you were headed to them. After all, I warned you that your phone was tapped and you probably made your appointments over the phone."

How do you answer something like that? I didn't try. I just said, "Yeah, well, O.K. I'll let you know if I hear anything."

A few nights later, when once again it was time to conduct a discussion group and bring my group from the outside to visit my group on the inside, I immediately looked for Bud. I wanted him to tell me what was going on. Why was he wasting everyone's time?

For the first time in months, he wasn't there. I looked around to see who might relay a message to him and found it difficult. Bud was obviously a loner. Besides, a few of the other men had warned me about speaking to him because they felt he was an informer. A couple even thought that Bud might be an FBI informant. It was difficult to pick someone in that room that could be trusted.

Even though Bud was, for all outward appearances, a lone maverick, there seemed to be one guy that always sat next to him and with whom he usually left the meeting. Prisons make strange bedfellows. Bud had the look of a dignified executive, his friend resembled a derelict. He was thin, gaunt, and had a face that looked like the map of Alabama. This particular evening, after peering over his shoulder a couple of times to see if we were being overheard, he slipped a note inside a book, placed it on my lap, and in a conspiring tone whispered, "They came and got him last night and he can't come in here anymore."

When I asked who 'they' were and why did 'they' come and get him, he once again looked over his shoulder and said, "You know, the 'company'. They came to Bud's' cell and took him out. He can't ever come back here again, so I'll have to relay his message. It's gotten very dangerous for you. You are under complete surveillance and being watched every minute."

I couldn't help it, I laughed in his face. Vaguely I remembered him as being the one referred to as 'Old Nutsy' who claimed to have a cure for cancer from the electric currents that ran through his body when he placed his hand on you. Actually, the whole incident might have been very funny if Bud hadn't wasted so much of everyone's time. Even though it was a dumb question, I had to ask, "Are you a member of the CIA also?"

Damned if this nut didn't say, "Shhh, no one besides Bud knows that in the institution. It was strictly a chance accident that we ended up here in the same institution together. I've known Bud in the "company" for several years, but we were in different divisions. I was in the intelligence division."

SURE HE WAS!

The note that "Old Nutsy" slipped me on behalf of his friend Bud, was dated Dec. 14, 1977.

"Thanks for all your help. I really appreciate all you have tried to do. As of yesterday, I can no longer see or contact you in any way. So for both of us, I'll keep away. Chris will explain some of the things that have happened this past week."

He wasn't even going to give me a chance to tell him face to face that I thought he was a liar, worse yet, psychotic. When I spoke to Willworth of TIME Magazine he told me that there are a lot of crazies who spend all their lives trying to convince people to believe in them. Their families usually do because they want to. Sometimes lots of other people do too. Who knows, maybe such crazies don't want to admit even to themselves that they are nothing more than con men who got caught. The whole prison experience can be so traumatic in its constant boredom that diversion can be welcome.

It seemed that Bud had trained himself to live in an unbelievable dream world, and there is no question that he really believed in it. What I couldn't understand was how so many others who should have known better, got caught along with him in this dream existence. Could it be there is a little bit of Walter Mitty in all of us? The complexities and intrigues proved too much for me to handle. I was no match for the CIA nor did I have the facilities to check out Culligan's stories. So I had to drop it. I don't know about being watched but I would be willing to bet that the phone at our home was being tapped during that time.

One interesting footnote to this whole episode was several months later, during the spring of 1978, a few months after Bud had been released; an invitation arrived in the mail. The envelope was heavy and the invitation embossed and engraved. In part it read;

"Brigadier Roland B. Culligan requests the honor of your presence at a cocktail buffet dinner in honor of his retirement from the Central Intelligence Agency and the United States Air Force."

It noted the date, time and place was to be in the officer's Mess Club at the base in Orlando, Florida. I stood there looking at what I had just received, picked up my car keys and headed over to Congressman Levitas' office.

Levitas was in Washington. Mary Ann was there, however, and when I showed her the invitation, her eyes widened. She urged,"Maybe you ought to go into Elliott's office and use the Watts line to check on this. See if it's a fake."

Once again, I was back at 'our desk', and checking on this absolutely fantastic story that was supposedly settled months ago. After a few minutes, the manager of the Officer's Club at the base answered and the conversation went something like;

"Hello? Hello. Who's in charge of parties on the base?"

After fifteen minutes of being switched around to every office in the base, a Mr. Ferguson, who was in charge of the officer's mess, came on the line. The connection was bad, but I was able to get through and ask, "I'm calling in response to an invitation that I received to a dinner at the base. Is it at all possible to have any sort of a function there if you are not a member of the Armed Forces?"

"Certainly not. We check the host against his military records."

"Well, I'm calling in reference to an invitation that I received from a Brigadier General Culligan." "Mmmm, oh yes, let me see on my list here. Oh yes, here it is. He is listed to give a dance in the Mess on the 12th of the month."

"Whom shall I say is calling?"

Well, I left my name and a message that I wouldn't be attending. A few days later I received a call from Bud that he had gotten my message at the base and was sorry that I couldn't attend.

That was it! Too many questions remain unanswered. Was he or wasn't he a CIA agent? I felt then as I still do now, there is a story there. People with far more resources than I weren't able to crack the truth. We all seemed to go just so far and then no further. God, I would have loved to known the real truth there. The CIA was bigger than I. Did I open the door to the lady or the tiger?

ARLENE PECK
CONGRESSMAN ELLIOTT LEVITAS, 1978

Chapter Seven

THE WILSONS OR: BABY BROTHER AND THE BOSTON STRANGLER

During my Bud Culligan CIA involvement, two new members joined the evening discussion. They were brothers and although not Jewish, came Wednesday nights out of curiosity and returned when they found that they enjoyed the evening. I suppose that they had been in a couple of times before anyone really noticed them. It really wasn't until Peter came over and introduced himself, that I gave a second thought or really paid much attention to him. Some of the other men were keeping me busy with their problems at the time, and unfortunately, a lot of guys got lost in the shuffle and were never noticed. The program had grown so, and, even though eventually the outside guests would average around ten people it still wasn't enough to go around when 60 to 70 men were attending the weekly meetings. Peter made a point to see that I was to know who they were. It was mostly out of concern for his brother. He had heard, via the grapevine, about the success of the 'Group' and thought, since he was getting transferred soon, that his kid brother might benefit by being part of the alliance we had going. Peter's manner was very respectful, and he seemed reluctant to leave his brother unprotected.

Peter was something out of a grade-B movie. He looked the part of a hood. He was average height, slender build, and had pretty blue eyes. If it had not been for his pock-marked face, he would have been attractive in a degenerate sort of way. His mannerisms had that streetwise stance I had learned to recognize. That's why his obvious concern for his brother was so touching and out of place.

Baby brother was named 'Giggy' and they loosely resembled each other. Giggy was the better looking of the two. His teeth were nice and his smile was engagingly shy. Not very many of the men were typed as either 'shy' or 'wholesome', but that was the image that Giggy managed to convey.

Initially, what made them different from the other men was that they were in prison together. Within a very short time, they began to open up and expound upon the reasons that brought them into the Atlanta Penitentiary.

Peter mentioned something about their being in for transporting stolen paintings. Coolness has never been one of my attributes so I blurted out, "Well, I suppose that the family that steals together, stays together. How did your parents take it, having both sons imprisoned?"

They gave a long sideways look at each other as though sharing a private joke and finally, Peter responded.

"They didn't really have much choice, and as far as the staying together, there were really four of us. We had two more brothers. You could kinda say we came as a matched pair, like book-ends, you know?"

I noticed the way "were" came out, so I asked what "were" meant. Peter, who usually did the talking for the two, studiously considered the veins on the back of his hand for a minute or two before answering, "Yeah, well, ya see, we had two other brudders, kid brudders and they had a shoot-out, like at the O.K. Corral, ya know? Except, in this case it weren't no corral, it was a bank robbery. Ya know? I mean, they were on their own at the time. It didn't have anything to do with what 'Giggy' and I were involved in. You could almost say they were like free agents."

Giggy finally opened his mouth and chimed in, "Yeah, they was younger than us, twenty-five and twenty-seven."

Peter finished with, "Yeah, we don't look it, but I'm thirty-seven and 'Giggy' over there is only a kid of thirty."

With the choir boy face that 'Giggy' had, I believed him and became curious about what the rest of the family was like. Casually, I asked, "What kind of business was your father in?"

Peter uncomfortably shifted positions but just as casually answered, "Oh, he was blown away years ago by a dissatisfied customer. He was a loan shark."

During the entire first conversation and most of the subsequent ones we had, brother 'Giggy' rarely had a word to say. He seemed perfectly content to have his older brother speak for him. Occasionally, he gave me a timid smile, and blithely looked over with his baby blue eyes, especially when Peter would attempt to illustrate the extent of the injuries they had encountered during their capture. For a while there he was getting pretty graphic. Once he pulled up his sweat shirt and delighted in showing us his stomach.

"See that, see those scars. He poked at various places on his stomach. I ain't supposed to be living from all des holes that got put in my gut. The both of us didn't almost make it. That's why we spent so much time in the hospital. Yeah, that's where we made the acquaintance of the Boston Strangler."

I had been going into the prison long enough not to be surprised by too much, however, the Boston Strangler picked up my interest.

I had seen the movie and wanted to know if it would be at all possible to get either of them to open up and 'tell all' about the famous case of the strangler. Were they really involved with the notorious Albert de Salvo? Could they be persuaded to discuss what they knew about him? You better believe they were. They were eager to speak of every aspect of their previous business. It was times like that, when I sat listening to the gory details that I sometimes wondered if I were getting as sick as some of the men who had committed these crimes. The sight of blood may upset us, yet, how many of us read avidly every word about the Manson murders? With the same fascination that I scrounged through the evening news looking for all the really brutal parts of the California killings, I listened to these brothers as they related how 'Giggy' had allegedly sauntered up to Albert de Salvo, (The Boston Strangler) and coolly stuck a shiv into his body fifteen times. Now, sticking a knife into somebody once is not your everyday run of the mill incident, but 15 times? That shows a person with a definite problem. That was the reason Peter was leaving the institution before his kid brother, and why he seemed so concerned that 'Giggy' should become involved with some outside interest.

Peter was very impressed that 'Baby Brother' had received an offer from a publishing house to write a book. Not exactly knowing how to reply to something like that, I sputtered, "Gee, I can't wait to see the movie."

Until I saw the unbelievable inefficiency with which the prison system is run today, it was incomprehensible that the powers that be would let a maniac like Albert de Salvo reside in a regular prison and not in an institution for the criminally insane where he belonged. By the time Peter made that statement about the murders, I knew that there were many Albert de Salvo's roaming the halls of our state and federal prisons. The way Peter told it, Albert, the Boston Strangler, and 'Giggy' shared a psychiatric ward. And, if so, who was I to be sitting there having a casual conversation with the nut who killed the other nut?

After a few weeks, I mustered up some courage and asked Peter if he would bring in any clippings that he might have concerning their case.

"I'd like to know why you are where you are and maybe find out something about your background so that I might better understand and get to know you guys a little better."

They loved it. As usual, 'Giggy' smiled and Peter did the talking for the both of them, "Sure, I got a lot of them, and I'll bring them the next time we come in."

They both seemed delighted that they had been asked to show their 'clippings' and were flattered that there was 'outside' interest in the story of 'Baby Brother' and the Boston Strangler."

The following week they were waiting by the door as a welcoming committee and as soon as I entered the Group, Peter stuffed a handful of photocopies of clippings about the crimes that he had committed. He apologized to me for having only a partial list of his latest crimes but nodded his head when I said, "Don't worry, I'm sure I'll find it very interesting reading."

Was it ever! After going through the clippings, I was thoroughly confused. When we had talked earlier, I was told that Peter was the one who was thirty-seven and his younger brother 'Giggy,' the one who had done the de Salvo murder, was supposedly thirty. According to the newspapers, the killer of de Salvo was named Robert Michael Wilson and he was thirty-seven. Now, I was wondering who in the hell was 'Giggy' and who the older brother really was, or even if they were really brothers. The papers also stated that Robert M Wilson (whichever of the brothers he was) was one of the most dangerous and vicious individuals that the arresting FBI agent who testified had ever had the occasion to know.

Wilson and his brother had been charged with interstate transportation of stolen property. They, along with two others, had broken into the home of a Rhode Island school teacher. They bound and gagged the teacher along with other members of the family, and stole over $20,000 worth of paintings, along with several valuable rugs and some silverware. According to the clippings, they then brought the paintings to Florida from Boston on a commercial airline. They thought they'd have a better chance to sell them down there. There were able to make a terrific profit and sold them for over $75,000. The only problem they encountered during the transaction was that they picked an undercover agent from the FBI to sell these paintings to. As a matter of fact, the agent had even rented an apartment on Treasure Island especially for this transaction.

The papers then went on to state that this nice, polite and sweet looking man, whom I had been feeling sorry for, had been arrested 19 times. Along with his many 'standard' crimes, 'Giggy' also had murder, assault, and robbery on the list. 'Giggy' (Robert) had also been charged with attempted murder, accessory to manslaughter, counterfeiting, weapons offenses and other crimes in addition to the de Salvo murder charge. For such a young guy he had certainly been a busy person. The most gruesome part of the story was that in 1972 Wilson had been sentenced to prison after he was convicted of cutting into pieces the body of a Boston man, John J. Rooney, before dumping it in the Charles River. No wonder the FBI agents at their trials kept the audiences morbidly enthralled with stories about the criminal's violent tendencies.

According to the articles, when de Salvo was stabbed to death in Walpole Correctional Institute in Massachusetts in 1973, Wilson was tried for conspiracy to murder more than once, but the trials resulted in hung juries and he was then freed. They, the jury, probably had difficulty believing any of the charges against him after gazing upon his innocent choir-boy face. I did find interesting Peter's attitude on 'forgive and forget'. One evening, I brought into the institution a man who was president of Hemshech, which is the organization of survivors of the concentration camps during World War II. Part of his program was to show a movie about the Holocaust, and after, we began a discussion on the terrible experiences he had encountered during the war.

Somehow, this led into a conversation about Rudolph Hess, the man who had been the lone resident of Spandau prison for his heinous war crimes. Peter entered the discussions for the first time. The fact he would pick such a topic to make his debut was surprising, but also impressive was the articulate way he presented the case in defense of Hess. His feelings were;

"Well, keeping a man in a cage accomplishes nothing. Hess had spent the better part of his life locked up as a political football. The time has come to forgive and forget as nothing has been accomplished by holding Rudolph Hess in prison for as long as he has been imprisoned."

It was with much restraint that I managed to hold back and not blurt out, "You SOB, why is it always that the non-Jew feels this way when it comes to carrying a grudge against the Nazis? Why the hell don't you just say what you really mean?"

The only way I was able to hold back my growing hostility was when the fleeting thought entered my mind that maybe that was how he felt about his own imprisonment. The more he spoke, the more I realized my hunch had been right; he was substituting Hess for him. The attitudes he held on forgiveness for these horrible crimes was somehow related to the feelings that he felt should be directed to him. It was obvious that he was rationalizing in his own mind when he said, "What is accomplished, if year after year, a man is imprisoned and kept away from the rest of society?"

It would be interesting to know if this man's victims, at the time of the crimes, were allowed to feel anything other than fear.

The forget and forgive attitude that prevailed in prison was amazing. Men, who by the wildest stretch of the imagination, shouldn't be forgiven, ever. These men, who never showed the least bit of compassion in their lifetimes to anyone other than themselves, ironically become avowed champions of human rights. In fact, so many of these men adopt it seems, a socialistic attitude in prison. It is usually the guys with any intellectual capacity at all that become intrigued with the concept of socialism and the first thing they revert back to upon release is capitalism.

The following week, when I entered the room and expected to see the Wilsons, they weren't there. I had just about given up on them when the door opened and both came in, a little breathless, but anxious to talk. That's what the men liked best of all about the people from the outside coming in. It gave them a sounding board for their frustrations while re-enforcing a feeling that someone cared. In the case of the Wilson brothers, they seemed to enjoy a sense of amusement from the reaction they were able to evoke from the 'outsiders' toward themselves and their crimes. The first thing I did when we had a chance to speak was ask, "I cannot believe that grown men would be so vain as to lie about their ages."

"Peter turned to gaze at me with those pretty blue eyes and innocently said, "Whatcha talking about?"

"Giggy, or Robert Michael Wilson. Whichever, are, according to the newspaper articles you gave me, said you're not thirty years old, but thirty-seven. Peter has to be older. Damn I thought that when I reached thirty-three I was entitled to lie a little, but you? Jack the Ripper, serving a sentence from now to eternity and you bother to lie about your ages."

They both looked a little sheepish and finally 'Giggy' laughed.

"Yeah, well, we had you going though; we really do look much younger, don't we?"

I had them there. I pressed on, "Listen guys, not to change the subject, but I really find it hard to believe that part in your press stories about your cutting up that man in Boston. Remember? The one whom you chopped up into little bitty pieces and threw into the Charles River for fish 2tbait? Good G-d, I get nauseous just cutting up chickens."

Very calmly and casually he looked at me and said;

"Oh, it's about the same."

He was talking about cutting up people from experience. PEOPLE!

This threw me so that I uttered out the first thing that came to mind, "But what did your mother think of all of this?"

Both of them made faces of disgust and 'Giggy' snorted, "She was a dishbag."

I asked, "What's a dishbag?"

My look of pure puzzlement broke them up and when they were finally able to stop laughing and catch their breath and 'translated'.

"Douche bag. She was a douche bag."

So much for good ole mom, family togetherness, and loving home life. At least they had the family togetherness. Freud would have had a field day with these boys. After that, there wasn't much to say except, "Oh."

It was time once again to change the topic, so I attempted to get onto the subject of de Salvo.

"How did you and Albert de Salvo get into the hospital together?"

'Giggy' looked over at Peter and said, "Well, I had hepatitis and they put me in with him."

Now, it just seemed to me that the Boston Strangler should have been in a mental ward, and I said so. I then asked if that was where they became roommates. I never received an answer. 'Giggy' decided to avoid the issue, and he leaned over and whispered, "Did you know that de Salvo was selling 'choker chains' while he was in prison?"

I didn't know what a choker chain was, but whatever it was, it sounded funny that the Boston Strangler was selling it.

When it came to the men and their exploits, they had absolutely no hesitancy in relating their experiences in graphic detail. The exception to this rule was usually the high organized crime figures. In the case of the Wilson Brothers, even though 'Giggy' seemed to be shy about speaking out, there was a sort of pride in telling those of us who came in from the outside the gory details of the 'bum rap' that they were in there for. I never could figure out if they did it to test us for the shock-value of our reactions, or if they had a definite pride in relating the crime they had committed. However, I never had a man in there tell me that he was in there for child molesting or rape. Perhaps they didn't consider them crimes of stature, or federal inmates travel different roads down the paths of crime. The state prisons get the mom & pop grocery store robbers, and more of the crimes of 'passion'.

Most of all, the men never seemed to express any remorse for what they had done. Sometimes I got the feeling that there are those who couldn't be rehabilitated even if they were reconceived.

This is not to say that they do not have humor and intelligence, and some, a few, did show remorse. It's just that there are so many who care about nothing. To them it is a cold, hard fact. That's how the Wilson brothers looked upon life. I do know that there was closeness between the two brothers that was special. I wondered what, if anything, would happen when the inevitable came and they were separated. I didn't have long to wait; Peter was moved to Louisville. 'Giggy,' for the first time, remained alone. He sat throughout the subsequent meeting quieter than usual. He approached me at the end of the meeting.

"Hey, did you know that the pockmarked one is gone?"

Then it dawned on me that he was talking about his brother.

"He wants you to start a branch office in Louisville. He's gonna write you about what to do an' all."

I started to tell 'Giggy' about having his brother get in touch with the Jewish Welfare Federation and various rabbis in the Louisville area, until I remembered that they weren't even Jewish and didn't even know what the hell I was talking about. All they had known was that they liked the 'vibes' that they got from the Wednesday evenings and wanted it to continue in another time and place. For a short time, they didn't feel like a regulation number, but as individuals who could express themselves. I had the feeling that 'Giggy' wanted to talk more, but that's the difficulty in having a one-to-one relationship in a program like mine. That particular evening, there must have been 55 or 60 men and only seven outside guests. As a result, the 'Group' members not receiving attention sat around waiting for someone to come by with a kind word. In a world of survival, you've got to have options. A kind word is one they look forward to.

Chapter Eight

PSYCHOLOGY, WITCHES AND ASTRAL PROJECTION

Bobby Berman, a semi-regular, came into the Group early in 1977 with his friend, Hornie Harry otherwise known as 'The Count' because he bit his victims on the neck. Old Hornie gave me his most charming smile, full of cavities and fangs, and a tattooed hand that had dirty fingernails and said, "Pleased to meetcha, is this the meeting where they bring the broads in?"

I told him that it was nice that he was in there for the cultural aspects of the program, as I was sure with a progressive attitude like his, he would be a delightful addition to the discussion group. Besides, I had been striving for a better class of criminal.

Bobby Berman had been coming into the 'Group' for several years. He was the one who managed to rob a bank, kidnap the teller and guard and then shoot himself in the hand before he was caught. As if he were not already loser enough, a high-rise apartment was built over the spot where he hid his loot. Bobby was no more than 5'2" and very slender with a long pointed nose and a face like a mischievous mouse. His little dark eyes would always dart around, full of interest. He would go for long periods of time between appearances because he said evenings such as those would depress him and he couldn't take 'caring' people. He was very excited and wanted to let me know that he was eligible for parole in only twenty months. He had moreover, written to the Atlanta Jewish Welfare Federation about a job. So far, he had heard nothing. In a prison one plans ahead, but twenty months! I told him not to worry and keep those cards and letters coming. Something was bound to turn up

Once when I was sitting next to Bobby, he looked very despondent and I asked, "Bobby, what's the matter?"

With a doubtful expression he looked up at me and said, "On all this earth, no one visits me. I haven't had a visitor for a couple of years, and its probably been longer than that since anyone has written to me."

He looked so very sad when he was saying this that my first reaction was, "Oh Bobby, don't feel that way, I'll write to you. See! Someone cares."

He dismissed me with a wave of his hand and said;

"I want a broad to write to me. A real live Mother F broad. You ain't a broad; you're one of the guys."

Now, it was my turn to look shattered.

I finally arranged to have a psychologist friend of mine write to him. She was a sex psychologist who had recently returned from a conference at the Masters and Johnson Sex Research Clinic. I figured she'd have lots to talk about. The last I heard, she was still getting enough material out of him to write a book of her own.

Looking back, the favored guest of the men, other than the pretty girls, were the psychologists. The men enjoyed them the most because they always seemed to do such fun things. One night, one brought in a hypothetical test that we all took. He came loaded with his xeroxed copies of the test that we were to take. We were split up into groups of four. I sat with three diverse, interesting men; Vinnie, Carlos, and 'Chicken Hawk'.

Vinnie was a chubby Italian, who was wearing a soiled undershirt over a roll of fat which he carried around him like a spare tire. He had once had his wife write to me from the prison where she was residing. Vinnie's wife was somewhere in a Georgia prison on death row for murdering her first husband for the insurance, so she could marry her lover, Vinnie. That in itself was incredible, because this beefy object of her passion was certainly no sex symbol!

Next, I had in this select group of four, a gentleman, and I do mean gentleman, named Carlos. Where other men are suave, Carlos was SUAVE. He was educated, charming and handsome. I understood that on the outside he had been a lawyer. Whether that be true or not, he certainly had the reputation of 'jailhouse lawyer'. From what we had been told, there were many who availed themselves of his talents. Whatever this man's field or profession, he would have been terrific in politics or psychology because people naturally gravitated to him.

No matter who came into the 'Group' from the outside, Carlos was the first they asked about upon leaving. A common response was, "He's so NICE, what did he do?"

Well, I never really found out. The charge was conspiracy and that can mean a lot of things. Somewhere I was told that narcotics were involved in this particular conspiracy. If that were the case, I didn't want to know, because I liked him and didn't want my attitude to change. I think I especially liked Carlos because he always spoke so highly of his wife and family and was so easy to talk with. Although he was extremely articulate in conversations among his select group of friends, he rarely entered into conversations in front of a roomful of people when we had our discussions. Whatever his crime, with his education and manners, he would have been a desired guest at any cocktail party.

Besides being absolutely charming, Carlos was also the resident warlock. As time went on, I became convinced that if he really wanted to, he could give a twitch of his nose and leave on other levels of astral-projection.

The other men frequently spoke about his 'powers' and 'readings' but I tended to scoff the whole idea off, until the evening I brought in a psychic. I knew many of the men were into meditation and decided to bring out a woman who had been quite often on the local talk shows. She was fairly well known. The evening we arrived, the room was mobbed and at least sixty men were waiting for the program to begin. It was a dubious question as to whether they were interested in the program or in the fact that she was young and pretty. Whatever it was, they were attentive. As she started to warm up to her subject, meditation, her eyes almost got a glazed look and then she stopped. She put her hands over her temple and slowly said, "I can't go any further tonight with my meditation as I feel other forces in the room that are fighting me. There are strong mystic forces in here tonight that make it difficult to continue."

As she half rose from her seat, she finished by pointing at Carlos and saying, "THERE!"

The repercussions from that evening came the following day, when the warden called and bellowed into the phone.

"MRS. PECK! What do you mean by having women brought into the institution and having the lights turned out and everyone told to hold hands."

"Why, Warden honey, whatever do you mean?"

Never at a loss for words, he sputtered, "Word has come back to my office that you are carrying on séances and other ungodly practices within the prison, and let me tell you now, I WILL NOT ALLOW IT!"

It took twenty minutes of pacifying on my part to keep him from snapping his fingers and stopping the program. The power held by prison officials is incredible. A virtually uneducated government employee holds a position that in most cases is not given on merit but, appointed, and he is allowed to run it like a kingdom. Men, who when they were in society and employing maybe hundreds of people, such as a Mike Thevis, end up as clerks or mopping the floors of these wardens and their equally uneducated and unqualified staff. They have a tendency to forget that it is the taxpayers who are paying their salaries. When conflicts arise when the rank outsider has not conferred what they consider to be the proper amount of respect they let you know who is king of this kingdom.

However, on that infamous night of the séance, Carlos took a seat next to me and, during our conversation casually mentioned that he had done a reading on me. I was instantly curious and asked, "So, tell me, what did you see?"

Never having had a reading before, I wasn't sure what was supposed to happen. It was with relief when that sexy Latin face broke into a grin and said;

"Well, Arlene, most people have a guide or what is called a medium. They watch over and help you in ways that this plane can't comprehend."

I probably would have giggled if his dark eyes weren't so piercing and looking into my very soul, but instead said, "Really, and who do I have watching over me?"

Carlos moved slightly, tilted his head a little to the right, and said, "That's what's so puzzling; everyone else I know has only one but, you get into such trouble that I see two for you, a man and a woman."

As an afterthought, he added, "I have a feeling that you're a handful, even for them."

I laughed it off with the quip.

"Yeah, well, when I was a kid, my mother used to tell me that if I'd been born a twin, she would have drowned the other one."

Truthfully, he was looking so serious and sounding so serious that the whole topic was beginning to make me feel uncomfortable. As soon as possible, I thanked him for his trouble and changed the subject.

A few days later, I had just finished reading a book called, Life After Life. It was written by a doctor who had filled it with actual case histories of people who had been clinically dead for a few minutes and brought back to life. What impressed me was that so many had the same experience of withdrawing from their bodies. As they went deeper into death, they had someone they had loved or known lead them through a tunnel into a bright light. Now, if they were going to make it back, this was usually the point from which they returned to tell about it. It was definitely a points-to-ponder type book and the whole concept, very impressive, so much so, that I got into my tacky orange Volvo and drove over to my friend, Rhalda's house.

Her house is situated on a slight incline, so I was very careful to put the brake on when I parked. We were sitting in her kitchen, getting into a really lively conversation on the subject.

"Look, who's to say? Anything's possible. I'd much rather believe that I'm not gone when I'm gone, rather than ending up as fertilizer for a mushroom in somebody's garden."

"Yeah, well it's still so spooky to be told that two people are acting as caretakers for you while you're on this planet."

While we were talking, Rhalda got up and went to get the pot to pour another cup of coffee. Two seconds later she let out a yell.

"Good G-d, Arlene, look at your car."

What I saw did not thrill me, as the damn car had started to roll down her driveway and it was picking up speed. At this time it was too late to do anything to stop it. About all that could be done was to stand there by the window while tears trickled down my face and watch my beautiful six-year old Volvo head for what I was sure was a disaster.

"Oh hell Rhalda. It's headed for your mailbox"

Just about the moment of impact it swerved and went around the mailbox.

"Oh no. It's missed the mailbox. But look, it's going toward the fire plug or maybe into the telephone pole."

But it didn't. It was crazy, but the damn car turned itself around and went between the fire plug and telephone pole and started, driverless, down the street. Now, that was a sight to chill the bones.

"Rhalda, I can't look! It's heading down to your neighbors houses!"

It had quickly backed itself almost a block down the street, gradually and miraculously turning toward the neighbor's window, then it stopped, just like that. It stopped before any damage was done, with a soft little thud, coming to rest about six inches in front of the neighbor's azalea bushes. If I didn't believe in the power of prayer before, I did then. For the first time in a long time, I was speechless. And for a couple of minutes, we were both very quiet. Finally I looked over at my friend. Her mouth was slack. She gave a little shiver and said, "Did you see what I did?"

Both of us were about to crack up and we did when Rhalda said, "Well, to tell the truth, remember what we were talking about the friends of whatever you have watching out for you that your friend in the prison noticed? Well, he might just know what he is talking about, cause, I tell you the truth, to me, it looked as though one was directing the car and the other one was driving."

It was too much. For the rest of the day I walked around like a village idiot, giggling to myself.

It wasn't until the next week that I was able to visit my soothsayer, Carlos, who had saved me a seat next to him. I was glad he did. He didn't know it, but we had some things to discuss. Carlos sat back and his dark eyes twinkled while I told him all that had happened to me the week before. I really expected him to say, "See what happens when you scoff and poo-poo your soothsayer. Never again."

The guys really seemed to enjoy the evenings when the program had a touch of the occult. They were especially receptive when there were tones of mysticism and astral-projection. Basically, it was because it offered the answer to the perfect crime.

"Judge, I don't know nothing about it. The crime was committed here, but my body was there."

I pointed out this possibility to my warlock, Carlos.

"Don't you think all this interest in the occult, mysticism, astral-projection and all is maybe just a copout, and really it's an escape from facing life as it really is here?"

Those eyes seem to flash in agreement with me, and he paused for a moment as though carefully phrasing his words.

"Arlene, it's not necessarily a facade that they put on to trick you. Most of the people here are playing parts because they have to, if only to get through the day. Most of the time you're not even aware that you are fantasizing, but you have to. You have to just to get through. And, after awhile, even the really crazy things that you see start to look normal."

That triggered my previous thought about the lack of logic that so many of the men have and now was as good a time as any to mention it.

"Yeah, well, what do you think are the reasons for so many of them coming in here unbalanced?"

Carlos leaned back shrugged his shoulders and continued, "Who knows, maybe the reason that men in prison do not necessarily have the same logic that normal people have is a chemical imbalance. Maybe it's the background, education, or lack of it. Whatever it is, the system is terrifying and normal people don't have to wake up and think, 'maybe I'll have to kill someone today.' You get out of bed in a nice surrounding and wonder what you'll wear, or eat, or maybe how you'll spend the day. In here, everyday, every one of us has had the thought cross our minds that maybe I'll kill or be killed today. It's an unreal existence and that's why after awhile, the abnormal becomes the norm."

There wasn't too much to say after that. He had said it all. I thought of Normie, the Bomber, and a few others, and I knew he was right. That's why the drift into the topic of life after life seemed so natural.

It was a topic that I had always found fascinating and was looking forward to a lively discussion that was sure to follow. Carlos was really a whiz on the topic so I directed most of the questions to him.

"Somewhere I heard that Jesus really didn't intend to form a new religion. Is it true that he just wanted to reform the Jewish religion?"

All wise, all knowing, he answered, 'Kabala' was the 'secret doctrine' and only the high priests, who were called the initiates, learned it. Basically, the people were given the same fundamental philosophy, the same codes and morals but the difference was in the explanation."

Was it any wonder that I loved these meetings?

"How does karma and reincarnation come into all this?"

Carlos's eyes were sparkling and it was obvious that he was speaking about a subject that delighted him.

"Well, it's said that when the early leaders of the church decided to teach the doctrines of the faith to everyone they decided to drop certain aspects to make it more palatable for everyone. One of these was the theory of reincarnation."

"Yeah, it must have been hell to explain."

Carlos nodded his head in agreement and continued, "Not only that, but it was also something that made life too complex and almost impossible for them to believe."

"Do you think that they were right in teaching this?"

He gave a slight shrug of his shoulders and answered, "Probably without it, the faith wouldn't have gotten very far or would have remained just a small sect for the intellectuals and students that were really into metaphysics."

As we talked, it was easy for me to see why Carlos looked upon his time in prison as a learning experience. He used so much of his time on the study of this topic that rabbis could have learned from him on the subject of kabala.

"O.K. Suppose I buy your theory of reincarnation. What's your explanation that people can't remember their former lives? Wouldn't it be wonderful if people could? Think of how much they'd know the progress that could be made."

"No, quite the opposite, Arlene. If that were the case, we'd never learn anything. Everyone would be too hung up on former likes and dislikes. True, our strengths would be carried over, but so would our weaknesses. No, it's better to have them on a suppressed form instead of an active plateau."

Somehow, whenever Carlos and I spoke on these subjects, I always walked away with the feeling that I had sat at the feet of the prophet. I loved what we spoke about, but usually understood very little of what he had to tell me. His conversations could become pretty heavy. I probed further.

"What do you mean by 'active plane'?"

"It's simple, what we have been before builds our character and intellect. It could be the reason that we're charming or hateful. As long as we have the free will, then we can go forth with it and make progress. If you think about it, the most important forces in our life and the very existence of man have been the invisible ones. Just think how much man could know if the original metaphysical structure hadn't been buried or lost through the generations?"

In an effort to appear knowledgeable I added, "Think about all that has been lost by not remembering what has happened in past lives."

Patiently he continued with his explanation, "Arlene, nothing has really been lost or forgotten by the subconscious. That's what acts as the storehouse for all the thoughts that we have, keeps a going record of our experiences. Think about it this way. Your past record shines through your conscious mind and present body. This is what makes the character and patterns in general that a person has."

"Well, I'm not sure I buy your whole theory but I'll say one thing."

"What's that"

"Well, if there is such a thing as reincarnation, then I want to come back as a tall, blonde, skinny shicksa married to a Jewish boy. I sure wouldn't have picked spending one of my lives as an inmate, even if it does give you the time to reflect."

The serious mood had been broken and Carlos laughed and said, "That's because you're a 'JAP' (Jewish American Princess) but, maybe you're right. If I had known better, maybe I wouldn't have spent the time as an inmate, either."

Our conversation was becoming more animated, more men were joining in the conversation and when I dropped the comment that, "Do you think that reincarnation is the reason that although I may forgive, I never forget?"

More than a few nodded their heads in agreement. Quite a few around the room were beginning to relate first-hand knowledge of occult experiences.

One man, who until this night had never spoken out, finally could contain himself no longer. He was semi-elderly, with sparse hair which he wore quite long, and he usually would be dressed like a hospital orderly, wearing all white. His eyes always seemed to have a look of deep concentration. In fact, for what of a better name, since he had never mentioned his, I mentally named him, 'Deep Thought.'

When the subject of life and the forces of the hereafter, "the life in the beyond", was broached, my semi-elderly gentleman sat there pulling on his white Van Dyke and shaking his head in agreement to everything. Finally, he sat up suddenly, straightened his bifocals and said, "If I might, I'd like to share an experience with you."

He fidgeted for a moment, as though he were nervous speaking before the 'Group', cleared his throat a couple of times, took a deep breath and continued, "Last year, I was suddenly taken to the hospital for open-heart surgery. My operation was early in the morning, and for quite a few hours I was in the operating room while the doctors were fighting to save my life. About three that afternoon, while I was in the recovery room, I remember being awake, but not awake. I was just sort of lying there and listening to the machine monitor my heart. It had a lulling effect, but I wasn't sleepy. I remember it doing the beep . . . beep . . . beep that it was supposed to. It still didn't seem as though it was connected with me.

Well, all of a sudden, there was a lot of commotion around me. I was watching them stick needles into me. I watched the doctors pushing down on my chest and I felt nothing. All the pain left me and I felt nothing.

His face took on an expression of almost relief as he added, "I clearly remember the nurse saying, 'Doctor, I think we've lost him'. Then the doctor was hitting me in the chest, shouting, 'Not yet. Not yet'."

'Deep Thought' continued in an almost peaceful serene tone.

"During all of this, the machine was still going beeeeeep, and the damnedest thing. I didn't feel a thing, yet I clearly remember standing next to the doctor and watching him work on me, like a spectator. I recognized me lying on the bed, but I kept saying to myself, no, the 'real' me is the one standing by and looking at the other. All the time, I was out of my body, looking down at them working on me."

He drifted off and his face remained peaceful.

"I can't explain it, but I didn't really feel afraid. While I was standing looking down, over to the side of me was my mother, and I remember wanting to ask her forgiveness for the things that I had done before she died. Before I could do that, she was asking my forgiveness. It was about this time that the doctor said, 'I think we'll make it, I think we'll make it, I think we'll make it.' Over and over he said that. I sort of remember my body being reluctantly drawn back and the next thing I remember was the heart monitor going beep . . . beep . . . beep."

With that, he leaned back in his chair almost with relief, though he added an afterthought to his occult reminiscence.

"But, you wanna know something? If that is what death and dying are like, I don't know. No, I do know. I'll never have that fear again."

'Deep Thought' had become uncomfortable after he realized that he had spoken before so many for so long. Out of embarrassment more than anything else, he laughed nervously and said, "I don't know how to explain it."

My favorite warlock, Carlos, smiled and said, "You just did."

It's hard to say how many believers in metaphysics, in ESP, in the power of the mind or in prayer, were in that room, but there was no doubt about the man's sincerity when he spoke. Long after the lights went out, or whatever happens there after hours, there was more than one person, besides myself, with points to ponder before he or she dropped off to sleep.

My third partner in our psychology study group of four was Robert Helm, alias 'Chicken Hawk'. He was the classic case of the battered child and neglected juvenile. Once when we were speaking during the early years of the program, he told me, "Aw hell, Arlene. You don't know what it's like out there. By the time I was nine, I was on my own. And, when I was twelve and they stopped bringing me back to the county homes, I had done everything that you could imagine."

He was right too, growing up and raising my kids in the 'Jewish Mother' syndrome where every move of the children is planned and accounted for. It was inconceivable that any child could be mistreated or uncared for. My oldest child was twelve at the time and he had never even ridden a bus by himself. No, it was hard to imagine.

Later, as we became friends, he began to write me occasionally, and I remember thinking when the first letter arrived from Robert that, "This man can't be a drop-out, he spells words that I can't even pronounce and his handwriting is beautiful." Robert had such a poor self-image that he didn't even know that he was a winner. It was up to me to convince him, and, if necessary, make him realize his potential.

I began by making a point to bring Robert into the discussions. This wasn't as easy as it sounds, because most of the men were reluctant to assert themselves in a group discussion until they were familiar with the people and surroundings. Sometimes, one had to pull them out of a shell. I was interested in hearing Robert's attitudes and feelings on the topics. Gradually, he began to open up a little, and when he did speak, it was obvious that this was a knowledgeable man. He was almost like a sponge soaking up information. Eventually, I began to bring in special books that I thought he might want to delve into further. I wasn't wrong. Within a couple of months, he walked into the Wednesday evening and shyly said,

"I've come to a decision. Now, don't laugh at what I'm about to say, but I've decided to go to college."

Laughing was the furthest thing from my mind and I told him, "Robert, that's wonderful! What made you decide and what kind of college can you attend . . . here?"

"Oh, there are all kinds of college classes available in the prison. You can get almost any kind of degree you want here. It's just most of us are not motivated to want it. I don't know what's made me get the education bug, but I really think I'd like to go for a degree. What do ya think? Think it's too crazy that someone like me would want to end up a college student?"

No, I didn't think it farfetched, or crazy. All Robert had needed for most of his unfortunate life was for someone, just once, to believe in him.

Robert was slight of build and he had a face that looked like a poor man's James Cagney. His age could have been anywhere from mid-thirty to mid-forty. As time passed and he enrolled in his studies, I became like Henry Higgins in 'My Fair Lady', and Robert was my prodigy. During this time, even his physical appearance began to change. His eyes sparkled with enthusiasm when he spoke of what he was learning or doing for that week. And, although he sometimes complained about the heavy workload that he was carrying, he spoke with a pride in his voice that I hadn't noticed before. In the early days of his transformation, Robert had a hair style that was reminiscent of old pictures of Fannie Brice. Once he became wrapped up in his new self-awareness program, the hair was cut, blown dry and very attractively styled. He cut his fingernails and spruced himself up. Eventually, even his speech pattern began to change. Robert now had a purpose and a positive one!

In my enthusiasm, I realized that he was too elegant for the institution, his cellmates, and the girl he left behind. She came into town and he was anxious for me to meet her. He was proud of himself and the transformation he had been making. Life was looking good and he was getting to the point that he wanted to share it with someone. Robert had been taking a full load of accelerated courses, and now he called in 'the girlfriend' from Philadelphia to visit him and meet his friend who had inspired the transformation. I was curious to meet her, because I was hoping that she would be someone who would continue where I had left off when he was paroled, which was to be shortly. She wasn't.

She called my home late one afternoon.

"Hey, Arlene, it's me, LaVerne."

"Who?"

"Me, LaVerne, you know, 'Chicken Hawks' girl from Philly."

"Oh, you mean Robert. Oh, it's nice you called, Robert mentioned that you'd be coming to town and that he wanted us to meet. Where are you staying?"

"The Regency, only the best, I brought a friend's credit card. Wanna meet me in the bar?"

We finally settled on the coffee shop, although reluctantly on her part. It's true that you can't tell a book by its cover, or a person by her bra size or lack thereof, but this girl was about a size D, droopy D, wearing a dingy tee shirt that proclaimed, "Pollution Sucks," without a bra. Once you got past that distraction, she had pimples, bad make-up and long straw-textured white hair with about three inches of black root showing. In between snapping her gum, she leaned forward, resting those enormous boobs on the table and delightfully stated, "Hey, what' cha do to that little guy, 'Chicken Hawk'? How bout that, a college boy? Course, I never finished school and it didn't hurt me none."

Our conversation went downhill from there and I reluctantly made the decision that although she may have been the girl for him when he arrived in the institution, she didn't have the 'class' he needed to leave with. And I told him so. He didn't say much, but he did send her home to Philadelphia before her trip was supposed to be over. I was getting so carried away with this project of mine; I almost patted him on the back and said:

"Don't worry dear, a mother knows."

Months went by and each time the college would have finals and grades would come out, Robert would send me his straight A's with a follow-up that he'd made the dean's list. I drew the line at signing his report cards, but I came close. Before I knew it, he was a senior and up for parole.

A few weeks before this event was to take place, Robert cut a class and came into the discussion evening. His appearance had changed drastically, and he now wore his hair in a fuller, blow-dry cut. He'd filled out a little, but most of all, he carried himself with a sense of pride. It showed in the way he moved. He no longer had that whipped-dog expression on his face that was once so apparent. Still, something was wrong. All evening he sat quietly, and when we broke up for the social half-hour he came over and said, "Arlene, I've got good news and bad news."

"So, tell me the good news first."

"Well, my parole has come through and I'll be able to get out of here before long."

"Robert! That's terrific, what could be bad news after that?"

"I can't leave now, I've got three more months to finish up college and graduate and the parole board is going to make me return to Philadelphia instead of letting me stay in Atlanta so I can finish up and get my degree. Do you think that there is anyone that you could speak with on my behalf so arrangements could be made so I could just finish up, get my credits and then go back to Philly if I have to?"

There was a time in the beginning years when I honestly believed that the prison officials and all those connected with prison life really wanted rehabilitation, but my thinking had become tainted through years of reality. The case of Robert was but one reason to become cynical. Maybe I could have overlooked the incompetent and sometimes vicious acts committed by prison officials, but not letting this man graduate? That really got to me. I was mad as hell and at a loss of how I could help.

Though one might expect the authorities would be interested in this man's getting a fresh start in a new place, I knew differently from past experience. As it turned out, I was absolutely right. I had left that night promising to make a few calls to see what I could do, but nothing could be done. They were going to send this 'criminal' back to his original environment, which had been terrible to begin with. I was able to arrange a job for him and an apartment.

"Mrs. Peck, this is Mr. Knowles, Robert's case worker. Have you got a minute? I'd like to discuss something with you."

"Sure, it's nice to know that there is someone connected with the prison system that actually cares what happens to any of the men, what can I do to help you?"

"Well, as you probably know by now, Robert has been running into dead ends each time he tries to get someone in the courts or the parole board to give a ruling that will allow him to stay in Atlanta so that he might get his degree from college."

"Yeah, I know, I've had the same thing happen out here. People from the Jewish Community, who've been impressed with how far this man has come, have gone out on a limb and assured him living arrangements and he has a job waiting here when he gets out, one that won't interfere with his attending classes. Frankly, at this point, we're at a loss as to what to do now. Any suggestions?"

Well, he hadn't helped any, but a few days later Robert called from the bus station and said that he was on his way to his 'previous environment' and he would keep in touch. We spoke briefly as the bus was leaving in a few minutes.

"Robert, promise me that you'll finish school just as soon as you get settled in where they send you. You've gone too far to let everything slide back now."

He sounded hopeful, but hedging.

"I'll try, I really will."

I knew, even then, that although he had all good intentions, and somehow the goal that he had been working so hard for would never be attained. I couldn't feel disappointment in him because I felt then, and still do enormous pride at how far he had come. But, I knew how Henry Higgins felt. My prodigy would never get to the ball, or in this case, graduation, as his final triumph. And, although I never felt that it was he who let me down, there was a terrible sense of loss that he didn't quite make it.

A year later, I received a call late at night and it was Robert. He just wanted to let me know that he was O.K. and staying out of the 'joint'. We talked for a while, and most of what he said was music to my ears. He had been working steady; he was settled in an apartment. Most of all, he was staying out of trouble. He even had a new girlfriend. She was a University of Pittsburg graduate, a teacher and Jewish. I'm sure that somewhere, because of me and my program, there was a Jewish mother of a Pittsburg graduate tearing her hair out.

The real shame of Robert's situation was more than his not being able to continue college. It was a system that was so untrained and unqualified that even my interest in men like Robert came under suspicion. Our hands were tied. The final decisions were up to the Bureau of Prisons which was engulfed with red tape. The men were reduced to really being only a number. We, the taxpayers, are the ones who bear the final burden of such a system. Even if help is offered, so many obstacles are placed in the way that usually those who are trying to help give up in pure frustration. The prevailing attitude of those who run our federal and state prisons is that the men in there aren't worth any efforts in their behalf.

True, many in there aren't and should be locked away from society forever, but occasionally, a Robert will turn up and what happens to them? The housing and job offers that were made available to him cost the public nothing. Each time outside help is discouraged, they might give up and eventually go on to another project.

The psychologist discussion leader of that winter evening in 1976 had given us a hypothetical situation. We were told, "You are leaving this place to start a new world. On this world, you will take only nine people from this list of fifteen that will be allowed to go. You are to discuss with your group and agree on which of the nine you wish to take along with you."

I scanned the list and found; a pregnant woman, a carpenter, an artist, scientist, social worker, professional athlete, housewife, civil rights worker, philosophy professor, college student of the humanities, a Rabbi, a construction worker, wealthy elderly person active in charities, and a woman active in the liberation movement.

For the next thirty minutes or so we broke up into our groups of four. While we were in these groups, we were to discuss who we wanted to take along with us, and most important, why.

Although every group was as diverse as mine, one person on the list was selected by everyone, without exception, the artist. The psychologist directing this exercise was surprised, because the artist was the person who was usually omitted from the list when he gave the question to other groups. Never in all his experience had everyone in a room voted the same way. On this particular night there were probably fifty men there and the vote was unanimous.

I didn't want to sit there and tell the psychologist I knew it all the time, but I did. The surroundings are so ugly and drab in that place that beauty has to be the thing the men miss most. He never had guys look at him in the eye and say, "A lot of us don't know what a bird chirping sounds like, or a dog barking, but if you ask us what it's like to hear a man getting stabbed to death, we can tell you about that. If you ask us what it's like to hear a man screaming because he's getting gang raped by four other guys, we can tell you about that too, cause we hear that every day. That's reality to us!"

I had heard that conversation more times then I cared to remember, so I knew how important beauty was to them. Of course, a lot of them thought of beauty in the form of a good-looking woman, but they missed beauty, and an artist would be high on the list of people that these men needed most. That place was really ugly. Not only the physical surroundings, but the system itself was terrifying. In order to bring some color into their lives, many of the men had taken up painting. Some of the work they created was really incredible. They had a show once or twice a year, and people from the outside were allowed to buy these paintings. As expected, many times paintings were done of landscapes and seascapes, which testified to art's lure, escape into beauty.

A renowned sculptress once visited the 'Group.' The men were interested in looking over the pictures of her work and hearing about her techniques. She was delighted to see their interest in sculpture in the institutions. Maybe this talented lady could be persuaded to teach a class for the inmates. At the suggestion, everyone broke up into laughter and one of the more vocal ones said, "That would be nice, but I don't think they would allow it."

I knew they had painting classes, but it didn't make sense to me why they couldn't allow sculpting classes and I said so. This amused my 'Group.' Their answer made sense.

"Ya see, in order to have a sculpting class, you gotta have certain tools, like picks, hammers and chisels. We think the administration might frown on that sort of thing, but anything is possible. Anybody that can arrange a day out for the inmates just might be able to do it."

Then, as an afterthought, one of the men leaned over and whispered to the lady;

"How are you on chiseling granite walls?"

Chapter Nine

THE DAY THEY HAD OPEN HOUSE AT THE BIG HOUSE

Years ago our federal prisons practiced the policy of visits. Our institutions and penitentiaries would allow people to come in from the outside and have tours that went through the place, which was really kind of tacky. Thankfully, through our "enlightened" period, this had been cancelled. However, occasionally they'd let certain tours go through the institution to show them what facilities they have and don't have. On one of the coldest days in January of 1977, a call came in from the Director of the Bureau of Jewish Education. It seemed that some members of the Jewish Community had requested a visit through the Federal Prison to see the conditions. Because of this request by a few, the prison administration decided to allow the entire group to join this tour. Rarely was anyone from the outside allowed to see what really went on behind closed walls. It promised to be an interesting day and I was looking forward to the 'tour' with mixed feelings. In five years of weekly visits, the only parts of the building that we had seen outside of the meeting rooms were the dining hall where the men had the Passover Seder. Although the men would be on 'exhibit' in a way, they had also spoken of conditions many times and it would be nice to see first hand what they were speaking about.

It would have been nicer if another day, other than the coldest day in January had been picked. Most of the tour was outside and we were freezing our southern 'tushies' off.

We arrived almost on time, with a few stragglers along the way, me being one of them. The reason I arrived 'almost' on time was because the guard in the tower waited until I had parked my car, locked it and was halfway to the entrance before he announced over his bull horn, "Halt!"

"You will have to move your car. You are not in a designated space."

Typical.

There were about twenty of us there, and the priest and guard were ready to escort the visitors into the conference room. First, we went through those double, in-out, open-shut gates I had come to know so well. Once the group was through the gates intact, we were ushered to the left, up a long stairway with white marble walls, which was in the process of being painted or redecorated. We were told that it was to be the new waiting room for groups like ours, because the entrance was too congested. The room itself was very plush, so incongruous with the rest of the institution. It had a nice, long expensive looking conference table. It brought to mind the many times the men had raised questions about expenses laid out for the administrative offices, reminiscent of Las Vegas in all its fineries while funds weren't available for a much needed library for the inmates. The walls were carpeted no less. I supposed it was to muffle the screams. Despite all the times I had been in there, I was still learning things I didn't know before.

According to the information we received that day, the Atlanta Federal Prison was the armpit of the prison system, the cesspool of the world, the top of the heap or the bottom of the barrel. It all depended from where one looked. In fact, we were given a dubious parallel between the prison system and the educational system. The local state prisons and juvenile halls were the kindergartens. The minimum-security prisons, such as Danbury, Connecticut and Allentown, were the high schools. When one got to the graduate level, the all-time college of the penal system is my Atlanta Arms. The men who enter here, according to the priest, are incorrigible at their nicest, most sophisticated and cunning of all the inmates in the entire prison system. We were told that these men had done the grossest acts against society. One of the guests inquired, "How do the men who live in this little community you have here get their supply of drugs, if not through the guards?"

I had wanted to know the answer to that myself. The answer we received from the priest was, "Well, many people do come into the institution day after day and no matter how well someone is searched, it is still possible to miss something. Besides visitors, delivery men came into the place from the outside, and there are even inmates who have outside contracts."

He ran his hand across his grey flecked beard as if debating with himself whether to say what he had planned next, and continued with, "And, last but not least, with the enormous staff of 500 that we have, it has not been unknown to have employees of the penal system itself supply the drugs. Although we have been able to control the flow of contraband, it is nearly impossible."

This question and answer session went on for a few more minutes, and finally we were told by the guard that we were ready to start the tour, but first the ground rules. He seemed to delight in exaggerating his 'schpiel' as though his purpose was to impress upon us the really serious excursion we were about to undertake. With an undertone of intrigue, he stated, "First, stay as close as possible to each other, otherwise, someone could mingle with your group and try an escape. Further, we are responsible for your safety, and believe it or not, there are professional pickpockets in here who could bump against you."

The priest's eyes narrowed a little and he told the group, "Would you believe that last week, nuns were in here for our Catholic program and they had their purses stolen? They just left them for a minute and had them stolen!! Catholic nuns, for G-ds sake, NUNS!"

He managed to convey this message that he would have felt better about it had it been someone from the Jewish group who'd gotten ripped off. Anyway, because of this, all visitors into the prison had to check their belongings at the entrance of the building in airport type lockers. Thankfully, I'd brought my coat. They had neglected to tell us that the better part of the tour would be outside in what felt like a blizzarding windstorm. Living in the south tends to give one thin blood and it was definitely not the day which we would have chosen for an outside stroll around that huge institution.

Herded together like cattle, we went down the same way we had entered and started on our official tour. This part of the building was lacking the long, plush carpeted 'conference rooms'. It was really depressing, and I believe I said as much to the guard who was stabbing his teeth with a dirty toothpick.

"Didn't I read something in the paper recently about how this particular institution was to be closed because it was one year younger than G-d and ready to be condemned?"

The priest looked up at this and said with a sardonic grin, "I'm afraid when this place is closed, the last warden it will have hasn't even been born yet."

All during the walk we were told to stay together because the place was loaded with psychotics. Someone in our party drawled, with an unbelievable southern Jewish accent, "Mr. Guard, I vant to ask ya'll should answer a question for me, if you shouldn't mind?"

"Yes?"

"Vell, da question is, vat are da muschigie, er crazy peoples doing here anyway? If dey shouldn't be here and der crazy, then vat in da voild are they put into da jailhouse and not in the crazy house where they should be, if you'll pardon mine expression."

Eloquently put! Guard Tidbit continued picking his teeth and drawled right back, "Wa-ll, to tell the truth, they just got too many of them in there. Cells are crowded; hospitals are crowded, whole damn place. Ya know how it is; if its only got room for 500 patients and you got 600 residing there, then they're gonna cure the less violent crazy ones and just medicate them and send em on back to the prison in 90 days. I'll grant ya though, they should be off somewhere in a mental ward."

All the while he was saying this; I heard a scream coming from down the hall from one of the cell blocks.

The cell blocks we passed both on our left and right were a far cry from the plush offices of the man who resided on the other side of the bars. There were 600 people in these cell blocks, which was 5 stories high, with 4-6 people to a cell. Some of these were 6-8 men cells. The bottom part of these cell blocks, those that we were able to see, were littered with candy wrappers and ripped cigarette packages. Some men were sitting, lined up on chairs watching T.V. A little further along, we were allowed to glance into the visiting room. I felt sad for the families of the men. There must have been a better way to make it easier for them than the present system. As we approached, a mother was leaving with a couple of small children with runny noses. She had tears in her eyes and kept dabbing at her eyes with a ragged tissue. Although it was cold outside, she had beads of perspiration along her top lip and was pushing stray wisps of hair that fell across her forehead. Along with them were other people who were leaving the room. Of course, everyone was escorted by two guards, as were we, one at the front of the group and another bringing up the rear. I wondered then, as I do now, why on earth the authorities subject the inmate's families to seeing all that. Why is the location of the visiting room in such a place that the visitors have to pass through the gates and watch them locked behind before they are escorted to the visiting room, past the cell blocks? It's just not right for the kids to see.

The visiting room itself is large and one has to walk about five steps to enter. At the threshold, however, there are two more guards who sit at a table to watch and make sure that not too much hanky-panky goes on. Usually, a search of the visitors and their belongings when they first arrive is made. All around the room are vending machines, and I wondered who had the concession for them. Later, I found out quite accidentally that one of the guards who had recently retired had the concession.... How? Briefly, the thought entered my mind to maybe ask the priest on this tour.

"Who gave a guard the right to have a concession in a federal institution?"

But I chickened out and figured; maybe I wouldn't because I didn't want to be escorted out before the rest of the group.

I was glad that we didn't go in the visiting room, because for the first time, I felt that we might be imposing. I didn't want to stop and stare at the people. I hadn't felt that way earlier, because until then, I had been walking through a place which was already familiar to me. It was like visiting a friend that I hadn't seen in a week or so. Until then, I didn't realize that we were only a small percentage of the prison population. It really seemed strange to be spending the better part of the day walking around there and not recognizing anyone.

We were next taken to the dining room. Actually, it didn't look too bad. The men were fed by their cell blocks, but they could eat pretty much what they wanted, when they wanted. The room itself was quite large, and along the walls were cheerful but garish posters and paintings. It reminded me of a large Woolworth coffee shop. There were bins of not very sharp, stainless steel silverware that was absolutely sparkling. While we were standing there, wondering where to go next, the guard motioned us over to one side.

"Ya'll better move cause we got a group of 'holdovers' comin' in and they gotta eat now."

"What's a holdover?

"Oh, those are the prisoners who are being transferred from one prison to another. Sort of like a rest stop ya might say."

The priest, who was still acting as our guide, explained, "These men do not mix with the other inmates in any way until their papers come through. They even have their meals separate and at different times."

As we went out, the holdovers came in, and I suppose I felt just as much on exhibit as they did.

From the cafeteria, we went outside into the cold and learned about the mills where they make canvas bags, mattresses and God knows what else, for twenty-five cents an hour. We were told about the vocational programs, but we didn't really see any. We did see about thirty men lined up outside a building and when we asked who they were, the guard told us, "Oh, that's the medicine line."

I commented, "They don't look too sick to me. If they are, isn't it a bit cold to be standing outside waiting for medicine? That's a good way to get the flu."

The priest looked first at me, and then at the men with contempt and patiently explained, "That's the prison drug program, you know, the addicts."

"Oh! What are they giving them, methadone?"

That triggered the only laugh of the day from the priest and he chuckled, "Uh-hum. That's true."

My next comment fell flat.

"I told the guys to save the name of the doctor because in a couple of years I wanted to go see him and tell him to start at the knees and work up, up, up. When he gets to the top, he can snip it off, and make a cloning of what's left."

Tucked off inconspicuously, in this little complex of buildings we came upon the 'hole' which was otherwise known as segregation. It was a taller, red-brick building, heavily barred, and very isolated looking; extremely formidable. The men that are placed in this 'hole' are considered to have discipline and security problems. Although I had learned that even 'jailhouse lawyers' spent none of their share of time in the 'hole', being considered trouble makers, suits have been filed charging that solitary confinement is often used to isolate those troublesome 'writ' writers away from the other inmates where they couldn't do any harm, or good, depending on what side of the fence you are on. Others may have been 'holed' up for violating the prison rules for drugs or for gambling, sometimes for 'protective custody'. A man might even request to go there if the Atlanta Arms had become too small for him and someone else when violence potential was sensed.

We quickly passed that building and the priest acted as though he wanted to avoid all questions concerning it. I became curious and asked, "How do the men get transferred out of this place?"

"Oh, it can be easily arranged. Sometimes another institution has a skill that an inmate might want to pick up, such as computer programming or the man is a discipline problem in Atlanta and they want to move him out of there to get him away from certain people."

In actuality, it wasn't as easy as the priest made it sound.

We passed the hospital but were not allowed to go inside. One of the reasons given was that it had a psycho-ward, and it was not safe to bring visitors inside. I had been really interested to see the hospital facilities. In the waiting room, we had seen brochures about the prison which showed lovely pictures of a hospital, but according to the men, the hospital and its services were in reality, deplorable.

In the beginning, I had doubted their story. And later, I knew different.

I saw case after case from the hospital records describing how men were butchered by the complete lack of competent medical care in that institution. These hospital records were rolled up with copies of the cases inmates lawyers had pending in court. When these men recover damages, and they should, it will be the taxpayer who again is stuck for the tab.

One inmate's file described how he went into the hospital for a simple hernia operation and found that after surgery, his left testicle was lodged inside his body and has remained there ever since. The same surgeon, lovingly referred to by the men as 'Old Shakey' suffered from a condition which manifested itself in uncontrollable hand tremors. He had performed an operation for hemorrhoids and cut the man's sphincter muscle. The patient lost control over his defecation. Remember, American taxpayers pay these damages.

We had seen pictures of a lovely library that the pen supposedly maintained; however, the men told us what little library they had was poor and ill-equipped. Brandeis, a Jewish organization, donated forty or fifty thousand books. What happened to them? Within a year or two! Who sold them? Who pocketed the money? It seemed logical that since reading is such a passive exercise that the officials would encourage it as much as possible.

We did go into the exercise area, and da-mn! That place was big! So was the wall. The priest pointed with pride that the wall was six to eight feet thick, twenty-eight feet high, and sixteen feet deep. It was the largest man made wall until the Hoover Dam. About this time, my teeth were chattering and the bottom button of my coat had popped off and I was getting the full benefit of the January blast. I was dying to get back inside, to the cells or whatever, as long as it was out of the cold. Before we went in, we were shown the tennis courts, basketball courts, handball courts and baseball diamonds and stadiums. I made a mental note to tell the guys on my next visit that the place was a regular 'Grossingers'.

By this time, I had lost all feeling in my toes, and I was sure gangrene and frostbite had bitten my left hand. Fortunately, the priest suggested that we continue the questions inside the institution. We were then escorted back to the waiting room for another question and answer session. I let fire immediately.

"How much money are the prisoners given to leave the place with?"

Swinging Priest now had us seated at the table and he picked up a piece of chalk and started to answer the questions by drawing squiggly lines on the blackboard.

"One hundred dollars, but, they're not only sent out with the money, they are given a new leisure suit."

He ignored my comment, "I like the symbolism in that."

And he continued with, "Along with the hundred dollars, they are given paid transportation to their destination. If they had a bank account, then they were able to draw the money from that after sixty days. This gives them the time to get adjusted to their new environment, whatever that is. The reason for the delay on the money is there are some who, if they got their hands on real money after not having any for so long a period they would blow it and then be right back in trouble."

As much as I hated to agree with the administration, I did in this case, because I remembered the time Little Joe called from the bus station. Little Joe had been in the penitentiary for many, many years. One of the charges had been murder on a federal reservation. The morning that he finally received his parole, Joe called and asked whether I would meet him at the bus station to wave good-bye. I said 'sure' and headed to the station. It took all of fifteen minutes to drive over there and during that time the man had managed to get himself bombed. He was unconscious in the waiting room and looked as though a truck had run over him. This was at the ungodly hour of nine o'clock in the morning and he was about ready to settle down for the day in a nasty, torn Naugahyde bus station seat. There was a burning cigarette about to ignite the end of his yellowed, fingers and I debated for a minute or two if I should watch and see whether he hollered when it finally burned down. He probably wouldn't have noticed as the man was not feeling any pain, and I was afraid that he would be picked up by the police and put back in prison.

Little Joe mentioned that his bus wasn't due to leave for a couple of hours. At this point, he was in no condition to get on any bus and go wherever they were sending him. It took me a while, but I found a porter and slipped him a couple of dollars for the promise that when the designated time came he would see that "Little Joe" was put on it and sent with his money and suitcase. The porter agreed to watch out for him until departure time and see that he got there OK. A few weeks later, I received a call thanking me.

I was also thinking of 'Little Joe' a few minutes later, during the prison open-house. We were told that there were some inmates who, that no matter what they did to guarantee that they didn't return were so 'institutionalized' that they would return the first chance they got. It was the only way they ever knew. These men had been from foster home to juvenile hall to reformatory. Their lives had culminated in big crime and a sentence to the federal prisons, the biggest 'home' of all.

Mr. Tidbit (all guards always seemed to be named Mr. Tidbit) told us, "Wa-ll, you sure can spot one of these men too. They came in here smellin' like a goat, dirty mangy clothes and scuffed raggedy shoes, and within a week they got their hair cut, got clean, and spit'n polish on their shoes. Yep, you sure can tell one."

These are the men who don't know how to function on a non-institutionalized basis. I knew that my friend 'Little Joe' from the station was like that. Within three months he was back, but not in my 'Group'. After all the promises Joe had made, he was embarrassed to come in and say that he had been wrong.

The priest was giving his 'going my way act' and bubbling with charm act to those who didn't know him. He was charmingly answering any and all questions, and in addition to his squiggly lines, was now drawing diagrams on the blackboard. He was very intent on telling the visitors

"Are you aware that only twenty-five percent of the prison population has any visitors?"

Tibit unnecessarily added, "Which means that another seventy-five percent don't even have any kinda contact with the outside world. You wouldn't believe that some of these guys have been in institutions such as these for their whole lives, and as incredible as it sounds, programs like yours may be one of their few chances to talk with people who are straight."

While they were talking, I was thinking, it's funny, religion in the federal pen, at best, is distrusted. People, who came in with a program such as our discussion group, are genuinely interested or want to help. They can accomplish more than all the professional social workers or do-gooders who are paid to come in there to 'do their job'.

For many of the inmates, religion is a cop-out. Some will join everything, because it might impress the parole board. Some are natural 'joiners'. On the other hand, a man may sit and one day and look back at what a mess he's made of his life, and start looking around for something else. That search for something else can be religious, ethical or moral conduct, whatever turns him on. If he can find that something to hold on to, his 'time' can go ever so much faster.

We still served a purpose, even for those who couldn't have cared less about what we had to offer in the way of Jewish education. If, and this is a big IF, they walked away, as I think many did, from those evenings, lacking the hostility or hate or whatever brought them in, then our discussion group, whatever its 'ulterior motive,' served a real purpose.

Chapter Ten

THE DAY I WAS SET UP FOR THE FLIM FLAM

The phone rang as I was just heading out of the house. I was late for taking my daughter for her piano lesson and was annoyed that the phone rang as I was just heading out the door. In my eagerness to answer the phone I tripped, stubbed my toe, banged the hell out of my shin and shouted with unconcealed annoyance into the telephone, "Hello!"

I almost said, "dammit." A voice oozing with sweetness, said, "Mrs. Peck?"

At first I thought it was one of these 'market research' phone calls and I was ready to blast into her, but again I heard, "Mrs. Peck? My name is Susan and I was told to call you so you might schedule my name to go in this week with your 'Group'."

"Oh, well, I would love to have you go into the group with my guests for this week but I'll have to know some more about you. Who told you to call me, by the way?"

In a throaty voice she said, "Oh, my goodness. I must have forgotten to tell you, the men from Temple Yakkov wanted you to clear my name as a guest."

Despite my impatience, this intrigued me, as from time to time some of the men had wanted me to bring in a girlfriend, wife, business associate or whatever, and I just could not do it. I tried to explain this to my caller and she glazed it over with, "Oh, Mrs. Peck. I certainly have no intention of breaking any rules and I don't have any desire to go into the discussion evening as a visitor of anyone. I happen to be a lawyer and Mr. Dreck, who is the president of Temple Yakkov, invited me in to see the group's discussions. I am very interested in prison reform."

I didn't want to be rude, but I had to ask, "And, who is 'Mr. Dreck.' I've been going in for years and thought I knew the names of everyone, or at least anyone who was the president of Temple Yakkov."

She answered weakly, "Well, Mrs. Peck. You see, I'm a Jewish lawyer who is quite curious about your prison work and would very much like to become a part of your program. And 'Mr. Dreck,' although new to the group, has been elected president by the men who realize he is very much interested in the progress and aims of the men in it.

This all sounded like a crock of turdfeathers to me, but my curiosity was up. So, I said, "OK. I'll see what I can do about getting your name on the entrance list. We meet at my house promptly at five o'clock and everyone goes out together."

I gave her the address, but something about her 'involvement' in prison reform just didn't ring true, but I couldn't put my finger on it.

Wednesday came and Lawyer Susan was at my home a few minutes early so that we might have a chance to 'chat'. She was oozing charm and certainly looked the part of the young executive. She wore a tweed skirt and jacket. Her hair was pulled back severely, and her horn-rimmed glasses made her long face look even more angular. Somehow she reminded me of the girl who is in the commercials who lets loose her hair, unbuttons her blouse to show cleavage and throws off her glasses to say, "See, I'm a sex symbol after office hours when I use 'nofke' perfume." She didn't look me in the eyes when she spoke, which is not a very good trait, especially in a lawyer.

A few minutes after she arrived, the rest of the people came and we didn't get too much of a chance to talk further. I was more interested in watching her speak to the men in the group and see how she handled herself. This whole new election that Lawyer Susan had spoken of puzzled me. Why didn't I know the group's new president or vice-president and why had they never been regular members of our evening discussion? The question kept arising, why the new sudden interest?

Handle herself she did. For one who had never been up there on a Wednesday evening, Ms. Susan received a hero's welcome from the men, at least from the new president and his board of directors. Something was up and I didn't have long to wait to find out. 'Mr. Dreck', the new president came over to introduce himself. He was big and very powerful looking. He stuck a huge paw in my face and waited for me to shake.

"Why hi there Mrs. Peck, I'm the new president of Temple Yakkov and we certainly heard a lot about you."

"Well, that almost makes us even. I've heard nothing about you."

Mr. Dreck ignored my comment and continued, "Yeah, well it was what you might call a sudden election. However, me and my board members over there have what you might say is a slight request that we would like for you to handle for us."

"Mr. Dreck, you make that sound like it's an offer I can't refuse."

He gave me a big smile.

"Hey, that's good. I like a sense of humor in a broad. You see, for quite a while, the men in Temple Yakkov have been knocking around the idea of trying to get an outside bank account for the men in the group. They feel the need for one in case of emergencies."

"What kind of emergency did you have in mind? Usually, anything that happens in here is an emergency."

He smiled, but it never reached his eyes.

"Hey, you're a funny lady Mrs. Peck. Naw, the kind of emergency we're talking about is in case someone's mother died. They want to set up a fund to send flowers to the family. Or suppose Chanukah time. They want a fund to be able to send presents to their kids, you know, little things like that."

I had a feeling I knew the turn of events that this conversation was taking, but still couldn't figure out where lady lawyer came into the picture. Within a short time, I found out.

"Listen, Mr. Dreck. I'm sure that you and your board of directors wouldn't dream of doing anything that wouldn't be on a legitimate basis. Nor would it enter your mind to go up against the Bureau of Prisons Policies. But, any account that would be started under the heading of the Bureau of Jewish Education would have to go through them with the bureau handling the funds."

About this time, El Presidente sided closer with his illustrious directors, who incidentally also look very formidable and said, "Well, here is the plan that we have unanimously agree upon, see? Temple Yakkov is in the process of arranging to have a bank account, under the direction of the Jewish community and especially the Bureau of Jewish Education, but the sole executor is to be our very capable lawyer, Susan."

It wasn't too difficult to figure out what they were up to. Their plans were probably to have an illegal account where laundered money could run through it. But, it wasn't about to happen. Not if I had anything to do with it. They weren't going to use the Bureau of Jewish Education as a vehicle to do it.

I gave him my best evil eye and said, "Guys, I don't know what you have up your sleeve, but I'll be damned if I'm going to let you use me to do it."

Mr. Dreck smiled at me like a shark and said, "Aw, Arlene, nothin's wrong. We just want our legal counsel to aid and represent us in a little bank account for emergencies. You see, it's gotta go through your program, so don't make any waves about it, dig?"

I dug all right. I knew there was no way the bureau was going to justify sponsoring anything like that, so I really didn't worry about it getting clearance. If anything, I wondered more than ever what my new lawyer friend had up her sleeve.

One thing I knew damn well was that she wasn't going out with me again. I always tried to line up people as guests who were extroverted and made an effort to speak with everyone. This kid was spending too much time during that three hour period speaking to her three or four clients. I also didn't like the way that she failed to mention the fact that she had clients that she was planning to visit.

During the course of the evening, a group member casually mentioned to us that the next week there were plans underway for the prisoners to film our discussions on tape. He chimed, "Since you've done such a good job, we wanted to make a movie and show it to groups to see what kind of programs we ought to have more of."

Being an egotist, I could easily relate to that.

One week later, just as I was getting ready to drive out to the prison, Lawyer Susan called. I wanted no part of her, as there was no question that if the prison officials even thought that I were planning any clandestine banking arrangement, both the program and I would be out.

My nerves were still nervous from all the hiding I had to do from the Bud Culligan 'caper', and for a while, I just wanted to stay anonymous around that place. Nevertheless, she called.

"Oh, Mrs. Peck. I'm SO-O-O-O glad that I caught you. I just wanted you to know that I'm scheduled to go out with your group to-night, and I wanted to know should I meet at your house or at the prison."

Somehow, I managed to control myself and said, "Oh? Really? Who cleared your name to go in with me?"

I figured it was the prisoner's aide to the priest who had added her name to the list. He also 'happened' to be one of her clients, and member of the board of directors.

She airily replied, "Oh, I suppose it was probably the Bureau of Jewish Education."

I knew this to be a lie as well, because I was the one who made up the list and turned in the names of the guests for the evening. The bureau in turn called and gave my list to either the priest or his aide. Hell could freeze over before I let this kid in, but I didn't tell her that. Instead I sweetly said, "Well, I just can't imagine how your name was cleared, but I do know it wasn't by me. Moreover, I just have too many men going out there this evening, so do yourself a favor and stay home. It would really be a shame to drive all that way out there and not be able to get in."

Her voice was no longer cool, but taking on a desperate tone.

"Oh, but I just have to go out tonight. You see, they are going to make a film tonight, and I'm a lawyer, and I have to be there to see that the legal forms which have to be signed are taken care of."

They had thought of everything, but this girl wasn't getting past me! Just as firmly, as if I were telling one of my kids that she wasn't going to an X-rated movie, I said, "Well, tonight I happen to have the Israeli Counsel going with the group. He also happens to be a lawyer, so I don't think we'll need any of your services too much, so thanks, but no thanks."

I hung up, but something told me I hadn't heard the end of it.

I gathered up my people, Israeli Consul and all, and entered the prison. Despite all that had been said, there she was, waiting for me and my 'Group'. I have always found scenes tacky, but I was on the verge of one of them. Rather than make any comments, I just headed to the glassed-in desk where I reported our arrival to the guard and picked up the phone to speak to him.

"Hello? Mr. Tibit, it's me, Mrs. Peck with the people from the Wednesday discussion group."

"Hi there, well now, are ya'll are ready to go in now?"

"Well, not exactly. We're all ready, but it seems as though we've picked up an extra passenger who doesn't belong. See that girl sitting at the end of the room that looks as though she is trying to blend in with the people that I brought in?"

He pushed his bifocals down over his nose and looked up from under his scraggly eyebrows and with casualness almost comical. He was hiding behind large dark glasses busily studying a hangnail and looking terribly nonchalant. Guard Tibit, nodded his head and said, "Yep, I see her alright."

"Well, I just want you to know that she is in no way connected with me or the people that I am accompanying. So, in answer to your question, this part of the ya'll are ready to go in with the others that are here, all except her."

He scanned down his list, and said

"But, Mrs. Peck, she came by the window before you came in and announced herself present and had her name checked off the list, see?"

"Well, that's your problem sweetie. I didn't turn her name in."

Well, they escorted us up, but she was left standing at the gate. When we got to the meeting room, numerous TV video-tape cameras were set up, and we were told where to sit for a panel discussion that the men had planned for the evening. I noticed that most of the men on the panel consisted of the new 'Board of Directors' from the new officers from the recent Temple Yakkov election. Naturally, the moderator was to be its president, 'Mr. Dreck.'

The discussion was to be a 'question and answer' session for the Israeli Consul about the conditions in Israel. About fifteen minutes into the file, the guard came into the room and the new officers were called down, one by one, to the visiting room for a conference with their lawyer, Ms. Susan.

This caused much confusion, as the script had been pre-arranged and the many substitutions, stops and starts had to be adapted into the script. Another fifteen minutes passed and they all came back, really furious, because I hadn't let their Lawyer Susan into my 'Group.' At this time, I was getting a little hostile myself. When these few men spoke of the 'Group's' having her in and how much she was needed, the officers weren't speaking for the entire fifty or sixty men who were considered to be members of the discussion group. This was confirmed by most of the 'regulars.' The men confirmed my doubts.

"Arlene, we wouldn't let nobody set you up for anything, ever. We like ya too much. Ya better believe we'll get to the bottom of this and find out what's going on."

It was nice to know that this particular inmate, who was telling me this, was on my side. He was so ugly; he could have made a fist with his nose. When the Shadow said, "Who knows what evil lurks in the hearts of men?" He knew.

The only thing no one seemed to know was why the new officers were trying to get Lawyer Susan maneuvered into the Wednesday nights. Some suggested that even though the inmates can see their lawyers anytime they want, if she were part of the discussion group, they could have their private 'conference call' and set up whatever future plans they wanted together, like an outside bank account. Fine, but we weren't going to be the vehicle to arrange it.

As a footnote to these manipulations by the new electees, the president was taken to the 'hole' for protective custody, and the new leadership subsequently dissolved. The real nature of the conspiracy that was being formulated remains a mystery of sorts.

Chapter Eleven

THE FRENCH CONNECTION WAS MORE THAN A MOVIE

It was in 1975 when an extraordinary man entered my life and my 'Group'. Our friendship was to last the next few years. His name was Herbie Sperling and he was the first one to ever give me headaches. His involvement and subsequent arrest for being the possible head of the 'French Connection' was his reason for being in the Atlanta Penitentiary where he had been transferred from New York. However, on that night during the winter of 1975 when he walked into the meeting room, I probably never would have noticed him if it had not been for Jean Claude Pinto, who had brought him into the group. Jean Claude was a Frenchman and had served 8 years of a 30 year sentence for drug-trafficking. He was absolutely gorgeous, and if he were not remembered for that alone, he would always hold a place in our hearts for being the one who first brought Herbie Sperling into the Jewish Discussion Group. The contrast between Pinto and Sperling was so great that he looked all the more outstanding. Jean-Claude walked into the circle where we were having our serious discussion of 'Sex in the Synagogue' and in a voice that would put Robert Redford to shame, sexily inquired, "Pardon, madam, is this seat next to you available?"

Of course it was. I merely had to drive my seventy-year-old senior citizen guest speaker from her chair to make room for Jean-Claude.

"Oh, I'm so sorry, we will need two chairs. My friend 'Herbie' is sitting with us also."

That's when I noticed Herbie, not that it was easy to tear one's eyes away from Jean-Claude who was a beautiful six feet tall, dark skin and piercing dark eyes, long lashes and reeking with sex appeal. His green tennis warm-up suit, encased in an athletic build that was warming up every female in the room. Herbie motioned him off and said, "That's alright kid, I'll sit here and you get another seat there across the room."

I was hoping my disappointment wasn't showing, but if there had been a choice of who sat where, I much preferred the Frenchman. Besides, until then, I had always thought that the 'French Connection' was a movie starring Gene Hackman. It was just so difficult to visualize that beautiful 'bod' serving a sentence for the next twenty-five years in the penitentiary. At the time, I wasn't aware that Herbie Sperling was serving a sentence for life plus one hundred years. Life plus one hundred years plus life was and is still the most severe sentence in our penal system, and even James Earl Ray and Charles Manson have a chance of parole, but not our Herbie.

Pinto and Herbie had been business acquaintances and Herbie was the founder and head of another group fondly referred to by the FBI as, 'The Pleasant Avenue Connection' or the 'French Connection'. In his field, Herbie was one of the all-time greats. The man was eventually to become one of my favorites for being absolutely pure, pure thug. He was so corrupt, that he was a wonder to watch. He could instill fear with only a pause. Herbie always reminded me of 'Little Caesar'. He was short, with crew-cut grey hair and a compact, bullish body that had a Neanderthal quality with long thick arms like a gorilla. I'm not especially tall, but Herbie was very vertically challenged. He always commented on my 'stilts' when I would come in wearing long jeans and high heels. I think he hated being so short, and maybe as a result, he became aggressive in other areas of his life. His physical appearance was always extremely clean and neat and his personality hostile and abrasive. Nobody, but nobody crossed Herbie. His height never slowed him down in the least when it came to letting anyone know who held the power when he was around. Naturally, he was always the most vocal when he attended, and once he began to express interest in the group, all collective participation by the other men ceased. The back and forth banter dissolved because no one wanted to disagree with Herbie. It didn't matter what the topic of the night was, whatever Herbie's opinion was, that was it for the evening, or else!

Actually, I was either too stupid or too uninformed to feel any real fear from Herbie. I thought that he was just a cuddly teddy bear. Of course, at the time, I was unaware that the saga of Herbie was the story of probably the largest and most important organized crime investigation ever conducted in this country. The government named it 'Operation Undercover.' Yes, maybe I was too stupid and too uninformed. Somehow I just would not or could not connect the guys in my 'Group' to the very same ones I'd been reading about in newspapers around the country, and never, did I feel any fear concerning any of the friendships with any of the men, and especially Herbie. Herbie was what he was; tough, dangerous and yet he still reminded me of a teddy bear. Obviously all of the men did not have the same reaction to him as I did, and had it not been for the vengeance of a man, Herbie would probably still be on the streets and conducting his multi-million dollar business. It was the testimony of Ceil Mile, who, with one of his men, led to the indictments and massive arrests of Herbie and his operations.

"I'm working for Herbie, the greatest little guy in the world. A really terrific person. He's a little Jewish guy who speaks Italian. He's an ex-fighter, who's been in prison for most of his life. Really, a terrific guy!"

In prison, Louis was impressed that Herbie had been arrested in 1959 at the age of 20, along with Vito Genovese and Joe Valachi. By the time Louis began working for Herbie, Herbie was building a mansion in Belinore, Long Island, next to the canal. They began to refer to Herbie as the Baron of Belinore. Herbie's drug operations were protected from one end of the transactions to the other. By 1969 Herbie and a number of others had developed really excellent overseas multi-kilo connections. He would buy his drugs directly from the heroin laboratories in Marseilles and from the other heroin jobbers in Frankfort, Amsterdam, Montreal, Beirut, Paris, all over the globe. A virtual handful of wholesalers on Pleasant Avenue were bringing enough heroin into this country to supply most of the major street dealers from Detroit to Brooklyn. Louis was a favored employee of Herbie, possibly because his background was much the same. Both were sharp gangsters from Manhattan's Lower East Side. Both had been raised on crime.

Had it not been for a quirk of fate, Louis might have continued being one of the slickest of the Manhattan hotel and high-society apartment building jewel thieves. Until Louis's employment with Herbie, he had spent years, minus the times in prison, working these hotels and living in plush accommodations. When he retired from being a jewel thief, he became Herbie's key man in the preparation of heroin for street distribution in the United States. No one could match his considerable talents. He could spend hours; busily mixing concoctions of pure heroin with quinine, milk and sugar and when he would leave the premises, not a trace of paper could be found anywhere. The man was a master in his job. In return for his considerable talents he was taking in over five thousand dollars a week. Business was getting better and better.

The operation was running smooth as silk. When a multi-kilo heroin shipment came into New York City it was usually sent from 'friends' and 'connections' of Herbie Sperling through his London or French connection. By 1971, the French police were putting pressure on the major heroin laboratories and Herbie was also having difficulties with his London connection. The secret of Herbie's operation was his ability to buy direct from the European brokers or dealers. As long as he was able to keep these French and London and other European connections direct, his profits per kilo were up and his costs were substantially lower from what the avenue dealers had to pay. During this time, Herbie was one of the three or four men in New York who had these connections, and the moneymen were anxious to please Herbie. He was flying high. He would only concern himself with major deals that involved the 'big money.' Anything smaller, Herbie would turn over to one of his aides and let him handle the transaction.

The men that Herbie had working for him on the dock or in the airport would bring the 'new' merchandise to a designated motel for Louie to mix and package. Once they were ready, he would call one of Herbie's men or maybe Sperling himself and someone would be sent over to Louie to pick up the heroin packages. For years, the operation worked like that until the trusted aide, Louie, made a slip. Instead of having the packages picked up as it was always done, Louie got into his car and headed out to personally deliver the 'merchandise'. He walked into a trap. Federal agents were all over the place.

Now the feds were able to make a tie-in directly to Herbie When Louie was called to make his one phone call to the police, he called another member of the Sperling organization who in turn called Herbie. According to reports, Herbie, taking a chance, drove over to the motel where Louie had been performing his business. There Herbie discovered that his trusted, Louie Mileto had been cutting the heroin into more bags than he was supposed to. Herbie had been getting ripped off and Louie had been having a nice business going on the side at Herbie's expense.

A lawyer was finally called and Louie was released, but within days he disappeared and eventually a body was turned up, or what was left of a body. Louie had been so mutilated, that it was over two months until the police were able to identify the body from dental records. Actually, a state trooper found a burning car and when he and the fire department were able to put out the fire, a man's torso was found in the trunk of the car. That's all, a torso, no head, arms or legs, nothing to identify what it might have belonged to. It was only because the medical examiner found teeth inside the stomach that they were able to make a positive identification. The medical report stated that Louie had been beaten so severely, that he had swallowed his own teeth during the beating. Those teeth were to come back to haunt Herbie. Louis' wife Ceil was called and agreed to be a government witness against Herbie. According to direct quotes from her book, *Louie's Widow or One Woman's Vengeance Against the Mob*.

"It was the toughest decision I ever had to make. If I testified, Herbie would kill me, if he could find me. If I didn't testify voluntarily, he'd kill me anyway. Life against death, freedom against prison. The government really didn't leave me any choice."

According to her, once she began to put the pieces together and realized that Herbie was behind the murder, the rest was easy to do.

The government gave Ceil a new name and a new past. It is ironic that eventually, her new identity landed her in Atlanta. It's ironic, because that was where I eventually made friends with Herbie when he was finally put out of commission as a result of her testimony.

Before this, however, the government was moving in. Unknown to Herbie, Ceil had met with the federal agents. She gave them the locations where her husband Louie had held his 'business meetings' with Herbie Sperling and friends. Much of his business conversations had been conducted on the corner of Seventh Avenue and Fifty-Fourth Street in front of the Stage Delicatessen. The government men were able to 'bug' the mailbox where Herbie had stood to conduct much of his business. It was the information they obtained from that 'bugged box' along with Louie Wida's testimony that enabled them to break open the most massive drug operation this country has ever known. Although the trial lasted three weeks, it was about two years in the making. Finally, on July 12th, 1973, Herbie and ten other members of his organization were found guilty of conspiring to sell narcotics. The January issue of that years Reader's Digest had an article about the drug operation called, "Night of the Big Bust."

By Friday, April 13th, 1973, federal indictments were given in New Jersey and New York which named in sealed indictments, eighty-six co-conspirators in the 'Pleasant Avenue' heroin organization, headed by Herbie. Nothing like it had ever happened before, rounding up that many heroin dealers and middlemen in such a massive arrest. Nothing had been done before or since that could so dry up the drug supply of New York. Over two hundred and twenty-five agents were involved in the raid. The operation was so widespread that the Joint Narcotics Task Force, which included city, state and federal agents, was brought into the investigation. Ceil Milo, too, had her vengeance.

Of course, I knew none of this when I first met Herbie. All I knew was that Herbie, and his friend Leo Guarino who usually accompanied him, gave me headaches. Their personalities were so forceful, that for the first time, I walked out of the meetings with headaches. Within days of his arrival into the Jewish Group, Herbie became the new President of Temple Yakkov. Now, Temple Yakkov, the Jewish Discussion Group, had always had officers since its very inception. The men were very particular about how they elected their officers and board of directors, and how they ran the organization and discussion group. But out of the blue, within days of his arrival, Herbie was president! The men elected him because they decided this is what he wanted and Herbie was not one to be crossed. The vote was by show of hands. It was not wise to show Herbie that you did not vote for him. The next time a vote came up you just might not have hands to raise! I was not adverse to him being elected president. In fact, I even thought he might have some positive effects on the group because of his dynamic personality. And, he and Leo managed to take complete control of the 'Group' and intimidate the men to such an extent they were afraid to open their mouths. Herbie apparently took his position very seriously. He must have decided that he was going to have the most interesting program in the penitentiary. He ran it like he had run his business, by instilling fear. When he said that men should fill up the room, they did. When he said we were going to discuss this for the evening we did. It never mattered to him what the scheduled topic for the evening was to be. If Herbie didn't like it, the discussion was changed to something he liked better, like Meyer Lansky. Usually the change to topic would intimidate the outside guests or inmates, neither of which bothered him.

Once, a speaker was giving a dissertation on the political situation in Israel and Herbie went for the poor man's jugular.

"Whadda ya mean, treatin' a wonderful citizen like Meyer Lansky the way you people have?

With all he'd done for Jewish causes and all da help he's given to charities, he woulda been an asset to any country."

To give a little emphasis, Herbie pointed his finger in the man's face, all the while jabbing his finger.

"Aw, you don't really believe that, do ya?"

Emphatically, Herbie chose his words, "You're G-d damned right I do!"

The speaker, unthinking, because he didn't really know with whom he was speaking, answered, "Then you're full of crap!"

The room froze. You could have heard a pin drop as everyone was waiting. I was constantly at odds with him, but luckily we managed to keep it on a kidding basis. He took extra pleasure in driving me crazy and I usually fell for the bait, whatever it was. The speaker however, didn't have the same relationship with him, and everyone was waiting to see what Herbie would do. This time, Herbie chose to laugh. Because he laughed, the rest of the men laughed, but it was a very nervous laughter.

The speaker later told me that by this time he had realized what he had done, and if Herbie had danced a jig at that moment, he would have joined in. Watching Herbie was like watching someone balancing, barefooted, on the edge of a razor blade. He could fall either way. I watched him once, when he didn't have the control of the room to his liking. He used all the tricks of a high school kid. Remember, all the little diversions that one could use to distract the class? Sometimes you would pass notes to someone else, get up and sharpen a pencil, ask questions to change the topic, all the little 'shtick' that could be done, Herbie did.

Later during the social period Herbie sauntered over and patted the speaker on the shoulder.

"I gotta admit kid, ya got guts."

The guest speaker laughed back and said, "And Herbie, you have a sense of humor."

We both breathed a sigh of relief and it was only when we were safely out of the building that the speaker looked at me and said, "You know, I wasn't kidding in there. He's the only man that ever made me feel any fear by going in that prison. Something about him makes you hope that he doesn't carry a grudge."

On my next visit in, Herbie was waiting. He wanted to show me something 'special'.

"Hey, Arlene, come here. I got something to show you. Besides, I wanna sit next to you, cause you're a gorgeous hunk of womanhood."

"Herbie, I don't want to hurt your feelings, but I think you've been in here too long."

"Naw, I'm serious. Besides, we gotta stop meetin' like this. Anyways, I got something I wanna show ya ... SIT!"

I couldn't help giggling. He was a teddy bear. Sometimes I'm wrong.

"Listen, I got a book here for you to read. It's a special book about me. I want you to read it carefully, cause I might give a test and ask questions later."

I looked at the title, "Something Classy like the Pleasant Avenue Corporation".

"Herbie, it looks marvelous and it's all about you. That's terrific. I can't wait to read it tonight when I get home."

He had decided that I was to read, or at least start it, in front of him apparently, so that he might receive the full benefit of my facial expressions. With a tap of his fingers, his bodyguard, Rocco placed a chair under me so that I might sit and read Herbie's book.

Rocco had breath like a dead dog and a pimple on his nose that looked as though it would burst any minute. He was overweight and had nasty tattoos all over his arms ... really gross. That's probably the reason that Herbie kept him around. He needed someone to look as mean as Rocco probably was. Rocco evidently didn't talk. He just did a lot of grunting at appropriate times. They sat there, one on each side of me, while I looked over the book. While I was casually turning the pages, Herbie just as casually, but very proudly mentioned, "Ya know, Arlene. This ain't the first book that has been written about me. Course, they're all a bunch of lies, but I got others on the markets that have been written about me."

"No kidding? Herbie, I find that absolutely fascinating."

"Why? What's so fascinating about it, ain't I good enough to have books written about me?"

OH! He was, he was.

"Oh no, it's not that you're not a good enough topic. It's only that I was thinking ..."

He cocked his head to one side, and if I didn't know him better, I'd almost think he was posing coyly.

"Not so long ago, I met Dr. Edward Teller who was the developer of nuclear energy and the hydrogen bomb. When I went to the library to see what they had to say about the man, I was able to find only one book. Now, isn't it something that they have a whole catalogue about you? Amazing!"

Herbie modestly waved away my comment, "Yeah, well, I don't find it so amazing."

The conversation between Herbie and me ended, and I found myself seated between Herbie and his watchdog, Rocco. I realized I was really left with no other choice than to read the book, end of conversation.

I looked up at Herbie and said, "Herbie, I know that you've led a colorful life, but tell me, did you actually do all those things that the book said you did?"

He smiled like an evil troll and said, "Pure fabrication! Do you think that I could do such despicable things?"

I started to say yes, but luckily kept my mouth shut. Like I said, one thought better of it when it came to making Herbie angry.

However, when Herbie wanted to be a gentleman, he put his heart into that. He decided which inmates could sit next to the guests because as he put it, "Hey, listen, I ain't gonna let some of the scum in here sit next to them fine southern ladies you bring here. Most of these guys ain't got no class. They don't know how to behave next to a real lady."

Once, during a Passover Seder, after the guests were ushered into the dining hall, Herbie realized that there was no women's restroom because it wasn't a co-educational prison. In all seriousness, he set himself up as 'hall monitor' and offered to guard the men's restroom in case any woman had to go. He would see that nobody bothered them! The guy was all heart.

In the fall of 1976, my friend Sheila called and said, "Quick! I'm on Channel 2!"

"Why? What's on?"

Exasperated, she shouted, "Arlene, if you'll stop talking and turn on the Today show, you'll have a chance to see Herbie."

Our Herbie, it turned out, was the subject of the head of the Food and Drug administration speaking about their most famous and difficult case, which was Mr. Herbie.

Without a doubt he felt that Herbie rated right up there on the very top.

"And, when they arrested him, I believe that they were able to get something like eighty-six indictments on him. Yes, Herbie Sperling was really something. I don't remember running across anyone like him in any other case. Would you believe that when the man was finally arrested, a multitude of officers waited until the early morning until he finally pulled in his driveway? When they began reading him his rights Herbie pulled back and said, 'Are you guy's crazy? All I make is a hundred and eighty dollars a week, I'm a salesman."

He was then asked, "How come you live in a quarter of a million dollar house? How come you drive a Mercedes and have three other new cars? What about the yachts and big diamond rings that your wife wears?"

Naturally, Herbie had the nerve to look them back in the eyes and say, "Hey, wadda ya expect, I'm a good salesman."

As I watched the TV, drinking my coffee, I could almost see 'MY' Herbie while the federal agent was talking.

"Would you believe that when they searched the car and found a small ax and an arsenal of guns, the federal agents asked what they were doing in his car and Herbie had the unmitigated gall to answer back, "I'll be damned if I know but when I get outta this I'm gonna write a nasty letter to the rental company, they're not supposed to leave guns in their cars! You can be sure that's the last damn time I rent a car from Hertz!"

It wasn't hard to believe that, nor was it difficult to believe that when Herbie was finally arrested and was told that his own mother had been arrested at her apartment in midtown Manhattan earlier that day and was in a holding cell, Herbie's big response was to shrug his shoulders and answer, "Hey, that's her problem, don't lay it on me, the old lady has to take her own weight."

He looked at them straight in the eye and said, "Anyone who came in here to see me beg or plead is in the wrong courtroom. I'm asking the court for nothing'."

Then after taking a long last look at the judge he said, "I am and always will be a better man than you. I sentence you to think about me for the rest of your life. May G-d have mercy on your soul."

Tough to the last. However, never did I figure that Herbie would play a big part in the investigation that was soon to be triggered.

Chapter Twelve

THE NIGHT JULIAN BOND AND I BUSTED OUT OF PRISON

Early spring of 1978 was the beginning of the end. Julian Bond was the catalyst. He was the catalyst of my banishment and of what was to ultimately trigger off the investigation into the Atlanta Penitentiary that was to reach national proportions. The officials had really wanted me out of that place for a long time, but it wasn't until Julian Bond that they were able to seize upon an opportunity to once again bar me from the penitentiary. As the membership of the group grew, so did the caliber of outside guests that I enticed to be speakers. They made the mistake of insulting a national political figure who carried the issue past the prison administration's intentions.

In 1974, Julian Bond was America's first black vice-presidential nominee. He was presented to the nation as an up and coming figure to be watched. He returned to Atlanta, became a state senator and the local head of the NAACP. I had met him casually in 1957 once or twice. Mostly I remembered him and his brother, James when they cooked brownies in a local department store for 'celebrity day.'

During this time, the papers were filled with statements in favor of the PLO. With this in mind, he was scheduled as a guest speaker. He was also widely known to be in favor of the 'quota system.' He had been traveling around the country at that time giving speeches defending quotas and speaking against the Baake decision. Although we were usually restricted to bringing Jewish speakers, and Bond didn't qualify, the topic that was planned for the evening did. The Baake Case was national news at the time. It was the test case of a Jewish student in California who had fallen victim of 'reverse discrimination' and sued the university because he had been unfairly passed over for entrance into medical school. Since I had grown up in the fifties under the quota system, I had a natural abhorrence to any system that would let a straight 'A' student be passed over in favor of a 'C' WASP student because the institution already had their three percent quota of Jewish students. With those attitudes in mind, it promised to be a lively discussion. Both the men and guests were looking forward to the encounter. We received an 'encounter' alright, but not quite like the one that had been anticipated.

Because of Bond's fame, which had recently been expanded because he had a regular spot on "The Today Show"; it was quite a coup to arrange to have him visit free of charge. The man was making a fortune traveling around the country as a guest speaker. At that time in 1978, a radical friend of mine was working in the Georgia Legislature while it was in session. Through her daily involvement with Bond he agreed to come to the prison with her the next time it was convenient. I called the prison right away to get clearance for his visit. Specifically, I talked to the prison priest and got official clearance to bring Bond in. I felt that the prison powers resented anyone with a college education so I wanted to be sure there wouldn't be any difficulties bringing Senator Bond into a maximum security prison.

Once again before the appointed night, I called the prison priest who was the official liaison. Once I got his clearance I called again for permission to bring a tape recorder so that I might record this session for an article that I was writing.

Wednesday arrived and I met my friend, Temi, and Senator Bond on the prison steps. He looked crisp and fresh in a three-piece beige suit that blended well with his complexion. His skin was very light and his features somewhat Caucasian. In fact, he almost had an angelic, cherubic face that looks as though it belongs on the top of a soup dish instead of the senate. It's more than possible and highly probable that the innocence in his face didn't reach his heart. He was pushing forty, but looked like a man in his twenties. In a conversation with him, one can feel the charisma. The man is all charm and political grace.

Temi, who would have made a hell of a politician herself, arrived huffing and puffing behind him and introduced us. Whether Senator Bond remembered me or not, he gave the impression that he knew who I was. Behind him was the public relations man for porno king, Larry Flint, a talk show host, and a female newscaster who reminded me of a walking commercial for women's lib. She just walked angry.

Soon the rest of the outside group arrived. Since it was close to six o'clock and we were scheduled to enter, we hurried to the entrance desk to sign in. A 'new' guard had been assigned to check us which should have been a danger signal to me. He had salt and pepper hair, cut in a leftover from the marine's crew cut and eyes that were mean as hell. He stood like a centurion with one hand on his belt and the other holding a clipboard.

"Uh uh, Mrs. Peck. These here people that you got to go in with you here tonight can't go in cause you got ten people here and only five of them have been cleared to go in from my list."

I got a glimpse of the list on his clipboard. He was right. I knew something was up their sleeve. Then I noticed that the other guards around were suddenly very quiet, watching our discussion with great interest and with obvious amusement.

"Officer, I can't understand how that can be since two or three calls were made into Father Undall's office this week to make sure everything was in order. What seems to be the 'trouble' now?"

"Wa-ll, as best as I can rightly see, you brought in people here that are listed as 'undesirable', especially Julian Bond and that TV lady."

Sure, I knew what kind of undesirables we were. He was an uppity black and I was a loudmouthed Jew.

"Hey, wait a minute. What the hell kind of undesirable is Julian Bond? Senator Bond, a man who gets $2,000 to speak to a group, a man who as a vice-presidential nominee and, only last week had his picture on the cover of the Atlanta Journal Sunday Magazine as a future force to be reckoned with and yet he's to be denied entry into the prison as an undesirable?"

With absolute relish and delight in those narrow eyes he said;, "That's exactly what I'm saying."

"But officer, there are a roomful of men, sixty or seventy at least, who are waiting for us in the meeting room. You can't be serious that we are to be turned away and let then be disappointed."

"That's exactly what I mean, Mrs. Peck."

It could not have been made more obvious. Here was a situation waiting to turn into an incident. If it became another incident, they'd have an excuse to cancel the program and be rid of me. Of course I'm sure they didn't like Bond much either, and this was a way to handle the uppity black that he was. The priest and the other officials had seen the list for two weeks. They knew who was on the list. Now they said that Bond was a 'political undesirable' as well as the 'Lady Newscaster'. I walked over to another nearby guard, who was watching everything and casually picking his teeth, "Sir? Do you think that you could contact somebody here to clear up this misunderstanding?"

He slowly pushed back his metal-rimmed glasses and said, "Lady, I don't make the rules here, I just follow orders."

Before turning on our heels and storming out, I raised my voice and said, "Now what in the hell is going on here? I don't know what the priest is trying to pull, but he's not going to get away with it. He knew, he knew we were coming in here. Everybody knew. I had a feeling something like this was going to happen. I knew you've been trying to set me up, but dammit, I'm not going to let it happen! He knew it! He knew Bond was coming in. We're here, and we're gonna go in!"

About this time, Lady Newscaster received the news that she was among the few who weren't to be allowed in, and she reacted a bit more vocally than the rest. Rumor had it that she received her position because her father was the bureau chief of the network. I had seen her on TV a few times and was surprised at how much studio people are able to accomplish with make-up. She was short and pear shaped, and quite bowlegged. Wherever she was thin was in all the wrong places, like her lips for instance. My grandmother used to tell me, never trust a thin lipper; she usually turns out to be a bitch. You know, my grandmother was never wrong. Lady Newscaster's thin lips were closed tight. She had small eyes with thin eyebrows and skimpy lashes. Her nose was long and pointed and her dark eyes always seemed to be darting. Her taste in clothes seemed to run to dry and I wondered if the TV station made her arrangements? At the moment, she was trying for the image of Lois Lane, but was coming off more as something out of an old Joan Crawford movie.

She pulled a pen out of a gigantic purse, and just like in the movie, licked the end of it. She rapidly turned through a few pages of her pad and started to take down the names of everyone in the room that she thought remotely responsible for our present situation. Eventually, she cornered a guard and demanded, "Er, SIR! Where is the Warden and who is responsible for this fiasco? WHAT IS HIS HOME NUMBER? I WANT TO SPEAK WITH SOMEONE OF AUTHORITY!"

During all this, she was tapping her pad with the pen and looking around impatiently.

"Lady, I don't make the rules, I just do as I'm told."

Lady Newscaster continued, "Now listen you. Don't you try and give me a hard time. There's going to be big trouble around here as it is. I wonder if you people would like to have a television show made from this whole horrible incident."

She fumbled through her purse for change and stormed off in the direction of the telephone.

"I imagine the man who is responsible has no idea of who I am and the power I hold. Well, he'll find out."

I desperately tried to keep my cool and hoped she would speak up at this point. Since there was nothing else to do for the moment, I took out the tape recorder so I might have a chance to interview Senator Bond for an article that I had in mind for the Jewish Post & Opinion.

"Senator Bond, I had a million questions that I wanted to ask you, but now I've got it narrowed down to just a couple of dozen."

We settled ourselves in the waiting room after a few minutes of fiddling with the tape recorder. I started the interview with a few throwaway questions then gave him my big one:

"Didn't you come out with something that was pro-Palestinian?"

I had the feeling that Temi had told him this was one of the questions that I would hit him with and he laughed, "Heh, heh, you just think I did. Of course I didn't."

The way he answered left little doubt that he was kidding, so I pressed further. Finally, he gave a resigned look and said, "Well, in all seriousness, it's an incredibly complicated thing and would probably take up all your tape."

Despite all the commotion and complaining and phone calls Lady Newscaster was making to the various wardens, it didn't look as though we were going anywhere soon, so I said, "Don't worry, we got time . . . Talk."

Bond knew he was cornered, so he began to relate how the story of his PLO statement had started.

"It was about five years ago, or perhaps not that long. It was Sacramento, California, making a speech and someone in the audience came out with the statement, 'Hey, how should black people stand on the middle eastern situation?' and I said, we should stand on the side of justice and fight. The guy sat back with 'That's not good enough.' So, I said that we should stand with the side of the Palestinians."

He noticed my face and stopped and then continued, "Wait a minute. I just said that it caused a tremendous furor. So much in fact, that I received a lot of flack back from it. Finally, I was asked to speak before a group of Jewish leaders in the community to clear up my statement, and here it is; First of all, Black Americans ought to be interested in foreign policy questions; secondly, we have to have some interest to see some peace come into that area because we have an involvement and a big commitment to Israel; and thirdly, there has to be some homeland for the Palestinians. If it involves giving up the land in the '67 war, then, in my view, Israel has got to give up that land. At the same time, the United States has got to be a guarantor of the security of the pre-1967 borders."

All the time he was talking, I kept thinking, "Why is it no other country has been asked to return territory it won in any war? Why is it always the Israelis who get these demands? The PLO have a land, it's called Jordan. I believe I said something to that effect, and then, this articulate man, who's personality I probably would have found captivating had he not had such screwed up political ideas, continued with, "Well, my position is essentially what I believe to be the Jimmy Carter position."

G-d help us. That did it! The man was the president of the NAACP and representative of their views. Bond closed this issue with the remark that we officially, "Have no position anywhere around the globe except in South Africa."

No wonder the man went into politics, he knew how to straddle the fence so well it's a wonder that he didn't walk away bow-legged. Anyway, it was difficult to try to continue any serious discussion, as about this time we really started to get aggravation from the 'hacks', otherwise known as the guards.

Lady Newscaster was busily making phone calls, none of which seemed to help, all the while walking around saying, "But do you realize who we are?"

It was obvious she wanted to say, "Do you know who I am?" However, she managed to restrain herself. She finally did arrange for someone to come down to speak with us, but no one showed up.

Later, the evening duty officer arrived who was black. He walked over, dressed neatly in a navy sport jacket and grey flannel slacks, tall and imposing. I would have booked that he would have been favorable to our cause, unfortunately he wasn't. The guard seemed determined not to show any partiality to Senator Bond because he was a 'soul brother.' He surveyed us for a few minutes.

"Mrs. Peck, I'd like to speak to you for a few minutes, if you don't mind."

Without waiting for an answer, he walked over to the corner out of earshot of the others. Temi followed. 'Mr. Hack' looked at her and said, "If you don't mind, I'd like to speak to Mrs. Peck personally."

Temi's face fell only slightly, she gave a shrug, tossed her henna hair and said, "Humph, she'll only tell me later anyway, so there!"

His attitude became quite apparent when he looked over his shoulders and said, "I have just spoken to Assistant Warden Wpoopski."

Things were undoubtedly going to get worse. Wpoopski had had it in for me ever since the case of the missing tomato plants. He had never forgiven me for going over his head. Mr. Hack continued with, "I have just personally spoken to Assistant Warden Wpoopski and he had informed me that if you cause any sort of waves, of any kind, then I have the authority to cancel the program."

"What do you mean, cancel the program?"

"I mean, Mrs. Peck, that if you give us any sort of trouble at all this evening, then you won't be able to go in either."

I suddenly felt as though I was back in the fourth grade and my teacher was telling me I would have to stay after school if I misbehaved. Calmness has never been one of my attributes, but before I had a chance to act in an unladylike manner, Julian came over and asked, "Ah, what seems to be the difficulty over here?"

Thank God the man finally spoke up. I was wondering when he was going to get around to opening his mouth. I started to tell him, word for word, this latest ultimatum but before I was into my second sentence, Mr. Hack snapped his fingers and said, "That's it! No program tonight. Everyone can go home because they aren't going anywhere inside the penitentiary."

I thought a little power in some people's hands is a dangerous thing. I felt sure that I was included in this ultimatum, but I wanted to have him say it.

"Are you including me? I can't even go into my 'Group' to tell the reason why the others aren't allowed to enter?"

The two or three guards were standing around trying to ignore us and one mumbled something to the effect, "Wa'll their names aren't on the list."

Mr. Hack just stood there and stared back, so we gathered up our coats and headed out of the institution.

I was ashamed to go home, so we decided to head to a party at the Martin Luther King Center where Temi was to receive an award for some work that she had done. Julian was going to the King Center but stopped off for a drink with us at a pub called 'Underground Atlanta.' I was glad, because the fiasco at the prison had really upset me and I wanted to ask him what course of action to take.

Having a conversation with Julian Bond is like relating to a tranquilizer. The man never loses his cool and after five minutes of my pleas of, "How shall I handle the situation?"

Julian took a long, slow thoughtful sip on his drink, looked up at me and said, "Don't give it too much thought. I'll make a couple of phone calls and we'll take care of it. They just wanted to flex their muscles out there tonight and the only way to handle this is to flex back."

"But, if I can get you rescheduled, will you go out there again so we can test it?"

Julian pushed back his drink, nodded to the rest at the table and said, "Hey, listen, I gotta go, but you have a good time at the King Center tonight."

It had been one hell of an evening. The next morning bright and early, I had my kids and at the state capital where the legislature was in session and arrangements had been made for the Lt. Governor as a doorkeeper. I was anxious to tell her about my conversation with the Director of the Bureau of Jewish Education earlier that morning. It seemed that he had received a phone call from the priest at the prison telling him that the entire matter was now in the hands of Warden Handbury. The Jewish Bureau director had already received calls from our United States Congressman, Wyche Fowler, concerning the ousting of Julian Bond. Julian himself had called. As a matter of fact, calls had been coming in all day concerning the unfortunate incident. It had been reduced to an 'unfortunate incident'. Early that morning the phone rang and it was from the Secretary at the Bureau of Jewish Education, "Arlene? This is Dorothy, at the Bureau."

"Uh-huh."

"What on earth happened last night? We received a call first thing this morning from the priest, Father Fundhall. He says that you can't go into the prison again . . . ever! Do you know anything about what's going on?"

"Well, I know that he's an anti-Semitic SOB and has been looking to get rid of our program since the first day he saw the positive results that it was getting."

"Well, I just work here in the office, but you can't go around antagonizing people like that. He says it's in the new warden's hands. This new warden doesn't even know you, does he?"

"Listen, I'm not too worried. Julian Bond was there, the TV lady was there, obviously something's going to happen from this, I mean she's not going to let it drop, she won't sit there. Something's going to happen, I mean, they can't keep me out for G-d's sakes! I'm an integral part of that program. Anyways, don't you try, it's being taken care of. They're going to find out that they opened a Pandora's Box in not letting me or my guests in. I wonder if they've forgotten that Senator Bond was the president of the NAACP."

I hesitated, "Or, maybe that's the reason for the whole thing."

At lunch, I continued my discussion with Senator Bond. At best, it was a harried affair. Between bites of stale salad in the capital cafeteria I did learn that my fellow 'undesirable' was the father of five children. It was hard to believe that his oldest child was fifteen. Bond had dark brown curls, which may have started out as an afro, but nevertheless looked like a cluster of boyish curls. With his young face and athletic, wiry body he just did not fit the father image. We parted with Julian soothingly saying, "Don't worry; you'll be laughing at this whole incident. I said I'd take care of it and get both of us back in there, and I will."

"Well, I doubt if I'll be laughing about it but I believe you can do something, so keep in touch."

He grabbed a roll and said, "Love to sit and visit, guys, but the legislatures back in session and they need my words of wisdom if they're going to function right. 'bye."

And he was gone.

I sat there thinking, "What a great guy," not knowing at that time that it was to be the last contact that I was to have with him for months. All future phone calls into his office would be left unreturned. Even with all his reassurances, something still didn't sit right. The feeling lingered that it wasn't going to be as easy to get back in as he made it sound. They had used Julian Bond as an excuse, but I felt it was because they considered me a trouble maker. Well, maybe him, too. Every time that I had fought for the men was one reason for the authorities to want to discontinue the visits. The latest issue we had locked horns over was when I insisted that they allow the men to have a kosher food line. It was shortly before the Bond incident that the men had requested to have kosher food be allowed to be brought into the prison. I went before the various officials and the answer most received was, "We ain't got no funds for no special Jew food."

For once I was armed with the facts and when this reason was given I responded, "Aha! But a precedent has been started. Rabbi Meir Kahane, the founder of the Jewish Defense League was imprisoned in Allenwood. Since he's an Orthodox rabbi and was unable to eat the unkosher food served in prison, special food had to be sent to him from the outside. As a result, the law pertaining to the 'special' foods has been changed and if Rabbi Kahane could be allowed to have kosher food while in prison, then so should the men in my Group. The precedent has been established. What happens in one prison should be allowed to happen in all of them, and if you don't do it, we're going to do something about it."

When the authorities saw that the men might start legal action to get their rights, they backed down. The men got their kosher food. It was their turn.

Changes were beginning to happen. It started with the afternoon papers. The Atlanta Journal ran a large article about kidnapper Williams and how much this program had come to mean to him and how Mrs. Peck was directly responsible for his positive attitude toward Judaism. Attitudes that did not do much to endear me to the warden or his staff.

The afternoon mail brought a lovely letter from the men in my 'Group', in part it read, "Arlene, you did right in refusing to go up that night unless the Senator and TV lady were allowed to enter. This could very well be the catalyst needed to shake those bastards up. How can they possibly deny a Senator access to any prison?"

They had a point there, one that I had to pursue. The letter continued, "We have never heard of such a thing. What are they afraid of? Or, could it be that they deem us too articulate? Maybe he might have found out a few things about the inefficient and corrupt way things are run around here? At any rate, we are all in accord that you did the proper thing when you refused coming in without them. I, we, can only hope that you, and especially the Senator, will not allow these petty but pathetic despots to have the last say. Knowing you, we are sure you won't let that happen."

How prophetic those words were to be. In a strange twist of events, the 'Bond' incident was to turn the tide and to bring about an investigation of national proportions that has not yet uncovered everything.

Jean was another one of the guests who originally went in to the penitentiary as a member of the Jewish Discussion Group. As a result of the interest she gained from visiting our group, she gradually involved herself in the NAACP Sunday evening program. When she heard what had happened to me she thought it was rotten and came over to say, "Hey, listen. I had a brainstorm, I was thinking you might be able to get in yet."

"Oh yeah? How?"

"Well, now don't laugh but they got a meeting coming up. The president of the NAACP is in the process of starting yet another group which will include anyone I want to invite. The name of the group is called 'Crime Prevention.' What d'ya think of it?"

"Oh, I love it! I've always said, the originality of the men is astounding. So anyhow, along with being a sometime visitor of the Jewish Discussion Group, you're also turning out to be a head honcho in the program."

"Well, possibly, however, I think it might come down to your being very, very interested in my NAACP program."

"Huh? What do you mean?"

She was taking her gloves off slowly and enjoying every minute of her little story. Personally, I didn't think it very nice of her to tell me how she was allowed to enter and I wasn't. While I sat listening, she pulled off the other glove, ran her fingers through her short red afro and said,"Oh, I forgot to mention to you that tomorrow night when I go into the prison, I have a signed letter from the warden that I should bring four or five guests with me. Now, who do you think the other four or five visitors should be?"

Our eyes met and we both broke up laughing.

"Oh Jean, that's beautiful; but how are you going to get my name cleared? When Assistant Warden Wpoopski, or worse yet, the real warden see my name on the list, they'll never approve my visit!"

Jean took several seconds to answer, so perhaps she could savor my anxiety,"Ahh, but that's just the point. In this program, I don't have to clear names! The people that came in the NAACP discussion group have never been required to clear their names with anyone."

"But, why don't the NAACP group have any special forms to fill out and names to clear like the Jewish guys do?"

Jean passed over it with,"Great question, but like Scarlett, why don't you worry about that tomorrow . . . after you've returned from the prison."

All that night I was apprehensive; would I be caught, found out, dishonored, and incarcerated, whatever. I just did not want any new hassles when I went back to those prison doors.

I arrived at the prison early and was escorted to the waiting room by a new guard. I spent the next twenty minutes or so, looking vainly through the bars for Sara, one of my friends and realized really what a small number of men out of all who were there that we really knew. The men were having what they called 'movement,' when they moved on the 'hour' from one cellblock to another. I had no doubts when I first heard it also, and I commented,"Gee, where are the rest of the men in the group tonight? Aren't they going to come into the room?"

One of the men answered,"Oh, they're having a movement soon, and will be down after that."

All I could think to say was,"Huh?"

My friend Jean had not arrived yet, and it was a few minutes before the scheduled time to enter. A number of other people were there, a diverse bunch to say the least. There was a large black woman who arrived clutching her black Patton leather purse, huffing and puffing after having climbed the entrance steps. She was wearing a bright pink dress and a pink net hat. G-d, I hadn't seen one of those in years. In a few minutes I saw two young girls who I found out later were recently out of college. Both were stunning and I looked forward to seeing the men's reaction. Along with them were various men who were either NAACP officials or ministers. At the last minute, my friend Jean rushed in, I'd given her up for lost. She was out of breath and had stopped at my house to pick me up.

"Where the hell were you? I called earlier to say that I'd pick you up and I drove by your house and the kids said you had left. Don't your kids tell you anything?"

"Does anybody?"

"Oh well, never mind, did anybody notice you?"

"I fail to see how they haven't since we're the only white people here."

"Just keep quiet, I'll handle everything."

I was introduced to the officer on duty who was in charge of the program. He seemed like a nice enough man, not too different in appearance from the rest. He had somehow managed to wear an in-style suit without style. Atop his head was a bad toupee that was far more youthful than his face. He made a last-ditch effort at a mod moustache that somehow came off as straggly and faded. In fact, he looked soft of faded . . . maybe the word I want is seedy. I'll bet he once drove an Edsel. We were all introduced and taken to the waiting room where we were asked to leave our purses and coats. We were told that the door would be locked so our belongings would be safe.

"Psssst. Jean, why do they get to have their belongings locked up and guarded in a special room and all my people get are those little bitty cramped lockers up front?"

"Arlene, haven't you started enough trouble already? Don't make waves, save your questions for later, OK?"

We were led down the corridor into the meeting room. The guard, Mr. Dreck, explained the procedure of not taking anything out or in for anyone, no phone calls or any favors done for anyone, and so on. At a stab at humor he said, "Oh yes, no guns are allowed to be taken in there. The only ones who are allowed to have them are the inmates."

I whispered, "Ah, but which guards bring them in?"

And Jean pinched me.

Again, through the push-pull-click-click-iron bars, we headed for the visiting room and into the ante room. It was a brightly lit room with cheerful paintings along the walls. Many of the men started to wave a greeting to me and a quite a few recognized me. But at that moment, I did not want to be recognized.

I put my hands to my lips in a 'you don't know me' motion and they understood. It wasn't until we were settled and safely in for the evening that I could begin to act like I knew where I was.

The meeting opened with a prayer. I glanced over at the two young girls who were there for the first time. The expression on their faces made one think that their prayer might be to get out of there all in one piece. Following the invocation, we were welcomed by one of the officers who told us that the topic for the evening was about 'MOTHERS'. Somehow he said it as though it were half a word. I sat there thinking I was so old I remembered when it was a word of endearment. Actually the discussion was really quite interesting. The purpose of the Crime Prevention program was to let the outside community know some of the reasons these men are in prison; and if somehow by sharing their past experiences, maybe the others they bring in can benefit from their misfortune. At least that was the gist of the meeting. It always touched me that these men were trying to make themselves useful members of society by helping others in the prison community this way. They felt that it was their way of proving to the outside that the image of animals in the zoo does not always apply. It has been responsible for the rehabilitation of almost 20,000 juveniles who had been 'sentenced' to several hours in the institution and literally, 'Scared Straight.' In 1979, the filming of this program even won the Academy Award for best documentary, despite the four letter words that were liberally sprinkled throughout.

The men at the Atlanta Prison had long wanted a program such as this whereby they could work with the youth but were told time and time again, it was not allowed.

One speaker for the evening was an inmate, one of the vice-presidents in the NAACP group, and our men liked him. Sam, the speaker, always carried an attitude of confidence. His hair was cropped in a close afro and his wide smile was partially covered by a full mustache.

"When we spoke earlier of the mothers, we mean the influence of the parents that the children emulate. The pattern that put the men in here started long before they were arrested for the crimes that brought them to the Atlanta Penitentiary."

He had everyone's rapt attention, everyone except me that is. Too many men had given me effusive greetings and the guard looked at me a little suspiciously. I was nervous that they would recognize and usher me out of there, so I missed most of what he had been talking about. By the time I shook myself back to attention I caught the end of Sam's words which were, "I remember when I was a small kid and emulated the adults around me. I remember the first time that I did something that was dishonest. I stole from my uncle and thought I got away with it. I did other things that finally got me put in the state reformatory at the age of eleven."

That brought me back. This man standing before us had been on his own and headed for a life of crime at such a young age. I thought what a baby; my son is the same age. Sam continued, "The role models that I had, the very life that I had as an example, set me up to pursue one action after another that finally led me to Atlanta. I am a man serving a sentence of life plus one hundred years."

I leaned over to Jean and said, "I don't believe it; he's always so pleasant and educated. What could he have done to have gotten that kind of sentence?"

"And, even though I know I'll never get out of here, I want to feel that there is a purpose for my being here. If I can get through to teachers, leaders of the community, you ministers and mothers of small children and impress upon every one of you that you have to set the right example for what your children are doing, or going to do. How they will turn out is by how you are setting the example for now. If they pick up even a trace of indecision, dishonesty or criminal acts, when it comes time for them, they will think that it's alright for them."

During all this time that he was speaking, not a sound, no coughing or chair shifting could be heard in the room. When he finished, we broke up into small groups to discuss how we, as leaders of the community, could follow a plan to prevent crime in our individual classes, churches or organizations.

During the coffee and cake break I headed for Jean, "Psst... how come they get to have all these goodies with a cake and coffee break and we don't?"

"Arlene, don't start, OK?"

A little petulantly, I continued, "Humph, well it still seems like discrimination to me."

A man walked over to our table and began taking pictures with a Polaroid camera. It took me by surprise and I kiddingly asked, "I'll order three copies. What are you taking our picture for?"

With a big smile, he replied, "The Yearbook."

I started to giggle and Jean gave me a kick under the table and said, "Don't you embarrass me."

With as straight a face as I could muster at that moment, I asked him, "What do you call your yearbook? The every year yearbook?"

Oops I did it again! I hoped that in this situation he would see the humor in the comment. He laughed.

Before we left that evening, the inmate president of the NAACP came over to me.

"Hey, listen Mrs. Peck, we're with you. You think it was only the Jews that was insulted by what those 'Mothers' did. Hell no! They meant it as an insult to the blacks too by not letting Julian Bond in. We've already written letters to our senators and congressmen protesting this action and you'll be getting a copy of it."

It looked as though it was fast becoming a racial incident. How fast? I knew the following day when I received a call from JET magazine wanting an interview.

Now since I had made it back into the prison once again, without the benefit of my program, even though by dubious means, we could ask the question about Bond when the occasion arose, the question being:

"How come Julian Bond wasn't allowed into the Jewish group, but the chairperson of the Jewish group was allowed into the WCP and without clearance?"

I spoke with a friend of mine at the Atlanta newspaper and she thought it would make a heck of a story. I asked her to hold off its publication as it might give the officials an opportunity to disband my program entirely, which they wanted in the first place.

Some questions bothered me; why was Lady Newscaster still sitting on this story? How could a real newsperson let a story like this pass? How did she benefit in keeping it quiet?

Meanwhile, after Bond's complaint, Wyche Fowler called the prison and was told that Mrs. Peck did not follow procedure. She should have submitted Julian Bond's name in writing two weeks in advance. In five years of chairing this program it was the first time this rule had ever been discussed. The warden had cited that they hadn't had enough 'security' to protect Bond. This was curious, as Bond had recently spoken on two other occasions to the WCP, in the prison, without special security. I learned that Leon, the director of the Bureau of Jewish Education, was called into the warden's office to discuss the 'Mrs. Peck situation'. Later, Leon called me, "Arlene, we have a problem and I don't know how to handle it."

"And?"

"Well, there was a staff meeting at the prison today and, well, I don't how to tell you this."

"You don't know how to tell me what Leon?"

"Well, it seems that, uh, once you brought in a state senator and the media, and especially since that state senator complained to the congressman who contacted the warden, they sort of consider you persona non grata."

It was against my nature to refrain from saying what was going through my mind. Instead I told him, "Leon? Were you at this meeting?"

"Well, not exactly."

"What's that supposed to mean?"

"Well, I wasn't at the prison staff meeting, but I did attend the one with the warden, priest and the Assistant Warden Wpoopski."

"Leo, would you mind telling me why if the meeting was about me, why I wasn't invited. After all, I was the topic of the day, wasn't I?"

He hedged, "Well, I have to admit, you were discussed a little today and actually, I went to bat quite a bit for you."

"Terrific! I don't need you to go to bat for me. What I want to know is WHY I WASN'T I INVITED TO THE MEETING ABOUT ME! Could you let me know a little more in detail who arranged this meeting and what was said?"

Among those in attendance was Chaplain Kiggs, he always reminded me of Hitler. Not kidding, that's what he looked like. He was short and wore his black hair plastered down with greasy kid's stuff. I'll admit he was considerably chubbier than Hitler, and a little bit friendlier, but he wore that silly moustache and looked the same. Each time I saw him, I had this irresistible urge to salute and say, "Zeig Heil!"

The last time we had any conversation was the night there was a little pray-and-stay with Charles Colson of Watergate fame. Ole Chaplain Kiggs was standing off to the side like a lost tourist holding a camera, waiting to get a picture of the visiting celebrity. I figure he probably never had any fond thoughts about me since the time I had written a letter to my congressman questioning why the money that was supposed to be for the Jewish prison religious budget ended up paying for a new staff member in the Protestant chaplain's office. In fact, none of the officials seemed happy about my questioning the religious budget and why it wasn't going where the government had allotted it. Or, about the demand for a kosher line or Passover dinner. And, in places like that, they didn't want people around who would question or demand.

Next, in attendance, came the "Swinging Priest", Father Fundhall. The best thing that could be said about him was that he was anti-Semitic and was not one of us. He had twinkling blue eyes that lied and a charming, beguiling smile that also lied. That smile never reached his eyes. All this was packaged on a nice build. His gray streaked beard had started out as a goatee but had gotten out of hand. It was a shame that those nice blue eyes weren't sincere. The consensus of opinion about the "Swinging Priest" can be summed up in the words of one of the inmates in our group, "Yeah, so you think he's a nice guy. Well don't let him fool you. He's one of them and not to be trusted. He's a hack just like all the rest. He works for the prison system, and just because he's packaged different with dat funny collar he wears, don't let him fool ya."

You know, he was right. Soon a new regulation from heaven had been installed. Everyone to be cleared from the outside had to fill out a paper stating his whole past history, even if he had ever been convicted of a felony. It had as many questions as a job application, and we had 'Swinging Priest' to thank for it. The Jewish group was the only one to have this honor. Next, came the rule that the refreshments for the coffee break at our meetings were no longer allowed. Little by little, we were removed. It was all done with such a charming smile.

The topper came when he was installed as the prison priest. The 'day out' that we used to have was no longer allowed. It was like a bad marriage, like him or not, and we were stuck with him. After awhile, we just learned to expect every sneaky thing that could be done and tried to ignore it. When it happened the men were dependent on the priest's whims and misguided knowledge of Jewish laws and traditions. The men hated it. But, being such a minority, they really had no choice.

Our hostilities almost came to a head when they gave an open house tour. Afterward, when Father Fundhall was giving his canned speech, he came out with the choice comment, "And, before I came here I worked in a prison mental ward, so I suppose that's why I can relate so well to the men . . . and Mrs. Peck."

The man was a barracuda.

Last on the list of the 'terrible three' was Assistant Warden Wpoopski, He also had a 'special' place in his heart for our program. So much in fact, that through the years he managed to throw a monkey wrench into every positive program that we had planned. He was the one who called me into his office before the Passover Seder and said that there would not be sufficient government funding, although the Bureau of Prisons could afford to fund Christmas and Easter since they were 'social holidays.' There would be no funds for the Jewish holiday because it was a religious dinner. If the men wanted it, they would have to pay extra for this 'special dinner.' The social dinners of Christmas and Easter, however, would be free.

Wpoopski reminded me of the type who, when he was back in school, his playmates would tease for being such a nerd and now it was his time to make them pay. He resembled a shark each time he'd say;

"Well, well, well, and how are you, Mrs. Peck?"

It was times like those that I felt like saying, "Kiss my grits." He was short and squat, and when he stood next to Chaplain Kiggs they could have passed for bookends.

From the gist of the Director of the Bureau of Jewish Education's conversation, they had spent the better part of the day discussing what an undisciplined person Mrs. Peck was, and how conduct such as mine could not be tolerated in the institution. They also conveyed the impression to Leon that they simply could not allow men like Congressman Fowler questioning their actions. Fowler's interests arose directly from Mrs. Peck questioning too many things that were not her concern. Good grief. I had been banned from the place. How many are there around who can claim that distinction?

What none of us knew at that time was that the beginning of the end had already started, and the lid was beginning to come off as a result. The solution to the problem was not going to be to merely an individual who asked too many questions. No, time was going to have to come with some more answers.

After I was fired from my volunteer job at the Atlanta Penitentiary, I travelled with icon Rabbi Meir Kahane to various prisons in upstate New York where we began Jewish Discussion Groups.

This was the night when Julian Bond, President of the NAACP and nominee for Vice-President of the US, and I came to the Penitentiary. They would not let us in nor would they let the inmates out to visit us.

ARLENE PECK WITH WILLIAM MORRIS, CYRUS VANCE AND DEAN RUSK

ARLENE AT LUNCH WITH WYCHE FOWLER
INTERVIEW, 1981 NOV.

ARLENE AND SEC. OF STATE DEAN RUSK
MID EAST CONFERENCE, ATLANTA 1983

ARLENE WITH RABBI MEIR KAHANE
GREEN HAVEN STATE PRISON
1980

After I was fired from my volunteer job at the Atlanta Penitentiary, I travelled with icon Rabbi Meir Kahane to various prisons in upstate New York where we began Jewish Discussion Groups.

Arlene with Rabbi Meir Kahane and the Prison Rabbi 1980

Julian Bond and Arlene Peck 1978

This was the night when Julian Bond, President of the NAACP and nominee for Vice-President of the US, and I came to the Penitentiary. They would not let us in nor would they let the inmates out to visit us.

Chapter Thirteen

THE SHOCK OF RECOGNITION

After the Bond banishment, six o'clock neared and I was very apprehensive as to whether the people I had previously scheduled to meet at the entrance of the prison would be let in. Would there be trouble? Who would be there to watch out that everything went as it should?

He agreed to continue taking people out there on a weekly basis. I was still to see that the guest list was made up and decide who was to go out there each week, but he would be the one to take them in. He had good rapport with the men, so he would be the best one to try to see that Jewish content was brought into the institution. He was to become, along with one of the others, my connecting link to the program. I got him out of the phone book before he left for the prison.

"Mike, listen, be a boobie and stop by the house on the way out to the penitentiary tonight."

"Sure, what do you want?"

"Well, I've got a shopping bag full of Jewish newspapers, junk mail and my old Neiman Marcus catalogues to take out to the men."

"Yeah, sure, be happy to . . . is that all?"

"Well, now that you mention it, there is another little thing I'd like taken out there."

I certainly hoped that he was joking when he said, "No, Arlene, I won't take a bomb for the warden's office."

"Very funny, although it's not a bad idea. No, what I have is a xeroxed picture of me, a skinny ten pounds ago picture. I want the men to hang it on the wall in absentia until I return on Wednesday evenings . . . and, I also want you to tell the guys that like old soldiers, I SHALL RETURN!"

"Sure, I'll keep my eyes and ears open for you and let you know what, if anything transpires during your absence."

My family was delighted with the change of events. For the first time in six years, mommy was home. They may have been happy with the situation, a domestic presence to serve and clean up from dinner. However, it did not trigger any pangs of happiness nor generate any enthusiasm for me. During those six years I had felt like more than a 'mommy machine' and the men in the group definitely considered me 'chateaubriand' instead of the 'pot-roast.' I was at HOME! It felt strange not to be rushing out of the house at the dreaded hour of five to get to the penitentiary on time. My husband had never said so exactly, chauvinist that he is, but he never approved of his wife hanging around a MAN'S prison. He had the basic belief that criminals shouldn't be coddled. And what was I doing there in the first place. His mother always stayed at home.

Hoping that the group hadn't forgotten me yet I was feeling a little sorry for myself. I needn't have. Late that night, Mike who had been used, stopped by my house on his way home from the prison. He gave me a vivid description. He told me how the meeting had gone.

"Arlene, it was really something. I have never seen a lesson in love in absentia like that, and it's too bad you couldn't have been there to hear it."

At the moment, I heartily agreed with him and let him continue.

"And, they spent the first half hour praising you. They spent the next hour and a half putting down that SOB priest. I mean to tell you, the mood of the men was hostile."

I moved my chair closer, so as not to miss a golden word, and Mike began to warm up to his position of story teller. He made expansive gestures with his hands, and his eyes sparkled.

"Now, picture this; the room was packed tight, really crowded. Everyone's attention was on last weeks Bond incident. They were all there waiting to hear what had transpired during this week. The priest came in, and you know the man never sets foot in that room, but tonight, he was there."

He was saying it too slow for me.

"Yeah, yeah, go on, what happened then?"

"Well, O.K., I finally asked the priest, 'Why isn't Mrs. Peck allowed into the institution he said, 'Because she is barred.' But, why is she barred, because she's not allowed into the institution."

"Mike?"

"Yeah?"

"Would you mind telling me again what you just said?"

"What I said was, the priest was talking in circles, and some of these guys were professionals at that and weren't about to let that happen to them. They wanted answers."

"Knowing who they are dealing with, I doubt if they'll get any, but it's good that they had a chance to find out what has transpired since the week before. It's beginning to look as though this whole incident with Bond has opened a whole can of worms. How can petty prison officials run an institution of that magnitude as though it were their own personal social club, with their setting up the rules?"

Mike rubbed his beard, then scratched his head up toward his receding hair line and finally said, "Now, the real question behind the whole thing is the anti-Semitism and discrimination toward the blacks. You realize of course, they were behind the whole thing. In this particular incident, they were able to insult the Jewish Group and embarrass the NAACP."

"You know something it's really touching."

"What is?"

"Well, you know, the men are against this action as a unit. The Jews, Blacks, Muslims, all of them who came in to the discussion group. They were, are, ready to fight and write letters in support of this program."

Not only did Mike agree but he added, "You should have seen your old friend, William Williams tonight, he was terrific."

Williams, who I've written about earlier, had been coming into the Wednesday evenings for the past couple of years. He was still a loner.

"It was really something, this ex-hot-shot from J.B. Stoner's hate organization, writing letters to the Journal about how you've changed his life. But Arlene, he was best at the meeting. You really should have seen him. Williams sat and listened to Father Unhdall and his comments of why Mrs. Peck wasn't allowed and finally he stood up and addressed the group, but directed his comments to the Priest, 'How in the hell can you stand up there like you do? In fact, what is it you really do around this place? I've listened to all this that you've had to say, about why they were turned away and how Mrs. Peck don't follow procedure and it's a pile of garbage."

That seemed to inspire Williams further.

"I know this whole thing that's directed toward this program is an anti-Semitic action, and hell, if there was anybody that would know an anti-Semite, it would be me."

What soul searching it must have cost a man like that, who was teethed on hate and bigotry to admit that. Williams was getting angry but he must have figured that he had to wrap it up soon before he rapped the priest in the mouth, so he finished by saying, "And, it's been over three years since I've given an interview. But, I'll tell you the truth, I'm so damn mad over this railroad job you and your buddies are doing Mrs. Peck and her program I'm ready to give one."

All the men were angry, but William A. H. Williams, particularly. The priest, like Anthony, had praised and buried the program at the same time. I pressed Mike for more details, "Well, he sat in that room, knowing how instrumental he was in what had happened and couldn't seem to praise you enough. He kept saying what a cracker-jack program and that he could never deny all the positive programs that have resulted from it. This is the Priest talking about you, Arlene."

"Mike, TURDFEATHERS."

Mike was half-way out the door when another thought hit him and he turned back with, "Oh, yeah, he wouldn't admit that he knew anything of why you weren't allowed in or much less admitting to being one of the one's responsible for the banning. You really missed the best part, you would have enjoyed it when the inmate aide to the Assistant Warden Wpoopski stood up and said, 'You MOTHER.'"

(SEE! I knew it was half a word)

I know that the other 'Mother,' Wpoopski, was in the institution watching on closed circuit TV and directing the whole thing from his office. You people were telling Julian Bond that no one was around of any authority to help the people downstairs while they were getting the runaround, while all along you're part of them and giving directions from upstairs. You knew just how to go about embarrassing those people and what to say about how to embarrass those people. You were even telling them what to say to Julian Bond when you turned them away. I SAW YOU!"

"Oh Mike! He didn't, Oh!"

"Yeah, and when the aide sat down he crossed his arms and gave a self-righteous, 'hmmph'."

"What happened then?"

Well, all the other men in the room clapped and Father Fundhall gave a belligerent look and said, "Listen, I didn't come in here to take treatment like this. Mrs. Peck has been refused entrance to this institution and if you people are wise, you'll think better before you make waves."

One of the men sitting near gave a long look at the priest and then turned to the guys and said, "Ya, know, when Nixon had dat list for people dey didn't want in the White House, it was kinda prestigious thing ... do you think dis is sorta the same thing? You know the prison blacklist?"

According to Mike, as 'Swinging Priest' was walking out he looked over his shoulder and said, "She's been barred, and that's it."

He carefully motioned for one of the guests who had come in that evening to follow him out. As he walked out the door, the priest offered one of his most engaging smiles, lowered his voice so that hopefully none but the two of them were able to hear, with last rites of seriousness, and said, "Er, listen, we've been warned to expect some calls from pretty high places."

His voice went down a couple of octaves, in a conspiracy tone, "You know, people, that have no business getting involved with this. So, if you people are smart, you won't make waves, this prison has a way of forgiving and forgetting and, maybe in six months or so, maybe they will forgive and let Mrs. Peck in again."

"Hey, do you think if I say three Hail Marys, they might forgive me faster? Wait! I've got a better idea; the Archbishop is head-quartered in Atlanta. Maybe he should be informed of what's going on."

Mike was out the door but he hollered over his shoulder, "You've got nothing to lose. At least it's worth a try."

We secured an appointment with the archbishop for the end of April, 1978. It's a good thing that it wasn't for the last rites, we could have died waiting. But while we were waiting, and the prison banishment continued, new names were being added to the elite group of undesirables. One of these was Andy Andravitch. He used to introduce himself by saying his name rhymed with son of a witch and he looked like the Jolly Green Giant, but had the temperament of Captain Kangaroo. He was at least six foot four inches with a voice of a radio talk show commentator, which he was. He had also been one of the dependable program regulars in the discussion evenings for at least three years, but he had never gone in there as 'media.' Andy had always been a valuable addition to these evenings and the men enjoyed his visits. Word filtered back via the Bureau of Jewish Education that he was no longer allowed to visit on Wednesday evenings. This upset me but didn't surprise me. When he was told of this new directive, Andy's anger matched his size. His first reaction was to call me and say, "OK, that's it! I don't need this aggravation and I'm not going to let my self get upset. I'm getting an ulcer from all of this and who needs it?"

"Andy, calm down, you know this is what they want. The 'terrible three' want you, and the rest of us to get mad enough, or upset enough to stop going in."

He paused for the barest of seconds and continued with, "Well, I'm not going to fight them anymore. Tell the guys in your next letter that I said I'm sorry and I hope that everything works out for them. I've had it!"

The atmosphere seemed to be getting everyone down. It was important that the program be allowed to continue but all this aggravation, who needed it? The mood was re-enforced shortly after Temi called. It seemed Father Fundhall had also called her. He let her know that she was considered 'undesirable.' In her Tallulah voice she drawled, "Dah-ling, this is absolutely ridiculous and you haven't seen anything until I'm upset. The very idea! Taking it out on those poor men! Maybe I ought to talk to new friends in the press and let them see what real media is?"

She was right!

"Temi, I couldn't agree with you more! The only way that we have to make them understand we mean business is to stand up to them and not back down. Keep in touch with me and don't let this drop like the prison officials are hoping."

A day or so after our conversation the phone rang once again. It was radio personality Andy, with second thoughts.

"OK, I've calmed down. Do you wanna go to Washington to see the Director of the Bureau of Prisons and stop these bastards from stopping the program?"

I laughed and said, "What took you so long?"

Andy mused, "I was thinking about it. How would it sound to my kids that their dad got kicked out of a federal prison, before he had a chance to stay in?"

It was after midnight, the next night. The phone rang and after propping up a child who was sleeping at my end of the bed because she had a bad dream, fling over a husband who was dead to the world, I was able to catch it on the fifth ring. At a time like this I'm grateful that I have a husband who could sleep through a herd of elephants setting up camp.

"Mmmmmmmm ... huh ... hello?"

"Hey, Arlene, is dat you?"

At the moment I wasn't exactly sure but I decided to play their silly game.

"Er ... mmm ... huh I think so ..."

"Hey, Arlene, it's me, Alfonso."

Alfonso had been in the Group in earlier years. In fact there was a time that I thought we were going to be growing old together and finally his parole came through and he was done.

"I heard about the trouble you were having and I want you to know that if you need any help down there, or anything, I'm here."

The prison grapevine was already incredible. The word had already gotten around, even to the ex-cons, on the outside. I was starting to wake up now and beginning to get curious as to what ANYTHING was.

Anything with some of my group could cover a multitude.

"Uh, what did you have in mind?"

He didn't answer, but went on, "Listen, we ain't going to let those 'mothers' hassle you, so just in case you need a friend you got one. More, so don't you forget it! If somebody's giving ya a hard time, you just let me know and we'll burn his house down! Nobody will know!"

Considering the attitude of the officials towards my endeavors; revenge didn't sound like a half bad idea.

Oddly, during that week, 'Swinging Priest' called to say, "Hi there, Mrs. Peck! Just calling to inquire if the people we were scheduled to go into the institution at the next meeting know what time they are supposed to come out?"

Now, why in the hell was he calling when he knew that I wasn't the chairperson for the meetings any more. I could hear extension phones being picked up all over the place and the faint whirring of tape recorders. It's easy to get paranoid with that bunch.

"Mr. Unhdall?"

"Mrs. Peck! I'm referred to as Father Unhdall!"

"Oh, how could I have forgotten? Well, nevertheless, you know, it wasn't very nice what you people did?"

He started his conversation geared for the tape.

"I agree Mrs. Peck, and if certain restrictions required by the institution were followed, that wouldn't have been necessary. All the things that have transpired the past few days . . ."

His remark brought me around to asking him, "Oh, restrictions? Are these the restrictions that just the Jewish group has to abide by, or are they for everyone?"

"Well, I don't want to get into that, Mrs. Peck. All I want to know is, do the people going in the group next time know the hour they are supposed to be at the institution?"

He didn't seem to want to discuss all the things that were on my mind, like discrimination and finky deeds. I almost expected him to say, "Let's kiss and make up."

He quickly terminated the conversation with, "And, in case you've heard differently, it's not true that the assistant warden and I were there the night that you were trying to get in with Julian Bond."

"Sure! We were on candid camera and didn't know it."

And, on that cordial note, the good father and I ended our conversation. I later wondered what his reactions were when he saw the afternoon papers and the articles about the Bond incident.

The newspapers were beautiful. Both afternoon editions carried different versions of the incident. The 'terrible three' must have had a stroke when they saw the headings;

"PRISON BARS SEMINAR LEADER IN DISPUTE OVER SENATOR BOND."

It quoted William Williams saying that he "credited the program with changing his anti-Semitic views." Senator Bond called the prison action "arbitrary and capricious" and ended up saying that "Mrs. Peck had been barred, after she had attempted to take Senator Bond into the prison for one of her Wednesday night seminars two weeks ago." The articles went on to say that inmate participants had responded angrily to the news that Mrs. Peck had been barred. There had grown a certain bond of affection between the inmates and Arlene.

Some of the inmates sent me letters. They were all asking what they could do to help. When could they write? How could they go about changing the situation? They supported me all the way. Nice.

A day or so after the articles came out; Channel 5 (CBS) called to see if they could convince me to meet them at the prison and have their cameras film an interview with the institution as the backdrop. The interview was to be made by that. It was ironic why part of the news team was called 'trouble shooters'. They gave the part of the news that always seemed to be concerned with fixing someone's s phone bill or focusing on the reason why a welfare person didn't receive his check on time. Until the minute that

Channel 5 decided to show an interest in the Jewish Discussion Group, I never realized what a potential service they could perform.

It turned out however, that the real reason they were interested in this filming was because "Lady Newscaster" had been denied admission. They wanted to find out why she had sat on the story for a couple of weeks. We did tape an interview, but they never ran it, probably because they couldn't find out about 'Lady Newscaster.' Who knows, so much for the 'trouble shooters'?

Chapter Fourteen

THE ARCHBISHOP

The day of the appointment with the archbishop arrived, and Andy, Temi and I headed over to see him, fire in our eyes. The archbishop had been brought into this incident in the hopes that he would be willing to help. We were wrong.

The building that houses the Catholic Archdiocese was a modern building and from the difficulty we encountered in trying to set up an appointment, it might as well have been a fortress. We arrived on time and were asked to wait. Eventually, a stoic-faced secretary returned and motioned us toward an office and said, "You may go in now."

The archbishop sat there, behind a coffee table, in front of pictures of the Pope. His black frock was in contrast to the maroon, leather chair that he was sitting in. Temi sat opposite him, clutching her ever-present Louis Vuitton purse. It was the first day of spring and her outfit was appropriate to the situation, black and white. I sat there like Death! Titles have always intimidated me, and I had the feeling that we were being measured and found wanting. After all this, the man had the power to help us save our program.

The archbishop neither looked, nor acted anything like Spencer Tracy nor Barry Fitzgerald. He was tall, powerfully built, and had a ruddy complexion. His eyes were somewhat large and droopy. He had lots of teeth. My first impression was that they were sharp. In fact, that's the impression we got from him, sharp and shrewd. He had none of the warmth that we had hoped to find. He would smile and just bare his teeth, but the smile never reached his eyes.

He gave us a penetrating stare and began tapping a pencil on his desk and said, "Ah, yes, what can I do for you? I understand it's about a program at the federal penitentiary. You have a complaint about the priest that is in charge of this program?"

Andy leaned forward until he was on the edge of his chair and interjected, "Yes we do! We are members of the Jewish community who have been involved with the Jewish Discussion Group, which Father Unhdall has direct jurisdiction over."

During Andy's comments, the archbishop put his heavy lidded eyes at half-mask and nodded . . .

"UM . . . hmm . . ."

Temi continued, "Yes, and we have brought you into this incident in the hopes that you could be made aware of the overt acts of anti-Semitism that seem to continually occur under his guidance. We were hoping you could contact this priest at the penitentiary and see if some necessary changes could be made."

Barely letting her finishes the sentence, the archbishop put down his pencil, "Now, ah, these are very serious charges that you have made against a priest. A charge of anti-Semitism could have very serious repercussions; and before I do anything, or if I do anything at all, I want these accusations in writing."

Temi looked at him just as blandly; Andy shifted in his chair and I sat almost in a trance. I think it was his teeth that had me spellbound. I kept wanting to count them. There was no way we were going to put anything in writing, because they could use it to string us up by our toes. In fact, how did we put in writing that the "Swinging Priest" was a rat and looking to sabotage the program? All I could think to answer to the archbishop was, "Well, as a matter of fact, speaking of repercussions, I hate to think of what use the prison would make of anything that had been put in writing."

The archbishop stood up to signal that the meeting was over and cleared his throat, "Well then, that settles it. I'll be waiting to receive the charges in writing."

Against, our better judgment we left, agreeing to write a letter to be sent to the archbishop so that he would make contact with the priest concerning our complaints.

We did write the letter but, it was a good thing that Andy never got as far as mailing it, because no sooner had Andy arrived home than the Assistant Warden Wpoopski called him.

"Well, we in the institution have been made aware by the guard on duty that evening (the one with the bad hair-piece), that although you were present when Mrs. Peck tried to bring in Senator Bond, that you weren't nearly as vocal as she was about getting in. Quite possible, if you let sleeping dogs lie, then maybe, just maybe, we might be ready to let you back into the penitentiary. We've also been appraised about a possible suit that 'you people' have been preparing to file and we just want to put you on notice now that it would be a waste of time and money."

Andy thanked him for his interest, hung up and then called me.

"Andy? What do you think? Do you think they mean it?"

"Yeah, I think they mean it."

"Well, I don't care. It shows something else also."

"What?"

"Well, I think that it shows that somehow events are starting to zero in on them. Maybe these threats mean that they are beginning to get a little worried."

Andy mused that over and gulped,"Sort of like maybe they doth protest too much?"

"Yeah, something like that. Only..."

"Only what?"

"Well, true, maybe, no, maybe not, but I'm sure that the political press and television coverage is something that they don't want, but I just don't want them to take it out on the men and have them be the ones to ultimately suffer from all this."

How prophetic those words were to become.

Once the discrimination and anti-Semitic actions had been exposed, then the officials had no recourse but to make everyone have the same regulations. Now suddenly, the NAACP was having to fill out the same forms and get clearance for their names. And who got the blame for this 'new' change in policy? You guessed it! 'THEM JEWS.' The men, who a week earlier were all for fighting the 'fuzz' were now having second thoughts. They were beginning to feel that if I had public exposure from TV or went on a radio show, I'd never be able to get back in. Word came back to me that maybe the warden should receive a letter of apology. A letter of apology for an infraction of the rules that didn't happen. I wouldn't do it.

Incidentally, not only did Senator Bond never answer our phone calls, nor did he involve himself in any of later events, he almost became a liability by his inaction. The officials must have noticed that he did not give support to our efforts to get back in. Because of his dual role as senator and president of the local NAACP he was in a beautiful position to help the Jewish group, both inside and outside. But he did not help.

Georgia Congressman Wyche Fowler meanwhile was busy in his own prison related political endeavors because of the run-around that he had been given when he first inquired about Julian Bond. Fowler had begun a full-scale investigation. Murders were happening on a more then occasional basis and in the span of just a few short months, there had been quite a few. Fowler called for an investigation into them and the charges that were being made into 'graft and corruption.'

The evening news began to focus on the 'full scale investigation' that he was going to investigate. I decided when I learned that, to go back into my spy work, so I offered my services as an aide to the investigation. The first chance that I had to become really involved was when Temi called me up all excited, saying, "Have you had a chance to see the paper tonight?

There is a big article on how the prison program is in jeopardy. It calls for an investigation of their anti-Semitic practices."

"Uh-huh, I heard that but, I also heard on the six o'clock news that Congressman Fowler's office had a team of prison officials sent in for this 'investigation.' Don't you think that it's a joke he's getting the prison people to monitor themselves?"

Temi gave a throaty laugh adding, "Mmm, I would put it on the same basis as having a sex crazed sailor alone with a virgin for a long period of time."

"Except in their case, it's more like sending a Nazi in to check out the concentration camp. In other words, my friend Temi and I have serious doubts as to the wisdom of prison bureaucrats monitoring prison bureaucrats."

"Listen dah-ling, hope for the best. Have you had any contact with the Congressman's staff?" "Yeah, I mentioned to them that it might be a good idea to send one of these men as a guest into the group that is still meeting on Wednesday, without me. Maybe then the men would be able to talk freely. They wouldn't have to worry about retaliation as they would when the warden was present in one of the 'official interrogations.'"

"And? What was their reaction?"

"Just about what I expected. They thanked me and said they would contact us when they needed any further help."

Before Temi hung up, she said, "Well, look on the bright side. Maybe Wyche really does mean to clean up this mess and we'll be hearing from him."

"Don't count on it."

Later in the day the mail brought a descriptive letter from one of the men of the group relating how Assistant Warden Wpoopski had been beaten up at the horse show the previous Sunday. A horse show! The place was turning into a regular resort with high walls!

"Wpoopski approached an inmate and accused him of being drunk!"

Now, a statement like that made to an inmate by a Federal Warden is sort of astounding, considering he was speaking in a prison where things such as that aren't supposed to be even possible.

"Wpoopski allegedly said, 'The man is drunk; guard, take him to his cell!' The inmate tried to shake himself free; Assistant Warden Wpoopski went to grab him and then all hell broke loose. The inmate broke away, Wpoopski landed on the ground, and two hundred cheering inmates formed a circle around him so that the cavalry, or in this case the guards, couldn't come to his aid."

My husband thought it sort of tacky that next day when I sent a get well card to Wpoopski, but I thought it the very least that I could do.

Chapter Fifteen

THE INVESTIGATION

During the spring of 1979, things really began to pop. At this point it was long past things happening to me personally. It had started as a test between the officials and Bond, and had grown to proportions that no one initially had visualized. The media smelled a story and they were right. The inmates sensed that they now had an opportunity to get the kind of publicity they needed to help change the deplorable conditions within the prison. Congressman Wyche Fowler must have recognized also that this would be a good opportunity to get some much needed media coverage. After all, it was an election year. There had been almost a dozen murders there within the past year, and supposedly this was what his investigation was about. However, it couldn't hurt that the press was going to cover every statement he uttered about this 'deplorable situation.' Basically, everyone knew that nothing ever happens with these prison investigations, and after a week or two, or maybe a month, they'd come out with a report that says everything is fine and things would go on as they had before. The men in prison didn't have much confidence in this investigative team sent down to investigate Fowler, especially when they found out that it was made up of a lot of prison officials who would check out other prison officials. The inmates called them 'hacks' from the very beginning. Despite many negative encounters within the system, I had still, somehow, managed, up until this time, to carry a shred of optimism into my attitude concerning Congressman Fowler and his investigation. All signs pointed to a white-wash but I wanted to give the man the benefit of the doubt. Maybe he really did mean to find out the truth. The inmates almost took it as a joke. During the first week they were there, the prison officials were walking along one floor inspecting while an inmate named Dominique Orsini was getting himself killed on the floor below. Whoever did him in had the 'Chuptza' to do it almost literally under their very noses. Some joke. Orsini was later to play a bigger part in the Senate Investigation, but at the time, we on the outside just thought that it was another one of the murders that plagued the Atlanta Prison so regularly.

According to the papers, Orsini, 55, a Corsican born drug smuggler was found stabbed to death in the prison stairwell. From his picture in the paper I recognized him as one who came into our evenings from time to time. He hadn't been a regular member of my Group. Orsini reportedly headed an international drug ring that poured more then a ton of cocaine and heroin into the United States between 1968 and 1972. There was talk that he had been part of the 'French Connection'. He was convicted and sent to the Atlanta Federal Penitentiary in January 1977. The official excuse for the man's death came out of the warden's office was some foul-up had happened in the marshal's office and the paper work was responsible for the 'unfortunate incident.'

I remembered the excuse the warden had for Louie the car thief; they managed to 'lose' him for a year and four days beyond his sentence! They must have forgotten about him because he was in the hole for ten months.

Meanwhile, each night on the evening news, Congressman Fowler would bask in the media exposure and let the public in on the progress of his investigation. Usually the prison would be in the background and Wyche Fowler would look directly into the camera and say things like, "I have called for a thorough investigation to be done. We will get to the bottom of the reasons for the violence at this particular prison."

Probably, I thought the reason the place was falling apart, was because I, mother Earth, was not allowed in there anymore (with my chicken soup).

Meanwhile, Jack Anderson's aide, Jack Mitchell, called. We had been in contact since I had presented to them the incredible story of William Williams and the 'hidden papers.' At that time Anderson and his staff discounted it. The story seemed far-fetched. After all, who, back then could have believed all the land deals and stock swindles allegedly involving Senator Herman Talmadge? Anyhow, we had kept in contact and when the Atlanta Prison story began to be picked up by Associated Press, Mitchell called, "Arlene? Hi, it's me, Jack Mitchell."

"Hi, yourself."

"What's been happening down there? Things are starting to filter up here that everything is not as it should be at your prison in Atlanta."

"It's not 'my' prison anymore and without my direction it's going to pieces. Murders, dope, graft, corruption and plain old incompetence are plenty prevalent around that place. It's almost a joke. That's been the norm since I first started going there."

"Yeah, we got your clipping about how you and Bond were kept out. That's why I'm calling you now. We caught a copy of the Atlanta Constitution today and there was a large article with a plea for the men in the prison to write to the newspaper to tell what was really happening there, as the media has been refused admittance. Phone calls from the press aren't even being taken. What do you think? Think there is a story there that Jack might want to look into?"

"I know there is a story there!"

"O.K. As soon as you get concentrated call us on the 'Jack Anderson private watts line'. You know us, all the news that's fit to print!"

"Yeah, I know, nothing would make me happier, as soon as I have something that you can use, I'll call back. Maybe you can come down?"

"Maybe."

We hung up and I just set my mind in a whirl. The headlines were screaming daily about the latest rash of murders. Questions were being asked. Were the killings tied together in any way? Why wasn't the press allowed any information? Then the brainstorm hit me. Although I wasn't allowed entrance technically, I was still acting chairperson of the Group. I scheduled whoever went into the Wednesday evenings. Why couldn't I add someone from the press on the list of people to go in. That's when I thought of Jodie.

Jodie was not your everyday average newsperson. She worked for the same television station as Lady Newscaster but that's where the resemblance ended. She certainly didn't even vaguely resemble Lady Newscaster, not in the least. Not even her lips were thin. Jodie looked as though she had been built by Mattel and the dark headed Barbie Doll had been modeled after her. Nothing stayed still when she walked and it was all in perfect precision. We had remained friends, despite the fact that when I was with her I always felt like a wren standing next to a peacock. Rather than discuss anything over a phone that I figured was bugged I headed over to her apartment to see if she would work as a link for me with the press and men in the group. She was always short of cash but her apartment was very posh, leftover from a nice settlement from a past divorce.

It was lunchtime Sunday. I rang the door for minutes, no answer. Then it dawned on me that maybe she had 'company' and wouldn't be answering the door bell. I headed back to the car and had just started up the engine when I noticed her door open a fraction. I cut the motor and headed back to her apartment. When I was in view, Jodie motioned me to come in so I followed her back to the kitchen where she was busily pouring coffee. In my torn jeans and scuffed sneakers, once again I felt insecure.

"Jodie, I don't believe it!"

"You don't believe what?"

"That you obviously just got up and you've got your eyelashes on, that you're walking around in a lounge dress that's cut up to your armpit and down to your navel. I mean that you really look like this when nobody's around . . ."

She fluffed out one of her Barbie Doll tendrils that had fallen behind her ear and said, "Well, to be frank, I was expecting someone else at the door. Good G-d, what time is it anyway? It feels like the crack of dawn."

She gave me a yawn and continued, "What could be so all fired important that you came over here at daybreak on a Sunday morning?"

"Jodie, it's 1:30 P.M, it's the shank of the day." "Daybreak."

"O.K. Listen, I won't stay long. I just want to ask a favor, OK? You know the problems that I've been having with the prison and all?"

"How would you like to play detective?"

"Arlene, boobie, I'm not a violent person."

"Jodie, you wouldn't have to do a thing. Really, it'll be fun."

"Arlene, I don't want to hurt your feelings, but you've been married too long to remember what someone who's single rendition of fun might be."

"Kidding, listen. Would you be adverse to going into the discussion evenings on Wednesday nights to see what you can find out about what's going on in there?"

"That's all? I wouldn't have to smuggle anything or anyone in?"

I had intended to keep the call from Jack Mitchell secret, but then I figured that it was probably my ace in the hole to help entice her into making the trip in for me. It worked!

"You mean he works as a special reporter to the real Jack Anderson?"

"The same, and he's cute, too, I've seen him. Meanwhile, all you'd have to do, for the time being, is go in each week and find out what you can that I can use against the administration. Hey, do you think that you could have the station wire you to go in so that you can tape the conversations?"

"I doubt it, don't they have those little metal detectors that you have to go through on the way in?"

"Oh dammit, you're right, oh well, it's just as well."

I wouldn't give her the satisfaction of saying that on her body they'd notice an extra lump.

Jodie was hooked. The day after she had attended a meeting of the Temple Yakkov, she called me. Jodie had gone into the meeting and enjoyed her visit so thoroughly that she had forgotten the original reason for her visit.

"Hi Jodie, what happened last night? They gave you all sorts of information to relay back to me, right?"

In her breathy voice she purred, "We-ll, not exactly, but, oh-h-h they were adorable. And their manners were so nice. I took a cigarette out of my purse and six of them rushed over to light it."

That's funny, I was thinking, they never did that for me.

"In fact," Jodie continued, "they were all so sweet, especially the kidnapper, William Williams! He is just like Yogi Bear."

"Jodie, I can sense this conversation is not leading where I had expected it. If you'll remember, I held expectations that you would have picked up some information that would be useful in relaying to my contact in columnist Jack Anderson's office. Jodie, what did you talk about? Did you find out any earth-shattering revelations about the rash of murders that were front page in the papers all week?"

Instead, she proceeded to tell me, "We-ll no, not exactly, but we just had the best conversation on auras, and really got into a terrific conversation on astral-projection."

"Good G-d, you what!"

"UM-hmmmm, we really did, but you know they really found it difficult to believe that I personally had an out-of-body experience."

Yeah, so did I. If I had her body, I'd never leave it for a minute. So much for friend Jodie and her training as a super-spy proved to be.

My next opportunity came later that day. The afternoon paper carried an article of the beating of Assistant Warden Wpoopski at the horse show. The article stated that the story had been from a reliable source who had close contacts in the prison. I was that reliable source. The reporter who ran the story called and asked if I knew of an inmate who had been released that he could interview for a series of articles that the Atlanta Journal was planning to run.

I told him, "Sure, come by and pick me up. I'll take you to see Hal, my aging hippie. He owns a worm farm."

Hal was the one who had ground his forty acres of grass, circled by a crop of corn in Kansas. He had called a few times and said how well he was doing. I was glad for him and I was curious to see for myself.

The reporter, Clyde, looked like a 'Clyde'. He was driving a staff car with the paper's name in big letters all along the side of it. That wasn't too cool. The interview was supposed to be anonymous. I have a basic distrust of reporters. He didn't further my lack of confidence in the men of his profession by his appearance. Clyde was dressed neatly in a sport jacket and trousers. However, they were mismatched and the jacket had stains on it and his pants zipper was traveling at half mast. He looked like one of the Smith Brothers in the cough medicine advertisements. Maybe he looked like all three. It was a toss-up if he had more hair on his head or his face. It was everywhere! Usually, I'm also suspicious of men who wear beards. In most cases, it's to hide weak chins! Moses was probably the exception! In Clyde's case he gave the impression of being a well groomed derelict. Promptly at 2:00 p.m., he arrived and tooted his horn outside my door. Before running out to his car, I tucked a couple of notes into my purse that the men had written. The car was a disaster area. After apologizing, "Er, you'll have to move a couple of things to make room."

"Move a couple of things. It looks as though you're saving up for a paper sale. How on earth do you see over the dashboard?"

"Yeah, well, it's a staff car."

"So I noticed."

The rest of the ride was in silence.

We drove to one of Atlanta's better neighborhoods. Hal sat us outside his home. He had put on some weight and was sporting a bushy mustache, but looked good. Gone was the image of 'reject.' Now he was to be thoroughly enjoying the new statutes of legitimate businessman with his worm farm. Hal escorted us into his new middle class living room that was decorated in Jewish provincial with a lot of white and gold.

Clyde set up a tape recorder to make sure that we got every golden word and Hal invited us to sit down. With his ole familiar leer that I remembered so well, "Can I offer you something? Tea? Maybe? Heh. heh."

"Hal, I'm on a diet, does it have any sugar in it?"

His grin returned and he said, "No, no sugar, a lot of things maybe, but no sugar. Try it, you'll like my tea. I use a special brew. Heh. Heh."

"I'll just bet you do."

Hal just sat there looking as though he were enjoying the whole darn thing.

Clyde began, "Hal, what do you think will be accomplished from this full-scale investigation?"

Mal reached over to get a match and lit up one of his never ending Camels, "Come on, you know the answer to that? What do you think is going to happen when you have hacks investigating hacks? Do you really think that it's going to be anything but a white-wash?"

Clyde probably knew that would be the answer, but he said, "Do you really think that's what's gonna happen?"

"Sure. They'll run around for another week or so doing their investigation and then go home and things will be back the way they were."

I hated to think that he was right, but that seemed to be the general thinking of all the men I had heard from. Throughout the week, the mail had brought many letters saying just that.

"Hal, what about the drugs? How do they get the drugs into the institution?"

Mal leaned back, put out the cigarette and lit up another.

"Oh yeah, it's pretty prevalent. Guards bring it in and sell it. Also, there is a valium line, and the men go to the line in the morning to get their drugs. Instead of swallowing them, they put them under their tongue and spit it out to sell it later. Everyday after breakfast, lunch and dinner, they line up for what we call the 'bot line'. That's the administration's idea of rehabilitation, these guys walking around like zombies not bothering anyone."

Clyde wanted to press the point of the press black-out so he said, "What's the reason that the news people can't get in to find out what's going on?"

Even I knew the answer to that and said, "Because they're afraid that the news reporters and television people will get inside the place, talk to the inmates, and find out what's really going on."

Hal nodded in agreement.

"She's right! Have you checked the Bureau of Prisons budget lately? It's probably bigger than the defense budget. They don't want the taxpayer to know what's going on with their money. That's why they want nothing to do with the first amendment. That's why they read the inmates mail, so nothing can get out that they don't want.'"

The men had made a big point about the poor hospital care so I questioned, "What kind of medical help does a man receive when he's in there?"

"Well, there are a lot of unfortunate men, who besides being criminals, are mental cases. Man, you really got a lot of crazies running around in there. They are eaten up with hostility, and most of the time the cause of their going into the joint was a result of this hostility."

I remembered that William Williams had told me earlier that he was never able to get to see a psychiatrist either.

Clyde commented, "Isn't one of the reasons for the lack of 'special medical care' because they don't have anyone to counsel the men? That's where the incompetence of the administration comes in?"

"Possibly, but the incompetence is everywhere. The average guard is someone who is only concerned with his tenure, retirement and putting his time in. Man, you got 'hacks' there, who are so damn incompetent that if they didn't have the job, they'd more than likely be in prison too."

Hal stopped, looked at our faces and said, "You think I'm kidding? Did you ever notice that the guards carry hip radios rather than guns? The reason is simple. Prison officials wouldn't dare give them guns because they're so darn dumb that the inmates would have them in no time."

Clyde was busy turning the pages in his little pad. He'd turn his head to the side a little as though somewhere inside his head he was getting directions for his questions. Then he'd be off on another thought.

"Er, Hal. Obviously there are so many ways to kill a person, so many places that you can quickly do it. Why does it happen?"

Hal was nodding his head and continued, "Sure, it's over dope, money or sex. He owes the shylock money and can't pay or won't pay. He got some bad dope or couldn't pay for it, or his sweetie left him and they had a lover's quarrel."

Which brought us to another point? I asked.

"Is there much of that in there? Give me the details."

Hal gave me one of those, 'don't be naive looks."

"Yeah sure, from the warden down, they have the attitude that not only is homosexuality condoned but almost encouraged, as they think it cuts down on tension. It doesn't, but that's how they justify what they do. There is only one state in the country that really discourages homosexuality and tries to avoid it and that state is Mississippi."

I didn't know that, but evidently Clyde did.

"Yeah, they also allow conjugal visits. I think Oregon and maybe one other state are starting pilot programs for the men. They keep the fags to themselves and allow visits every six weeks."

Now I thought we were getting down to the nitty-gritty.

"OK, now, what about rape?"

"What about it?"

"How big of a problem is it in the Atlanta Penitentiary?"

"Well, in order to be raped, you have to be pretty weak. You know, like a dog smelling fear. People give out certain emotions which can be picked up on. Maybe he is effeminate when he comes in. Or, maybe he runs his mouth and makes a lot of enemies, whatever. I've seen very young men come in and no one lays a hand on them."

To emphasize his point, he rubbed his hand across his chin and continued with, "Ya wanna know why, because they stand on their own two feet and keep their mouths shuts! Most of all, they'll tell you the minute you press them. I don't swing that way and leave me alone. It may take a blow or two, a very minimal amount of violent feeling and then, it's gone."

He looked at my face and laughed, "What's the matter, did I shock you?"

"No, that's not it. I was thinking about all that propaganda about ten guys raping some poor bastard in the shower. I received a letter earlier this week from one of the guys in the group describing how prison officials not only condone homosexuality, but make it a point to put two in together as cellmates. Hal, you wouldn't have believed what I saw during visits to the state institutions. I saw whole sections, where the younger inmates were housed together; and it was so damn obvious that the inmates were all having love affairs with their cell mates. And, do you want to know what the warden told me when I asked about this situation?"

"Arlene, I have a feeling you're going to tell me anyways."

"You're damn right! He justified housing the gays separate as being better for them to be together. That way, there wouldn't be all the commotions and fights like when they're housed with the rest of the inmates. At the time, it made sense to me, but I don't know now. Maybe a better system of 'releasing tension' should be instituted. Instead of putting a 'strange one' in the 'hole,' like Louie, with his red cars, maybe they should be able to see a 'shrink' on a regular basis.

Clyde made a note or two and then said, "Maybe if a few of those tax dollars were spent on getting a few good 'shrinks' there wouldn't be so many of them coming right back."

Hal made a face and said, "Sure, prison officials publicly make a lot of noise about recidivism, but let me tell you, secretly, they're thrilled every time someone returns. That means that he can go right back to that clerks job that he was trained for, or maybe they get another experienced hand to work in the cotton mill."

I asked Hal whether he agreed with the inmate's desire that the causes of the murders should be looked into, rather than how to solve who did them.

"Oh, no question about it. If your staff people in places like the Atlanta Arms knew how to handle situations, if they had training, a lot of these murders could be avoided."

Clyde prodded him with, "Slight assaults and minimally threatening situations are turned into formidable and alarming cases by a staff who are at a complete loss at how to handle things?"

I added my two cents.

"Even I've seen the administration encourage hostility between factions in the inmate population."

"We had it in our group, remember?"

Clyde was busy writing and looked over at me to continue, "Well, OK, remember that now. Since our complaint, all the other groups are being required to fill out forms for the guests they want to bring in. As long as I can remember, no other group had the restrictions we had or had to submit to insulting forms before they could go into the institution. Now, since our complaint, they have been told that they could no longer just bring in their outside visitors, as they had in the past. When they, too, were told they would have to clear the names of their guests with the institution ahead of time, and in writing, the NAACP protested."

Clyde's pen was flying and he questioned, "What happened when they protested the 'new rules'?"

"Well, they were told that it was the fault of 'them Jews'. I mean it! They could have started a war if so many members of the NAACP, including the president and several of the vice-presidents, had not been attending the Jewish Discussion evenings. It was avoided because the men were aware of who and what was behind this action."

Hal hunched up his shoulders and leaned forward.

"You read and hear about the murders, but you don't read about the cuttings and beatings that don't get reported. These you don't read about. You don't read about how many of the guys walk around there spaced out from drugs that they got from the guards. You know you don't even know your terminology in referring to these men."

Clyde was busy writing and I asked, "Terminology? Isn't a prisoner, a prisoner?"

"Hell no, you got guys living in there who are convicts, some who are inmates, and others who are residents."

"What's the difference?"

"Well, a convict is one who's going ten years or better, hard time. An inmate is one who is doing five years or better and is usually in for a nonviolent crime. And, a resident is someone who is doing under two years."

Clyde agreed and elaborated along the same lines, "I've been told that it's most often the resident, the guy with the least time, who does the most moaning and groaning. Also these are the guys most likely to snitch."

It made sense of sorts, as these were the men who were least likely to withstand pressure, because of their typically white-collar background.

Hal said, "Anytime you have no outlet for your emotions, there is a potentially explosive situation. Programs such as these discussion groups are outlets for the men to express themselves and release a lot of the hostility in a positive way. Media is not allowed near the men, and when the men are allowed to speak to the outside community away from the prison officials without fear of reprisals, it's a healthy situation."

"Well, it's healthy from the inmate's viewpoint, and lets the public know what is going on behind the walls."

As Hal put it, "Graft, corruption and all the rest are so easy in a place like that. When you have a place without access to the 'civilians,' a bad situation could be made into a horror."

Clyde began to sneak glances at his watch. He was getting ready to head back to the Journal to write up the story for the afternoon paper. Hal noticed that the interview was about to be wrapped up so, as he walked us to the door he tugged at Clyde's arm and said, "Hey listen, before you go, I want to see you write something that will make some changes in the parole system."

Clyde reached into his pocket and took out his pad and pencil once again and began to record Hal's comments.

"Well, you have about two or three interviews before you go up for parole. In the first one, they want your parole plan. You get the 'skinny' from everyone around, you know, 'what is a good parole plan comprised of?' Er, you got a job waiting for you, that's a good shot. You got a little money in the bank, you're accepted by your friends and neighbors, that's fine. That's all you know about putting a plan together, cause let me tell you your case worker isn't telling you what an acceptable parole plan is."

During all this Clyde was writing furiously and now looked up and nodded his head saying, "You mean, you gotta learn from your fellow convicts what to do and not do?"

Hal brightened, "Yeah! That's it, what little you can find out. Then you get your point's sheet, which shows how many points you're going to get toward parole if you meet certain criteria. If you're in for violent crime, non-violent crime, a drug crime, first class, second class, a family, a high school education, all the things mount up. You got a total of so many points. The more points you have, you're supposed to have a good chance of making it, the less points, the less chance. But, they don't in reality take that list into consideration. I've seen guys go in there with more points than the law allows and never made it."

I knew he was right, as I have seen men leave who I never thought would make it. And others, who we were really rooting for to get out and never, did. Most of the time it never made sense why they picked someone for a parole. Hal had gotten an intense look on his face.

"So, Hal, what was the criterion that they gave for parole? Can you tell me?"

He threw up his hands in frustration.

"Nope, you never know. Trying to find a job in the street as part of your plan is almost impossible. There isn't anyone beyond those walls who is going to assist you in getting employment. Your case worker isn't going to, hell, neither is your counselor. Groups such as yours, those who come in from the outside perform a great service to the guys. You help to set us up with a job, living facilities, whatever is necessary. Don't let us down."

He turned to Clyde, "When you write it up, tell it like it is."

Clyde snapped shut his little notebook, gave Mel a long thoughtful look and said, "Well, I'll give it a try."

The ride back was uneventful. It was a sunny spring afternoon, the kind of day that made me glad to be on the outside. Each of us were deep into our own thoughts. Clyde was probably collecting his thoughts for his story, I was just starting to appreciate the power of the press. I hoped for once that I had met a factual reporter who would tell it like it was.

Chapter Sixteen

THE FOX PROTECTING THE HENHOUSE

By May of 1978, things were absolutely beginning to jump at the prison. It was incredible. Men were being murdered on a regular basis. Good Heavens, if you're not safe in a prison, where could you be safe. The local newspapers and eventually the national ran articles about the rumors of suspected graft, corruption and incompetence in the Atlanta prison. Then low and behold, Georgia's Freshman Congressman found a cause. I really believed that they were going to look into the murders, the results of the murders, and what could be done to correct the problems within that institution.

"Mrs. Peck? This is Warden Handbury's secretary calling from the warden's office. I'm calling to tell you that the 'independent investigation committee' is going to be at Congressman's Fowler's office tomorrow between one and three o'clock, and I would like to find out what time you'd like to set up an appointment with them?"

What did they mean, set up an appointment for the warden's office to meet with the congressman for this investigative committee? And, the call coming from the warden's office. What kind of meeting could it be if the warden had anything to do with it? My G-d, were they calling everybody like they called me? It sure smacked of intimidation. They should be completely independent of each other and have nothing to do with making calls from the Warden's office. We set up an appointment for the following day and I began to organize thoughts in my head that I planned on discussing with them. First and foremost on the agenda would be to find out how they had the 'chutzpa' to make phone calls in the manner that they were doing. Something told me that I just might need a witness. I gathered up my tape recorder and Temi and early the next afternoon headed for the congressman's office.

Although we arrived on time and no one else was waiting, we were left cooling our heels in an outer office until finally we were ushered in to see this committee.

The 'independent investigation committee' was comprised of two gentlemen who looked grim. Although one was black and the other white, they seemed to share the same attitude. The mood of the room, to say the least, was hostile. Although the day outside was a glorious, sunshiny afternoon, it never reached this office.

The white investigator introduced himself, "Ah yes, Mrs. Peck. Congressman Fowler has been called away to Washington. He regrets that he cannot be here. I am investigator McCume from Washington," and nodding to the other gentleman, "this is Mr. Williams."

Since Temi had not been called to speak to their 'committee,' they obviously decided not to acknowledge her with an introduction. Mr. McCume had that same marine appearance that I had seen before; thinning, sandy colored hair, cut not stylish, but neat. His pressed sport coat and pants resembled the official uniform that Marines wore. He had a very 'civil service' bearing, almost as though he could click his heels at any moment. Mr. Williams, on the other hand had a little flair. He seemed to study us with a little less of a frown and what appeared to be some interest in his eyes. He also had a pad and pencil which was only fair, as we had brought along a recorder. Temi seated herself on an easy chair. I chose a small 'love seat', although that was certainly not what I was feeling at the moment. Both McCume and Williams were in straight back chairs, it went with their military bearing. The black investigator couldn't seem to get comfortable till he finally ended up slouched deep in the chair, his fingers stroking his meticulous Van Dyke and looking at us through tinted sun glasses. For a moment or two we all just sat there, eyeing each other. Finally, I spoke, "Sirs, the men have been extremely concerned that this investigation will turn out to be a white-wash. They feel that prison officials monitoring the other prison officials are like the fox protecting the henhouse. The very fact that Warden Handbury's office called me to say that you gentlemen would be here at Congressman Fowler's office from twelve to three to set up the appointment was not the way it should have been done."

They exchanged looks between them while I continued, "Now, with me, it doesn't matter. No one's paying my salary. I don't have any relatives there, no one special to visit. But think, if I were an inmate's wife and I were called to discuss information that I might have about the warden, his staff or anyone there, it sure as hell would have intimidated me if I had received a call from Mr. Handbury's office. In fact, that's enough to give anyone who might want to come forward twinges about going further."

Again, the looks to each other.

"Uh huh, well, Mrs. Peck. We're not here to discuss that, or why you presently aren't allowed into the institution. That's between you and the warden."

Uh oh, they knew about that, huh?

Temi, in a calm, articulate manner so in contrast to my own mood of the moment, interjected with, "Gentlemen, you fail to realize how important this program is to the men. Many of the hostile feelings that have arisen between the staff and the men can be traced directly as to how poorly the issues, such as this, have been handled by your staff."

"As for example," I butted in, "sixty men were waiting there that night to attend this meeting and they walked away with the frustration of not knowing how or why we were not allowed in." Inspector McCume impatiently cut me off with, "I TOLD you Mrs. Peck, we are not here to discuss your prison situation. This committee has been called to look into the murders at the prison, not your trivial encounters with the prison officials."

I almost blew a gasket but somehow, "And, while you're investigating, did it ever occur to you that maybe, just maybe, it might behoove you to look into the reasons for the murders, as well as who did it. Maybe you'll find that that is just as important."

Temi couldn't stay quiet and she enjoined, "Just suppose, that a man has been having a hard time from his case worker, who just might possibly be uncaring or incompetent and feels terrible frustration at finding any solution to what looks like a hopeless situation."

The 'committee' looked bored. Temi continued, "Now, just suppose that this same inmate has just been given a hard time concerning his parole from this same uncaring or incompetent caseworker when he leaves his office, returns to his cell block and runs into someone that he might have had an argument with, two months previously and wham! An argument which would have probably, under normal circumstances been forgotten, turns into a murder."

Mr. Williams spoke for the first time and said, "Really, Mrs. Peck. I fail to see how this hypothetical situation has any bearing on what we're here to discuss."

Somehow, it wasn't very surprising to find out they would feel that way.

"Mr. Williams, how many case workers are there working in the institution?"

Through clenched teeth, McCume answered, "Eight, eight case workers."

"for twenty-three hundred inmates? My, my."

The afternoon paper had run an article titled, "Polish Prince Robbed by Inmates!" Maybe it was time to pick up that train of thought and see what it might have.

"OK gentlemen, you say that you aren't here to discuss the issue of whether I ever go back into the institution, but many of the incidents that we are here to discuss are tied up with other things. It's just possible you might be able to do something to help with positive results."

Temi broke in with her usual flair. She pushed her enormous pink tinted sunglasses up over her nose, and with a theatrical wave of her ring filled hand said, "You can't say there is just one solution to these killings!

Like society, the prison is a complex picture. And, if there aren't programs to utilize or interest or capture a man's intelligence or imagination, there is no hope!"

They were starting to look at us with that 'get to the point' look. I continued impatiently, "The retaliation by Assistant Warden Wpoopski in keeping me from my program may possibly, just possibly be what was responsible for what happened to him at the horse show. Violent actions were almost inevitable as a result of the harassment that the men undoubtedly felt about Assistant Warden Wpoopski's response to Julian Bond and myself. And the shame of it is, the whole thing is so damned childish. Here, let me read you this letter from one of the inmates, and I quote,'plain assaults are turned into murders which could usually have been avoided if handled properly by the staff. The attitude of the prison officials encourages an atmosphere such that otherwise mere slights by inmates form the justification for assaults with dangerous weapons'."

I looked up and said,"If that sounds like something you've heard before, you did. But you told me that you failed to see how my hypothetical situation had any bearing on the situation."

He sat there nodding his head, cleared his throat and said,"May I say something?"

He didn't really require, or expect an answer, so he continued,"I've sat here and heard you read the letters and expound on your feelings about the inmates and how you feel they have been mistreated by staff. Let me ask you a question Mrs. Peck, where do you think the officers and the administration come from? Don't you realize that they are your neighbors and are trying to do a humane job and so forth? So far, the only thing that seems to be truth to you is taking for face value everything that the inmates have told you. I just have difficulty in understanding, are you really here to hear us or to try to understand what we're talking about? Or, have you come to the conclusion that everything that you've been told by the inmates is absolute fact?"

The first thought that I had, and it almost came out of my mouth was, "What the hell difference does it matter what I believe?"

How did we get on this trend? How could we get our point across? I tried to say, tactfully,"Sir, it doesn't really matter what I think. I'm sure there are many wonderful and dedicated men in there running the institution, trying to do whatever they can to help. But, there are some bad apples in the barrel that encourage some of these actions such as supplying drugs, homosexuality and the like."

McCume's face appeared colder. He answered with,"What about the inmates? Is there a possibility of their maybe bringing contraband in?"

Oh hell I thought. How did I end up getting on the defensive side?

"Certainly, a good amount, or even a large amount is probably getting in via the inmate population, but how does it happen? Who shuts their eyes to all of it, Mr. McCume? More important, why have men from my group been put in the hole for wanting to give testimony to you and your men? I fail to understand when the point of this committee is to gather information, why men within the institution are not allowed to speak with you."

McCume broke in, "That's not true! Anyone that wants to speak with this committee has and will be allowed to!"

Like hell they were. An illustrious senator from Georgia, Wynch Fowler had brought himself down from Washington a couple of hot-shot prison officials that would give just the white-wash to his investigation that he wanted. He was getting a tremendous amount of TV and press coverage from their findings and finding too much wouldn't serve the public interest as he saw it. Looking him right back in the eye, I said, "Fine, then here are the names of the men in my group who have been sitting in protective custody since they announced the fact that they wished to testify before you. As a matter of fact, here are two more names written on this piece of paper of guards who are 'supposed' to be supplying the inmates with contraband. I understand that one made so much money, he could retire."

I handed the papers over and sat back waiting for a reaction. Finally, McCume stuck the papers in his pocket and said, "We'll look into it. However, Mrs. Peck. It is not guards that bring in contraband. Whatever is there has been brought in by inmates."

Temi calmly agreed by logically stating, "OK, I'm sure there are men in there who probably get drugs and such in. We're not saying they don't."

I interjected again, "Right, but we're saying that if you look into the names that we've just given you, and if you'll release these men from the 'hole,' you and Congressman Fowler just might uncover what this committee is supposed to be looking for. For instance, a couple of names on that list like Jason Lynott and Gary Biach wish to speak with you and might have a lot to say that a 'real' investigation might want to bring out."

Warden McCume looked at his watch, but damn, I wasn't going to let him off the hook that easily.

"And, while I've got your attention, there are programs such as the one that we had that are desperately needed in there to release this hostility that gets bottled up. Usually their only outlet is a violent act. Which incidentally, is what you're investigating, the causes and effects! The bright minds that are in there could possibly be channeled into educational endeavors. Many of the men from our group have gotten college degrees. And, Mr. McCume, you can be sure that when these guys graduate and get out, they aren't coming back in. Part of the administration's responsibility should be to generate this type of . . ."

McCume cut me off and almost rose out of his seat. He leaned forward and said, "How do you think that this program got where it did?"

I answered, "With every kind of hassle you can imagine!"

"Mrs. Peck! If the administration didn't want this program, or any program, there isn't a program in the prison that they WOULD HAVE. Those programs got in there because the power people felt there was some benefit in having them!"

I really wasn't in the mood to go into how progressive this particular staff at the prison was. Although they really did not want to get into it, I made sure that we spent the next ten minutes discussing how and why I felt they were wrong. The people in there, both in and out of the group, were not being treated fairly. And, we were only able to continue because of our determination. It was difficult to constantly overcome the obstacles that Assistant Warden Wpoopski and 'Swinging Priest' had put before us.

There was silence in the room. Temi broke it by clearing her throat.

"Ah, one more thing. This program has not cost the federal government one dime! It cost no one any money, and other positive programs have begun from this."

Mr. Williams smiled for the first time since we were there. I thought maybe we were finally getting through to him, "Well Mrs. Peck. It seems as though you've come with a shopping list of complaints. Are you sure you don't have a few more complaints to make before our next interview comes in a few minutes?"

"Well, Mr. Williams, I hope that you realize that what I had to say aren't our personal complaints. These little comments that we've made here today have been from the men."

"A probe like this is a good thing for a freshman congressman to latch onto. It gives him a cause. It would be nice if maybe your report could generate some changes in the prison, changes for the better."

"Oh, I quite agree, Mrs. Peck. That is if changes are warranted."

I thought, "Oh no, no changes are needed. The whole system is terrific."

It left me feeling as though Temi and I were the enemy. It gave us that old walking on eggs syndrome. My suddenly quiet cohort prodded me, "What about the commissary?"

We spent a total of two hours sitting in the congressman's office and left with the feeling of futility.

"Oh yeah, thanks, Mr. McCume. Are you aware that the inmates have to sometimes pay twice the retail price of various products?"

McCume gave me an amused look and said, "Mrs. Peck, I rather doubt that, and I'm sure there must be some mistake in your figures."

"Oh no there's not! Recently, I placed the order for the Passover matzo and it was to be thirty cents a box. I know that for a fact, because I ordered them. That's the price the penitentiary paid. However, when the men went to buy them, they were charged ninety-two cents. Shall I list more?"

Why did I get the feeling that they were watching me with unkind eyes?

"No, we will naturally look into your charges of 'alleged mismanagement' of government funds. Is that all, Mrs. Peck?"

No! It wasn't! We went on to tell the committee about the cases of Louie who had been kept past his sentence longer than any other inmates in the federal system, due to 'incompetence' that according to them, he didn't exist.

"He was killed, after he was put in the general population by a staff who knew he was supposed to be in protective..."

Investigator McCume straightened up straighter in his seat and narrowed his eyes. The veins in his neck were actually throbbing.

"Now wait a minute! That was not true! Are you trying to accuse the institution of knowing that the man was in danger and didn't do anything about it?"

"OK, Mr. McCume calm down. I'll agree. It was an accident. But these accidents should not happen because that accident cost that man's life."

Mr. McCume broke in with,"Do you really believe that?"

I figured before arrangements were made for me on death row I would semi-retract that statement and said,"We-ll, I question it. But, even if they didn't know, they should have known, because it cost that man's life!"

The other investigator, Mr. Williams who had been sitting quietly taking notes most of this time spoke up and said,"Mrs. Peck, you're talking about an institution that deals with thirty thousand inmates year in and year out. More than that, when you consider all the internal papers to process and so forth, it's a lot of paper work to keep up with. I agree, Mrs. Peck, it was a very sad occasion. But the fact is that the institution did not know, nor did the Bureau of Prisons, that this man was in protective custody and cannot be held responsible for it."

"OK"

The meeting was winding down and so were we. It seemed there was no way we were going to speak the same language. Tired and frustrated, I said,"Yeah, well, if it's too much to keep up with your inmates in an adequate way, I suggest that maybe you put in your report that the prison system should be revaluated. Records of the inmates ought to insure the safety that prisoners are entitled to."

Temi adding, in her very definite way,"You know, we feel the crux of the problem is that the system is designed such that people who should long ago have been fired are merely transferred rather than being removed."

I couldn't resist adding, "Which reminds me, I have heard a rumor that Assistant Warden Wpoopski has been transferred to another institution, to teach of all things, mob control. Is there any truth to that?"

That seemed to catch them off guard, but both men looked me in the eye and McCume said, "No, of course not! Assistant Warden Wpoopski is on leave of absence until Monday."

We didn't believe it. I bet they didn't really expect us to either.

There really wasn't too much more to say, so we gathered up our purses, papers, tape recorder. They didn't seem particularly sorry to see us leave.

In Congressman Fowler's ante room, we noticed a meek little man. He resembled the man in those old comic books who used to get sand kicked in his face because he was so puny. He looked as though he hadn't had a good meal in years. In addition to his slight appearance, he wore 'granny' metal frame glasses. All he needed was an umbrella to complete the Wally Cox image. We figured that he was probably the next appointment for the 'committee'.

We were half-way out of the door when he walked over to us hesitantly and introduced himself as another reporter from the Journal. He said that he had stationed himself in the congressman's office in the hopes that someone would speak to him. No one wanted to talk to him about the investigation. That is until he met us! Temi and I took him down to the coffee shop and filled his ears with enough information to enable him to write a full-page spread in the evening's paper. Once again, I was the mysterious 'unnamed reliable source.'

Things were quiet for the next few days. Passover time was upon us, and for the first time in five years, I would be missing from the prison Seder. Several friends were planning to go. They had been invited because of their participation on Wednesday evenings. Andy, Temi, and I were still banned. Even Senator Talmadge had personally called the warden to request that I be allowed to attend, but it still was a no go. No one knew when I would be allowed to return, if ever.

As it turned out, it was an evening that I would have loved! The next day I received calls telling me what I had missed. My neighbor June started with:

"They were adorable! Just adorable! After we arrived and we're finally taken to the dining hall, the Rabbi and Cantor were escorted to the dais where they were to sit and conduct the service."

Without too much enthusiasm I said, "How nice."

Really, I was hoping that she would feel the sheer hurt in my voice, that everyone else was able to attend Seder without me! Still, she did not stop, "Oh! And Arlene, then the men pointed out that the chair between the Cantor and Rabbi was saved for you. We noticed for the first time that that place was not only set, but there was a large framed picture of you that the men had placed there. You would have loved it and it's a shame you had to miss it. The part you probably would have liked best was when they dedicated the service."

"Why, what was so great about that?"

"We'll probably they should have dedicated the service to G-d, but no, they dedicated it to you. You were Elijah! The invisible angel who visits all the Jewish homes during their Seders and, drinks some wine."

"Really? All that happened at Seder, in front of God and everybody?"

"Right."

"Hey, wasn't too bad after all. June?"

"What?"

"Did they give you an idea where they thought the information should be?"

"Well, one of the men mentioned that he knew of your acquaintance with Jack Anderson and that would be a good place to start. Personally, I thought Sixty Minutes would be pretty effective."

"June?"

"Do you think they would pay any attention to me if I did get in touch with them?"

"I don't know. Depends on what you've got to say to them. Why don't you wait until you get the information that they have for you? If it's as strong as the men told me, and if it can prove enough graft and corruption as they say is going around that place, then you might just be sitting on the story of the year. Wait a couple of days and see what you get."

The other guys in the group had promised to raid everyplace that information was accessible and send out proof of the corruption and graft. Boy, the guys had really given me a mission. They were counting on me and I didn't know if I could handle it or not. But I was going to give it a try. Now, someone had to get this information to the news, or to the senators or somebody who would listen and still remain anonymous. This was one time I didn't want my name at the forefront. The package itself was six inches thick of death reports about men who had bled to death from stab wounds, from lack of attention to these wounds, legal briefs, news of staff, who, if it were anywhere else would have been fired for incompetence years ago. There were also suits against the prison brought by inmates because of damage to them directly caused by the prison personnel. It took hours to wade through the stuff. Much of it was in legal terms I didn't understand.

Unsure of my next move, I called June next door and said, "Well, the package came, now what?"

"Well, what did it say?"

"It said that the whole damn prison is either incompetent or corrupt."

"Does it prove any of those charges?"

"I think so, I'm not sure. I don't understand this legal talk."

While we were speaking, I shifted around some of the papers and looked again,"I don't know, some of these documents look pretty official to me."

"Well, why don't you call your contact in Jack Anderson's office?"

"Yeah, that's what I was thinking; they'll know what to do with this and how to use it."

"You're right! Let him tell the world! See ya later, I gotta run."

My next call was to Washington. I managed to get through to Jack Mitchell, Anderson's aide. He asked me questions for almost an hour, then said, "Hey, Arlene. It really sounds like you've got some dynamite stuff that they want to get out. Listen, tell you what. I'll relay some of the really pertinent information to the old man right away and you keep in close contact with me as things come in. We wanna know about it, OK?"

"OK?"

Within a couple of days, and with a lot of effort, I weeded the garbage from the 'real' stuff. It really was dynamite. A day or so later, I called Andersons' office and passed along the information. During this same time I made another call to Congressman Fowler's office to tell them that I had acquired a bit of information that should be acted upon. They thanked me for my efforts and said someone would contact me further. No one ever did. However, Jack Anderson's office called backed though, "Arlene!"

"What!"

"Hey, listen, I've got something that I wanna read to you. My boss is going to read this commentary tomorrow over the air tomorrow morning on Good Morning America. You are really going to like it. Now listen, how about this part, 'The Atlanta Prison system has the nation's most unfeeling and heartless prison officials, who are completely unresponsive to the needs of the men incarcerated there.' What do you think of that, huh?"

"I think it's terrific!"

"Yeah, well that's not all, there is a good chance that I might be able to do a little investigative reporting for Anderson on the case and fly down to Atlanta. Do you think you can get me into the prison so I can see for myself what's going on in there?"

"Yeah, shouldn't be too much trouble."

"O.K. I'll call you tomorrow, and remember, don't forget to watch for your story on the Good Morning segment tomorrow!"

My little girl Marla was so impressed that she was selling my autograph to the fifth grade! For the salary I was getting, which was zilch, I was starting to put in an awful lot of time sifting through papers, contacting various news media, and spending all day answering the phone; but things were moving. The clock was ticking.

Chapter Seventeen

THE TALK SHOW

Speaking of phone calls, toward the end of January of 1979, within a day or so of Anderson's talk on national television about the conditions that were prevalent in Atlanta, I also was invited to speak on the same subject locally. WRNG radio's station manager called and inquired if I'd would I be interested in coming on Reggie Eaves Show? Would I!

Reginald Eaves was at one time Atlanta's first black police commissioner who had been appointed by Atlanta's first black mayor, Maynard Jackson. They had been roommates at college, and were both success stories. Jackson had gone on to become mayor, while Eaves had a distinguished and controversial career. He had been director of penal institutions in Massachusetts. His two year tenure with the Atlanta police department culminated in a department scandal and open warfare between the two old friends resulted. Who was it who said, 'Never borrow money, nor take a job from a friend?' During his temporary withdrawal from public office, radio station WRNG had offered him a job and Reggie was in 'show biz.'

Reginald Eaves and I went back a long time; however, I wasn't sure if he'd remember me or how we had come in contact a few years earlier when he had first moved to town. Our local Jewish newspaper ran an article about Atlanta's new black police commissioner who was also Jewish. Finding someone with those qualifications is about as rare as finding a one armed paper hanger and I was in dire need of someone with just what he had to offer.

Sammy Davis, Jr. was the only other black Jew that I knew of, and he wasn't available. Several of the men in my discussion group were Muslims. For several weeks they had been asking me to bring in a Jewish 'brother.' Until I read the article about Mr. Eave's being a member of our tribe, I knew of none. Weeks later, I received a phone call from the warden's office.

"Mrs. Peck! Why do you continually do the unauthorized things that you do concerning your relationship with this prison?"

"Why, Warden, Hon, what on earth could you be talking about? I can't imagine what I could have done that you feel is an infraction of the rules?

"Are you aware, what am I saying, of course you're aware? The Commissioner Eaves, Police Commissioner Eaves and a bodyguard who was incidentally wearing a gun tried to enter the institution and was turned away at the door. He said that he had been invited to speak at the institution by you."

"Well, my goodness. I certainly hope you let him in."

"Of course I didn't! Under no circumstances could we let a man such as a police commissioner into the place. What possessed you to think that you could bring him in?"

"Well, frankly warden, I fail to see why the man couldn't come in."

"Because I won't allow it! That's why! And, besides, do you realize how much extra security a police commissioner would require?"

"Oh? Is he involved with the law? Gee, I never knew that he was a member of law enforcement. I scheduled him in because he's black and Jewish and I wanted the Muslims to have someone to identify with."

"Mrs. Peck . . ."

"Yes?"

"You don't fool me for a minute . . . Click . . ."

I might have been able to pull it off, too, however, Mr. Eave's office told him the wrong date and he was there a week early, with a body guard who was wearing a gun!

The prison officials probably had a stroke by his presence, and I hated to miss it. We hadn't spoken since then. When I called him to apologize for his having wasted a trip, I invited him over to my home for Passover dinner. He didn't come.

It probably would have been easier to reach Sammy Davis, as repeated calls into Eave's office brought no response. Finally, I was able to get his appointment secretary to schedule him for a Wednesday the following month. We would be discussing the problems at the prison and the investigation and we would receive calls from listeners.

This time it was my daughter Dana who was selling my autograph to the kids in the fourth grade!

I arrived at WRNG an hour early with a handful of notes, a camera to record the event for posterity, and goose bumps down to my toes that no one would call. I'd have to be sitting in front of a microphone for the entire session making a damn fool of myself. Everyone at the radio station seemed to be very busy. A trim receptionist ushered me to a waiting room until it was time to go on.

The studio was nothing like what I had envisioned. The waiting room was small and bare except for a standard couch, chair and coffee table. While I sat on the couch fidgeting, I found myself facing a glass window where the present WRNG "Ring Master" a man named Neil Bortz was finishing up his show. He was a man whom I had listened to many times. From his voice, I had conjured an image of a gorgeous individual. Boy was I ever wrong! He was really yucky. He could see me also through the glass window. Apparently our first impressions of each other were mutual. When it came time to give the lead in for Reggie's show, I heard his strong, distinct voice announcing, "Well, for those of you who want to stay tuned to Reginald Eaves' show today at six, he is having a guest named Arlene something giving a talk on colanders or string beans or something."

"You miserable SOB," I thought, "If anyone was driving home and considered keeping their dial tuned in, you just killed it." I briefly thought about making an obscene gesture at him, but changed my mind when the station manager came in to brief me on the talk show procedure. It was getting close to six now, and Mr. Eaves still hadn't arrived. During the last half hour wait, I had made six trips to the bathroom. Something told me that it was going to be a long show and at that point my nerves were beginning to get nervous.

At what seemed to me three seconds before we were about to go on, Eaves arrived and coolly put me at ease. We really had more time than my nerves had told me. The news was on and during this time he showed me how to place the earphones and speak into the mike. I felt like raising my hand for permission to run back to the bathroom one more time, but it was too late. The music was on and so were we!

The familiar lead-in music was playing. Then Reggie Eaves was saying over the air to thousands and thousands of people, "Good afternoon ladies and gentlemen. Welcome to the Reggie Eaves show. Today we have a question. That question being, what is it that Reggie Eaves and Julian Bond have in common? Is it they are both black men? Well, that's true. Is it because they're both graduates of Morehouse College, and have fought for the rights of blacks? Well, that's true, and I suppose that we can go on and on about what we both have in common, but I suppose there is one thing that stands out that you don't know, that we have in common. No, what you don't know is that Julian and I attempted to go to jail and we were locked out. Can you believe that? Both guests on our program today are going to talk to us about how attempts to make life a little better are foiled by the prison officials."

He briefly touched on the Fowler investigation into the murders. My throat went blank along with my mind, as he was talking. I kept looking at the phone with all those unlit buttons out of the corner of my eye. I was praying to myself, "Oh, please, don't let me sit here with a voice that won't speak and no one is calling."

I turned my attention back to what he was saying. "Welcome to the show and let's talk about it." Look, I wasn't petrified, I could speak and I found myself telling him, along with those thousand others who might have been listening, the story of Julian Bond at the prison. Suddenly, all the lines were popping up and Reggie noticing it also said, "Well, let's go to the phones."

First on the dials was my son Keith, and his question was, "Mrs. Peck, aren't you afraid to go in to the penitentiary?"

I laughed and said, "No, darling, I'm not afraid of the prisoners. I'm afraid of the administration. I'm afraid the warden might have a contract out on me if I keep stirring things up. But no, I'm not afraid of the men, as they've always been very nice."

Reggie chuckled and said, "I got a feeling you're a troublemaker. Do you think that there might be some truth in my feelings?"

"Just possibly. Maybe, it's because I question too many things that I've seen over there through the years that are wrong with our 'system.' Honestly, I went into that program years ago with a very law and order attitude that the 'establishment' was always right, but gradually I've got to admit they've changed me."

He led me into the, "Case of the Missing Tomato Plants" and a few more stories. Then we went to the phones. The next caller commented, "I think that one of the reasons that she's rocking the boat is because the prison officials hate to see the truth about certain things that are happening that she sees."

"No, I don't think that's the reason so much. I think the problem has come about because they don't want us, the public, to see how our tax dollars are wasted."

Reg agreed, "They don't want trouble makers. Prisons are 'big business' and they don't want questions being asked."

We began to answer the calls faster and I found I was really enjoying myself. Calls were coming in about homosexuals, prostitutes, and all sorts of things. Reggie left the switchboard for a few minutes and asked, "What about the men? How do they feel about this Fowler investigation?"

"Well Reggie, the men are paranoid that the investigation is going to be a white-wash.

You can't have prison officials checking out other prison officials. They're retaliating against the men because of it. What little library they had was taken out, classes were disbanded. Why? What can possibly come from their report except a week or so from now they'll come back and say, 'yeah, everything's fine, we're gonna need more money allotted to the prison. The staff does not need more money; they've got more than the national budget now. They need other things that they're not getting. The administrations going to probably get what it wants out of this, but it's not going to filter down to the men."

Zip, another call. It was a man and the voice sounded very familiar:

"Er, hello. Ah, I have to believe that the courts were reasonably correct and the inmates are guilty and in there for a reason. So why, after five years, does she continually go in there, especially in view of the problems she's had from the officials who obviously don't want her? Why does she insist on continuing to do this? Why does she leave her family to go in and do this?"

My host gave me a look that said, "Uh oh, here comes one of the crazy calls that we often get." Eaves and the caller really began to get into the topic, before Eaves cut him off. The tone was definitely not friendly. About that time a commercial came and Reggie and I had a chance for a few off-air comments. He almost apologized to me about the last caller and said, "Well, eventually you get a few weirdoes or hostiles who call in."

I wasn't sure if I should tell him, "Oh, that's O.K. don't worry about it, that was my husband."

"THAT WAS YOUR HUSBAND?!"

I almost hated to upset him, but I repeated it. Eaves was flabbergasted, "But, but, the caller was so hostile!"

"Of course he was. When it came to me and my prison, the man's attitude is positively vile. He's never understood what compelled me to go in there. To tell you the truth, when it comes to me and my prison visits, he would rather have had me, cleaning dishes and cooking dinners."

Eaves looked at me, a smile tugging at the corners of his mouth. He didn't say so exactly, but his eyes had the expression of, 'That's my sort of soul brother!'. Instead all he said was, "I wish I had known. I would have talked to him longer before I cut him off."

Then it was time to take the calls again. I had told many of my family to call in, but mostly it was strangers that were doing the calling. Later I found out that over eight hundred people called in and weren't able to get through during the show.

The feedback the next day was pretty positive from my friends and relatives, and when the letters had time to arrive a few days later, they were absolutely amazing! Most of the listeners were in complete agreement with the basic theme of the evening's topic, the waste of tax dollars in our federal prison system. It rarely receives the attention that was focused on it that night and even the inmates appreciated it. The cheer would go up through the Atlanta prison.

Maybe the subject was one that I found easy to speak about, or my host was smooth and knowledgeable putting his guest at ease, but Eaves and I worked together like Frick and Frack! One of the callers inquired of Mr. Eaves, "How come you didn't make changes when you were involved with the police here, weren't you able to? Were your hands tied?"

He shook his head affirmatively, and said, "Oh yeah, I had no control over prisons here, but we did change around the system when I was commissioner of penal institutions in Massachusetts. Mrs. Peck is not exaggerating, the conditions are horrible!"

I chimed in with, "There is a lot of mental stress that is forced on prisoners daily."

Eaves shook his head conspiratorially and asked, "Well, why should we spend good dollars to rehabilitate these men in this prison, a maximum security prison at that, with the most hardened criminals?"

Was he baiting me? Acting the devil's advocate? I was a little angry.

"Who are you kidding? They don't want rehabilitation in our federal prison system. They discourage it and the aim of our government Bureau of Prisons is not to rehabilitate! And, let me tell you Mr. Eaves, I can say this based on experience, because I traveled around to the state prisons, and this Atlanta Penitentiary is twenty years behind some of the state prisons that I've seen which are really the pits!"

He winked at me and I finally realized that it was a put-on, "Aw, com'on, what do these programs do to take their minds off their problems, especially programs that bring in rabble-rousers such as Julian Bond and Police Commissioner Eaves..."

"All right, you're kidding, but seriously, programs like these don't cost a dime and they still fight them tooth and nail!"

In a more serious tone, Reggie continued, "It's true, when a man is dehumanized while in prison, he loses respect for himself, the public and everyone. He goes out and acts accordingly. If you dehumanize him, you can only ask for an animal to return to the streets."

"Amen!"

The controversial sentence of Haldeman and Erlichman was paramount in a lot of the caller's minds. More than a few called in to ask questions like;

"How did the inmates feel when they saw the Watergate criminals serve brief sentences at resort facilities, and leave on furloughs to attend their daughters' weddings and enter private hospitals when the other inmates weren't accorded the same privileges?"

People have a tendency to hear what they want to, and somehow more than a few formed the impression that I was super-liberal, which was so not the case. Their calls were the most fun. My favorite was a woman who called long-distance to give me pure southern hell! From her tone it was easy to see that she felt that I was one of those 'damn Yankee liberals' who had taken over where they didn't belong. She called from a country town to say, "Er, am I on? Huh? Oh! I'm on? Wa'll, I just wanna say, are you for just for opening the doors of all prisons and just lettin all prisoners free?"

Reggie gave me a 'here comes a crazy call look, and I tried to keep a straight face.

"No, I don't think that they should open the doors and let all the criminals out."

For a couple of minutes she sputtered and finally she said, "Wa-ll you and Mr. Eaves sound like ya'll are just hell bent on letting them out! Every livin one of 'em!"

He said, "No lady, I'm not for seeing that 'breakers of the law' are set free, but, maybe you should do what you can while they are there, do what you can so that they won't return. In fact, it's your tax dollars that I'm looking to save."

That flustered her so that she ended her call saying, "Shore! Let em all out! Let all them murderer's and rapists out to run free!"... Click

People like her can't be blamed though. I suppose that years ago, before I had become involved with prison reform, my thinking ran the same way. Except, that was before I realized that penal institutions are big businesses and a big waste of our tax dollars.

The program must have hit home. Even a few of the prison guards called in and quoted to me the facts and figures of keeping an inmate in the institution. Even their voices sounded like ex-marines. I could see the tight little neckties and short hair cuts as they spoke.

All too soon, I heard the sign-off music and I realized my chance at revealing all about the prison system was being cut short. I had lots more to say. I could have gone on all day. I almost wished I owned the station, and then they'd really hear something.

Reggie summed it up with, "It's not a very sexy subject and we've got to think about it seriously as taxpayers, and if we don't think about it seriously as taxpayers, then what we're going to do is wind up spending a lot of money incarcerating people and running out of time."

"That's true. But, you're spending more now by not having some of these programs and basic things that the men are entitled to and keeping a hostile situation going whereby the men are kept at each others throats. Reggie, I'm not kidding when I tell you that it's the general practice over there where they set up situations where the men are pitted against each other. This comes strictly from the inside. Maybe this investigation ought to concentrate on making some solutions for these practices that are commonplace over there and shouldn't even be happening in the first place."

"Arlene, our time is up, but you've given us lots of points to ponder. Maybe we didn't solve the entire prison problem during this past hour, but hopefully some of our listeners are better informed and maybe will be watching the Fowler investigation a little more closely. Thanks for being a guest on WRNG, and we were off.

My hour in the limelight was over and during the drive home I wondered if we had really accomplished anything. Thousands and thousands of people were listening to the show. What was going to happen now? Did it make any changes? Was anyone from Fowler's investigative committee listening? Anyone from his office, who might relay the word back to the congressman that the public was interested? Calls of concern had come in. What was he going to do now? We had barely touched on the topic, but, like Scarlett, 'tomorrow was another day.' And tomorrow, Jack Mitchell, from the Jack Anderson office would arrive.

Chapter Eighteen

NORMAN, THE BOMBER

As the years passed, each of the men became special to me, some more than others. The personalities of some were so infectious that even after learning about their crimes I just couldn't help liking them. Others, because of their crimes, held a fascination that made it more and more interesting each time I met them. Some just showed me what was wrong with prison injustice in general. There was one that touched me maybe a little bit more than the others because he was the only one the other inmates said really didn't belong in there. I noticed him first at the first Passover Seder because he was such a character. As I got to know William Williams better, I realized that Norman had been the catalyst for the initial change in Williams' attitude towards the Jews. When I got to know Norman better, he taught me that things really weren't what they seemed.

Norman the Bomber was really a pussycat. It wasn't until he was released a few years after and we met that I began to realize how weird one could get living within the institution. Of course, he could have been that way before I met him, but I'm getting ahead of my story.

Norman was a pleasant type. He had been a bona fide pharmacist who loved to play the horses. Far be it for me to stereotype a person, but he looked like an unmade bed. Some of the men managed to look like they had been outfitted by Brooks Brothers, but not Norman. There was a distinctive walk that the men got after prolonged periods of being cooped up. Well, Norman had it. The reason he walked so funny might have been because his shoes were too large. He always looked as though he were about to trip over his feet. In fact, he did a lot of that also. He wore droopy white socks, which wouldn't have been so noticeable except, his pants, which were baggy, were also hitched up above his ankles.

He wasn't exactly heavy, but he had a loose, un-athletic build that always seemed exaggerated in white t-shirts worn hanging out over his loose khaki pants. Gorgeous he wasn't, with his fuzzy, thinning brown hair that was too long and a receding hairline. A couple of times I thought about mentioning that he might avail himself one of the nose jobs offered in that place, but I didn't want to hurt his feelings. Most of all, it was his eyes that made one wonder what his problem was. They were really strange. Right in the middle of a perfectly normal conversation, his eyes would get a look that would make one think he had left this planet.

If that wasn't distracting enough, he had hairs sticking out of his nose and ears. Sometimes they would just sort of wave around like big antennas that would make conversation with this nice man all but impossible. Norman had never married, and it was probably a blessing. I could see his contact with women to be that of polite, never passionate contact. Everyone seemed to like him though, the ones on the inside and the visitors who came in from the outside. Norman had a really droll sense of humor and would break up the men with one of his outrageous statements at a very serious time. During the first Passover Seder when some of the professional do-gooder social-worker types were in attendance at the dinner, one of them had the really stupid idea that the men should stand and give a three minute essay on 'What Passover Means to Me.'

Herbie, who was sitting at my table leaned over and said, "What jerk thought of dat essay crap? How much ya wanna bet you get some really stupid answers?"

He was right. The first four men who stood and gave their essays were not Jewish and were members of either the NAACP or the Muslims. Their speeches went something like, "I'm so grateful to the administration that we have this chance to sit with our fellow Jews and break bread on this very profound occasion. Passover means that we will be able to break bread with our fellow Jews in the Soviet Union and in Israel, if only in our thoughts."

We, who knew these particular guys were Jewish only for this night so they might be able to have a better meal, found the whole series of speeches funny as hell. But, because of the seriousness of the occasion were able to refrain from breaking up that is until Norman the Bomber spoke. He pushed himself from the table, pulled himself to his full height, looked around at the group and said in a somber tone, "What does Passover mean to me? What does Passover mean to me? Well, it means that spring is here and the horses are running at Hialeah, they're running at Churchill Downs and they are even running in New Jersey. It means the Braves are playing again, and the New York Dodgers are once again training in Los Angeles."

He said this with a look of deep reverence and broke everyone up, except the do-gooders who had thought up this little exercise.

Norman was the only one of whom I ever remembered any of the men saying, "He was framed."

In the beginning I really discounted the cop-out plea, because I had heard it all before. I kept remembering how I had been told that over and over in spite of the fact that most of the men in there were not first time offenders and had long rap sheets of offenses they still tried to make the argument that they were 'framed.' Norman changed my mind. There was something about him and his sense of humor that made you want to find out more about him. Other than knowing that he cut out pictures of horses to hang up in his cell instead of pin-ups and centerfolds, I knew very little. He had been a cellmate of a notorious kidnapper, William A. H. Williams and was possibly the first Jewish person with which Williams had ever had any contact. Williams told me about the good vibes he'd gotten from his friendship with Norman. In fact, everyone seemed to have nice things to say about Norman, and around that place, compliments were a rarity. But when I tried to speak to him he was so spacey I suspected him of being on drugs, but I couldn't be sure. His sense of humor was so outrageous, his face would look so serious that before you laughed you had to stop and think, "Maybe he really means it." Then he would get that goofy look on his face, shake his head from side to side and continue with the conversation. Then I had to laugh.

The men had told me earlier that he had lived with his mother and an older sister, whom I figured to be somewhere in her fifties. They had found him a constant source of embarrassment. His pharmacy was somewhere in Kentucky, because that's where the horses were. Somewhere along the way, a few of his neighbors thought him a little strange also, but mostly his crime was the fact that he was a Jew. They just didn't want him in the neighborhood. The rent on his store was raised, and when he refused to pay what he considered to be an outrageous price, the store was mysteriously blown up in the middle of the night when no one was around.

Even when I got to know him better I thought maybe he had a screw loose. But, I could not help liking the guy. Finally, one evening, he came in dragging his feet as usual, pants hitched up to the hilt, looking like one of the seven dwarves as he reluctantly approached me.

"Er, Arlene did ya hear, I'm getting out of this place?"

Then, his face broke out with a smile that went from ear to ear and he said, "I made my parole. How about me taking you out to dinner in a couple of weeks when I get outta here? In fact, if your husband doesn't like you going out in the company of a convicted felon, I'll take him too."

"Sure, I'd love it!"

One night a few weeks later, sure enough the phone rang and it was Norman calling from the airport.

"Do you have a little while? I'm in between planes. And I've got a couple of hours, so can I come over and say hello?"

"Oh, Norman! You're out! That's terrific. Stay where you are and I'll drive over to the airport to pick you up."

"No, that's OK. I'll just catch a cab and see you in a few minutes. You just get some coffee in the pot."

I was curious to see what he looked like out of the prison walls and whether I'd even recognize him. I wondered if they had made him presentable enough to catch a plane. Soon enough he arrived but the guy who came to my door just barely resembled the one I had grown to know in prison. Gone were the nose and ear hairs, the shuffle, and the demented look he carried around with him.

The man standing outside my door was dressed immaculately in a brown leisure suit and beige sweater, and Norman was wearing an air of confidence. I invited him in for food and although he refused a meal, we sat over coffee for the next couple of hours. Before he was merely pleasant, but as we sat drinking coffee he was now articulate and interesting. I commented on the change and even in a different voice he said, "Arlene, don't you realize that it's a protection to live in a fantasy world in there? Things that are normal to the outside world are not normal in there, and after a while, you're not normal in there either."

In prison, all he wanted to talk about were races or horses or both, but now, we talked about everything. We discussed the 'criminal types' that inhabit the 'Big A'. I remember saying, "Surely society wants prison reform, but I never really saw any evidence of it while I was there."

Once again, I was told what I had been told by the men numerous times and most recently by the priest.

"There are many cases in there that are there legitimate. There really are a few that shouldn't be there. Most of them are guilty, and what's more, not only are they guilty, but they have no intention of changing their ways when they get out of there. You have to realize that this is a maximum security prison, and when a man is sentenced there, the government is telling the officials that these men are to be warehoused. That's what the judge is saying when the guys are sent. He's saying they are beyond rehabilitation and it's a waste of time and money to try. They are not to be rehabilitated. This is the policy."

He was right, I hated to hear it. It went against all my preconceived images of what the institution should be. This particular conversation also went against my preconceived notion that I'd ever have a lucid talk with Norman Finklestein. He was articulate and told it like it was, without the weird face.

I kidded him with, "But you have to admit that we get a better class of prisoners in my group."

"Yeah, you're right, you don't get the run of the mill criminal who ran around shooting people when he got caught stealing something, but you still got very dangerous people."

Norman elaborated, "Your usual run of-the mill criminal is crummy, and the reason the fellows in the 'Group' aren't is because federal laws only cover certain areas. The feds only have jurisdiction over certain things like car stealing from state to state, income tax evasion and extortion."

I knew he was right and said so, "But Norman, I thought there would be a lot of people in there for tax evasion and there aren't."

Now, it was his turn to look at me as if I was weird, and he shook his head as though with all my years of going in there I hadn't learned anything.

"Of course they're not. You don't get those people in a maximum security prison. Those men go to Allentown or other minimum institutions. What you find there are bootleggers, especially in this area."

"Bootleggers? I thought that went out in the 1930's."

Somehow, I had visions of the stereotype in the hills and it all sounded so silly, but he was right. The government frowns upon people making their own liquor which is a federal offense.

"We've got a lot of guys in for armed robbery, interstate firearms violation and narcotics offenses."

Norman continued between thoughtful sips of coffee. At that point I believe we were on our third cup. I was becoming curious about how a man with Norman's background and education spent the last three years of his life in a place like that. Mostly, I wondered what the men who were the nucleus of my 'Group,' the Jewish inmates, were in there for, so finally I asked. Norman carefully unwrapped a stick of gum, folded the paper and stuck it in his pocket. Finally, he said, "If you're Jewish and in prison, it's usually for checks, securities, IRS, forgeries, nothing heavy . . . nothing heavy. I was one of the few heavy Jews in there."

Now, as I said earlier, I thought he was sort of chubby and un-athletic looking, but I couldn't really consider him heavy, and told him so.

Norman again looked at me as though I were spaced out, laughed and said, "Boobie, 'heavy' there doesn't mean 'fat'; it's serious, it's violent, it's a crime of great magnitude. Very rarely will you find a Jew in prison who's in there for violence."

His face took on a grimace and he continued with, "I was unique. I was the only one there during your stay that was ever connected with violence."

He paused, and then continued, "Well, maybe one of the very few."

"Norman, I heard a few stories about your alleged 'bombing'."

"What kind of stories?"

"Well, how your store had been bombed after the landlord put up the rent and how it had been done after hours when no one could be hurt. Norman, if no one was hurt, then how were you convicted of a violent crime?"

At this, his face took on a pained look. Looking down, he said, "Arlene, my crime was living where I lived. It was a 'restricted neighborhood'.

They wanted me out and the guy who 'got it' was my neighbor. They set it up through the insurance company for money. They set the whole thing up for money. They wanted money from me and they wanted me out of the neighborhood. Well, they got both."

His face started to take on a look of intensity and he continued with, "I wouldn't give in on either. I wouldn't leave and I would not give them money. They had it set up this way when they got me convicted. They framed me, they railroaded me, and then they gave me such an extreme sentence that they figured I'd cave in and give them money. That's why they sent me to Atlanta, because I never cooperated or buckled. That's why I got such a severe sentence. The probation department recommended probation. Their federal probation officer recommended probation. The judge ignored it because he was part of the whole thing."

This segregationist treatment I couldn't understand, until he told me something I could relate to.

"The judge didn't like Jews, and he figured that I had something to do with it and was getting what I deserved. That was the kind of judge I had. He really threw it to me."

I felt for him and said,"But they knew it was your first offense. How could they justify actions like that? This was the 70's in Louisville, Kentucky?"

"Arlene, there was no difference between that court and the ones in Russia and Germany. In fact, I'm surprised that they gave me a belt to go in with. They should have given me a rope and chain to enter with, because that's the kind of court that I had."

He looked me right in the eyes, from eyes, that were no longer muddled and said,"And think about what I'm saying. Haven't you seen that kind of mentality yourself throughout the years with many of the prison officials? What about the warden? Hasn't he fought the program every inch of the way? What about that two-faced priest? Doesn't he set up obstacles every step of the way when it comes to the Jewish program? Do you think that his 'Good Catholics' have to contend with the same grief and aggravation that you have to go through?"

"But why don't they?"

"Because the man does not want the Jewish program to continue. He's jealous of the success that your group has had. He takes it as a personal affront. Do you know that at one point, he patterned a discussion group exactly after the one we have going?"

"No, what happened?"

"None of the guys trusted him, they all thought was just a hack and instead of all his 'Good Catholics' going to the Catholic discussion evening, led by him, they all came into our group. That's one of the reasons he hates us. That, and the fact that he doesn't like Jews."

About that time, the kids came home and changed the mood. For once I didn't really know what to say. By the time I made snacks and sent the kids outside, another twenty questions that I wanted to ask were running through my mind. Norman's comments to me about the 'chain and a rope' triggered something that I had been wanting to ask for a while, but hadn't had the chance until now. I was afraid it might be a tacky question.

A few times as we were leaving the prison, we noticed a big Trailways or Greyhound bus parked in front with a load of new men who were about to enter the institution. The guard told me that they had been parked outside until we left, because they always had to wait until visitors leave. It was hard to believe that thirty or so men were kept sitting, cramped, waiting for us to leave.

I watched the U.S. Marshals and guards make a line from the bus door to the front door of the prison. As each man left the bus, they were given a bag of supplies and escorted up the stairs. A few of them seemed to be having trouble carrying everything because they were handcuffed. I wanted to know how long they would have to travel like that and asked Norman. He seemed to get a kick out of my question and was delighted to give me an answer, "Well, I didn't travel with them. I went by car with the other guys. They dropped them off at the county jail and then came to the Atlanta Prison. But, we were handcuffed and chained together."

"Sure, chained at the waist. And, if you are really bad and have a history of escape, then they shackle you. They put chains around your feet. It looks like something out of the middle ages."

"Norman? I know you're telling the truth, but, I mean, if I hadn't seen with my own eyes all those men lined up outside the prison wrapped in the chains, I'm not sure if I'd believe your story of all those men traveling on the bus and chained together. How many men does it take to transport all those men to the prison?"

He shrugged and said, "I really don't know. I did all my traveling by car. Oh, I suppose twenty or thirty men in transit, with maybe only a Federal Marshal and the bus driver."

"But isn't it dangerous? All those inmates and, just one or two men guarding them?"

In all the movies I had seen, they traveled on airplanes with a guard for each prisoner. At this point, Norman was also conveying the attitude that he was being patient with me about answering what were to him obviously dumb questions.

"It doesn't really matter how many men are guarding them, Arlene. As long as everyone is chained together."

"Oh, everyone is handcuffed?"

"Yeah, but along with the handcuffs they have a long chain that passes through a loop and winds around each guy so that everyone is chained together."

Now, this really worried me, and I had to ask the question that undoubtedly Norman would consider the dumbest yet, but it had to be asked.

"Norman? What do they do when someone has to go to the bathroom? I mean, it could be very embarrassing."

Out of all the questions I could have asked at that moment that was the one he wasn't expecting. Again, he looked at me like he didn't know whether to be serious, tugged at his ear, and said;

"Yeah, well, that's a good trick. You stand there and everybody goes, or waits, depending on their mood."

Now, I know it wasn't supposed to be funny and he didn't mean it that way, but I started to giggle. I couldn't stop laughing and finally it started to catch on to Norman also, and when I had finally calmed down he said,

"OK character, what the hell is so funny."

That set me off again, and while I was wiping the tears away, "Oh, I can't help it, I've got this image of thirty guys all chained and handcuffed lined up outside this tiny vestibule in the gas station and one of them has his zipper stuck."

"Yeah, it could literally be murder on a man with a kidney condition."

Norman mentioned that the prisoners are dropped off at different points and that no one knows who is going where. Obviously things could get a little complicated. The justification for this policy is to prevent informers from reporting on future prisoners. And, speaking of being in transit, it dawned on me that all the time we were speaking, he technically was en route. He had to have a travel permit. I had forgotten that they had to go through a probation period and report to a probation officer each time they traveled from place to place.

Norman told me, "In my case, I'm lucky in that I have an understanding probation officer who plays the horses also and permits me to follow them."

"How long?"

"Oh, reasonable as long as I'm en route."

But I wasn't talking about the days that he traveled.

"I want to know how long do you have to report? Days? Years? How long?"

He pulled at his ear again and said, "Oh, I don't know. As long as I'm on probation. Five years, maybe four now."

It was so nice that he had been able to stop by because for once I was able to ask everything you wanted to know about prisons but were afraid to ask.

"Another question, O.K? How do some of the men who are in there for white collar crimes relate to the really scaly, icky-looking men I've seen roaming those halls with pink rollers and cars sticking out of their afros and scars all over their visible parts?"

Norm nodded his head in acknowledgement and said, "It would be frightening to a man at first if he weren't street-wise or mentally strong. Of course, during my tenure there, I witnessed things that were really funny. There were some really incredible things that happened while I was there."

He was speaking about an article that had been in the paper recently about a couple of men who had gone over the wall.

"I remember prisoners going over the wall, waving to the other prisoners and saying, 'I'm going, I'll see you next Christmas'."

He picked up his spoon and started making marks in a napkin.

"They had a guard tower here in front, one in the middle and one on the edge. They had guards on the ends, but for some reason they never put a guard on the middle tower who could see the escapees. Luckily for them, there was an indentation in the wall where they could go behind and they go up. They waited and when the guard left to go to the bathroom, they went up the wall and stood on it. In fact they took a practice run. They went up there twice just to see if they could do it and when they saw they could, they went 'goodbye'. Everybody in the yard saw them except the guard."

I guess I must have looked incredulous, because he said, "That's true! In fact, the guy that did it I think is the only guy who escaped from the Atlanta Pen twice."

At this point I was laughing so hard I found it difficult to ask, "Do you remember his name?"

In all seriousness he looked at me and said, "Yeah, I think his name was Morris Johnson. I'm not kidding, it really happened."

"You know, it's nice that we've been able to have a long talk like this. On the discussion evenings, there are too many men, and I never have the chance to find out the answers to a lot of the questions I had. As long as I've got your attention, is it true that much of the drugs that get inside that place do so because the guards bring it in?"

He waved his hand nonchalantly and said, "Oh sure, drugs are easier to get from the outside into that place than on the street."

He continued, "Don't look so surprised. And what doesn't come in from the staff gets in via the visiting room. It's a good place for people to pass things. There are a lot of exchanges of dope coming in from the outside."

He explained to me how it's done, "See, they put the money or drugs in a balloon and swallow it. When they go to the visiting room, they are strip searched. But, after they are searched, they go and bring the balloon up, then pass it to the prisoner and he swallows it."

While Norman was in prison, I thought that he was a little spacey and a lot weird. He told me how easy it was for a man who was not mentally stable to end up a real mental case who should be institutionalized. He told me how, after three years of being there, he was finally allowed an outside job.'Outside' in that case, meant that twice a day he would walk outside of the sliding bars and into the vestibule or entrance room and pick up the mail. He described the thrill of something like that. People who led normal existences couldn't understand. That's when I first realized that there are different degrees of freedom. I was glad that he had regained what I felt sure he had lost while in prison, his prospective. He seemed like a different person.

Norman was free, now, to follow his horses or whatever. Who knows, now that he was out maybe he would follow the girls.

Chapter Nineteen

STANLEY THE TOUCHER

In 1977, the officials had me under close security. This was after 'Harry Swinger and the hospital incident' which they could never prove, and the case of the missing tomato plants. The last thing I needed was to be called to the warden's office again. It was only a matter of time and inevitable. Stanley came into my life one night when we had a packed house. He walked up next to me and made sure that he was going to be noticed. He touched me. Stanley was a toucher. He probably didn't mean any harm, but whenever he spoke to people, he just had to touch them. He was also a pathological liar. Everyone had to hear the story about how in real life he was a heart specialist. When he wasn't saving lives in surgery, he was wheeling and dealing in real estate. According to Stanley, he owned half the property in his native Miami Beach and was in the process of negotiating options for the other half.

If he hadn't have been such a braggart, no one would have noticed him. He was slightly paunchy, and had hair like a Brillo pad, with button eyes under fuzzy reddish eyebrows. He had that roasted in the sun of Miami Beach complexion that made him seem more of a misfit. The other men considered him an oddball and ignored him whenever possible. Stanley was the class loser from the 'School of Hard Knocks.'

It was a little more difficult for the people who came in to ignore him because they were more concerned with being polite. My friend Judy was one of these. Judy was sexy, newly divorced and loved to go braless, especially in the prison where every little jiggle had an appreciative audience. Throwing in a 'Judy' every now and then kind of spiced up the religious evenings. It kept the men from taking the discussions for granted. By never knowing what to expect, they would attend more frequently.

One particular evening, when everyone had broken up into the social hour after the discussions, I was standing in a group, deep in conversation when Stanley the Toucher snuck up behind me, stuck one of his pudgy fingers in my back and said, "BANG! BANG! Gotcha!"

That was not the place to play those types of games. Jumping three feet, I yelled, "Stanley, what in the hell do you want? Don't fool around, you almost scared me to death."

"Well doll, why don't you introduce me to your good looking friend?"

"Stanley, why don't you go away."

"Aw, come on, why do you have to talk to me that way? Listen Doll Face, your good lookin' friend and I might have a lot in common."

Resigned and having little choice in the matter, I replied, "OK, Stanley... Judy, have you met my friend Stanley, the doctor?"

Now, Judy was my friend from her pre-divorce Hadassah days, when she was the all-American chubbette with drab brown hair. This was until the divorce. Then she lost thirty pounds, bleached her hair, had a silicone job, burned her bra and discovered hip huggers, bodysuits and lots of chain belts. She had given up being nice for being sensuous. She batted three pairs of false eyelashes at him. Stanley meanwhile was chomping on his lip, all the while flecking imaginary pieces of lint off himself and anyone's shoulder he could reach. In Judy's case, she was aiming a bit lower, but she was a pretty fast mover, in more ways than one. She kept her cool, and instead of laughing in his face, seriously said, "Oh, this must be the famous doctor you told me about. I've heard so much about you from Arlene and the other men."

Thinking she actually believed it, Stanley maneuvered her shapely body over to the corner of the room, where under the watchful and wistful eyes of the entire group, he began to tell her the story of his misfit life, "Yeah, well the other guys here are just jealous of me. They know that I don't really belong here and am just a prisoner from trumped up charges. It was really a bum rap, the whole list of phony excuses that put me in here. Boy, when the government is after you, they're going to find something to pin on you."

This particular week, Stanley was the heir to a large fortune from a family owned movie theatre chain, practiced heart medicine as a sideline and was only in there on a trumped up security charge. Like a trooper, sexy Judy stood there batting her false eyelashes, tossing her sun tipped hairdo, looking as though she actually believed all he was feeding her about his family empire. There was only a trace of an amused smile on her face. I was only able to catch bits and pieces of their conversation as I was involved with several new people who had come into the discussion that evening. At the point I left. It was just in time too, to see Stanley stick out a rather fleshy lip in a definite pout and make the comment, "You just can't imagine having to live in a place like this, especially when you don't belong in here. It's like being on the ocean alone, with nobody to pull you back to shore."

Judy, originally from Brooklyn, answered him in a phony southern accent, "Oh-h-h, I know just what you mean, I can understand, really I can.

You just don't know how difficult it is for a poor woman alone out there. I am the mother of two defenseless little children and no one to hire me."

Judy had at that minute a fabulous job with the Jimmy Carter Campaign staff and wouldn't have traded it for the world.

"Well, I may be temporarily out of commission, but I've still got some high contacts in high places, and babe, I'm gonna set you up with a managing job at one of my families theatres in Miami Beach."

After Judy sent out radar to me that said, 'get this creep away from me,' I moved her over to another group a few minutes later.

Judy, grateful to me as she wiggled away, called over her shoulder, "Sure, sure, Stanley, you do that."

There is a big rule in the Pen that touching of any kind is strictly forbidden. Actually, it's one of the very few attitudes of the administration with which I've ever agreed. Those who break the rules could endanger the entire program. So the men do not look kindly on those like "Stanley the Toucher" or another from the group, 'Ronald the Flasher,' who might be the cause of unfortunate incidents. It was not with undue surprise that the next time we went in, Stanley was missing. It seems that after the last week's session, a few of my Muslim converts, who appointed themselves my 'protectors' cornered him in the shower and said, "You ever touch Mrs. Peck again, we break your arms, understand?"

Things were quiet for a few weeks. Stanley was off our backs and away from the meetings. Although things had been going smooth, I knew it wasn't to be a lasting situation. A few weeks after Stanley's last visit, the phone rang one day as I was busy carrying in groceries. Arms laden with bags and out of breath, I answered, "Hello, hello?"

"Mrs. Peck, this is Warden Pagen. I would like for you to set up an appointment with my secretary immediately and come to my office at the earliest convenience."

"Sure, would it be possible for you to tell me why I'm supposed to be setting up this appointment?"

"I would prefer not to discuss it over the phone, Mrs. Peck, however, I will transfer your call and you can set up the appointment... in my office... click..."

Oh G-d, I needed this. For once I couldn't even imagine what Old Broderick was upset about. Why this command performance? The meeting was scheduled for the following day, for two o'clock. After dressing as a dowager matron and decking myself in the family jewels for confidence, I arrived at the Warden's office promptly at two o'clock. As usual, he kept his part of the little game. He kept me waiting outside in the entry hall which I had grown to know so well. After the standard half-hour wait, a Mr. Tibut came out and ushered me into the inner sanctum of his office where an intimidating silence permeated the room while this man with a high school education ruffled his papers finally gave a loud, "Harr-urrtph, ah, lets see, what is it this time? Ah yes, Mrs. Peck, a letter has come to our attention from one of your, ah, shall we say, 'visitees' and an inmate."

To my left were two men I had never seen before, but they had the same look of white on white shirts and short haircuts as everyone else around that place. I didn't know who they were. Briefly, I wondered if they were there for protection, like the nurse that the doctor has in attendance while the gynecologist is giving an exam. Finally, to break the silence, "Err, Warden, would you be so kind to tell me why I have been summoned to your office and who wrote this letter that seems to be the reason for it?"

The two men gave sidelong looks at each other, and appeared extremely serious. The warden took time to light a Marlboro. I just knew he smoked Marlboros. During this time, while the room was quiet, I could hear the faint whirring of a tape recorder. I sat and worried. Maybe I was the cause of a prison break and they found a letter damning me on one of the escapees.

"Well, Mrs. Peck, are you acquainted with a female Caucasian woman Judy Stacked?"

It was not the time for bad jokes but I tried, "Warden, I'm not sure I should answer that question without being in the presence of my lawyer, but ya got me. Her name has been on my guest list so, I suppose I'll just have to come clean and admit it and hope for the best. What is she guilty of? Smuggling in a machine gun to a cell block?"

Once I admitted knowing her, they exchanged looks and with a smile of self-satisfaction, the warden continued, "Mrs. Peck, this is not a subject to make jest of. We have received a call from Ms. Stacked pertaining to a letter that she has received from one of your inmates. It was a letter making improper advances to her, and offering said Caucasian false employment of dubious character. She has filed a complaint to our federal government office about the said letter."

He sat back in his desk, looked at me smugly and said, "What do you have to say about that?"

I looked around and all three were sitting back in their chairs looking as smug as though they had broken a million-dollar opium ring. For this, we all pay taxes? I didn't know whether to laugh or kill friend Judy. Instead, I sweetly reached over and said, "May I see said letter?"

I had just finished reading it already. Reading upside down papers on my teacher's desk was one of my specialties in high school.

It was true! That jerk 'Stanley the Toucher' had written a letter. A suggestive letter in which he offered Judy employment in Miami Beach at one of his family's supposed theater houses. I found that extremely funny, because Stanley, the fictious heart doctor, was really the ticket taker in a movie house that he had tried to rob. Naturally, he had botched the job and that's why he was incarcerated. But why did Judy call the warden to complain about the letter? That just didn't make sense. After about ten minutes, I was dismissed with a wave of his hand and the comment, "Of course, Mrs. Peck I will not allow such things going on within your program, even if it means cancelling the program. We do not allow clandestine affairs with the inmates. Ms. Stacked, of course is never to come in to the institution again. And, most certainly we will be watching you and your involvement in the program most carefully."

I found the whole thing pretty silly and was still trying to figure how anyone could have a clandestine affair with anyone when one of the participants was behind bars. I told the warden that I would certainly give this my personal and immediate attention and would confer with him in the very near future.

Finally, I was allowed to leave.

Now, Judy was a fun friend with a strange sense of humor, but at this point I was ready to gleefully strangle her for being the cause of my wasted day. The first thing I did when I reached her on the phone was to can her. Skipping the niceties like, 'how-w have you been?' I went into a tirade, "What kind of a friend are you? How could you play a perverse joke and call the warden, instead of me, if you received an obscene letter?"

Judy said, "Listen, I'm at the stage where I'm grateful when I receive an obscene anything. What in the hell are you talking about?"

About this time we were both shouting into the phone and I came back with, "Did you, or did you not call the warden with the complaint that Stupid Stanley wrote you an obscene letter?"

"Judy, as one of my oldest and dearest friends, do you promise that you don't know what I'm talking about? You didn't make any phone call to the warden?"

Then she came up with the clincher, "May the only affairs I have be community affairs if I'm not telling the truth? He's got to be talking about another Judy Stack."

While we were talking, she had been thumbing through the phone book and damned if she didn't find what she was looking for. There was another Judy Stacked in the phone book.

A few minutes later Judy called me back, laughing and she said, "Are you ready for this? Better yet, are you ready to apologize for misjudging me so badly? I called the number in the book, which is obviously the one Stanley found since he didn't know my ex's name. He looked up the address that was listed in the book, wrote his letter, and sent it to the other Judy Stacked."

Talk about a fluke of fate.

"Judy, you're kidding. There can't be two of you?"

"Wait! You haven't heard the best of it yet. She, like me, is also divorced with two children. So, when the letter offering me employment arrived from the Atlanta Penitentiary she couldn't figure out how some nut in prison had gotten her name and address, and in her efforts to track down who and why, she ended up on the phone with Warden Pagen."

"You mean it was the other Judy Stacked who called and complained to the warden about the letter that you were supposed to receive?"

"Right!"

There wasn't too much to be said after that except maybe, "Da-mn!"

I really did feel guilty for misjudging my friend. I wanted to redeem myself in her eyes by calling the warden to allow her to re-enter the prison. The warden, as usual, lacking in any sense of humor declared that the ban on Ms. Judy entering the prison still held. As for Judy, the episode didn't seem to leave any lasting scars. However, what upset her more than being kept out of the program was being labeled 'undesirable'. She had strived so hard to change that image. The only thing that cheered her up was the fact that the FBI did a very strict security check on her before she was allowed to go to Washington for her new job. She passed with flying colors.

She was cleared to work with one of President Carter's Georgia staff, but somehow her clearance didn't reach as far as the Atlanta Penitentiary. That's only one of the reasons that I almost enjoyed bugging the authorities there.

I was bugging them. I knew it, they knew it, they didn't know how to handle me and I wasn't going to let them get the best of me. At this point they probably would have done anything to have another, different program. But now it had become a battle of wits between us and them. Each time the men, through me, were able to get away with even a minor infraction, it gave us a sense of victory that somehow, the system could be beat. How long this was to continue, was another story.

Chapter Twenty

I WAS A SPY FOR NATIONAL REPORTER

My contact with the national media was Jack Mitchell who was a columnist and Jack Anderson's aide. He had given me their 'special hotline news' number long ago when I had become involved with the William William's papers. I had kept that number close to my heart and in the back of my head, with the thought that some day it might be necessary. Well, the time was here and now and it was necessary. If I could get Anderson interested, I knew I could make a huge impact because his columns appeared in hundreds of papers across the country. Now we had the ammunition that was provable and I was going to knock that prison on its ass! Not just for the prison system and not just for the country, but because I'm a vindictive female and everything that the guys felt, expressed my sentiments exactly. It bugged the hell out of me that the inmates had been right. The end result of Fowler's investigative team was the white-wash they had predicted. It was mind-boggling that the U.S. Congressman who was in charge of the entire fiasco, absolutely refused to receive any information concerning the institution or graft that had occurred within those large granite walls. Somebody had to do something. He obviously wasn't going to. The question was, 'where do we go from here'?

Jack Anderson and the power he wielded seemed like the best opportunity we had going at the moment. Therefore, with more than a little anticipation, I dialed that 'special hotline news' number, "Mitchell? Hi, it's me, Arlene."

"Oh, hi, what's happening down there? Anything that Jack can use in his column? He's very interested in the situation down there, especially since your congressman Wyche Fowler hasn't seen fit to answer any one of the four calls that we've placed to his office."

"Really, a lot is happening down here, but none of it seems to be getting out to the public."

His voice picked up considerable interest, "Oh yeah, like what?"

"Well, judging from the mail and information that is arriving to our house each day, it looks like the men have made me the liaison from the penitentiary to the press. To tell you the truth, my kitchen table is filled with a mountain of papers, documents and just plain ole complaints that the inmates have sent me."

"Oh yeah, can you tell if any of it's important?"

"Jack, I don't know, but they're afraid to give it to the committee for fear that the men might be put in the 'hole' and the information destroyed."

"What do you mean they will end up in the 'hole'?"

"Well many of them that want to testify are put in segregation to prevent them from testifying. Personally, I think that all of this material should be gone through and I'm not the one to do it."

"Yeah, it sounds like something Jack would be interested in. I'll get back to you."

He said that he'd check with his boss, Anderson, and get back in touch with me. Within a few minutes the phone rang again.

"OK, Jack wants to run a column on the situation down there. He's disgusted that Fowler hasn't even answered his calls and wants me to fly down tomorrow morning to follow up on this. Can you meet me?"

"Sure, I'll be happy to, but . . ."

I almost died of embarrassment having to admit that after all the months since our last meeting in Washington, over the William Williams Papers, I had forgotten what he looked like.

"I'll be wearing a goatee and moustache and a brown suit and a brown shirt. How will I find you?"

"Well, since you've seen me I decided to find out if blondes have more fun, so, look for a blonde."

"OK see ya then, oh, by the way, do they?"

"Do they what?"

"Have more fun?"

"Sure, if they're tall, young, and skinny."

"Oh, one more thing. Can you get me into the prison to see for myself what's happening?"

"No problem, you're coming in on Wednesday, so I'll slip your name in along the guests that are already scheduled to go in so no one will notice."

He had another thought and laughed, "Arlene, there is an old Jewish expression I should tell you about."

"What's that?"

"From your mouth to God's ears. See you tomorrow."

Click.

Mitchell was arriving early in the day so that we would have plenty of time to go through the information that he had sent. I should have known better, as it's a fact that no matter who comes in or when they arrive, it's always the last gate in the terminal that I have to walk to. Naturally, the shoes I wore looked terrific for walking the streets but were terrible for airport terminals. I was exhausted before the trek was over and ready for traction by the time that we reached the car!

Mitchell arrived looking just like Van Gogh, with his ears intact. Other than the goatee, he was pretty average looking; height, weight, etc. except his eyes. They reminded me of still waters that ran deep and dirty. There didn't seem to be a shred of innocence behind them. They were the kind of eyes you would expect from someone working for Jack Anderson.

He walked with a fast pace. I asked, "I'll go get the car, while you pick up your bag."

He answered, I won't be staying that long. This overnight's all I brought."

"Oh, OK, you can walk with me to the car. How was your flight?"

"Terrific. I sat next to a lady named Laverne who grew up wanting to be Dolly Parton, but wound up waiting tables at The Waffle House."

"Was she the one who got up in front of you with the Red marks below the knee caused by white boots and wearing the cheerleader hair-do?"

"The same."

I liked his style. We took the scenic ride through town back to my house where the real work began. At least we attempted to get some real work done, but everyone was curious as to what someone working for the 'real' Jack Anderson looked like. By mid-afternoon, half my friends had stopped by, on one pretense or another, and he seemed to be enjoying all the female attention. His eyebrows even lifted a little when Jody, the last of my friends who had no desire to get into real estate or public relations breezed in wearing another one of her navel dresses. She told us that her TV station was arranging to interview the men in the group the following day. Jody had gotten the men's names during her last visit into the institution. Probably the men were hoping that the station would send her for a private interview, rather than a male newscaster. I wasn't sure if Mitchell's expression of interest stemmed from the news that she brought, or the skinny halter neck top that she was wearing.

He destroyed the neatness of my files in about two minutes and raped the papers that I possessed. Really, he took everything that he could carry and said that he would return them later. The rest he spread on the table and working with precision weeded out the facts from the fiction and the pertinent from the unnecessary. Loosening his tie, he whistled through his teeth, "DA-MN! You got a powerhouse of information here. No kidding, this is some dynamite stuff here! Has anyone else seen this information?"

"Nobody wanted to."

"WHAT?!"

"Well, you know what happened when Jack Anderson tried to call Congressman Fowlers' office, they wouldn't talk to him?"

"Yeah, so?"

"Well, when I tried to tell them that I had information that should go before the committee, they did nothing but thank me and said someone would contact me, but no one never did."

"Son of a bii-tch..."

He was sifting through the hospital records and was hunched over the table, intent on what he was reading. From time to time, he'd point to something.

Again, another low whistle, "Jesus! Look at this. If this information checks out, we've got a whole column on each one of these hospital records. Did you know about this before?"

"Sure, but no one would listen. For a long time, the guys would tell me about a doctor they had out there that they lovingly referred to as 'old shaky'."

He laughed and said, "I can see why."

Jack stuck a medical report in my face, "According to this, a guy goes in for a single hemorrhoid operation and 'old shaky' cuts the sphincter muscle where his patient leaves with no control over his defecation."

"If you think that's newsworthy, I'm almost embarrassed to tell you about the inmate who had a hernia operation."

He gave a sidelong look, waiting for the other shoe to drop.

"Would you believe that after the operation the man is now missing his left gonad?"

"Can you prove that?"

"Sure! See, there's his hospital record, and I've got the lawyer who is handling his case against the government. He's stopping by later to fill you in on how the case is coming along."

I made some sandwiches for lunch and Jack was still sitting at the table, shaking his head, muttering under his breath, 'Holy shit! He made a mistake and took the whole da-mn thing off?"

The day wore on and Jack had three piles of papers that he had labeled; take home, garbage, and dynamite! By the time the kids returned from school, we had spent the better part of five hours going over the folders that had been sent.

"Christ! How in the hell did they get their hands on this or even send it out! It's a good thing that the warden doesn't know that you've got this stuff. He might send one of his 'hacks' to get you."

Rather than laughing along with him, my sense of humor disappeared completely. He scared the living hell out of me.

"Jack?"

"Yeah?"

"Do you think anything could happen to me because I know all this information?"

"Yep."

"Oh my G-d, what?"

"Lightning will strike you if you even consider discussing the story with anyone else before I have a chance to write it up and have it printed."

The hours were rolling on and pretty soon it was time for Mitchell to leave to be on the 'program' for the evening. Right on the button, my friend June arrived, wearing a large loose top, so that she could fit any notes that the men might have wanted to send out. It was also the way we smuggled in the weekly 'newsletter' that I wrote to the men. It was the only way that I was able to keep the prisoners informed of the outside happenings. Things were much too 'hot' to send anything through the mail. I was even cautious of the letters that they sent me, so instead of having the men address my mail correctly, I had them write in care of 'Modine Gunch'.

I introduced Mitchell to June. She laughed and said, "I hope you're not wearing your press card, in case we're searched!"

Jack seemed to consider that and said, "Do you think they might do that?"

He brought up a good point and I told him, "Well, we've never been searched before, but that was before. At this point in time, almost anything could happen. It's very possible that with all that's going on, the outside people coming in will be looked upon with more suspicion than usual. Why? Do you have anything that might identify you with the press?"

He reached in his back pocket, took out his wallet and press cards and said, "Do either of you have a little notebook that I could take in? I don't usually travel unprepared, but I don't think that it would be a good idea to walk in there with the big steno pad that I usually carry with me on assignments."

"Good thinking! Now, if I can only find a piece of paper. It's a good thing you didn't ask me for a pen or pencil, my kids usually leave me a broken crayon or eyebrow pencil to write with. Ah, here it is. OK, you're ready to go now. Promise you will give me a call just as soon as you leave the penitentiary and let me know what's happening, OK?"

"Sure. But tell me, who should I talk with when I'm in there? I mean, how will I know how to get the information?"

"Ask for Chico. They'll know who to sit you next to."

"Well, how will I know what he looks like?"

"You can't miss him. He's six-foot four, weighs 200 pounds, and is, in his own words, 'mean as hell.' Chico's face looks like a chunk of Stone Mountain granite. It would scare dogs and little children, except that he smiles and jokes a lot for a man that mean. It's all been set up with the guys beforehand so they'll know who to steer you with and what to tell you. OK. Go!"

They left and headed down the driveway towards the prison in the midst of a blinding rain storm. I hoped it wasn't an ominous sign of things to come. My feelings at that moment were full of resentment and rejection, and the rain didn't help my mood in the least! It wasn't fair that I didn't have the pleasure of seeing the men's faces when they realized that we had managed to sneak a reporter in where no other press had been before. The prison had a room reserved for the press, but even then, the reporter only saw or heard what the prison officials wanted them to see or hear. Many times the men had mentioned that they were sure that the room was bugged. So you can imagine what the reporter heard. They heard what the men thought couldn't be used against them. They were afraid of retaliation by the administration. There was a good chance that our meeting room was bugged also, but there was still more of an opportunity to speak on a one to one basis without being overheard.

I was very apprehensive as to whether they would then get through the gate and the guards, but they did!

Mitchell returned looking much like the cat that had eaten the canary. Or in this case, conversations with inmates who sang like canaries. Everything you always wanted to know, but were afraid to ask, or better yet, were unable to ask was discussed that night. Earlier, during the afternoon, Jack had mentioned that he was only twenty-seven but there was a lot of mileage on him if that be the case. However, returning from the penitentiary, his eyes were shining like a kid. When I asked, "How'd everything go?"

"Beautiful, it was just a very interesting evening to say the least."

I nodded, "Yeah, I know just what you mean."

He was gathering up the papers that he was taking back to Washington for Anderson and getting ready to head out the door to catch his plane when he said, "Now, you're not a reporter, you couldn't know in terms of that what an evening like I spent tonight could mean to give you the right perspective about what's happening in our Federal Prison system. It is absolutely mind-boggling what's going on in those places, and especially that one."

"Well, reporter or not, somebody should write about what's going on in there. Did you get enough for a column?"

"Lady, I got enough for a book!"

"Mitchell, nothing personal, but if you don't go back to Washington and do anything with the information that I gave you, I promise I'll come after you and cut your heart out with an emery board."

He smiled and said, "Hey, stay cool. You'll see."

Then he was gone, back to Washington, eager to write the scoop. His boss would be happy, and I would have a week to agonize about what he was going to say. He had gotten what he had come for, spoken with the 'cream of the criminals,' my 'Group' and, if his smile were any indication, he went home one happy reporter!

Eventually, Warden Pagen made it a point to let me know his viewpoints on my behavior. I didn't have the pleasure of seeing his face when Jack Anderson wrote about me being the Atlanta Federal Prisons resident activist but he knew alright. A few days after the column was printed nationwide, the warden wrote me a nasty letter stating that I was never to set foot in the institution again. The feeling was really starting to hit home: Somebody in there didn't like me!

Chapter Twenty-One

CONGRESSMEN HAVE FEELINGS, TOO!

Jack Mitchell's plane headed back to Washington to meet with his boss, Anderson. I went home and sat down and wrote a semi-nasty letter to Congressman Wyche Fowler, stating my dissatisfaction with the way his investigation was going. If they wouldn't answer my phone calls, maybe they'd read my letters. Somebody up there had to listen. Three or four days after my letter was sent, a letter arrived from his office. It stated that his office had been trying to reach me for several days, and would I please call the congressman's office as soon as possible and set up an appointment with him for the next time he was in town. I found that encouraging, as maybe now I could find some safe place where I could, in good conscience, get rid of these incriminating records after what Jack Mitchell had said. I was beginning to feel it might be dangerous to have them around. The letter arrived on Saturday, and before I had a chance to call into his office on, my phone rang on Sunday afternoon and GOOD GRIEF . . . IT WAS CONGRESSMAN FOWLER!

"Hello Arlene, this is Wyche Fowler."

Gone was the laughter that I had always thought he had in his voice.

"Oh hi, I received the letter from your office yesterday. When can we make the appointment?"

"I don't think we are going to make it. Whatever has to be said, I think we can do it over the phone."

Uh oh, I was getting bad vibes. The receiver I was holding almost iced over. I cleared my throat and said, "Emummph, well, I've been trying to reach you about this prison situation for over a month. All I get is your aide, Alonzo, who keeps telling me not to worry, you're working on it. Meanwhile, my program has gone from over sixty men to maybe eighty."

He brushed that off shouting, "I have half a million constituents. WHY DON'T YOU CONTACT ELLIOT LEVITAS WHO'S YOUR CONGRESSMAN! Also, it's been reported to me that you're going to campaign for my opponent in the next election. I don't like that! You can write him your rude letters!"

"Really Wyche, I don't think that my letter to you was so terribly rude. All I did was mention that you are completely inaccessible, and that I have papers from the men in the institution that you can pick up. If that's not convenient then I can bring them over. Frankly, they're making me very nervous keeping them around the house so, if you don't want them then I will turn them over to the media."

I stopped myself from saying that he'd end up looking like a damn fool if that happened. He was beginning to boil now.

"I don't care whom you speak to. I'm running this investigation as I see fit. If you don't like it, then go to one of the other four hundred and sixty-five congressman and talk to them!"

Before the man hung up on me, I could tell the conversation was heading in a direction where he was going to hang up, so I mustered up all the 'Southern charm' within me and said, "Wyche, it's not even a matter anymore of my part but the men in the prison don't trust your committee and have been sending me information that I want to turn over to you."

There! I said it, for all the good that it did. All my congressman did was raise his voice even louder and say, "Listen! This isn't the first time I have gotten involved with prison work. I did this when I was a legal aide at Emory University. Like I told you months ago when we spoke at a party, you can't always believe what these men say."

Didn't he realize that he was in the big leagues now? In what I hoped was my calmest coolest voice, which now was beginning to quaver, I continued, "True, maybe they don't always tell the truth, but these men have been sending me documented information that backs up what they say. They don't want to give this information to the prison investigative committee. I hate to say this but they don't trust you or the committee."

Sometimes my tact is in my tushie, and this was one of those times, "WELL, I don't care! I DON'T TRUST THE INMATES!"

Then in a loftier tone, Fowler continued with, "This is a federal government investigative committee from the justice department. What do you mean that the men in the penitentiary don't trust them?"

It was difficult to believe that a United States Congressman could be this naive but he was actually saying these things.

"Congressman Fowler?"

"Yes, Mrs. Peck?"

"Are you aware of how your terrific independent committee called me into your office for an interview?"

"Yes, of course I am."

"Then if your committee is having everyone call the warden's secretary from Handbury's office it's a wonder that you've gotten anyone to go before them. Good heavens Wyche, you're a lawyer. You know that's intimidation!"

"Now listen, MRS. PECK. I am running this investigation as I see fit! I started this because no one gives a damn about these people, and I care about my constituents!"

Instead of saying, as I should have, "Da-mnit! Show it!" I said, "Wyche, the men want to have me turn this very sensitive information over to you, not your committee. However, a few of the men in there did want to speak to this committee."

A longer than necessary pause and then, "So? Let them come forward and speak to the committee."

"Well, Wyche, that's not possible at the moment. One of them was even put in segregation. He has names and documents of corrupt guards and higher-ups in the staff. In fact, all the men who weren't allowed to speak to this committee are still willing to talk. Would you like their numbers and see that someone gets in contact with them. Preferably you . . ."

"I?"

"What?"

"You heard me, I said no. I have no intention of going into the Atlanta Federal Prison to make personal visits to inmates you feel want to visit with me. My committee is doing a thorough job of checking out the problems and when I need your help, I'll call on it."

Now, it was my turn to get hostile, "Oh? So tell me, will you also be as accessible to me as you were to Jack Anderson when he was trying to reach you?"

"I don't care about Jack Anderson. I don't care about the president of the Atlanta Paper. I represent my constituents and not the press. And, you can send to Washington any information that you think you have for me."

He then proceeded to rattle off his Washington address, of which I was well aware. He finally finished with, "If you have an inmate that wants to talk, then I'll give his name to the committee. If you don't like how I'm running things, then go somewhere else. Leave me alone!"

Boy! Talk about hostile tone! All I had tried to do was see that the men got the congressional investigation that they very much wanted. The following day, Wyche called a press conference and announced that the committee had done a thorough job. But just as the men predicted, nothing was said about the real problems. The inmates had said that Fowler would say that the prison needed more funding, better security and that the present staff was competent. The inmates were right. The end result was a white-wash. They had predicted it.

Where did we go from here?

Chapter Twenty-Two

ORGANIZED CRIME

Despite the Fowler lame-duck committee's white-wash attitude, things were happening. Like with Watergate, the press pursued the scent. Each story that I fed to the newspapers fanned the mood for another. The administration had warned me time and time again that rules had to be met and I had to go by the code. This time they were going to get it. Armed with the new Supreme Court ruling, the inmates were not to be denied access to the press, so I began to arrange interviews on television. Some of the guys almost seemed to launch a career in show-biz they gave so many interviews. Our local affiliate of CBS began to run conversations with the inmates, much to the dismay of the warden. But this time, we went by the book.

The television interviews were arranged via my Barbie doll friend, Jodie. I would schedule her into the institution as a guest of the Wednesday evening discussion group. At the end of the meeting, the names of the men who wanted to speak with the television station would be duly recorded in her notebook. Then she would return to Channel 5 and see about arranging interviews for ones she thought really had something to say.

Once this was done, the station had to get permission to interview them. This wasn't easy as the law says that the men are allowed to be interviewed only if proper channels are followed. But, thank G-d it could be done.

The first to be cleared was Carlos, which delighted us all. Because he was so handsome and articulate, he would be able to do much to dispel the stereotypical image the public held of the average criminal. Nothing about the men in my 'Group' was average. According to the plan, the reporter was to talk with him and a couple of the others to find out the feelings of the men inside. The final result was on the six o'clock news and it was terrific.

The reporter opened with a scene from outside of the building, which was impressive to say the least. He stood alone, stark, against the background of the prison walls. Then the camera followed, with much dramatic flair, while the reporter stood waiting to enter the room where the interview was to be held. The iron bars slipped open and then BANG... shut behind him. When Carlos arrived on the scene he looked crisp and clean, and expressed himself eloquently. Then, they had a quick cut back to the warden, wet head and all. The contrast was very effective. To the outward viewer, the interview seemed terrific, however, the men inside did not agree. A day or so later, I received a letter that stated that most of the men had been unhappy. The feeling was that out of the hour and a half that they were interviewed by CBS, "The T.V. station only chose to put in three and a half minutes of only the sensational content and didn't get to the core of the problems that were discussed."

Two days after this, the CBS affiliate had another chance to film the reactions of the inmates to the reports of the investigation committee that had now been made public. Channel 5 blew it again. This time, only a little more than a minute of air time was devoted to the reactions of the men. Among those they did were William A. H. Williams and Leo Guarino of the French Connection and the Pleasant Avenue Connection. Williams was now sporting a grand handlebar mustache, and except for the weight that he had lost, he looked very much as he had after the kidnapping.

During all this time, things weren't dull around my house either.

Jack Mitchell sounded rushed and said, "I haven't got much time as I'm heading out to cover a story but I wanted to take a couple of minutes out to let you hear what Anderson will be running in his column. I think you'll like it."

"Did you spell my name right?"

With a sigh, he said, "Yes, I spelled your name right. Now, will you listen to what will be running in almost seven hundred papers in a few weeks."

"Jack, I will be delighted."

"OK. How's this?" Now we have sent Jack Mitchell into one of the worst of the federal prisons, with the help of inside contacts." ME!

"Right, you. With the help of inside contacts, we slipped inside the Atlanta Penitentiary. Nine inmates have been murdered there in sixteen months. Mitchell tried to find out why."

"Did you?"

"Be quiet and let me finish. Conditions were intolerable. They are daily in danger of being raped, abused, beaten, and murdered. Inside the Big A, Mitchell met with a dozen inmates, without the knowledge or consent of prison officials."

"ME AGAIN!"

"Right, remember Old Shaky?"

"Sure, who could forget the cause of the missing gonad . . ."

"OK, now dig this, One physician, who has just been removed from surgical duties, was known among the prisoners by the derisive nickname, 'Dr. Shaky.' Prison records were smuggled out to us as evidence that several inmates had received improper or haphazard medical treatment. How do you like that?"

"Jack, that's terrific! When do you get to the part where you spell my name right?"

He laughed and said, "The hell with the rest of the article. I'll get to the part that you want to hear. "Both black and white inmates agreed there is little racial animosity inside the walls. Black organizations seem to have constant access to the prison, perhaps because more than 40 percent of the inmates are black. But Jewish discussion groups led by prison activists, are you ready?"

Now I laughed, "Oh Jack; don't stop now."

" ... led by prison activist, Arlene Peck, has run into repeated resistance from officials."

"Jack, you wrote a terrific article."

"I know, listen to the last part. The complaints about conditions inside the Atlanta pen, of course, came from inmates with axes to grind. But, inmates interviewed separately, told the same basic stories. We have also spoken to prison social workers and lawyers, who confirmed the complaints of the prisoners."

"Jack, no kidding, I love it, what do you think will happen from here?"

"I don't know, but after Jack Anderson runs a column, something usually does. You keep me posted if something comes up. And Arlene, good luck. I liked working with you."

"You too, keep in touch ..."

The story appeared under the heading, "A Horrible Look inside the Big A." Our story was just beginning to be told!

Chapter Twenty-Three

THE THREAT ON MY LIFE

The Anderson column had been run. The prison report had been published and discounted by the inmates. Just as the inmates had predicted, the administration was to receive more government funding, but to be used for more security measures for stricter enforcement. They had severely clamped down on the freedom of the men within the prison walls. The men inside were even more unhappy and the situation seethed with hopelessness.

No more were the pages of the newspapers filled with the news of the penitentiary happenings. Life was beginning to slide back to normal, or so it seemed. That was before the letter arrived.

I had just returned from lunch with Jodie. It was a couple of hours until the kids returned from school and there was a novel waiting to be read. My mind was on the bathing suit that was waiting to be put on. Just as I was ready to stretch out in the sun with a good book, I saw the mailman's truck heading up the street. I decided to walk down the drive and pick up the mail, planning to read whatever came, while savoring my hour in the sun.

One envelope stood out among the others. There was no return address. Usually I just ripped them open, but this letter aroused my curiosity. It didn't look like junk mail. The envelope was heavy duty, like the kind used in government offices. It was neatly typed and addressed to me. I walked back into the house, opened it and had the living hell scared out of me. At first glance, it was typed on that kind of onion skin paper that the men from the prison used to write their letters on. But, instead of being another of those letters that were nectar for my ego, it was my first and hopefully last, threatening letter.

The heading was puzzling, in that it was addressed to Hal Bulliver, who was the publisher of the Atlanta newspapers. Good Grief! It was written to him, but it was about me. It also 'explained' the vandalism that had happened at the Atlanta Jewish Community Center.

The previous Sunday, the Center had been broken into during the night and persons unknown had destroyed everything in sight. Swastikas had been painted on every available wall. No one knew who did it or why it was done. I even wrote an article in my column in the Jewish Post and Opinion questioning whether it might have been a redneck reaction to the TV program 'Holocaust' which had recently been shown on television. Well according to my hate letter, it was caused by men.

It said in part, " . . . vicious trouble making people like Arlene Peck who were the cause of incidents such as what happened at the Center; and if her own people can't shut her up, then what happened there would happen again and again."

As I held the typewritten pages, with shaking hands, I read how Mrs. Peck had,

" . . . disgraced her people and she better learn that she'll really be in serious danger if she doesn't learn to keep her mouth shut."

The kicker came later in the letter though, "The people hate the Germans because of the actions of one man, Hitler, yet there are many fine Germans."

YUCK! There were six copies sent to various people. Three of the six copies had been sent to people who were directly connected with the prison. One had been sent to the warden, another to the prison rabbi, and one to the wholesaler who supplied the food to the institution. By these clues it was simple to figure out that whoever it was who sent the 'hate letter' came from within. However, they were careful to type everything so it could not be traced.

They made one mistake; they enclosed a copy of the Anderson column. Carefully underlined in the column were passages they had wanted special attention brought to. In fact, the letter writer even wrote in the margin, "Initiated by Arlene Peck!"

Now, it might be possible to collect all the carbons and see if there was a fingerprint or two and then check those prints against the employees of the prison. With trembling fingers, I dialed the police. All the while I was dialing the number I was praying, "Oh G-d, don't let me get killed by some psycho out at the prison. My little babies need a mother to raise them, at least let me live long enough to get my first facelift . . . Hello? Hello, yes officer, I like to speak with someone about a threatening letter that I have just received in the mail."

"I'll have to connect you to that department."

For the next ten minutes I was switched around like a yo-yo until an understanding sergeant listened to the letter and promised to send out two of Atlanta's finest. Actually, that was not the most encouraging news that he could have given me. Atlanta, Georgia at present, was about the highest in the nation in violent crimes.

Eventually, two undercover types, wearing jean, came out. As usual, in these 'team' situations, one was black and the other white. Both seemed a little on the 'mod' side. The white officer introduced himself as 'Frank' and carefully got out his pad and pen to take down the information. His partner never said anything, but seemed to have a purpose in sitting back and watching everything very intently. Now and then he would nod when the other one spoke. After a few minutes of Frank telling me not to hold out too much hope in catching the man, I anxiously asked, "But, there is a way to catch whoever wrote that letter, isn't there?"

"Well, we'll do what we can ma'am."

"Yeah, well, I'm sure of that, but what, exactly, do you do? Do ya'll contact the FBI and run a check against prints? What?"

"We-ll, I shouldn't count too much on the FBI doing much of anything in a case like this."

"A case like what?"

As though it were an effort, Frank carefully unfolded the letter and read it once again.

"Yep, just like I said, you got a letter here that is somewhat threatening, but not enough."

"What do you mean, not enough."

"Well, if they had made a direct threat on your person, or better yet, if there had been a homicide, then we could get the prints immediately."

"Officer?"

"Yes?"

"Don't you think that's a bit drastic?"

He spent another few minutes explaining how law enforcement bureaucracy worked and then headed for the door, case solved. I headed him off with, "Officer, listen. I know that letter has come from within the prison."

"Probably."

"OK, and we also know that there were seven copies that were sent out. Now, it's very possible that among the copies that were sent out, probably a print was left on one of them."

"I suppose it's possible."

"Please, officer, if I get them sent back from the various people who received them, can't you just run a check against the employees inside the penitentiary? It's got to be someone working there. Maybe you can pin it down this way? Especially, since we also have their handwriting in the margin. Can you check the handwriting against the prison file and find out who maybe wrote it?"

The officer, who looked like a clean-cut hippie, ran his hand over the back of his neck, looked at his partner with that 'how soon are we off duty' look and said, "Mrs. Peck, even if you did find out who wrote it, there is absolutely nothing that we could do. They haven't done an overt action to harm you."

"Officer, you wouldn't have to do anything. All I'd have to do is let some of the men in my 'Group' know who did it."

That was possibly the wrong thing to say, as he snapped shut his pad, shook his head and said, "Lady, we can't be a party to any hit service that you might have going from inside."

With that, they said good-bye and left me holding the hate letter. Things were quiet for the next few days, but receiving the letter had frankly unnerved me. I even called Congressman Fowler's office to report the letter. They actually laughed. I was also having misgivings about being in the 'super-sleuth business.'

Then I got a bit of information that really blew my mind. My friend Shirley called and said, "Remember when we were speaking and you said that you needed some definite allegations with proof to show the authorities?"

"Sure, I remember that conversation, that was before we realized what a farce the 'committee' was and that they actually had no desire to have documented proof."

Shirley cut in, "Never mind that. Do you still have someone who might be interested in what's going on there?"

"At this point, it's hard to tell. I suppose that I could get back with Jack Anderson if nobody else. WHY? What do you have in mind?"

Her voice lowered a little as though she were afraid of being overheard.

"Would you believe that, somehow, I have a friend who came into possession of a letter? But, this isn't just an ordinary letter. It was taken from the files of Warden Handbury. Not only that, it was written personally to Norman Carlson. Did you know that Norman Carlson is the Director of the Bureau of Prisons in Washington?"

"Shirley, how in the hell do you have sources that can get into the warden's office and lift his private files? No, on second thought, I take that back. With the way the week has been going, I don't want to know. Is what you have anything that can be used against anyone in the prison administration?"

She gave an evil little chuckle and said, "No, not since mass beatings given by prison officials are allowed."

Bingo!

"OK, I'll come by in a little while and see what you've got."

To tell the truth, I was getting paranoid, and at that point, I was pretty sure the phone was tapped. Rather than take the chance of speaking on the phone, it was easier to drive over to the school where she was teaching and pick up the letter.

Shirley never ceased to amaze me. There are some people who never seem to lose their cool, except with their own children. She was one of them.

Shirley taught kindergarten and even if ten tiny tots were hanging from her side, she never lost that Gucci-Pucci look. My G-d, she even managed to put her eyelashes on first thing in the morning. She had just dismissed class when I arrived, out of breath but eager. She handed it to me with a very smug look.

"Take a look Arlene, and tell me if this isn't something that will make headlines."

I took a look and she was right.

"Shirley, where in the hell did this letter come from? Cute. It's written to Norman Carlson, the head of the Bureau of Prisons in Washington."

Another Mona Lisa smile from Shirley.

"I told you, it was taken from the Warden's very own private files."

"Amazing, absolutely amazing. This letter is really something else."

"True, true. It reads like something out of a scene from the movie Cool Hand Luke. Incidentally, did you know that the real 'Cool Hand' Luke is now coming into the Wednesday night evenings?"

"You're kidding, the real one? You mean he wasn't just a movie with Paul Newman?"

"Sure, the real one. Only, he looks nothing like Paul Neman and he's a nice old man. The only part that the movie probably got right was how they broke his body. He's really crippled . . ."

"Boy, I would have loved to have met him . . ."

Shirley shoved the letter back under my nose with, "Arlene before you go on another tangent, think! Do you remember when the investigation committee came out with their report? One of the biggest complaints was the over-crowding of the prison."

"Yeah, I remember."

"OK, remember when they transferred a lot of guys out of the Atlanta Prison into a lot of prisons around the country in order to relieve the tension that was caused by the overcrowding?"

"Yeah, I remember that also."

"OK. finish the letter."

"I did. It was really incredible."

"According to what we got here, the ninety-three men who were transferred from the Atlanta Federal prison a month or so ago were taken off the bus en route and had the hell beaten out of them."

The letter was a complaint that had been written by the executive director of the National Prison Project protesting to the head of the Bureau of Prisons about the treatment that these men had received. There was another letter written to the Honorable Robert Kastenmeier, the Chairman of the Subcommittee on Courts, Civil Liberties and the Administration of Justice. Until now, the media didn't have a glimpse of this, and it sure as hell was NEWS! Shirley stood there, zillions of kids running around her in utter chaos. She brushed back a strand of her frosted hair with a manicured hand and said, "Do you realize that it might be dangerous to have this sort of information? Do you also realize that no one knows of the 'happening' between the parties involved?"

I sat there reading the documents when I was finished, went back and read it a second time. Finally, Shirley said, "Well?"

"Da-mn! It's just so hard to believe in this day and time that these things are going on in a Federal Institution. It makes you believe that we're living in 1984."

"If I didn't know the people we're dealing with. If I were just a 'civilian' taxpayer from the outside, I could not believe all that's happening."

"Tell you one thing. It's brightened my day considerably."

It wasn't too long after that things began to pop. Everyone from the media on down to the committees who were 'supposed to be investigating' wanted concrete evidence, instead of allegations. This letter says the men who were beaten are suing the U.S. Federal prison system. If that's true, then that's pretty concrete.

While she turned a record over that she was playing for the kids in her class she nodded her head in agreement.

"Arlene, according to this letter, the inmates were in handcuffs and leg chains when all this happened!"

I stuffed all the papers back into my purse, anxious to show this explosive stuff to someone, but I wasn't even sure who. Someone had to do something about all this, but whom? Shirley returned to her little monsters. I turned and waved good-bye. I felt I was fast losing my own self control. I now had some leverage; I now had proof and credibility. Added to the Anderson column, the evidence was convincing. Now, the press or the political parties had to listen. I knew Congressman Fowler wouldn't listen, so maybe it was time to contact Senator Sam Nunn, the Chairman of the Senate Committee on Organized Crime. He might be more concerned. And then maybe I could get that growing stack of documents off my kitchen table! Once I made the decision, I called the office of Senator Sam Nunn who headed a Senate Committee investigating organized crime. Within a very few hours I received an answer.

"Mrs. Peck?"

"Yes?"

"This is Keith Atkinson. Senator Nunn has requested that I call you concerning some information that you might have on our committee on crime."

Immediately, my first reaction was to take the Fifth, but I didn't know any organized crime news to hide. Instead I told him, "Well, I'll only be too happy to help in any way that I can, except the only organized crime that I know about is on the part of the prison officials. The inmates in my 'Group' are all pussycats."

He surprisingly laughed and said, "I doubt that. But, if you do have any information on misdeeds of the prison officials, we want to know that also."

"OK. When would you like to see me?"

"Well, you realize that I'm calling from Washington, so as soon as we can get on this we'll give you a call back?"

"Great."

Later that afternoon two men presented themselves at my door flashing identification, official government badges. Keith Atkinson turned out to be the Chief Counsel for the Permanent Investigations Committee on Organized Crime. The other gentleman was an investigator for them, although I still didn't have any idea of what they did or what their committee was.

Somehow, I had had visions of Keith Atkinson looking like what a man in his position was supposed to; wrinkled, shoestring tie, thinning hair and chewing on a big cigar. Well, I got the cigar part right, anyway, but the man was gorgeous! That is, if you like the type that looks like a younger, taller Burt Reynolds. The other man could have blended into my mafia group in a minute. He was Italian and all business. Both of them looked like 'big guns' to me. I was hoping that they were the cavalry.

They sat at my littered kitchen table. By this time, I literally had boxes and boxes of files that had been smuggled out to me from the prison. Even the Chief Counsel was impressed and commented, "My G-d, where did ... how did you get all this confidential information?"

"The men raped the warden's files ..."

Occasionally, Keith would light up a tapered cigar, while his Italian compatriot sat puffing one cigarette after another. For two hours, while they poured over material, Keith looked over at his partner; put down the paper he was reading and pointed, "Take a look at this. Do you know who this letter is from? Leo, Leo Guarino from the Herbie Sperling Crowd."

Then he looked over in my direction.

"You certainly have some big name friends here. We've been working on some of these people's cases for a year or more. These were the pussycats that you were talking about, right?"

"The salt of the earth! You would have loved Mike Thevis. He was a regular in the 'Group'."

The craggy investigator lifted one of his ample eyebrows and commented, "Mike Thevis? Not the Mike Thevis who at the moment is number one on the FBI's most wanted list. Not the same man the FBI has been searching nationwide for. He hasn't been seen since he has escaped from jail. Not that Mike Thevis?"

"The very same."

"Mrs. Peck, you wouldn't have heard from him at any time since his escape, would you?"

Thinking that the man was joking, I continued in the same vein when he said, "Oh sure, he's in my basement at the moment. We brought in a printing press for him."

From the look they exchanged, it was obvious that these men were serious!

"Hey, listen, Mr. Investigators, I'm kidding. I'm a big kidder."

Both turned to me and Atkinson said, "Mrs. Peck, if you did happen to hear from him, what would you do?"

Instead of making another bad joke, I looked that gorgeous Burt Reynolds man straight in the eye and said, "Why, I'd call you, of course!"

Before they left, I casually mentioned the two murders that had happened recently that no one had yet reported. I had been waiting until the last minute to drop that bomb, but they already knew about them. They knew, but the papers didn't yet.

Keith told me, "True, this information has not come out to the public, but, we are well aware of it and are very carefully looking into the situation."

Then as a warning he continued, "Frankly, we'd prefer not to read of the cases that are under investigation in Andersons or anyone else's column until we have a chance to look into it."

"OK. I promise not to breathe a word about the little tidbits that are being sent in daily if you really mean to do something about their complaints."

"Of course we mean to do something about these complaints. Why do you think that we've flown all the way down here if not to look into these allegations?"

I had saved the best till last. It was time to get down to the nitty gritty.

"OK, if you're really going to do something, not only about inmate crimes, but the higher ups in the system, what are you planning to do about the really deplorable conditions at the Lewisburg Federal Prison?"

"Aw com'on, I find it hard to believe that you're not aware of the bus load of men who were beaten by guards who met them with riot gear and helmets while under the warden's supervision. These were the men who were being transferred from Atlanta. You might find this letter interesting; it's from the head of the National Prison Project. According to him, there is a hell of a lawsuit pending against the taxpayers as a result of this action."

I passed the letter to the investigator. He read, and then commented;

"Hmmmm, you know, Mr. Fenton, the warden has been involved in a number of investigations related to the use of staff violence and brutality in his past institutional administrations. Pretty heavy charges they're making against the warden."

I took the letter back from him and said, "From the looks of it, it's more than charges. At least they're backing their charges up with law suits from these men. Tell me, do you think that Senator Nunn is going to look into it much. It costs the American taxpayer when something like this happens, right?"

Atkinson hedged, "Well now, Mrs. Peck, right now these are only allegations. As for Mr. Keith, we are calling for a truly impartial investigation. What does seem strange about this whole incident is that the warden of Lewisberg, Mr. Fenton, has been involved in a number of investigations related to the use of staff violence and brutality in his past administrations."

They looked at each other and then back to me, as though to see how much I really knew. Finally Atkinson said, "Yep, we've heard something about that."

"I thought you might have. What I want to know is how a man with a past history such as this is allowed to continue. What I really find ironic is the fact that these particular inmates were being transferred and dispersed throughout the Federal Prison System because of their violent nature."

"Well, it sure looks as though we've got our job cut out for us, doesn't it Mrs. Peck?"

"Yep, it sure does. One more thing, before I drop this and go on to something else, I want you to notice this little memorandum among the papers from Warden Hanbury's files. It's about the working conditions in the prison machine shop."

In the letter, J. T. Kelly, the machinist foreman wrote Warden Handbury about his concern for the elevators, their maintenance and repair.

"I am fearful that there is some safety factor that is unique to elevator mechanics that I am not aware of which could result in damage to personnel or equipment. It is my hope that I will be relieved of this responsibility or trained to do the work."

Kelly further stated, "The electric gates are dangerous, and as an unlicensed electrician I do not feel qualified to repair them. Because we are without the benefit of proper safety equipment in this area, two inmates and myself climbed to the top of the gate to heat, bend, and weld sections together. Thankfully, no one was injured and the gate was returned to service by the end of the day. I am not used to working with one hand and holding on for dear life with the other."

Further, in this lengthy mono, Kelly related how the windows fly open when gusts of cold wind hit them. He spoke of the temporary repairs, "Repairs can only be accomplished by sending an inmate to climb the icy bars. I fear that he will fall or be shot by an officer who was not given advance notice. I feel that this project is outside the scope of the machine shop."

I gave them a few minutes to take all this in and then lashed out, "OK, Mr. Investigators, I know that funds for repairs are supposedly limited, despite the fact that the Bureau of Prison budget is way up in the hundred millions and that it costs almost $25,000 (remember, this was written in 1979) of taxpayer's money each year to keep a man in that hellhole. But, if the building is in such disrepair as the committee states, then how do they justify the plush redecorating and renovation of the Warden's and other staff's offices? Rumor has it that state offices come complete with a fireplace! Maybe these funds had best been spent in the machine shop?"

Atkinson flashed a cute little dimpled smile and said, "Whoa, wait a minute here. I'm not the enemy. Remember, we're the good guys?"

A little contrite, I answered him, "Yeah, I suppose you're right. It's just that I get so da-mn discouraged when I see programs such as our discussion group fight every inch of the way. They're educational, harmless and cost the taxpayers nothing. Volunteers and media and yes, even politicians should be allowed free access into the panel discussions, religious and educational programs."

"Well, maybe now that people are looking into the situation, a little of that can change."

"Mr. Atkinson?"

"Yeah?"

"Reluctantly, I'm starting to realize you can't fight the system."

"Think so?"

"Yeah, but I'll tell you, before I sink into the senility of senior citizenship, I'm sure as hell gonna try."

I reached in my stuffed purse and took out pictures that had been in the morning paper. There was a giant size picture of strippers that the ex-Baptist preacher turned warden had arranged to be brought in to the institution. They were gyrating for the inmates. One picture even showed a stripper with a boa constrictor being wrestled to the ground by an inmate.

The mafia looking investigator lifted his heavy eyebrows, looked at the picture with definite interest and didn't even bother to suppress a smile. I said, "I don't know. I got flack when I attempted to bring in women that were seventy years old and this is what the warden deems proper for the Memorial Day program. I don't know, maybe they don't think educational and religious programs are the proper constructive solutions."

'Burt,' as I was now beginning to think of him, slipped on his coat, winked and said, "You don't really think the situation's that bad, do you?"

"No. Worse. Listen, before you go, don't forget about the guy, Jason Lynott that I mentioned to you who was put in the 'hole' because he wanted to talk to Fowler's committee. He was put there because he had information that was against the system and specifically the staff at the Atlanta penitentiary.

'Burt' slowly took his slim cigar out of his sensuous mouth, squinted his sexy blue eyes, and waved the cigar smoke away absentmindedly. He started to say something, but must have thought better of it. As he snapped shut his briefcase he said, "OK. we're going to do our job. Now you are to do yours. No one, no one, media or anyone is to know we are here, understand?"

I understood that on this day, in June, 1979 when this Permanent Investigation Committee on Organized Crime told me that I wasn't to speak to anyone, that it was important to listen to that and do what they told me. Being a yenta, it was difficult to keep my mouth shut, but I managed. That's why I was astounded to turn on the evening TV news and hear all about their visit. The lead story went something like, "Channel 5 has learned that investigation from a U.S. Senate sub-committee made a secret trip to Atlanta to interview an inmate at the Atlanta Federal Penitentiary. The secret trip was not related to the prison investigation conducted by Congressman Wyche Fowler. Instead, it was authorized by Georgia's Senator Sam Nunn, vice chairman of the Senate sub-committee on Permanent Investigations."

Next, they showed Sam Nunn sitting at his desk in Washington, discussing how his committee had become aware that there was 'organized crime' going on in the prison.

"There have been shocking allegations. My committee has been looking into this scandal and will report to the public shortly with what they find."

Then, they shot back to the news commentator who went on with, "We now know the identity of the inmate interviewed, however, for his security and safety; we cannot divulge the name of this man. Also, the specific areas of investigation are still a closely held secret. Nevertheless, the long-term nature of the senate investigation could indicate the charges that this inmate has made go well beyond the limited scope of the Bureau of Prisons inquiry made earlier this spring."

It had to be Jason that they were speaking about. The really sad thing about this whole 'scoop' was that two months earlier, I had tried to give this inmate's name to Fowler. I had also contacted CBS's Sixty Minutes.

No one seemed to think it was worth even following up and finding out what the guy had to say, until finally Senator Sam Nunn got his committee to look into it.

Shortly after the news, Shirley got in touch with me and said, "What did you think of the evening news?"

"Da-mn! I should have known. You gave the story to CBS, didn't you."

"Well, like they say, all the news that's fit to print . . ."

"You know something Shirley?"

"What?"

"Something tells me that even though I've been instrumental for putting everyone together, I was still not aware of the enormity of the situation that I've ... we've ... gotten ourselves into. What's going to happen now? Are they going to move Jason to another institution?"

"They already did."

"Do you know what he's going to testify on?"

She paused for a couple of seconds as if deciding to trust me with whatever she was thinking. Evidently, since I was in this far, she decided to fill me in on what was taking place.

"Well, what's probably going to happen, is something that should have happened long ago. Those SOB'S working out there are going to finally get what they deserve. Jason is in protective custody and he's talking to the committee about the misappropriations."

"What misappropriations?"

"Would you believe that the warden took vacations in a mafia chieftain's condominium? How about the money that we both know was supposed to be spent on libraries and prison programs that never got used for that."

"Yeah, I saw a copy of Fowlers report that said that there are between 60,000 and 80,000 paperback books in their library that we know do not exist."

"Boobie, before this is over, that's going to be the least of their worries."

"Keep in touch ... Let me know what's happening."

The real follow through on the T.V. broadcast was to see the perspective on the Nunn Committee not being allowed to become a three-ring circus. Things were quiet for a day or so till I received a call from Mitchell at Jack Anderson's office.

"Hey, Arlene? Chuck Colson of Watergate fame is going inside the prison tomorrow for a born-again session. You think you can get the word into that place that he can be trusted? If anyone wants to get any messages out to us they can do so through him."

"Sure, I'll get the message in, but you know, it's funny."

"What's funny?"

"Well, the men have sent out a few letters saying how the new preacher-warden had been having 'pray 'n stays'. Somehow Jack, I don't think the answer to the murders is Bible thumping."

"Let me know what happens, Jack, OK?"

"Sure."

The message must have gotten through. We spoke the following week and Jack casually mentioned, "You know Arlene, you're not too popular with the men as of late."

"Well according to Chuck Colson, he told me that he had conversations at length with some of the men.

Since you were responsible for having me smuggled in and a lot of their privileges were cut down as a result, some of the men aren't too happy and sort of blame you. Colson seemed to think that you used a religious program to smuggle in a reporter."

"You're da-mned right I did! How in the hell else were they going to let anyone from the press in there?"

"Hey listen, I'm not complaining. It got me in there, but I'm just relating to you what Chuck said about what the men felt."

"Terrific, thanks."

Both the evening and morning papers carried an account of Colson's visit and his observations. It was with relief that I noticed that he didn't mention to the press what he had told Jack. Bad publicity, I didn't need. I was worried though. Never did I think that any of the inmates could be unhappy with me. That's why I wrote an open letter to the guys the following week to get my own feedback on what they were feeling about me. If what Colson had to say was true, I was in trouble. In that place it didn't pay to have too many enemies. The letter was written, "To whom it may concern."

Mostly, I was the one concerned.

June, my friend and next door neighbor, was to read the letter to the men and report back to me. June had been a participant in the program for a couple of years. She had an insight into the men and their feelings. Her judgment could be relied on as to what the truth really was.

The men liked June, and it was easy to understand why. Although her kids were grown, she had still kept that youthful look. She must have been gorgeous in her youth. She was still a knockout. I am sure that even in pre-puberty she probably never had a pimple. Her enormous blue eyes revealed a shrewd business woman.

If there were any hard feelings in there due to any of my actions, June would be able to find out, come back and tell it like it was. The meeting night arrived. June stopped by briefly to pick up my 'open letter' and in a cloud of expensive perfume she was off in her long white Cadillac. When the meeting finished, she came directly to my home. I was on pins and needles, tenterhooks, and itching to hear.

Lighting up one of her non-stop, filter cigarettes, squinting her eyes from the smoke June said, "You don't have a thing to worry about."

"You'd level with me . . . You mean that June?"

"I mean it. Nobody's mad at you, at least not the inmates."

"June, start at the beginning and tell me what happened tonight when you went in."

She settled herself in the comfortable chair and began her detailed report of how the men reacted to the letter and Chuck Colson.

"The group was smaller tonight, partly because the guards didn't leave us alone for a minute. Remember, when we used to go, never was there anyone to watch what we did or whom we spoke to? Remember?"

I did and said as much.

"Well, tonight, after the guests were settled, I brought out your letter and read it to the men. There is no truth to the rumor ala Colson that they are upset with you in any way about your prison activities. Quite the contrary."

My face must have reflected like a mirror because June caught my expression and said, "Was it bothering you that much?"

"No, not much. I just feel as though the weight of the world has been lifted off my shoulders. Really, I suppose that it had gotten to me more than I wanted to admit when I had heard of how many 'enemies' I had made in that place because of my activities."

With a carefully manicured hand, June quickly unfolded her notes and settled back to relay her message from the 'inside'.

"Remember 'old Nutsy' from the CIA? He was the sidekick of Bud Collier, wasn't he?"

"Of course, who could forget old Nutsy? The guy who could cure cancer with the healing current that ran through his body when he placed his hand on you?"

June winked in my direction and said, "Now, you know that was the excuse that he used for touching any female who came in."

"Well," June continued, "According to him, Chuck Colson was in there on a 'born again' mission and had a meeting with thirty or forty men while he was there."

"Yeah, that I already know. That's what Anderson's office had called about. You know something?"

"Uh-uh, what?"

"Every time I see one of those 'I found it' bumper stickers, I feel like sticking one over their noses that says we never lost it! For 4,000 years!"

"You got a point there. What you didn't know was that the men he spoke with were a carefully selected group chosen by the warden. Everyone there was there by 'special request' except old 'Nutsy.' The important thing that I found out was what they didn't discuss."

"What was that? I mean, what did they avoid discussing?"

"You. Nowhere in their discussion were you mentioned. Which means that whatever Colson heard about you had to come from other sources. Simple arithmetic gives you three sources; inmates, administration and clergy. Deduct one for the inmates."

When she said that, it sent a warning chill up my neck.

"June, you know what I've been thinking? If the warden or any of the hacks are coming down hard on the men and blaming it on me, that could be dangerous!"

Probably to calm me down, June waved my comment away with, "Aw, listen, you're taking this far more serious than it really is."

"Probably, but I never feared any of the men there. I do fear the staff that they've got running the place."

June rose and headed for the door. She suddenly stopped as though she had another thought.

"Almost forgot. Nutsy said that at one point during the Colson meeting he couldn't stand it any longer. He stood up and said, "Are you aware that these men here are a bunch of yes-men, who have been selected by the warden to tell you about conditions here? If you believe any of this CRAP about how happy we are with this so-called staff here then you're crazier than I thought. After giving Colson an earful of what the prison clergy meant to him, he then stormed out and Colson went back to his 'pray'n stay'."

June's eyes got a gleam in them.

"But I've saved the best for last! When I read your letter of concern, all the men spoke out in unity about how much they think of you and all the positive feelings they have. By the way, none of our boys were 'invited' to see the famous Mr. Colson."

"I wouldn't expect them to be."

"No, but do you know how many of our programs from the Jewish Group that the priest has tried to implement in the Catholic group?"

"I don't know. I heard that he was having men come in like we did and was using the same format that we have."

"Right, but did you also know that he has control of the telephone and he uses that control to get a good attendance for his group."

I didn't understand what she was talking about, so June explained further, "It's really very simple. He wants his group to have a large attendance to look good on his brownie sheet with the Bishop. So, if they don't go into the priest sponsored programs, they don't get to make a phone call to their wife, girlfriend or kid when the time comes. He also scheduled bingo games in competition with the Jewish evenings where the men can win medallions or tennis warm-up suits and things like that."

"Da-mn!"

With that, she was out and I sat there thinking, "Now what?"

What next indeed! Shirley called.

"Turn on the CBS news tonight at six o'clock! I think you might find it pretty interesting."

"Do I ask you questions?"

"Always."

"Never mind, just watch it! You think that you can be the only one with surprises."

We just chatted about things in general, not about the prison situation. But whatever surprises she had was going to have to wait until after the evening news. I watched every night religiously. Six o'clock arrived and there, in living color, on the screen, was Jason. He was in silhouette, but without a doubt, it was him.

The newscaster began with, "An Atlanta attorney has evidently, while masquerading as a high-ranking official of the Justice Department, been involved with a swindle that involved large sums of money."

At this point, almost everything Shirley was doing surprised me. Evidently, she had been meeting with the higher-ups, compiling information on her own. Frankly, it was starting to bug me a little. She was being so secretive. I was dying with curiosity, and every time I'd asked her, "Hey, how did you find out about all this," she'd give me one of her sly laughs and say, "Hmmmm, wouldn't you like to know?" Well, I did want to know. I didn't want her to have the satisfaction of knowing more than I knew. So, for the rest of this particular conversation he introduced the lawyer, Stanley Galkin. He represented a major heroin smuggler who had touched off an FBI investigation that later attracted the attention of the United States Senate's Sub-Committee on Investigation.

They then shot to a picture of the heroin dealer, Leslie 'Ike' Atkinson and continued the narration.

"This is the heroin dealer, former army master sergeant, Leslie 'Ike' Atkinson. In 1975, he and several co-defendants, some of them in the military as well, were convicted on the charges of smuggling Asian heroin into the United States on military aircrafts. A federal judge in Atkinson's native state of North Carolina sentenced him to forty years in prison." That is how Leslie Atkinson arrived at the United States Federal Penitentiary. I didn't know either the lawyer or the inmate, but the story was beginning to interest me.

The commentator continued, "That is how Leslie Atkinson arrived at the Atlanta Prison and met his new lawyer, Stanley Galkin, a man whom Atkinson now believes was responsible in milking him out of more than a hundred thousand dollars in cash."

The screen shot from the picture of the lawyer to, "Good Grief," it was my tall Burt Reynolds look-alike from Sam Nunn's subcommittee, Keith Atkinson! He was closing the door to a car, but the shot didn't show who was sitting in the passenger seat. From the brief shot the next picture to flash on the screen was Jason, except you couldn't see who he was. You only heard the voice. It was a voice that I instantly recognized. Before he spoke however, the newscaster introduced him.

"This man was also an Atlanta inmate. Because he is now being held at a secret location on the authority of the Senate Sub-Committee, we have agreed to maintain his anonymity. This man was already an inmate when Atkinson arrived and they became relatively well-acquainted in part because they shared the same attorney."

Now came the good part. Secret inmate Jason, whose testimony Congressman Fowler had rejected, spoke of how he had used this lawyer, and as a result of this relationship, other inmates approached him and asked if Galkin would represent them in matters they had pending at the time. It was an association that Atkinson would live to regret. By the time he was transferred from Atlanta, the FBI was already deeply involved in an investigation of a hoax in which Atkinson was the unknowing victim. They then left Jason and zeroed in on another newscaster speaking of how the FBI had confirmed its investigation into the lawyer, Galkin, but they would not confirm the identity of his accomplice who masqueraded as the high government official in the hoax.

"Late this spring, the Galkin-Atkinson relationship was one of the items at the Federal Pen which attracted the attention of the Sub-Committee, which was already deep in its investigation of organized crime and narcotics traffic in our Federal Prisons."

Next, came a shot of the two men who had come to my home. With them was Senator Sam Nunn, and they were taking Jason from the federal courthouse to the place that they were keeping him hidden.

Once again, we were back to the shadow figure of Jason speaking of how his lawyer requested large sums of money. In return for this money, Galkin could guarantee the release of Atkinson and other prisoners. The interviewer asked how he could accomplish this. Once again, Jason's testimony was dynamite.

"... from the cooperation of the Deputy Attorney General in Washington, D.C., Mike Egan. The number three man in the Justice Department."

According to the story that unfolded, Galkin led the men to believe that he had friends in the Carter cabinet in his hip pocket. Among them was Mr. Egan, who was completely unaware of the hoax or the lawyer. When the heroin dealer demanded proof before payment of this proposition, Galkin offered to bring into the institution the Assistant Attorney General. Atkinson agreed but had no idea of what the real Michael Egan looked like. According to 'reliable' sources which at this point I was pretty sure meant Jason, Galkin managed to 'con' Atkinson.

"On the morning of the hoax, Galkin arrived first at the prison, telling his client that the associate attorney general was on his way from Washington. A man who is believed to be a close associate of Galkin's arrived shortly after supposedly flying from Washington. He arrived at the prison, flashed a set of credentials and signed himself in as Michael Egan, U.S. Justice Department. The meeting was brief but apparently impressive, as the heroin dealer believed that his freedom was eminent. A down payment of at least one hundred thousand dollars was agreed upon by Atkinson."

All of this was in cash, naturally. The news continued that Galkin expressed the fear later, after it was over, that Atkinson would have him killed. This was not the sort of crowd to make angry. Obviously, Galkin was in agreement with this. According to the news report, the FBI now believed him to be spending his time in Canada, at large.

The whole story was so bizarre. A Pandora's Box had been opened and there was no way to tell where it was going to stop. The Senate Sub-Committee was becoming deeply involved. Jason even said as much during the interview when he told the reporter that he," . . . intended to follow to the end the statements I have made, and, this means to a Senate Committee in Washington."

One of the first questions that should have been asked of this committee was who was paid off at the Atlanta Penitentiary so that this imposter could walk in freely to milk this inmate out of the money. Someone pretty high up on the staff had to know of this, but whom? I knew that it was only because of Jason's real hate for the past and present wardens that he had even agreed at all to speak to this committee. A lot of things were going on that I was no longer aware of. The one thing that I knew though, was that the tip of the iceberg was showing and getting bigger. When I spoke to Shirley earlier, she mentioned that a crew from New York television was heading down the following day to interview her.

Chapter Twenty-Four

PRIME TIME: THE HIT MAN

Weeks passed. It was July already, 1978. I had begun to think that the investigation had come to a halt. Wyche Fowler's committee had fizzled and ended up a fiasco. Congressman Sam Nunn seemed to become less than intense in his investigation after that first flurry of excitement. It had been at my request that the 'secret inmate' had been picked up and spirited away into protective custody. At least that's what it appeared. In reality, he and the Committee on Organized Crime Investigation were preparing for the biggest senate hearings since the Joseph Valachi days of 1969. Valachi's hearings focused on the mafia, but this investigation would center on alleged criminal activities inside the Atlanta Prison, activities of both inmates and authorities.

Senator Nunn arrived looking cool and crisp in a summer suit. I waited until all his election year conversation was over before I slid a note over to him that suggested he not leave before we had a chance to speak.

ARLENE WITH SENATOR SAM NUNN 1978

Senator Nunn had a youthful, bland face. He was quite bookish and had the appearance of a well dressed CPA. He pushed his glasses up on his nose and added, "Wait until everyone leaves and we'll be able to talk more freely."

It seemed as though everyone had a personal question to ask him, but occasionally, I would receive a look of reassurance. Finally, my turn arrived.

"Senator Nunn, I don't know if you remember me but . . ."

Sharp politician that he was, he cut in with, "Of course I'm aware of who you are. My investigators on the senate sub-committee reported back to me that you were quite helpful in the investigation."

"Yes, well, when I put you in contact with some inmates out at the pen, I had no idea how far-reaching it was going to be."

"Sure, well, things are really beginning to pick up. Each day, new information is coming out. You been in close contact with Keith Atkinson in Washington, haven't you?"

With the fond memories I had of the Burt Reynolds look-alike I almost said, "Not as close as I'd like."

Instead I chimed in with, "Uh-huh, but not since he and that other gentlemen you sent walked out with half my papers. You're aware of my program aren't you and how I was prevented from continuing with it?"

His eyes narrowed just a tad as though he was trying to remember exactly what the circumstances surrounding it were. Within a second or two he brightened and said, "Wasn't it when you brought Julian Bond out?"

"Yes, but that wasn't the only reason. What caused my sudden disappearance was the fact that the men coming into the group were too articulate. It was dangerous for the powers that be who run that place, to have the unity that the men were beginning to have."

Nunn added, "You mean divided they fall?"

"Exactly, and in my case I happened to see too much corruption concerning staff."

Nunn nodded his head in agreement when I continued, "You know the things I'm talking about; guards bringing in drugs, favors accepted by the wardens and staff as to how certain budgets were spent."

I drifted off and he picked up with, "Yeah, well, we're getting a lot of people coming forward now."

"I know. A few of them from the inside were in the Group and wanted to speak to the committee. Have they helped any, Senator Nunn?"

The first smile came on his face, "Oh, they have, they have."

He seemed to be interested in what I was saying, but I knew that I had to wrap it up shortly. There was an aide standing nearby who kept looking at his watch. Finally, he tugged at Nunn's sleeve and said, "Senator, we have to leave to make that appointment."

It was probably a ploy to keep him moving, but Nunn sounded sincere when he told me, "Listen, we've got a lot of things happening in the next few weeks, things I'm not at liberty to speak about now. Investigations will be starting that I think will clear up a lot that's been going on."

"Senator, nothing could make me or the men inside happier. But, from the reports they've been able to send out to me, they're afraid that these hearings will take on the circus quality of the Valachi hearings."

Nunn assured me, "Well, that's something we want to avoid. My staff has been working 24 hours a day with this thing. In the next couple of weeks we'll be starting televised hearings. There, the men will know we're serious."

It would be nice if he was as well meaning as he appeared. Whatever was to happen, there were indications that this whole damn case was about to burst open.

The same night's evening news confirmed the sensational aspects of Nunn's opening investigations. My one 'secret inmate' had now become plural. This time the man speaking to the committee in silhouette was no longer Jason, but Gary Bowdach.

Gary Bowdach hadn't been a member of the 'Group' for quite awhile. Actually it was since the time he turned state's evidence and began to testify against his fellow inmates that he told some very hairy things.

Gary first came into our discussion group sometime during the winter of 1976. He was tall, muscularly built and attractive in a 'street' way. The typical late 1950's guy hanging around the corner candy store in New York, wearing a black t-shirt with his Camels pack rolled in his sleeve.

Usually he had a cigarette dangling out of his mouth. He'd arrive, usually in white orderly clothes and sit in his chair leaning against the wall, biceps bulging and feet hooked under the legs of the chair. His personality was outgoing and forceful, yet he had never impressed me as being anything but a small-time hood. Whatever his crime, he was vague about the details. Later he was to become quite descriptive in his various specialties when he spoke to Nunn's committee. The last thing I pictured him to be was a mafia hit-man. Once he came to me, "Hey, Arlene, I got a problem I need yo' help with."

Frankly, understanding him in that excessive New York accent was a problem.

"I got a kid being Bar Mitzvah, and they won't let me visit him for the Bar Mitzvah. Do you think you can help me out?"

"Gary, did it ever occur to you that this is a maximum security prison and house calls are pretty much ruled out?"

"Yeah, but I also know that you arranged a day out program and until then I ain't never heard about visits around the city by the inmates either."

"Gary, don't count on me this time. It can't be done."

A few weeks later he waved me over. He was proudly holding in his hand a photo album.

"Hey babe, come here. Take a look at my kid! His Bar Mitzvah party! Wadda ya think? Some good looking kid, huh?"

He was pointing out his family, "That's the wife, and the aunt and cousin . . ."

There was obvious pride in his voice as he showed around the pictures that had been taken. He spoke often about his family, and probably because of the sentiment in my distorted thinking, he became one of the 'good guys'.

Apparently, the inmates and the prison officials felt differently. It was during the rash of murders in the spring of 1978 that Bowdach suddenly disappeared. Later it was to come out that Gary was to have acted as the middleman for the 1977 murder of Vincent G. Papa. Papa, the man I mentioned earlier, was suspected of masterminding the theft of 398 pounds of heroin and cocaine from the property clerk's office at the New York Police Department, including 57 pounds of heroin left over from the famous 'French Connection' case. He was murdered on July 25, 1977.

The FBI listed the filing of Papa as unsolved, but Papa had made dangerous enemies in the mafia while in prison. It was widely believed that he had turned informant. Inmates, on occasion had commented to me, "Hey listen, Papa set himself up for what took place. He talked to the feds and then came back and said, 'Hey, nothing' happened to me, nothin's gonna happen either.' The guy talked so much in the joint that someone finally had to show him. He didn't get away with it."

It seemed logical when I heard that. Whatever the reason, he was killed as he was returning from the jogging session. Whoever did the actual murder repeatedly stabbed Papa with a prison-made knife in a dark corridor of the penitentiary.

Surprise! Surprise! A prison guard was implicated for smuggling $2,500 to arrange a 'subcontract' for the murder. This same guard suspected of smuggling the money in was caught red-handed a few weeks later bringing liquor into the cellblocks for inmates. Amazingly enough, or, maybe not so amazingly, the guard was merely asked to resign and not put behind bars himself.

Bowdach let the committee in on the 'system:'"Senators, believe me when I tell ya, for certain inmates, the penitentiary is a 'country club'. Anything you want can be arranged. From murder to morphine, all you have to do is put your order in. I've seen inmates drunk and falling, so messed up on narcotics they couldn't walk. You had all the dope you wanted, you could drink whiskey. About the only thing you missed was women."

"Where did you get your steaks? You mean you ate steaks? Where, in your cell?"

"They brought them in from the kitchen. Anything you wanted, you just ordered. You put your order in."

"Put your order in to who?"

"Whoever was running the sandwiches."

"So they had just sort of a food operation going, too?"

"A catering service."

Later in testimony to the committee, inmates accused the kitchen officer, John Carroll of delivering heroin for one of the 'kingpin' drug operations. He also rated the Atlanta Penitentiary as the number one institution in the country in drug and weapons availability. It was not surprising that Warden Handbury petulantly commented to a reporter, "The Senate investigators have not shared their information with me about the happenings in the prison, and I think this has been a little unfair. Everybody in the bureau has been in the dark. I've made half a dozen telephone calls trying to find out information about the investigation."

My G-d! The man was upset because they weren't letting him know what was going on. Who in the hell does this warden think they were investigating? Surely there had to be somebody else besides him, right?

He also seemed not to be worried about any actions being taken against him, even though he was directly responsible for his staff within the prison. He in fact, stated to the press, "I work for the federal system and I have been transferred many times in my career. I seriously doubt if I would be replaced as a result of the continuing murder spree."

However, back in August of 1977, I was completely unaware of what was happening outside of our Temple Yakkov. I thought that Gary had merely been transferred. Shortly after Bowdach's departure, Herbie Sperling from the 'Pleasant and French Connection' was also whisked away. At first, I didn't see the tie-up until word filtered back that Herbie, who had also been one of the heaviest drug businesses in the Federal food and Drug administration, was somehow involved in Papa's killing.

Yet, during those weeks, the air in the meeting room seemed to be charged with electricity that was difficult to put into words. The men seemed to be pumping me for information as to where Herbie and Gary had been taken. Immediately after his departure, I received a frantic call from Herbie's mother, long distance, from Chicago.

"Is this Arlene? The head of the Jewish Group? The one that my boy Herbie attends while he's in Atlanta?".

"Yes, I am."

"Well, darling, this is Herbie's mother and we are absolutely frantic! No one seems to know why he has been put in solitary. Even his lawyers have been kept away from him. Will you be a darling and see what you can do to find out where he is? I'll call you tomorrow."

I tried to find out what I could, but no one was able to help me locate the whereabouts of Herbie. The guards seemed evasive and the inmates weren't talking. I never connected the transfer of Herbie with the disappearance of Gary Bowdach until much later, after the 1978 luncheon where Nunn mentioned that the upcoming news might have a few surprises.

Within a very short time of the Herbie Sperling transfer, word was relayed to me from several sources that Gary Bowdach was a rat. At almost every meeting someone would saunter over and casually ask about Bowdach.

"Say, what do you hear about Gary? Does he ever get in touch with you and tell you where he is?

It's like he just disappeared off the face of the earth."

I thought the continued interest strange, till I eventually learned the curiosity of the other men wasn't due to concern for Gary's health. Because instead, they were hoping to discontinue any future health that he might have. News of a contract on Gary first came to my attention when a friend of Herbie's sat next to me one night. I knew something was cooking. I asked, "OK, friend, what's been going on these past few weeks? Something's strange, and I know it's got something to do with Herbie Sperling and the disappearance of Gary Bowdach. Am I right?"

Herbie's buddy ran his hand through his full head of white hair and gave me one of his looks that I never knew were favorable or not.

"Yeah, well, somehow the hacks think that Herbie had something to do with some crazy things. Herbie's been sent away."

"And Gary?"

"Well, word is out that Bowdach is spilling his guts out testifying about anybody that he ever knew, including Herbie."

This was a subject that I wasn't sure I wanted to pursue. Herbie was not the kind of man that I wanted to have angry. There were times I really could have gotten myself in over my head. I really didn't want to know too much. The investigation was going at a fast clip now. Things were in the hands of Senator Nunn and his investigators. They still had most of my papers. I was in doubt as to whether I would be called to testify or not. I was hoping to go before this committee because I did feel there were things that should be told. I had sent the message to Nunn via Atkinson that I was available.

I really didn't want to push the topic of Herbie Sperline and Gary Bowdach. Visions of the violence Herbie was capable of appeared before me. It was definitely better to keep Herbie happy. But it appeared that Bowdach had made a lot of people unhappy, especially Herbie.

So much so, that a contract was out for a hit on the hit man . . . for a quarter of a million dollars.

When my phone rang in February of '78, I wasn't aware of all this.

"Hi, Arlene, how ya doin? It's me."

"Me? Me, who?"

"Me, Gary, Gary Bowdach."

"Gary, where've you been? You disappeared so suddenly?"

"Yeah well, things came up that made it sort of imperative that I leave suddenly. Didn't you hear that there was a price on my head for the testifying that I've been doing?"

I hadn't actually heard, but all at once it made sense. I didn't want to know where he was, but he let me know he was in a state prison in Georgia.

"Gary, what's going to happen to you now that you are talking about people that you could end up dead talking about?"

"Wadda ya mean? There's been a lot of talking about me among the guys?"

"Of course, there's been a lot of talking. They think you're a rat!"

"Humph ... Who am I gonna protect, the scum of the earth. I saw my chance and took it. What? I gotta sit here for more years than I can even think about to protect some lowlifes that don't even deserve to live."

"Be that as it may Gary, but you realize that it could really be dangerous to your health when you start speaking about some of the 'Atlanta Arms' residents."

He didn't sound too worried and laughed, "Well, frankly, the security is so tight on me that just to go to the bathroom I got three federal agents walking with me to hold my hand."

Then he nonchalantly said that our phone call was probably tapped.

"Yeah, well they can go looking for me all they want, they ain't gonna find me. Let me tell you, I'm not gonna take a bum rap for someone that don't deserve anything. And, what you're going to be reading in the papers in the next few weeks is only the beginning. When my story comes to trial, it's going to top the Valachi Papers."

Somehow his words had a ring of truth in them, but again, it really wasn't a subject I wanted to delve into. Too many people were making me their best friend and telling me all. I wasn't sure it was very safe at this point to even know the little bit that I did.

I kidded him back, "Gary, I never knew that you were a celebrity. Maybe I'll save those cards and letters you sent me. Think they might become famous?"

"You never can tell, doll, but you can be sure before this year is up, when shit hits the fan, that you'll be hearing about me."

"Maybe one day, in that case, when I write the great American novel, I'll devote a chapter to you."

"Believe it when I tell you I got something comin'. It's not going to be in any way small."

He was right. Sometime, around the first of August, 1978, I turned on the national news and there he was. He was speaking to Senator Nunn's organized Crime Committee. He had mentioned to me about getting a new face and identity. That must have been the reason that his back was to the camera. He spoke in a flat voice devoid of emotion, but I would have recognized that heavy New York accent anywhere.

"Yeah, I set fire to three buildings. Arson for profit is about the easiest thing to get away with next to homicide."

One of the investigators leaned forward, savoring his minutes on prime time television and tapped his pencil nervously on the desk.

"Mr. Bowdach, in addition to your arson for profit business, would you say the mob-linked torch jobs that you did were a lucrative line of work and what percentage of the insurance profits did you receive?"

"Ten Percent. However, that wasn't really a lot. But, professionals can easily make one million dollars a year by taking only ten percent of the insurance payments and staying busy."

The same investigator pursued Bowdach further while seeming strained to keep his voice steady.

"Mr. Bowdach, did you take those arson requests for any one person?"

Once again, without emotion, Gary replied, "One job we did was for Santo Trafficante."

Trafficante was the head of the mob's activities in Tampa. Trafficante was also the prime suspect of the House Assassinations Committee into the deaths of John F. Kennedy and Martin Luther King Jr. When the committee issued its 686 page final report, the organized crime figures listed were Carlos Marcello and Santos Trafficante as 'the most likely family bosses of organized crime to have participated in such a unilateral assassination.' Naturally, both these men denied any knowledge or connection with Kennedy's murder. It was spooky, that a man like Gary Bowdach, who I had considered a lightweight punk, was involved with the 'biggies' in the world of organized crime. With my insight into people, I would have probably picked Charles Manson as a baby sitter.

Gary's testimony continued, "We had a meeting between my partner and Trafficante. It was gonna be a torch job that was gonna be on the day of the Super Bowl. The owner, a friend of Trafficantes, was gonna be there that day so he'd have an alibi."

"What kind of alibi did you have in mind."

Gary hunched down in his seat, still only his back and formidable shoulders were shown for the millions of television viewers who were watching with rapt attention at this first hand glimpse of murder and arson for pay.

"We, my partners and me, drove to Tampa. There, we were given a key to the warehouse, and told where the flammable fluid was waiting for us in the building."

Nunn broke in, "Did you or the others, Mr. Bowdach, take any steps to draw the suspicion from the owner?"

"Oh, yeah, sure. Our instructions were to make it appear that the burning was done by people who would not want the business in the neighborhood. We wanted to make it look like neighborhood blacks burned the building."

To emphasize the point of the high level mafia connections that were involved, Nunn repeated, "Once again Mr. Bowdach, who ordered this particular arson?"

Slowly, Gary repeated, "Trafficante, Santo Trafficante," "He's the head of the mob in the Tampa area, and close to the family of the Massachusetts Don, Sam Cafari. To tell you the truth, although arson wasn't my specialty, I did OK. That month, my partner Manarite and I burned down four buildings."

When Gary had been in the meeting room, many times it seemed as though the men paid little or no attention to him. Well, they certainly noticed him now. Everyone from the Justice Department to the inmates sat in rapt attention while Gary spoke. The evening papers were full of Gary and his 'hit man' confessions. In the articles, an agent of the FBI, David Jillison, described Gary as being the most dangerous individual that he had ever encountered. The agent had stated to the press that under a grant of immunity, Bowdach was able to get a reduction on his current fifteen-year sentence. He was in for usury, lending money at illegal rates of interest. Later he was to run into trouble with the federal witness protection program, but that was later. Now he was enjoying the limelight. According to Agent Jillison, Gary had a most impressive record.

"The FBI located seventy-eight of Bowdach's loan customers. All but five refused to testify against him saying they'd rather be jailed for perjury than 'dead'."

One of the committee asked Gary, "How did you enforce your own rules for payment?"

Gary made a non-judgmental shrug, "Well, actually I had a variety of ways. Usually my customers were used car dealers who were hard pressed for cash. All it usually took were baseball bats to make them pay their weekly payments. Sometimes I had to resort to knives or guns."

Each night's news became an adventure to watch. I hadn't taken Gary seriously when he called a couple of months earlier and told me to, "Watch the papers." Go figure.

Sam Nunn, was basking in the publicity. Nunn then asked Gary what happened to his loan shark partner, Louis Cicchini, who disappeared in 1970.

Bowdach said, "He's dead."

"How did he die?" Senator Nunn asked.

"He was killed."

"Who killed him?"

"I did." Bowdach said casually

He continued his story as if he were ordering breakfast:

"I got distrustful of my partner and had pretty good reason to believe that he was talking to the cops. I felt that if I didn't take the appropriate action, instead of Mr. Cicchini being dead, I would be."

Bowdach said he had taken Cicchini into partnership over the objections of his boss, Brooklyn loan shark Julie W. Sirowitz. He said Sirowitz was a partner of Fromk Mari, whom he identified as a mafia member of the Bonnano family in New York.

The Senators exchanged a look and then Nunn continued, "How exactly did this murder take place?"

"Well, I went to meet him with four of my friends at Sonny Brock Motors."

"That was a used-car business in Miami that I used as a loan-shark front."

"And?"

"Well, when he came forward to shake hands, one of the guys hit him with a piece of rolled-bar steel pipe."

"And, did that kill him?"

"Naw, he went down, but he was still conscious."

"What happened then?"

"We dragged him in the office where one of the other guys shot him with a spear gun."

"Did that kill him?"

With this Gary laughed and said, "Damn SOB wouldn't die. It deflected off his rib and I finally had to shoot him with a .38 revolver. The first shot penetrated his arm and backed him up,"

Bowdach took time out for a sip of water.

"Then I shot him one more time. Got blood all over his Ban-lon shirt. I watched it spread in the area of his heart."

Anxiously the Senator urged him on.

"What happened then? What did you do then?"

"Whadda ya think? We hauled him off in a blanket and buried him with 100 pounds of quicklime in a shallow grave near Interstate 95."

This man could off-handedly describe such a killing and blithely mention that he buried his partner in a grave with 'quicklime' to speed the decomposition of the body. I sat there watching the back of his head, awed and frightened.

No one had ever been charged in the Cicchini murder ...

"Mr. Manarite and I were very close because of the fact that we did a murder together and did an attempted murder together. We automatically performed what we call a marriage between two people."

Most of his associates were famous underworld characters whose names didn't mean anything to me until Gary described the attempted murder of Louis bash, who had fortunately or unfortunately escaped. That had made me sit up! I couldn't believe it! Louie had called me only the day before the newscast. Herbie was not the only one that Gary spoke about in colorful terms. He seemed determined to involve everybody! He spoke of purchasing guns from the police chief of Opatocka, John Ripa, who had been since fired from his post. He spoke of how criminals used the freedom of information act to learn what the federal government knows about their activities and to figure out whether informers are being used. Then Bowdach went after the 'biggies'. He told of delivering an envelope full of money, "It was for Meyer," Bowdach said.

In a brilliant piece of deduction, Sam Nunn asked, "Has the name Lansky ever been mentioned?"

Almost in exasperation, Bowdach sighed, "Senator, in the circles I traveled in, you didn't have to. When you talk about the Pope, you don't mention Pope who."

All in all, Gary named more than 30 underworld figures with whom he had worked or came into close contact. Besides his testimony being colorful, he was also very graphic in his descriptions. The man had a definite eye for detail. His 'special memory' eventually led to the indictment of Herbie for the murder of Vincent Papa, his past partner in the 'French Connection.'

During the middle of September 1978, Gary decided to no longer cooperate with the Senate Sub-Committee and with good reason.

Actually, he had better than good reason. A hit contract was out on him. But that wasn't what made him decide to tell the committee to piss off.

The realization hit him that once he had finished being the 'star witness' for the Senate Committee hearings, he would be released from its protection and once again put in the custody of the U.S. Bureau of Prisons, the incompetent Bureau of Prisons. Far too often in cases such as this, the officials of our Federal Prisons somehow manage to 'lose' an inmate until he turns up dead. Then they issue a statement that it was a 'bureaucratic error.' It was not an issue whether these men deserved to live or not, they're despicable beyond belief. However, they're entitled to protection by law, and if the law is wrong, then change it. You can't let these men die as a result of an 'unfortunate bureaucratic error.' Within a very short time, he discovered that one of his fellow inmates was the son of famous mobster Joseph Bannano, whom he had testified against.

It took four days of complaints to Washington to finally get him transferred to another facility. It's a wonder that he managed to stay alive for those four days. The prison officials as usual, marked it off as a bureaucratic error. According to Gary, "I started getting a lot of stares and dirty looks from some of Bonnano's friends. Ya didn't have to be a genius to know the implications of their hostility. I wanted to go off somewhere in the boondocks, NOW!"

Gary is suing the government for $6,037. This was the amount he claims that his wife, Kathaleen, spent during the 1958 period when she was trying to avoid discovery by the Herbie Sperling organization. His wife was told by U.S. Assistant Attorney, James Fagan that she should leave Atlanta because her life was in danger. Bowdach asked the court, "For G-ds sake, don't release the lawsuit to the public record, it would tell the places where my wife stayed during the time she was hiding."

As a result of this request, no public record of the suit exists in the U.S. District Court.

Even though Nunn commented to the press, "I think it's incredible that they did not check out the prisoners in that institution. I wrote Attorney General Griffin Bell asking him to personally take an interest in Bowdach's case due to his extensive cooperation with us."

So much for the Bureau of Prisons efficiency. They knew that Gary would need extra protection. It's no wonder that when Bowdach refused to testify further to Nunn's committee he felt that he had been set up and said, "I told them to 'kiss off'. Why should I expose myself further? My mother would get very upset if I was to get myself killed."

And, for the first time there was a quiver in his voice when he said, "I hope they don't hit me in the face; I'm so pretty, I have my family to consider. I have my children to get through college. If I do nothing else in life I'm going to send my kids to college."

After that, he said, his voice trailing off, "Well . . . I'm ready."

During this time, I spoke to the reporter, John Turner, to whom Gary had called and relayed his story. Turner said Gary called him from his undisclosed institution and spoke nervously to him about the real possibility of his days being numbered. Gary was quite vocal in his criticism of the witness-protection program that was supposed to guard him.

Not long after Gary made this statement another murder occurred at the Atlanta Penitentiary. The front page story concerning the latest killing on April 29th, 1979 described the Bowdach statements, the murder of Papa and the indictment of Herbie for the killing. He was accused of paying three other inmates $2,000 for the killing. Bowdach allegedly arranged the pay-off.

The day this news made the papers, I sent my weekly letter into the 'Group.' Everybody at that time was very busy not knowing anything about

Gary, but we all did. At the bottom, I put a postscript kiddingly, "Tell me guys; can I believe anything that I read in those lying Atlanta newspapers?"

I was told that a few looked innocently at the ceiling and others chuckled and said, "I wonder what she's talking about."

Only the Shadow knew.

Louis bash had been released from Atlanta sometime in 1976, but he had been a delightful member of the 'Group' in the early days. His age was somewhere around sixty-five and he was exceedingly hard of hearing. He was also very vain about both. Of average height, with graying hair and a moustache, he always took pains to dress neatly in the prison khaki uniform that many of the men wore. I noticed that if there was a pretty girl in attendance for the evening, he seemed to make an extra effort to hold his stomach in and sit up a little straighter. Usually, Louis always managed to be a few minutes late, so he could create a little confusion finding his proper chair. Because of his deafness, he usually cupped his hand over his ear and spoke louder than normal. Personally, I found him delightful and cheerful. Much later, when we had the day-out program, three minimum-custody men were to be allowed out for the day. I asked if Louis could go. The request was denied, and for the first time I was made aware that Louie was in prison under the heading of 'organized crime.' I could easier see him feeding the pigeons in the park than being a part of any violent actions.

Several months after our first meeting, I noticed that he was less cheerful than usual. Usually his smile was infectious. When he appeared the same the following week, I questioned where his previous good humor had gone. The answer was simple.

"Well, Arlene, you know I got a son. A boy, Kenny."

I nodded my head and he continued, "He's really a good kid, lives in Miami, and drives a cab."

He paused, for me to take this in, and then continued, "Well, he used to come see me, but I don't know, he doesn't seem to wanna anymore. I think he's kinda embarrassed to come out here, ya know?"

With that, he gave a shrug of his shoulders and dejectedly walked over to the corner of the room and sat down quietly. His spirits seemed to be down in the depths. He was still on my thoughts when I returned home and tracked down the kid's number. Louis also had a married daughter whom he had mentioned, and I was able to get Kenny's number through her. The nerve of that kid not wanting to see his father. Finally the kid came on the phone.

"Kenny?"

"Yeah?"

"This is Mrs. Peck. I have just left your father."

"Oh yeah, he mentioned ya. Something about a program that he goes to."

"Good, I'm glad that you know who I am, especially since you seem to have forgotten that you have a father."

"When's the last time that you've written, or better yet, gone to see your father?" (Silence) "The man is over sixty and not in the best of health. Don't you think that it would behoove you to take a little time out from what I'm sure must be a busy schedule and try and fit a visit to your dad in?"

The kid mumbled something about trying to get down the next week and hung up the phone as soon as he possibly could. I forgot about the call and was surprised a few days later when the phone rang and it was Kenneth. I was delighted to see that my prodding at him had worked. I knew that Louie would soon be back to his old self.

Actually, I had misunderstood the reasons that were behind Kenny's infrequent visits to Atlanta. It was when he spent a Friday night at our home that the real reasons behind his apparent lack of concern began to surface. Louie's son had a mental block about his father's being in prison.

He hated the visits to the Atlanta Arms. However, once Kenny had friends and a place to visit in a real home when he came to the penitentiary, then the visits to his father became a frequent thing.

Louie gave me credit for bringing this change about and he never forgot it. After he got out, like clockwork, I would hear from Louie every few months. He would let me know how well he was doing and what a swinger with the 'girlies' he was. Occasionally, he'd send a card, covered with near naked bathing beauties from someplace like Fort Lauderdale, and scrawled on the back would be a cheerful message that he wanted the men in the prison group to know that usually he was a 'dirty old man' down where the girls were.

Shortly after the news headlined the story of Gary Bowdach, Louie called, "Hello, Arlene, this is Louie, Louie Nash, How ya' doin?"

"Fine Louie, I'm fine. More important, how have you been? I read about you in the papers."

"Oh yeah? Did you see me when I went on television to show what a no good, lying louse that Bowdach is?"

"I haven't, but, I have a feeling that you'll tell me about it."

"Ya shudda seen me! That snake Bowdach went on testifying and making up all kinds of lies. I finally couldn't stand it no more, so I called up channel 10 in Florida and told them I'd give them a story to let them know what Bowdach was really like."

"And, did you?"

"Oh yeah, I let em know what a doper, lying, faggot, which I caught in an unnatural act with a black man and an ex-used car salesman he was."

I almost laughed. He was so serious in what he was saying, but he was speaking with such enthusiasm that it sounded comical. This is until I remembered what a really dangerous person he was speaking about. I should have bit my tongue.

"Louie, it sounds like you were terrific. Do you think that Gary had a chance to see you on television? Maybe you might tell Nunn's committee the same things."

"Yeah, I'd tell them what a lying scum he was, but all these lying politicians aren't interested in the problems and issues. All they care about is their personal welfare. Rippin' off the country, that's all they're doing."

It was obvious to me that the main reason Louie had made this particular call was to see if the men in the Atlanta Prison had seen him. And, maybe, to find out what they thought about the accusation that Gary had made about Louie being an informer. We ended the conversation with Louie relishing his victory over Gary.

"Gary knows what a fool I made outta him. He's scared of me because he doesn't know what hit him. They ain't gonna believe him no more cause I made such a burn outta him."

"Louie?"

"Yeah."

"Can't they stop Gary from talking?"

"The committee is crazy if they use him, he's already been discredited as a liar. A lying no good faggot!"

"That doesn't matter with the government."

"The man was a used car salesman, I tell you. When he met Louie Chicchini, he was a car salesman for G-ds sake."

"Yeah?"

"Those people that he mentioned wouldn't bother with him, he was a nothing. He is a nothing."

"O.K. Louie, but why did he pick on Herbie?"

"Cause Herbie gave him a nice way out. Herbie gave him confidence. When Papa got himself whacked out, Gary knew there was friction and G-d knows what else he knows. The trouble with some of these guys is that they bring their troubles on themselves. They do too much talking, and guys like Bowdach sit around listening, waiting to use it against them. Barracudas, that's what they are. Gary Bowdach never had any motive in his life. He shot one of the witnesses on his case, shot him six times. Ya didn't hear nothin about that, did ya?"

"Not that I remember."

"And, I wanna tell ya somethin else."

"What's that Louie?"

"Foist of all, there outta be a law against a man with a record, a man whose a bum in the foist place, being used against a man that ain't got no record."

"Who didn't have a record?"

"Bowdach testified against a judge, didn't he?"

I wanted to get back to the question I knew Louie could answer.

"Louie, isn't it true that if the people Gary is talking about catch him, he's dead?"

"Naw, nobody's gonna be lookin' for him."

"I find that pretty hard to believe."

"He's a has been. He took knowledgeable things and acquainted himself with them. Then he related himself to them. That's all that happened. He was always a frustrated tough guy. He always wanted to be a tough guy and he couldn't get no recognition. You know those lies he told about me being an informer?"

"Uh huh."

"Well, I wouldn't let him get away with that. I went right to the top and said, 'Put up or shut up!' So they took him right outta the scene and put him back in the can."

"Louie, what kinda man was Papa?"

"He was OK. He didn't try and make nothing' worse den anybody else. They had a loop around him cause when he was a Springfield..."

"Springfield?"

"Yeah, Springfield Penitentiary, he didn't want no 'protection' that they wanted to give him. He said 'I don't want no protection cause I'm no rat'. They sent him from Atlanta to Springfield and he hollered so loud that he didn't need no protection that they just sent him back."

"And he got killed."

The least of Bowdach's problems at the moment were Louie's impressions or threats to him. After the talking Gary had been doing, he'd be lucky to alive, because no matter where this guy went in the world, it wouldn't be far enough.

Louie's call wasn't the last one that I was to receive that evening. No sooner had I hung up the telephone than it rang again.

"Hello, Arlene, this is Keith Atkinson."

Oh G-d, I thought, my reason for fantasying infidelity. However, unaware of my churning emotions at the moment he continued with, "Word has come to me that you had some information for the committee."

I knew that he was referring to the allegations that had been made in reference to misappropriations of government funds. One of the inmates had recently sent me a list of invoices that I knew the committee wanted. One of the items on this list indicated that Warden Handbury spent two thousand for drapes for his office.

"Well Keith, I've been getting all sorts of interesting mail. There have been some very interesting articles in the press as of late about your investigation. When are you coming back down here to interview me in person again, you cute Burt Reynolds look alike you?"

With that, he gave a sexy little chuckle and said, "As a matter of fact, I'm in Atlanta right now."

"Oh? Are you here to see Gary or Jason?"

Keith hedged, "Well, that's not really pertinent to my question for you."

"Oh? And what's that?"

"Usually, you're a fountain of trivia, what kind of tidbits do you want to send me back to Washington with?"

"Keith?"

"Mm?"

"I'm glad you mentioned that. How about the list of firearms purchased in preparation for a riot? Right, OK, that's interesting."

"Would you like to hear about the x-ray machine that is being installed? The one the men will have to walk through several times a day."

"What about it?"

"Well, the men are worried that at the very least they'll come out of there sterile or possibly dying with cancer."

"OK, we'll look into it."

Last, a question that had come up of late.

"Keith? How are you at checking out rumors?"

Again, that cute little chuckle.

"We do that also."

"O.K., Why don't you check and see if you can find out any info about the priest out there being a member of G.A."

"What's G.A.?"

"G.A. is otherwise known as 'Gamblers Anonymous'."

I told him that I had been fed the story that the priest was a heavy gambler and took many trips to Vegas to support his habit.

"Keith, how is this guy able to finance the junkets that he supposedly takes and the habit that he is supposed to be supporting on the salary that a prison priest makes? Do you think that he might be letting some of the inmates help him in return for any favors that he might give?"

Keith seemed to think about that for a few seconds and finally said, "I don't know, but you might have hit bingo with that. Let's look into it. Thanks for the tip."

Chapter Twenty-Five

THE FRENCH CONNECTION RETURNS

What had been accomplished by the investigation? According to the men, they felt that the end result would be more restrictions, more control over them and fewer privileges. The result of the investigation in the case of the Atlanta prison was the use of and sometimes abuse of the unlimited use of funding the inmates had. In July of 1979, the cost of living shot up for the inmates inside the Atlanta Penitentiary as federal authorities ended the era of unlimited free postage. Gone were the days when the prison could depend upon Uncle Sam's generosity and paid for by your tax dollars. The Federal prison postage bill amounted to more than 1 million dollars. Which, in 1976 was an enormous amount of money. Also, prisoners were disappointed that their letters were stopped. Some were even opened for inspection when they were deemed necessary, according to Warden Handbury. The mailroom did the sealing. The sealing was done by machine, he said. Under the old system, the unlimited letters were not opened. Handbury said that sections were read if the prisoner was beginning to be a problem. One of the more outspoken of what he felt injustices, caused by the federal government and the Atlanta penal system, was Leo Guarino who had been arrested with Herbie Sperling. Towards the end of April, 1979, he was released and called me a few hours before he was to fly home to New York. I invited him to come over and spend a few hours filling me in on what life was like in the Big A during those months of 1979.

He arrived looking like a banker and I couldn't help but exclaim, "Leo! You look terrific!"

"Yeah, I know!"

"My G-d, look at you! Pin stripe grey-vested suit, grey at the temples . . ."

He joked, "Yeah, the prison did that to me. I had a head full of black hair when I went in."

"And I cannot believe you have black patent leather shoes on!"

With that he looked down and said, "That's what they gave me. I'm gonna hafta burn 'em when I get home."

We kidded for a few minutes about what a dignified executive he was returning home as. Then the topic of the book I was writing about the men in the prison came up. Before speaking, he leaned back luxuriously, took a sip of his cognac, and thoughtfully looked at his nails as if deciding to get a manicure, and in a heavy Yankee accent said, "OK, I'll level with ya. Ya wanna know how the book is gonna go, I'll tell ya. Dis book is marketable, sellable. It's what people wanna read!"

"Leo? Do you really think so?"

In a typical New York Italian gesture, he leaned back again, waved a hand in my direction, rolled his eyes and said, "Listen, I don't need to lie to ya. You got something good here. I've seen the books they published on us. I ain't no prima donna but it was pure garbage. Life is an open book, but they don't know nothing' about me. I'm a pretty private guy when I wanna be. Those books that were written about me were pure garbage. They got them from some newspaper clippings. What do they know? You've got an insight into us, like the Godmother."

Leo paused slightly, even lifted an eyebrow, and said with relish, "In fact, I can be a pretty mysterious person. They don't know anything about Herbie either, uh, maybe what dey got from the public files, but I'm tellin ya' kid, you got an insight into us that nobody else has."

"Do you think the public will believe it?"

"Sure, listen Arlene. I've got no reason to lie to you. The area of your book is one of the areas that they don't have very much written about. Prisoners write prison books and they're depressing. Nobody wants to read 'em. Do gooders write books and dey don't know what in the hell they're talking about cause they ain't never been in the 'joint' before. They're writing about fiction. They got creeps out there teaching classes on penal reform who never been in a joint in their life."

"Leo, why do you like the idea of my book? What makes it something that's going to sell?"

A broad smile came over his face and with relish he said, "If you get good promotions you gonna have a hell of a seller. Let me tell you, I'm tellin ya' it's marketable cause you got an insight into us and that place that few ever see. No kidding, I ain't bullshittin ya. It's gonna be a winner. Don't you realize that you head the only female run prison program from a maximum security prison in the country?"

He was obviously enjoying his role as adviser and I thought it almost cute. One of the nation's 'top criminal figures' was sitting in my living room going over, point by point, advice as to how I should handle the 'Yankee' agents and publishers.

"Now, listen to me, you're not to go in there with your hat in your hand, cause you got dynamite material!"

He was playing the part of the 'Dutch Uncle' and guiding me in the process of publication.

"Naw, I ain't worried about the book being a winner, but you listen to me. What kinda agent you get working on this for ya? What kinda promotion had he got planned for you?"

"Promotion?"

Leo threw back his head and forcefully said, "Sure. You gotta have posters all over. You gotta have something that's shockingly graphic. I mean, Arlene, you got good taste, there's no question about it."

Here was a man that could put fear in the hearts of the powerful and yet the aspect of 'show biz' delighted him.

"Leo, what sort of graphic posters should I use? I know! How about having the guys posed up against the wall in chains under the caption of 'Men in Hell'!"

Leo seemed to consider this for a few minutes and nodded in affirmation, "Yeah, yeah, something like that . . . something! How about them being beaten up with a rubber hose? No kidding, people are interested in prisons; they're interested in reading about them. They wanna live other people's experiences vicariously."

You know something? He was right! People do want that, and at that moment, I was dying to get him on the topic of his own colorful experiences. Eventually, he reluctantly left the realm of his interest, which at the moment was a screenplay that he had in mind based on his life story.

"Leo, what did you do before you met Herbie? How did you get in prison the first time?"

Gone were the animated expressions that were on his face a few seconds earlier. He looked somber, almost reflective.

"I knew Herbie when we were both kids. It was during the early 1950's and we were friends. That's what got me in the first time, conspiracy for drugs. I was using at that time. I was a kid in my early twenties and I sold drugs to a guy that was an agent. I ended up in the can and the same thing happened to Herbie."

"Leo? Speaking of Herbie, I've got a question to ask you about him?"

Bless his little heart. He lifted an eyebrow as if to say 'don't ask too many' and then guardedly said, "Oh?"

"Well, not really so much about Herbie. I wanna ask you what's going to happen with him and the testimony of Gary Bowdach."

Gary was a subject that none of the men seemed to mind discussing and immediately he responded, "What has America come to Arlene? When a man can get on national television, let's forget about guilt or innocence, fact or fantasy, or whatever he's saying, but get on national T.V. in front of the United States Senate and talk about how he pulled his gun out and shot his partner in the chest and seen the blood seeping through a Banlon shirt! Now, only a Jew would recognize that a guy he just killed was wearing a Banlon shirt."

Leo had straight face, but oh G-d it was funny. After choking on my cigarette, I broke in, "You're right, that is very tacky."

"Arlene, I'm not kiddin, have you ever heard anything . . . Naw, I'm serious. Stop laughing!"

If it wasn't so serious, it would be ludicrous!

"He notices that the guy was wearing a Banlon shirt, and the senate, and the congress, and the media condone what dis guy did."

It was a difficult fact to dispute because someone must have condoned it, as Bowdach is free in society today. This brought me to my next question.

"You know, what I can't understand, is how Gary, who testified, is out, walking the streets. And Jason, who didn't testify about anybody except for the prison officials to Senator Nunn and his committee, is still sitting in jail. And he never murdered anybody!"

A smug expression crossed Leo's face, almost an 'I told you so' look, and he pointed a finger at me to emphasize his next comment, "Ah! But, since Jason testified against the system, this is the reward that he reaps. They've fostered the misinformation that the guys an informer and it's a prevalent thought throughout the whole system."

"But, he's not an informer."

"I understand that, but dis is what dey did. The guys in there think he's an informer."

Now THAT was ludicrous. Jason gave testimony on the staff graft and corruptions and he's the bad guy?

"Who do they think he informed against, Leo? He didn't speak against the inmates, Jason informed against the officials."

With the utmost patience, Leo explained, "Arlene, I understand that. You know it and I know it. But the problem with the jailhouse is that the men don't know the full story."

That upset me because I had submitted his name as one wanting to appear before the committee. Possibly I had put Jason in this precarious situation. This was an unexpected turn of events.

"Who do they think Jason was talking about?"

"They don't, that's the problem with jailhouse rumors. Guy's don't know the full story, OK? Initially, it was that Jason was only talking about prison administration. Then . . ."

"Then what?"

"Well, then it came out. Well, they put him in protective custody. Why would they put him in protective custody? Guy's aren't used to the subtle moves of government in situations like this. This is 1984. You're a thought criminal, OK?

He paused only to take a gulp of his drink and his eyes held fire,

"They took this guy, Jason, and left him in solitary confinement. Now, ya got a lot of guys in there with third grade educations, guys that are mental defects and what not, and one of these guys will take a shot at this guy."

"You mean Jason?"

"Sure, they're going to think, oh well, it's obvious that if he had not informed on one of us, he wouldn't need protective custody. So obviously, he's got to be an informer. Those guys in there don't think too clear or too straight."

"But Leo, don't they know that Jason is in protective custody for testifying against the administration?"

In his heavy New York accent, "Naw, they don't see it that way. They don't know the full story. Most guys don't have the opportunity to check it out. And oh, Jason . . ."

He trailed off . . .

Finally, I interjected, "Listen, I know that some of the stuff that I fed to the press and that Jason told Nunn, were against the staff. The Lewisburg beating was one instance! Did you know that Jason had a letter that was stolen from Warden Handbury's file that first told of these beatings? He had it smuggled to me and I passed it along to the press."

During all this, Leo was getting there looking at me intently and finally he said, "Naw, I'm not surprised. Hey listen, I know they got a lawsuit against the government about those beatings, but you gotta understand Arlene, these aren't the stories that get filtered down to the men. They're going to be led to believe that he was an informer. Now, on the other hand, you take this guy, Bowdach. He gets up on national TV and acknowledges that he murdered two people in cold blood. TWO PEOPLE IN COLD BLOOD! They take this guy, dey gives him parole, they put him in the street and they give him protective custody."

Briefly, Leo paused to collect his thoughts before continuing with, "Presumably the government is giving him some type of employment because the guy isn't qualified to work anyplace, right? They're going to take care of him and everything because he's on their side. He can do no wrong because he's on their side. But, if a guy tries to hurt me physically and . . ."

At this point in the conversation, Leo looked over at me with a little glint in his piercing eyes. Eyes that openly said it would be dangerous to make him angry.

"I'm not the type of guy to go to law enforcement, and if I protect myself, I'm an enemy of the state."

"Why?"

"Because I'm not cooperating wit' them. But, and here comes the good part, if tomorrow I want to cooperate with them, and tell them I murdered ten people, then that's right because then I'm on their side. Arlene, what's going on in this country is frightening. I've had people from Europe that know. They tell me what's going on over here is pre-war Germany."

As a final thrust to this conversation, he looked at me in the eyes and said, "I'm not bullshitting ya, I am not bullshitting ya."

It was getting too interesting to stop his train of conversation, so I baited him a little, "Getting back, do you think the Nunn Committee accomplished anything?"

"Well, on the new trials coming up there's a question if they're gonna use Bowdach, because his credibility has been discredited."

"Alright, forget Bowdach . . . Leo, I gave so much information to that committee, prison reform stuff."

"What's that mean?"

It was obvious to see from the way his body tensed that this was something that made him bristle.

"They yell over the loudspeaker, "THE MOVE IS ON!" OK now, if you're in the middle of being in the toilet, in the middle of taking a shower, ya have to hurry to get out of the door, but before ya got a chance to get out, they holler, "THE MOVE IS OFF!" and you're stuck wherever ya are. That's just one of the terrific improvements they've made."

Unfortunately, I knew he was right when he spoke of Atlanta having one of the most backward prison systems in the nation, despite the millions upon millions of tax dollars poured into it each year. The men in the place feel that the only result of the investigations is that every stool pigeon in the place is gonna come from under the rug and say, "I know something".

"Sure, listen, we gotta control crime. There's no getting away from it. But, the political chaos they're fostering in the country, and the images depicted on TV are crazy. It's just not so that every cop is a hero and every criminal is an idiot."

"That's because you know a better class of criminal."

"Aw, com'on, I'm serious. Listen, it's no getting away from it. You're gonna have people in prison. Fine, but give them human conditions to live under. Ya can't beat a man psychologically 24 hours a day, 24 hours a day, Arlene. Every man knows that he is in prison, even if he's asleep."

He was serious, and for once, I refrained from making any kidding comments. He continued, "Guys talk. They have nightmares and what not. Now, if you keep a person under that continuous type of stress, they're gonna crack. I consider myself one of the strongest. I gotta tell ya I feel like people been hittin' me since I been in there."

I knew that he's been rounded up with the 'French and Pleasant Avenue' mass arrest. I asked, "How long were you in there?"

"Five and a half years. And, right now I'm on parole. They got me on a rubber band. I'll tell ya the truth, Arlene, dis time I sure as hell don't wanna go back. Half my life has been wasted in prison."

When I asked him how it happened, a look of sadness came over Leo's expressive face, and the emotion carried into his voice when he said, "How does it happen? You're looking at the final product. I was a young kid when I went in. Spent all my twenties in the can. You come out and you're close to thirty. Everything passed ya by and you want everything. All your old friends got all the material things and ya think that's the answer to everything."

Things got quiet after he said that. His mood was pensive when I finally asked, "Was it the answer?"

"Well, for a while we did a pretty good job of getting what we wanted. Herbie kept going back to jail. I stood out for a long time. I was very circumspect, and I was on the lam, got married 'n all, and Herbie kept going back on violations, for bullshit, alright? But ya see, once ya come back, something happens to you. It's subliminal, it's difficult to explain . . . to put into words. They take the steam outta people. Ya see, I got some spirit left. There are guys in there that are like vegetables after a while. You know, it takes somethin out of you when you see guys who you thought were 'straight', eyeing young convicts that come in, like sharks observing helpless bait. It does something to you when you see that."

The mood was no longer the cheerful, carefree one of a few hours before. I was glad that my kids came in about that time. During dinner, the topic of conversation was still the prison, but it was off him personally. It was a pleasure to feed the man, as it had been a long time since anyone had enjoyed my cooking like he obviously seemed to. The kids were no longer surprised by the various guests who drifted in and out at our dinner table. But the conversation, it was obvious, held a strong fascination for them. Now and then, between bites of home-made kugel which he was devouring with relish, he would jab a fork in my direction and continue his advice to me about writing a book on prisons.

"Ya know, you might want to put into your book a little Jewish history, which since I'm Italian, I'm sure you're more familiar with than I am."

"How so?"

"Jews, traditionally, have never had prisons. I'm talking about the Orthodox Jews. I think they have something in the, er, what is it, Torah? Or, whatever, where they banish people rather then put them in prison because they believed that it destroyed the human spirit. You may wanna get a little erudite in your introduction and say why you're against prisons, and couple it in with Jewish philosophy, but not bullshit liberal philosophy, I mean real philosophy, huh? Think you can do it?"

"Leo, no one has ever accused me of being a liberal."

"I'm not saying you shouldn't punish people for crime, but look at the other countries that are doing something right, Sweden, Norway, whatever. Find out what they're doing and we're not."

The kids were dying to find out what being out felt like, and finally my daughter Marla could hold back no longer and said in a rush, "What's it like on the first day that you get out of prison?"

With complete candor, Leo looked at the kid and said, "It's a terrible thing being in a place like that. And for a guy like me, who people in dere look up to as the epitome of sophistication, so, er, if I get this kinda response, I can imagine what guys with less success, the type of feeling they got. I mean, I gotta home, car, swimming pool, and family, something to come home to!"

He was the exception. Most didn't have anything or anyone waiting for them, "So," I ask, "What happens when you don't have anything? How do you adjust?"

Between bites of kugel, he said, "Most don't adjust. Arlene, 24 hours a day in that place, you're a sub-human. Then they expect you to get out and adjust yourself to society. They ain't got a chance in hell of making it!"

Then, changing his train of thought, he said, "The really sick part of all this is that as a direct result of the investigations and the attention that was brought to the place because of them, you got that 'mother,' 'Father Fundhall'. And now, the warden's going around the city giving speeches on prison reform, of which I might add, they know nothing about."

For the remainder of the afternoon and up until it was time to catch his plane Leo filled me in on how the priest used pressure on the men.

"The priest has the right to give you a phone call. What he does is he decides who will have the right according to how he conforms to his way of doing things, like participating in his programs."

Now, it dawned, "Oh, so if you want a phone call out you . . ."

"Right. So if your wife is sick, or you want to talk to your girlfriend or little daughter, or whatever, you participate in one of his programs, then you're a 'good guy' and then you get a phone call."

"Oh-h-h, so that's the way he makes his programs a success?"

"Sure, you get a little phone call, play bingo in his games and win a little warm-up suit, or medallion, cigarettes. This is how he gets his brownie points with the institution and the Bishop."

The rest got even better, "I'll tell ya something else. As a Catholic Priest, I can tell you dis, I know he's got problems with his vow of celibacy, if he ever took one."

"In what way?"

"I know a guy in the prison, that did a painting for him for what appears to be his girlfriend, paramour..."

While he spoke, I jotted down questions. Somehow, the answers had to be found. It had been months since I had been into the institution. The warden who had replaced 'Broderick', Warden Handbury, had never met me and it didn't seem as though he was ever going to. How these questions, could be answered, or better, how could a confrontation be arranged? Impossible! Yet, fate works in mysterious ways. The afternoon paper held the answer.

Chapter Twenty-Six

THE BUIIDING IS BAD!

Within a few hours after Leo was on a plane back to New York, Georgia Congressman Wyche Fowler called a press conference and announced to the world that the Atlanta prison should be closed as soon as possible. He further stated that a bill was up before the U.S. Congress to do just that. One of the biggest complaints was that the place was over-crowded. Of course, we know what happened to the Lewisburg prisoners that were transferred out of there, the ones that were beaten. Now, after much deliberation, congress met and decided that the place just needed tearing down. It was a bad, bad building. Bad sticks and bad stones. Not because of the problems inside, not because of the incompetence, graft and corruption. The evening news also had a small article that one of the local colleges, a small Southern Baptist school, Mercer University, was sponsoring a day of discussion with none other than the warden and swinging priest. The times were listed in the paper when they would be speaking. Wild horses couldn't have kept me away! I had been waiting a long time for this confrontation. The rest of the day was spent compiling a list of questions for these important men. As extra insurance, I called Jean and Jodie to come along. Calls were made into the various media to make sure that they would cover the talk. Armed with my friends, tape recorder, and hostility in my heart, I drove over to the college.

Jodie was wearing an outfit that jiggled when she walked. Maybe it was Jodie that jiggled. Whatever it was, I was glad because I was hoping that the warden would be distracted enough when he saw her that he wouldn't notice me. Unobtrusively we grabbed seats before his speech, which was not easy, as Jodie couldn't do anything unobtrusively, much less wiggle into a seat. Somehow my type of looks stood out in this small Bible belt school. Handbury was seated on the stage. For the first time I saw the man who had been responsible for my banishment. He was everything but the Baptist preacher turned warden. He wore an out-of-style off the rack sport coat and pants. He had long sideburns and his hair was dark reddish and worn in a slight pompadour. It was slicked back with G-d knows what to give it that wet-head look. It was difficult to see his eyes because they were behind pink tinted glasses with wire frames. It was those, and the large Indian turquoise jewelry that he wore, that gave him the appearance of a used car salesman.

My mother used to tell me never trust a man that wore Indian turquoise jewelry, or women who had lipstick on their teeth. His skin looked pale. I didn't think that I would be nervous finally confronting the elusive warden but I felt on the verge of hyperventilation. He had no reason to suspect that I was anything other than one of the 'interested persons' scattered in the audience. And yet, suppose someone recognized me as the 'troublemaker' and had me bodily ejected? Suppose I got up to speak and made an ass of myself? What if all those nice Baptists in the audience who obviously liked him, didn't like me or what I had to say?

It was obvious that no one in the room, other than the three of us, doubted his sincerity. He was speaking to an audience that had been meeting all day on prison reform. Since he, at this time, had no idea what I looked like, there was no reason for him to believe that this speech should be anything but a piece of cake to a receptive crowd. It was difficult to concentrate on the platitudes that were being given about him before he rose to open his talk. Finally, he rose and slowly walked towards the microphone, looking at me the entire time! It took all my concentration to place a bland expression on my face and listen.

"I hope that you are here because of your interest in the world of forgotten men and women and are here to help them help themselves."

He praised the program of education that this university had instituted within the prison and then moved on to the feeling of the public today in relation to prisons.

"I hope that you are aware that most offenders today are out on parole. Then, they are on probation and in community treatment centers, halfway houses and such. We know that most of those that are incarcerated are repeat and dangerous offenders. I must tell you that punishing criminals and deterring others from crime and protecting citizens from crime is gaining today.

He was taking pleasure in alarming us, "It's taken over a decade, but we are aware that rehabilitation is not the sole aim of prisons. It is one of retribution, deterrents, incapacitation, and rehabilitation. These are the objectives of incarcerations. Angry Americans, many who feel unsafe in their homes and on the streets, are demanding and forcing us to take another look at the justice system at every level; local, state, and federal, which are undergoing an incredible re-examination. Law enforcement is being criticized for being too lenient, for coddling and pampering the criminal. We are putting too many dangerous people back on the streets."

With a direct and forceful manner, he spoke about how congress had a bill before it now, Senate Bill 1437, and if it passes it will overhaul the federal criminal code. It will do away with parole, except in extreme circumstances. As he continued, I wondered how his talk related to prison reform, which was supposed to be the topic. But, still I kept quiet, while Warden Handbury continued, "The majority of the inmates in the institution that I serve have been in institutions like it on many occasions.

In our new atmosphere of 'get tough', we question the idea of rehabilitation as being the main goal of incarceration."

"Hell," I sat there thinking, "That's nothing new." Without those guards backing you up, buddy, I thought "You've got big trouble. You've got a lot of employees out there that need those men in there."

For over an hour the warden spoke on love and prison reform. The message was interspersed with the 'get tough' attitude that was needed to handle the men in prisons. Basically, the message was that nothing is or really can be done but to 'house these men' until they leave to recommit their crimes all over again. I sat there thinking to myself, buddy, that's nothing new. The highlight of the program was after the warden's speech.

Seated on the podium with him were four inmates who were recent graduates of the college. They had been invited to speak to an audience of mostly Bible students on how they were 'saved' by the education that had been provided by the school. Actually, after hearing them speak I had the feeling that it was probably true.

After another twenty minutes of testimonials, the last inmate rose to speak. He was tall and thin with piercing eyes, jutting cheek bones and had a panther's nervous grace. He wore his hair slicked back in the same style as the warden, even down to the long sideburns. He was wearing a very tacky pink polyester knit leisure suit. He slowly rose and walked toward the microphone in his ill-fitting suit and white socks. He stood for a moment, looking down at the audience, held out his hands in a futile gesture and finally said, with resignation, "How do you like my new suit? You should, you know, tax payer, you paid for it. You paid for it to the tune of sixty dollars. What is interesting about this particular suit is the fact that it was sold for sixty dollars to the prison and had a price tag inside for twenty-five dollars."

I looked over at the warden after this intriguing comment and he had slouched down a little in his seat with an intent look on his face while waiting for the rest of the statement.

"Now how do you think that happened? Not only did you Georgia taxpayers pay for it, but, coincidentally, the warden of the prison where I formerly resided, Reidsville State Prison, just happened to own the local dry goods store that alas just happens to be where this suit that you good taxpayers paid for was purchased. Luckily, when I got out, I was able to find more suitable clothes in order to find employment."

The statements of this inmate were obviously not what Warden Handbury had envisioned. It was hardly what one desires in a testimonial. He sat there like stone, neither looking to the right nor the left. It was with a sense of relief that the session ended and he headed hurriedly for the exit. He was halfway up the aisle when I managed to tug at his sleeve and said, "Warden, Warden Handbury, could I have a moment of your time?"

A bit taken aback he turned and said, "Why, yes, young lady, are you a member of the press?"

"I certainly am . . . would you like to see my credentials?"

"Oh no, that won't be necessary, I just wanted to know with whom I'm speaking."

G-d forbid the man should know. I would have never been able to get past the first sentence. Instead of further introducing myself, I plunged ahead with, "Isn't it true warden, that when Congressman Fowler had his independent investigation committee set up, it was your office that made the appointments for everyone? I mean the family, friends, all the people that the inmates wanted to come forward to give testimony against the administration?"

His eyes became wary and ice behind those cool pink tinted glasses. It was obvious that he could tell from my tone of question that this was not to be the favorable interview as he had expected. With a slight edge to his voice, he leveled a look at me and said, "Yes, yes we did."

"But, don't you think that this was intimidating for anyone who wanted to come forward to testify against you and your staff?"

Again, another steel look, "No."

"Why did your personal secretary make these appointments, warden?"

A small crowd was beginning to gather and he clearly was not enjoying it. I, on the other hand was loving it. I had been waiting months for this. This was the chance to let it all hang out. Put all the cards on the table. All the things I wanted to say to this man who hadn't answered my phone calls were going to be said now.

"It was at the request of Congressman Fowler and the investigation committee."

"But warden, why were some of the inmates put into segregation who wanted to give testimony that later, triggered off a senate investigation?"

This time, rather than answer, he just stood and looked at me coldly in silence. He made a half attempt to leave and I stood firmly blocking his path. This man wasn't going to get away so fast. And I continued, "Warden, surely you wouldn't mind answering a few more questions for the press here, do you?"

He looked around and saw that a small crowd had gathered. He couldn't get away. Obviously, he did mind answering but he answered in a low voice, "No, of course not."

"Good! Now, I'd like to ask another question. Do certain ethnic or religious groups bringing in outside programs encounter any discrimination? For instance warden, I was told that special Christmas dinners are given to the inmates at no charge, whereas the Jewish inmates are required to pay out of their own pockets for the right to have the Passover meal."

Before he had a chance to answer, I continued, "Incidentally, when this was questioned, the answer from the institution was that there was no religious budget for such a dinner, and even though the Easter and Christmas dinners are considered 'social' holidays, the Passover Seder and holiday is listed by your institution as religious and therefore not funded?"

Hostility was now creeping into his voice and with a tight smile he said, "Oh, but all the inmates are invited to partake in our delicious Christmas and Easter dinners."

"But Warden, that isn't the Jewish holiday so why should they celebrate it and not their own?"

The crowd around us had grown a little bigger and it was obvious that he would rather be anywhere but where he was at the moment. Reluctantly, the warden said, "Well, I really am not aware of that rule so maybe you should show me a copy of the particular rule to which you are referring."

I looked back sweetly, in wide eyed surprise and said, "Why warden, I had no idea that I would have to explain the rules of your own prison system to you."

Someone in the crowd asked one of their own questions. It was a question that I had fed to them earlier just in case he would allow for a question and answer session. Carefully, she read off a question from the list I had prepared for her. She said in a nervous, but clear voice, "Warden? John Caroll was one of the guards supposedly involved in the trafficking of narcotics. Is he still employed by the institution, and if so, why? Is it true that he had a law suit against you, Warden Hardbury, and once you reinstated him, the suit was dropped?"

Clearly taken back, the warden returned to his pious looks that he had during his earlier speech and responded, "Well now, Miss. I don't know about any lawsuit. But yes, the guard you mentioned is still working within the institution."

"Good heavens, why?"

"Well, I would certainly hope that a man is not guilty until proven guilty. In the case of John Caroll, it was never conclusively proven that he was guilty of the charges. Now, if you'll excuse me, I have a previous appointment and should leave."

I wasn't about to let that man out of sight until he answered a few more questions. Deliberately blocking his path I shot out the next question, "Warden, just a few more if you don't mind."

Clearly he did.

"Warden, is it true that it costs to keep an inmate one day in the federal prison the equivalent of a day in a luxury hotel? And, if so, why was Lou Almark kept one year and four days past his sentence? And, for how much is he suing the government as a result of this costly mistake by the Atlanta Penitentiary?"

In a clipped tone, Handbury answered, "I am unaware of any Lou Almark or lawsuit for that matter. When did this occur?"

"Sometime within the past two or three years."

His first smile tugged at the corners of his face. Clearly, he had the answer ready for me that he could relate to.

"Oh well, I didn't know about that. I wasn't there then."

I almost gave the report, "With an attitude like that it's no wonder the man was lost."

But, before I could say the words, the warden continued, "I have 550 staff people to know these things."

See, I knew it was big business. His smug smile of satisfaction vanished when I answered, "But warden, this man was lost for over a year, lost at the taxpayer's expense. Most of all there is a lawsuit about which you, as warden should know."

It was obvious that the interview was fast drawing to a close. He brushed aside a question from another observer about the inadequate medical attention and was gradually heading for the door. Quickly, I zinged in the final and possibly most important question. "Warden, I would like to ask you a question about an inmate, Jason Lynott."

"No Comment."

"Warden, isn't it true that this was an inmate who testified about you and your prison administration and as a result of that testimony is now residing in the prison with the highest ratio of assaults and murders in the entire prison system? Is this how he was rewarded for speaking before Senator Nunn's permanent committee on organized crime?"

With an absolutely cool and collected expression, the warden looked me directly in the eye and stated, "I have no comment about the gentlemen. That is privileged information."

Not content to let it drop, I pressed further, "But warden, on the other hand, didn't Gary Bowdach, a man who by his own admission was a murderer testify before the Senate Committee against his fellow inmates. And, spoke against the other inmates rather than against the prison administration and their graft and corruption and is now walking around as a free man?"

This time the warden didn't even dignify the question with a 'no comment'. Instead he brushed past me and said to one of his on-lookers, "I really am very late for another appointment. You'll have to excuse me."

I reached after him, "But, Warden . . ."

His voice rising for the first time with emotion.

"That is privileged information. I have NO COMMENT!"

With that, he was gone. For the first time I noticed the old adversary 'Swinging Priest,' trailing behind him. With his most charming smile, he greeted me effusively, "Why, Mrs. Peck, it's nice to see that you still have that same old fire. Still giving 'em hell, huh?"

"Mr. Fundhall, I enunciated the 'Mr.'. "When that outrage to injustice is gone, I'll be dead. But to tell you the truth, I only get fired up when I see the hateful things that I've come to expect from the place where you reside."

He winked those nice blue eyes of his in a conspiratorial look and said, "Mrs. Peck, that's your trouble. You just couldn't follow the rules. And you know, if you had followed the rules, then you would still be going out to your program today. Such a shame. I'll have to admit that your discussion group was the best one they have had out there and since you've been gone, it has not been equaled.

The unmitigated gall of that man! He just could not stand it that all his Catholics were coming to our group. I felt that if I had too long a conversation with this man, I would hit him or kick him in the gonads, that is, if he had any. It was really infuriating! As anti-Semitic as the man was, he was nevertheless the sole representative for the Jewish Discussion Group and there wasn't a damn thing we could do about him. The government had made him the representative of the inmates and that was it. It was a good thing he hadn't seen me earlier, or he probably would have tipped off the warden and I wouldn't have gotten as far as I had.

But rather than do what I preferred doing at that moment, which was giving him a good swift kick, I turned and called over my shoulder, "No, 'father', what you didn't like was that I couldn't be a hack for the system like you. You couldn't stand that or the fact that all your Catholics had joined our group."

Swiftly, I grabbed Jodie and caught up with Jean outside and we headed for the local pub to talk it over. Halfway in the door, my eye caught the headline on a paper that was in a vending machine. In large letters the article read, "Pen Closing!"

Once again, another murder had taken place at the Atlanta Federal Penitentiary, the second in less than a month. This latest brought the record to an even dozen. As usual, the officials were unable to do anything. They did not have any suspects or any indication of motive in the slaying.

What happens now? What is the end result of the landmark which has contributed, in a manner of speaking, to Atlanta's fame which now is on its way to being closed and presumably demolished?

The United States House Judiciary Committee has voted that the facility must be closed by September 1, 1984. When Congress Fowler's House committee declared that the prison should not be used in the future for the confinement of prisoners by any echelon of government, that such institutions should not be in urban areas, was it a cop-out? Is Fowler influenced by the fact that in recent years the penitentiary has been a stain on Atlanta's reputation? How does it reflect on him and his 'prison efforts' that the officials in charge have obviously been unable to do anything about such crimes? And, while the public at large might not be able to generate much sympathy for the inmates in the prison, it is obviously the responsibility of the federal government to guarantee the safety of those held there.

And, what about the logic of Fowler's final solution about building such institutions away from urban areas? The guards and staff that are in charge now are inadequate to handle the present solution. How on earth could qualified guards be found to work in the boondocks, and most of all, what kind of hardship would it place on the families of these inmates in their efforts to visit?

When Warden Handbury responded to questions concerning a congressional committee vote to close the Atlanta pen by September 1, 1984 and prohibit its use as a prison in the future, he said he would like to see a replacement facility located in Atlanta. He then cited the action that was taken by the House Judiciary Committee when they added an amendment to a Justice Department funding bill declaring, 'It' (The Atlanta Institution) had been the setting of many violent inmate murders and hundreds of dangerous incidents, primarily because the ancient physical condition of the building and the closure of this prison is essential to the development of a respectable federal prison system.

Turdfeathers! The building isn't bad. The system stinks! Billions of our tax dollars are going down the drain due to incompetent management and a lack of understanding of how to cope with a situation. Wardens are appointed in political payoffs and sorely lacking the training in management and the psychological knowledge that is needed. If this lack of qualified personnel exists at the top, imagine the caliber of the employees that exist at the lower levels. It is virtually impossible to fire any of our so called 'civil servants,' so when they are caught in gross misdeeds, they are usually transferred to another institution.

And finally, in the case of Julian Bond, what was the end result? Bond was invited to speak to my discussion group as a guest speaker. By the time I brought him, the officials were getting nervous with the attention that I seemed to be focusing on the institution. To bar Bond from the institution was a means to get rid of me and dissolve a program that had became too popular. Rather than having the desired effect, the once vice presidential nominee and present state senator complained to his United States Congressman, Fowler. Since it was an election year, the congressman welcomed the chance to have a little attention brought on the institution, especially since, according to Fowler's office, the prison officials were totally uncooperative with him in answering questions about Bond's rejection. No one counted on me being made the link between the inmates and the media.

When Fowler appointed his 'independent' committee no one expected anything other than a superficial 'investigation' and, after a few days, the results would be favorable to the administration. During this time, Fowler would have gotten the pre-election publicity that he desired and the case would be closed.

Instead, the inmates would not let this investigation be the 'white wash' that it had been set up for and eventually I was able to bring columnist Jack Anderson into the situation. Once his office focused the attention of the national press, I was able to get Senator Sam Nunn to bring in the United States Permanent Committee on Investigations and a full-scale Senate Investigation developed, the likes of which have not been seen since the Valachi hearings. It would truly be a shame if after all the hearings and investigations into the prison and the murders if the only thing our learned officials have learned is that the building is bad. The changes that were made at the time, such as installing metal detectors and, setting up searches for weapons, have not been the answer. In his address to the workshop at Mercer College, Handbury said, "Angry Americans are forcing federal prison officials to take a new look at their emphasis on rehabilitation. Clearly a get-tough mood seems to be growing." Maybe it's time that we took a 'get tough' attitude with the system that serves as a breeding place for unspeakable mental and physical violence.

And how did it affect me? Well, I saw the results of prison battles. Battles that were fought with crude knives, fashioned from files and pitchforks at times. It left its marks. Both on the men and me. It's impossible not to leave that place without scars. It hurts you to hear a man say, "You know somethin? I'd give both my arms right now just to have the chance to hug a woman for the first time in years. I've never been to a professional football game. I haven't seen a bird in years." It hurts when you hear a grown man tell you this.

It seems that the visions of what they lived through fade from their minds similar to that they might have seen a in horror movie. For myself, I know it's going to be a long time before the memory of those years dissipates, because the memory of those men still linger and is going to for a long, long time to come.

Epilogue

After a year and a half of banishment from the penitentiary, fate was to intervene and, once again I was to have contact with the officials in the Atlanta Prison. Nearing the winter of 1979 I had been appearing (as the lead, naturally) in a local production of the Broadway play, The Majority of One. Our version wasn't so ambitious and instead of Broadway, we played the Atlanta Jewish Community Center. The critics panned us, but what did they know? What the cast lacked in talent, they made up for in attitude and offered to present the play in a benefit for the men in the institution. After a hurried meeting between the Warden and his staff, a decision was made."If Mrs. Peck were to have anything to do with this benefit, the play would not be allowed into the prison. While they were rendering these earth shattering decisions, another brutal murder was taking place. This time to a civilian.

On the twenty-first of November, 1979, a young dietician, Janice Hylen, was viciously murdered while working in a room off the hospital. Once again, the officials that run the Atlanta Prison were 'shocked and outraged that such a thing could happen.' Georgia's 5th District Congressman, Wyche Fowler, called a press conference and stated that the institution must be closed as soon as possible to make the penitentiary safe for the inmates who seemed to be murdered there on a regular basis. Who is responsible when it is not safe for the inmate's families or participants in civic programs; or, in the case of Janice Hylen, a female employed on a consulting basis, to enter the institution without taking their lives in their hands? Certainly, our tax dollars pay enormous amounts into the penal system to see that they are run in a competent manner. A building in itself cannot be uncontrollable, nor can it be bad. The administration running the institution is that which needs tearing down, or changing.

According to inside sources within the Atlanta Penitentiary, the innate who committed this brutal rape and murder was a born psychotic killer. Only a few short days before he killed Ms. Hyland, he had been called into the Warden's office in relation to threats he had made against the female staff psychologist. Reportedly, she had complained to the administration that he planned to kill her, and that he was too dangerous a man to be left roaming the prison. Warden Handbury and the FBI agents who were called in gave a stern warning to this inmate, and advised him that he was being watched and he was not to commit the murder that he had broadcast throughout the institution. Shortly after this 'warning' he quietly entered the room where Ms. Hylen was working, closed the door and repeatedly raped, stabbed and decapitated her.

Within a few days of the murder, letters once again began to arrive at my house from the men imploring me to 'get the story out'. They described how the murderer was picked up in his cell once the lab men were able to match up his red hair and skin that were found under her fingernails. He reportedly 'kept stabbing her because he couldn't get her eyes to close'.

Allegedly, there is even a tape that the FBI supposedly had on record where he called his mother, stating that he was in a 'little bit of trouble' because he had killed somebody.' This was at his previous federal prison where he had also raped another inmate and almost killed him. Yet, this same man was allowed to enter, at will, the room where Ms. Hylen was working, stuff her pantyhose down her throat to stifle her screams and brutally kill her. Why did she not have a 'beeper' such as the male employees carry for protection? Only after this latest murder were the women employees given beepers.

The men complain that despite the money being poured into the Atlanta Penitentiary the results are not seen. As guards retired, replacements were not being hired. Knives were still plentiful. Inmates were asking about their own security and the security of the outsiders. The guards told them, "It's your responsibility to watch out for the outsiders that come in. You know all the bad guys. You take care of them and we'll turn our backs." Maybe it was time that we didn't turn ours.

Appendix I

The Letters

UNITED STATES DEPARTMENT OF JUSTICE
BUREAU OF PRISONS
UNITED STATES PENITENTIARY
ATLANTA, GEORGIA 30315

April 1, 1975

Mrs. Arlene Peck
1656 Lenox Road, NE
Atlanta, Georgia 30324

Dear Mrs. Peck:

    We trust that you and your family enjoyed a rewarding Passover Season. Allow me to express our gratitude for your concern and assistance with the Passover Services and Seder Meal at the Penitentiary.

    The main purpose of this letter however is to express concern over the activities associated with the Wednesday evening discussion group. It seems that for sometime an effort has been made to increase the number of female participants of the Jewish Discussion Group. However, the activities of last Tuesday evening and the near confrontation with the Black Studies Class caused us to reflect and re-examine the activities in this area. Because of this activity we are concerned about the security of our visitors and the institution.

    Therefore, in the future, we will require a balance or mixture of male and female participants in the Wednesday evening discussion groups. We do not want to terminate the very worthwhile activity. However, we do want the outside group to be no larger than six people and to have one male participant for each female, preferably husband and wife combinations. In this manner the group will be representative of the Jewish Community and will not create such a stir among the all male inmate population. This refers to the portion of the program you coordinate, since we've never had this situation arise with the group arranged by Mr. Marshal Solomon.

    We trust you understand our concern and will comply with our request. If you have any questions concerning this matter, please feel free to contact Associate Warden McKernan here at the Institution.

Sincerely,

M. R. Hogan
Warden

cc:
Rabbi Lawson
Rabbi Cohn

October 29, 1975

DOCTOR LEON SPOTTS
Bureau of Jewish Education
1753 Peachtree Road, N. E.
Atlanta, Georgia 30309

Dear Doctor Spotts:

This letter is on behalf of the Jewish Study Group of the Federal Penitentiary of Atlanta.

For some time now we have been extremely fortunate in having Ms. Arlene Peck lead our Group as we go forward rediscovering the humanity of life and what it is like to have others care and be genuinely concerned for one's welfare.

Certainly, it goes without saying, Ms. Peck is a true "Beautiful" individual. But more than this, she, through her interest and concern for us, has enabled the men here to share in the social dimensions and dynamics of the life and living on the other side of the walls that keep us in and the existence of the community out. In this regard we have all benefited greatly in our personal growth as a direct result of Ms. Peck's caring and demonstrated graciousness in giving of herself so that we too might not go unattended or miss the joys of life. We thank her from the very depths of our humble hearts.

Additionally, we ask that you be kind enough to express to her personally our deep and abiding appreciation for all that she continues to do so that we here might be a part of your world.

With every good wish, I am

Sincerely,

ROBERT L. HERN

1656 Lenox Road, N.E.
Atlanta, Georgia 30306

January 5, 1976

Mr. Norman A. Carlson
Bureau of Prisons
United States Dept. of Justice
Washington, D. C. 20537

Dear Mr. Carlson:

Because of my returning to Atlanta from a tour of Russia a few days ago I have only now opened your letter of December 9th and the copy of a letter you wrote to Congressman Elliott H. Levitas concerning my difficulties at the Atlanta Federal Penitentiary.

In your letter you state that I was informed my group should be restricted to six individuals, preferably husband and wives. That is true, however that is alson one of my questions of contension. I have been bringing a Jewish program and the women I occasionally bring out for the most part are Jewish legislators, presidents of organizations or other Jewish oriented programs. It would make as much sense to insist that I have Mrs. Elliott H. Levitas (only because she is his wife) attend if he would desire to visit our bi-monthly meeting.

Secondly, you state the warden felt six (including myself) volunteers would be sufficient for a group of individuals, numbering twenty-five. The last visit before my Russian trip fifty-two inmates were present. Rarely are there less than forty men present at the meetings and at times I have counted sixty. I have also been at the institution on more than one occasion when fifty or more outsiders were in attendance for the N.A.A.C.P. and A.A. groups. I understand, that recently, a seated dinner, complete with a band was given by the N.A.A.C.P.

The third point in your letter states that entertainers must come into the institution for their own personal benefit. I wholeheartedly agree, however, Mr. Ludlow Porch is certainly not an entertainer nor was he coming into the institution as anything other than an interested volunteer on an individual basis. I cleared his name with Father Caine well over three weeks ahead of the meeting because Mr. Porch is such a busy man. It was not until the day before the meeting that I was told that Mr. McKernin "changed his mind" and Mr. Porch could not attend because he was "media." I did note that during the same time a reporter for a local magazine was not only allowed into the prison, but she also had lunch and spent the day with Mr. McKernin. Naturally, he was mentioned in the article.

As far as a show being performed featuring "Miss Nude America" and two strippers, I have contacted one of the T.V. stations in Atlanta that does remember covering it and I am trying to document that.

- continued -

MR. NORMAN A. CARLSON —2— January 5, 1976

Along with your letter stating I should request a meeting with Warden Hogan and Congressman Levitas, letter of December 4th, I also opened one from Warden Hogan cancelling my invitation into the prison. I am enclosing a copy of that letter. He states among his reasons, my bringing cookies to the inmates which I have never done and tomato plants to the inmates. The plants were brought in with complete clearance by Father Caine and the prison officials cleared them! In fact, it took three guards to carry them in as the nursery that donated them sent several trays. They did so because they were through channels. I did not sneak them in as has been implied.

Lastly, Warden Hogan states that I said I was responsible for the transfer of Mr. McKernin. Not only have I not said that but I find it difficult to understand how he knows of anything that I have said as we have never met personally. This is despite my repeated request. I have invited Mr. McKernin and Warden Hogan repeatedly to attend our meetings to that they might see firsthand how beneficial our meetings are to the men. We are not a Bible class. This I have arranged through a few of the Rabbis here to be on alternate Wednesdays from 6:00 to 7:00 p.m. The group I bring in is a discussion group that is Jewish oriented.

I am enclosing an article from last month's Atlanta Magazine. Obviously, according to some, I must be doing something right. The best judge of that would be the men who by their attendence seem to agree. I was warned that long after Congressman Levitas' involvement in this matter was over, the warden would still be in charge. So, I had better not "make waves." This I do not disagree with nor did I mean to challenge. I do not think taking away my invitation because I "made waves" is what you meant when you said I would receive full cooperation from the warden. Continuing the worthwhile program for the Jewish group and specifically the thirty-five or forty regulars that I have been instrumental in getting interested in coming, should not be dependent on childish games of who can flex the most muscles. I had been scheduled to next attend on January 14th along with Stuart Lewengrub (Director of the B'nai B'rith Anti-Defamation League), Jacob Goren (Southeastern head of the Israel Tourist Bureau) and three other equally important guest. Please see what you can do to handle this regretable situation before then so they won't have to be cancelled. I will be anxiously awaiting your reply.

Thank you for the help you have offered and I feel I can expect.

Very truly yours,

Arlene Peck
Mrs. Howard R. Peck

cc: Congressman Elliott H. Levitas
    Ludlow Porch, W.R.N.G. Radio

1656 Lenox Road, N.E.
Atlanta, Georgia 30306
March 13, 1978

The Honorable Herman Talmadge
Room 109, Russell Senate Office Building
Washington D.C. 20510

Dear Senator Talmadge:

My name is Arlene Peck, and long ago when we shared the dais at an Israel Bond Dinner, I told you that my parents thought that you were the best thing since "chopped liver". My folks were Mollie and Aaron Greenberg and their relationship to you went back a long way - as far back as the apartments on Greenwood Avenue. I even think that they traveled with you to Washington for Truman's inauguration.

I am writing you for two reasons in the hopes that you can help. For the past five years, I have been the chairperson of the Jewish Discussion Group at the Atlanta Federal Penitentiary. The prison officials have never wanted this program and have done everything they could to stop it. All of this came to a head a couple of weeks ago when I brought Julian Bond in to discuss the NAACP position on the Bakee decision and the PLO. When we arrived at the prison they turned us away, after first insulting us terribly. The next day Julian called Wyche Fowler to protest this action against a State Senator and President of the NAACP. Wyche in turn called Warden Handbury to relate his displeasure at this incident. No sooner had he called when the director of the Bureau of Jewish Education was called into Handbury's office and given the ultimatum that if "he made waves, there would be NO PROGRAM, but Assistant Warden Watowski, Chaplin Riggs and Father Ondahl would no longer allow her (meaning me) to be the chairperson of this program." This was in direct retaliation because a politician got involved in something that wasn't their concern. The only thing that I have done to upset the prison officials is try to bring in a program that is informative and interesting. It has upset me greatly that men in this, or any other prison, have the power to make decisions like this.....and only for spite. I was told long ago by the previous warden (Hogen) that "They don't like people getting Congressmen and Senators involved in something (their prison) that is no concern to them.....and long after they are gone, the prison officials would still be there to run things as THEY see fit."

March 13, 1978
Page Two

    They also don't like the fact that I write for the Jewish Press (articles enclosed) and have tried to remove me because I'm "media", which I don't consider myself to be. The day I was cancelled as chairperson was the day that the enclosed Williams article came out. The only thing that it says is positive things about the program. The reason given "officially" about refusing Bond was that, "Mrs. Peck didn't follow exact procedure and clear him in writing two weeks ahead." This was on a Wednesday that Bond was not allowed to enter. The following Sunday I was invited into the NAACP program at the prison, and went - with no clearance. Since this time, I have found out that the Jewish group is the only one to have had this restriction of two-week previous written clearance and the rest of the non-Jewish and NAACP people just come with their people and enter.

    We are filing a protest to this discrimination in court and I will have our lawyer, Mr. Dennis Seigle, keep you informed. In fact, there have been other changes in procedure instituted by Father Ondahl that only the Jews have had to contend with. Please see what you can do to help with this deplorable situation. Wyche is being kept informed, also. Elliott Livitas became involved a couple of years ago when they wouldn't allow the men to have the Passover Seder because it was a religious holiday and the government doesn't pay for religious holidays. I was told by Assistant Warden Watowski then that Christmas and Easter are social holidays and, therefore, the men (non-Jewish) could have them.

    The second reason for my letter is to state how upset I am about the sale of arms to the Arabs. I know what a friend you have always been to the Jews and know you will do what you can to help. I am president of Technion, Women's Division in the south and would like to relay to my membership what your position is.

    I hope to hear from you soon about these matters. And, I'm thanking you in advance for your concern.

                                    Sincerely,

                                    Arlene G. Peck

AGP/jan

P.S. The group that I had scheduled to speak this last Wednesday evening were told by Father Ondahl that he had been warned to expect letters from people like you and that would be a mistake; that the prison has a way of forgetting and forgiving and if I stayed quiet they might forgive and forget and let me back in, maybe six months or so. He also told this group when asked why I need clearance for the Jewish group but the NAACP and others didn't that as of last Sunday everyone has to have clearance. That's nice, but it should have been for everyone or no one from the beginning.

May 18th, 1978

Dear Warden Hanberry,

I am most happy that you finally saw fit, after several months to finally accord me the courtesy of an explanation, although somewhat untrue, as to why I have been barred from the Jewish Discussion Group. It is most unfortunate that you extended me this explanation only after Congressmen's Elliott Levitias, Wyche Fowler, Senator's Talmedge and I believe Sam Nunn's office wrote or called requesting the reason. Not to mention the lawyer, Dennis Seigle, who also requested a reason as to why. He wanted it for his files on the discrimination case that the men are planning concerning this incident. Which brings me to my next point. Why are there two sets of rules concerning outside programs. One seems to be for the Jewish inmates and the rest for everyone else. How is it that I was able to enter the institution the very same week that I was told that I was barred to attend the NAACP Crime Prevention Program, without clearence. In fact, I was told that only our group has had to comply with these "special' rules and regulations. It seems very strange that only after the question arose as to this difference of treatment to our group that attempt was made to have the same restrictions for everyone.

I find it almost ridiculous that over a span of over five years that the 'charges' against me are such as, bringing tomatoe plants that were personally cleared by YOUR prison priest. Might I ask how I could smuggle in seventy-five tomatoe plants into the prison? On the night in question, it took the priest, three guards and myself to carry them into the prison. As far as the greeting cards, I believe they were Passover and Jewish New Year cards that were personally requested by the prison priest, first Caine and the Ohndall. It was expensive to supply them, I paid for them out of my pocket. However, I felt that I could not turn down the request of the men that was given via the priest and, complied.

2. I have no idea as to what you are refering to in regard to Bud Culligan, and, wish that you would be more specific.

3. As far as gifts, they sent me a painting, a very bad one, for my birthday. I was unaware that this was such an infraction of the rules and am sending it back to you. I do hope that you will return it to the men in the Jewish Discussion group with the explaination as to why I was not keeping it.

Now, as far as the last 'serious' infraction. I brought the camera only to take a picture of Julian Bond to be reprinted in the Jewish Press. I had no intention nor have I ever taken a camera inside the institution gates. In fact, that very same evening then Senator Bond was unfortunately refered to as an " Political Undesirable' I had called the prison priest, Ohndall and requested (for the second time that week) to bring into the group a tape recorder so that I might record his discussion on the Bakke decision. Incidentially, it is a Jewish subject, and I intended to write an article on the topic for the Jewish Press. It is interesting to note that on not one, but two occasions, father Ohndall gave his most gracious permission to bring it in.

As far as my personality conflict with the 'very good and able men who seem to have suffered the unwarranted attacks upon their professional and competent persons" I hope by now their sensitive souls have recovered, and that close scrutiny of their, and your households via these various investigation's uncovers nothing more 'serious' than my tomatoe plants. I must admit though that that through the years of seeing injustice and imcompetence that there have been times when my patience as a taxpayer was taxed. I do hope that you, as a man of the cloth will do whatever possible to change the attitude the men who work in these type jobs have. That of being their very own G-d image. Of course you realize that penal work, like anyother civil servant positions are paid by taxpayers such as myself.

I am distressed to hear that you feel that the content of the Wednesday discussion groups, led by me have been lacking in Jewish content. I am most interested to know on what you base this accusation since we have always had a very lively and interesting JEWISH DISCUSSION. My guest always had much to offer in their knowledge of our " faith heritage of enormous respect among us all." It would have been nice if you would have been available during your tenure there to see fit to let us meet with you to discuss this program. How dare you state that I took the program far afield from it's intent and purpose ! Since neither you nor your staff ever attended these meetings, what do you base this decision on?

Our Jewish Discussion group was not the Bible study class that your clergy felt it should be. Jewish discussion was and is just that. Every meeting was attended by the various leaders in our community, that brought in educational Jewish programs. Incidentally, I am well aware of Jewish leadership. I am presently the president of Technion. A Jewish womans organization in Atlanta of several hundred members. Last year I served as the first female vice-president of any synagogue in Atlanta, while my husband was the president of our congregation of almost eight hundred families. During this time I served as vice-president of Woman's American ORT, and on the boards of the Jewish Community Center, Bureau of Jewish Education, Hadassah, Adult Education committee, and the Children's committee at the Community Center. And, those are only the Jewish organizations that I've listed. In fact, I first entered the institution when my husband who, at the time was Worshipful Master of his Masonic lodge was invited to speak. He also was the founder and first president of the Synagogue Council of Atlanta. My family is among the founder's of the Jewish community in this city and at one time or another has either founded or served as president of every Jewish organization or synagogue here. So, I think that I am better versed to know Jewish program better than your prison priest!

As you stated, there are many other avenues of volunteer service to provide me with the rich and rewarding satisfaction for my personal interest. I feel sure with the wide realm of friends that I have in many fields that it shouldn't be too difficult to continue in the very rewarding one of prison reform. In fact, I'm finding it almost easier from the outside, without the fear of "not making waves" by keeping quiet about the injustice I have seen. You just might have done the men, and me a service.

I hope your investigation goes well and uncovers the core of the problems besetting you and your able staff. I do have one suggestion to make however, As you know, the appointment for the "independent investigative committee" and myself to meet was made from your office through your personal secretary. Even though we were to meet in Congressman Fowler's office. I can see how that might seem a tad intimidating to someone who would want to give testimony about staff and they had a relative inside the institution. I am sure a minister of a heritage that I have always held in such regard and have so many good friends would want to avoid even the appearance of evil.

      Sincerely yours,

      Arlene G Peck

P S I must have been doing something right as according to you, I have outlasted " three chaplains, two Rabbi's, two associate wardens of programs and now, two wardens: I feel thankful that during all this time that no one was paying my salary, as I feel quite certain that you would have had me fired long ago.

May 18th, 1978

Dear Warden Hanberry,

I am most happy that you finally saw fit, after several months to finally accord me the courtesy of an explanation, although somewhat untrue, as to why I have been barred from the Jewish Discussion Group. It is most unfortunate that you extended me this explanation only after Congressmen's Elliott Levitias, Wyche Fowler, Senator's Talmedge and I believe Sam Nunn's office wrote or called requesting the reason. Not to mention the lawyer, Dennis Seigle, who also requested a reason as to why. He wanted it for his files on the discrimination case that the men are planning concerning this incident. Which brings me to my next point. Why are there two sets of rules concerning outside programs. One seems to be for the Jewish inmates and the rest for everyone else. How is it that I was able to enter the institution the very same week that I was told that I was barred to attend the NAACP Crime Prevention Program, without clearence. In fact, I was told that only our group has had to comply with these "special' rules and regulations. It seems very strange that only after the question arose as to this difference of treatment to our group that attempt was made to have the same restrictions for everyone.

I find it almost ridiculous that over a span of over five years that the 'charges' against me are such as, bringing tomatoe plants that were personally cleared by YOUR prison priest. Might I ask how I could smuggle in seventy-five tomatoe plants into the prison? On the night in question, it took the priest, three guards and myself to carry them into the prison. As far as the greeting cards, I believe they were Passover and Jewish New Year cards that were personally requested by the prison priest, first Caine and the Ohndall. It was expensive to supply them, I paid for them out of my pocket. However, I felt that I could not turn down the request of the men that was given via the priest and, complied.

2. I have no idea as to what you are refering to in regard to Bud Culligan, and, wish that you would be more specific.

3. As far as gifts, they sent me a painting, a very bad one, for my birthday. I was unaware that this was such an infraction of the rules and am sending it back to you. I do hope that you will return it to the men in the Jewish Discussion group with the explaination as to why I was not keeping it.

Now, as far as the last 'serious' infraction. I brought the camera only to take a picture of Julian Bond to be reprinted in the Jewish Press. I had no intention nor have I ever taken a camera inside the institution gates. In fact, that very same evening then Senator Bond was unfortunately refered to as an " Political Undesirable' I had called the prison priest, Ohndall and requested (for the second time that week) to bring into the group a tape recorder so that I might record his discussion on the Bakke decision. Incidentially, it is a Jewish subject, and I intended to write an article on the topic for the Jewish Press. It is interesting to note that on not one, but two occasions, father Ohndall gave his most gracious permission to bring it in.

As far as my personality conflict with the 'very good and able men who seem to have suffered the unwarranted attacks upon their professional and competent persons" I hope by now their sensitive souls have recovered, and that close scrutiny of their, and your households via these various investigation's uncovere nothing more 'serious' than my tomatoe plants. I must admit though that that through the years of seeing injustice and incompetence that there have been times when my patience as a taxpayer was taxed. I do hope that you, as a man of the cloth will do whatever possible to change the attitude the men who work in these type jobs have. That of being their very own 'G-d image. Of course you realize that penal work, like anyother civil servant positions are paid by taxpayers such as myself.

I am distressed to hear that you feel that the content of the Wednesday discussion groups, led by me have been lacking in Jewish content. I am most interested to know on what you base this accusation since we have always had a very lively and interesting JEWISH DISCUSSION. My guest always had much to offer in their knowledge of our " faith heritage of enormous respect among us all." It would have been nice if you would have been available during your tenure there to see fit to let us meet with you to discuss this program. How dare you state that I took the program far afield from it's intent and purpose ! Since neither you nor your staff ever attended these meetings, what do you base this decision on?

Our Jewish Discussion group was not the Bible study class that your clergy felt it should be. Jewish discussion was and is just that. Every meeting was attended by the various leaders in our community, that brought in educational Jewish programs. Incidentally, I am well aware of Jewish leadership. I am presently the president of Technion. A Jewish womans organization in Atlanta of several hundred members. Last year I served as the first female vice-president of any synagogue in Atlanta, while my husband was the president of our congregation of almost eight hundred families. During this time I served as vice-president of Woman's American ORT, and on the boards of the Jewish Community Center, Bureau of Jewish Education, Hadassah, Adult Education committee, and the Children's committee at the Community Center. And, those are only the Jewish organizations that I've listed. In fact, I first entered the institution when my husband who, at the time was Worshipful Master of his Masonic lodge was invited to speak. He also was the founder and first president of the Synagogue Council of Atlanta. My family is among the founder's of the Jewish community in this city and at one time or another has either founded or served as president of every Jewish organization or synagogue here. So, I think that I am better versed to know Jewish program better than your prison priest!

As you stated, there are many other avenues of volunteer service to provide me with the rich and rewarding satisfaction for my personal interest. I feel sure with the wide realm of friends that I have in many fields that it shouldn't be too difficult to continue in the very rewarding one of prison reform. In fact, I'm finding it almost easier from the outside, without the fear of "not making waves" by keeping quiet about the injustice I have seen. You just might have done the men, and me a service.

I hope your investigation goes well and uncovers the core of the problems besetting you and your able staff. I do have one suggestion to make however. As you know, the appointment for the "independent investigative committee" and myself to meet was made from your office through your personal secretary. Even though we were to meet in Congressman Fowler's office, I can see how that might seem a tad intimidating to someone who would want to give testimony about staff and they had a relative inside the institution. I am sure a minister of a heritage that I have always held in such regard and have so many good friends would want to avoid even the appearance of evil,

                Sincerely yours,

                Arlene G Peck

P S I must have been doing something right as according to you, I have outlasted " three chaplains, two Rabbi's, two associate wardens of programs and now, two wardens: I feel thankful that during all this time that no one was paying my salary, as I feel quite certain that you would have had me fired long ago.

May 18th, 1978

Dear Warden Hanberry,

I am most happy that you finally saw fit, after several months to finally accord me the courtesy of an explanation, although somewhat untrue, as to why I have been barred from the Jewish Discussion Group. It is most unfortunate that you extended me this explanation only after Congressmen's Elliott Levitias, Wyche Fowler, Senator's Talmedge and I believe Sam Nunn's office wrote or called requesting the reason. Not to mention the lawyer, Dennis Seigle, who also requested a reason as to why. He wanted it for his files on the discrimination case that the men are planning concerning this incident. Which brings me to my next point. Why are there two sets of rules concerning outside programs. One seems to be for the Jewish inmates and the rest for everyone else. How is it that I was able to enter the institution the very same week that I was told that I was barred to attend the NAACP Crime Prevention Program, without clearence. In fact, I was told that only our group has had to comply with these "special' rules and regulations, It seems very strange that only after the question arose as to this difference of treatment to our group that attempt was made to have the same restrictions for everyone.

I find it almost ridiculous that over a span of over five years that the 'charges' against me are such as, bringing tomatoe plants that were personally cleared by YOUR prison priest. Might I ask how I could smuggle in seventy-five tomatoe plants into the prison? On the night in question, it took the priest, three guards and myself to carry them into the prison. As far as the greeting cards, I believe they were Passover and Jewish New Year cards that were personally requested by the prison priest, first Caine and the Ohndall. It was expensive to supply them, I paid for them out of my pocket. However, I felt that I could not turn down the request of the men that was given via the priest and, complied.

2. I have no idea as to what you are refering to in regard to Bud Culligan, and, wish that you would be more specific.

3. As far as gifts, they sent me a painting, , for my birthday. I was unaware that this was such an infraction of the rules and am sending it back to you. I do hope that you will return it to the men in the Jewish Discussion group with the explaination as to why I was not keeping it.

1656 Lenox Road, N.E.
Atlanta, Georgia 30306
May 19, 1978

Jack A. Hanberry, Warden
United States Penitentiary
Atlanta, Georgia 30315

Dear Warden Hanberry:

    I am most happy that you finally saw fit, after several months, to finally accord me the courtesy of an explanation, although somewhat untrue, as to why I have been barred from the Jewish Discussion Group." It is most unfortunate that you extended me this explanation only after Congressmen Elliott Levitas, Wyche Fowler, Senators Talmadge and, I believe, Sam Nunn's office wrote or called requesting the reason. Not to mention the lawyer, Dennis Seigle, who also requested a reason as to why. He wanted it for his files on the discrimination case the men are planning concerning this incident. Which brings me to my next point - why are there two sets of rules concerning outside programs? One seems to be for the Jewish inmates and the other for everyone else. How is it that I was able to enter the institution the very same week that I was told I was barred, to attend the NAACP Crime Prevention Program, without clearance? In fact, I was told that only our group has had to comply with these "special" rules and regulations. It seems very strange that only after the question arose as to this difference of treatment to our group that an attempt was made to have the same restrictions for everyone.

    I must have been doing something right as, according to you, I have outlasted "three Chaplains, two Rabbis, two Associate Wardens of Programs and, now, two Wardens. I feel thankful that during all this time no one was paying me a salary, as I feel quite certain that you would have had me fired long ago. I also find it almost ridiculous that over a span of over five years that the charges against me are such as bringing in tomatoe plants which were personally cleared by YOUR prison priest. Might I ask how I could smuggle in 75 tomatoe plants? On the night in question, it took the Priest, three guards and me to carry them into the prison. As far as the greeting cards, I believe they were Passover and Jewish New Year cards that were personally requested by the prison priests - first Caine, then Ohndall. It was expensive to supply them and I paid for them out of my own pocket. However, I felt that I could not turn down the request of the men that was given via the priest, and complied.

Warden Jack A. Hanberry
May 19, 1978, Page Two

2. I have no idea as to what you are referring to in regard to Bud Culligan and wish you would be more specific.

3. As far as gifts, they sent me a painting for my birthday. I was unaware that this was such an infraction of the rules and am sending it back to you. I do hope that you will return it to the men in the Jewish Discussion Group with an explanation as to why I cannot keep it.

Now, as far as the last "serious" infraction -- I brought the camera only to take a picture of Julian Bond to be reprinted in the Jewish Press. I had no intention nor have I ever taken a camera inside the institution gates. In fact, the very same evening that Senator Bond was unfortunately referred to as a "Political Undesirable", I had called the prison priest, Ohndall, and requested (for the second time that week) to bring into the group a tape recorder so that I might record his discussion on the Bakke decision. Incidentally, this is a Jewish subject, and I intended to write an article on the topic for the Jewish Press. It is interesting to note that on not one, but two occasions, Father Ohndall gave his most gracious permission to bring it in.

As far as my personality conflict with the "very good and able men who seem to have suffered the unwarranted attacks upon their professional and competent persons", I hope by now their sensitive souls have recovered and that close scrutiny of their, and your, households via these various investigations uncovers nothing more "serious" than my tomatoe plants. I must admit though that through the years of seeing injustice and incompetence there have been many times when my patience as a taxpayer was taxed. I do hope that you will do whatever possible to change the attitudes of the men who work in these type jobs. Of course, you realize that penal work, like any other civil servant positions are paid by taxpayers such as myself.

I am distressed to hear that you feel that the content of the Wednesday discussion groups led by me have been lacking in Jewish content. I am most interested to know on what you base this accusation, since we have always had a very lively and interesting JEWISH DISCUSSION. My guests always had much to offer in their knowledge of our faith. It would have been nice if you would have been available during your tenure there to see fit to let us meet with you to discuss this program. How dare you state that I took the program far afield from its intent and purpose! Since neither you nor your staff ever attended these meetings, what do you base this decision on?

Warden Jack A. Hanberry
May 19, 1978, Page Three

    Our Jewish Discussion group was not the Bible study class that your clergy felt it should be. Jewish discussion was and is just that. Every meeting was attended by the various leaders in our community, who brought in educational Jewish programs. Incidentally, I am well aware of Jewish leadership. I am presently the president of Technion, a Jewish women's organization in Atlanta of several hundred members. Last year I served as the first female vice-president of any synagogue in Atlanta, while my husband was the president of our congregation of almost 800 families. During this time I served as vice-president of Woman's American ORT, and on the boards of the Jewish Community Center, Bureau of Jewish Education, Hadassah, Adult Education committee, and the Children's committee at the Community Center. And, those are only the Jewish organizations that I've listed. In fact, I first entered the institution when my husband who at the time was Worshipful Master of his Masonic lodge, was invited to speak. He also was the founder and first president of the Synagogue Council of Atlanta. My family is among the founders of the Jewish community in this city and at one time or another has either founded or served as president of every Jewish organization or synagogue here. So, I think I am better versed to know Jewish programs better than your prison priest!

    As you stated, there are many other avenues of volunteer service to provide me with the rich and rewarding satisfaction for my person interest. I feel sure with the wide realm of friends that I have in many fields, that it shouldn't be too difficult to continue in the very rewarding one of prison reform. In fact, I'm finding it almost easier from the outside, without the fear of "not making waves" by having to keep quiet about the injustices I have seen. You just might have done the men, and me, a service.

    I hope your investigation goes well and uncovers the core of the problems besetting you and your able staff. I do have one suggestion to make, however. As you know, the appointment for me to meet with the "independent investigative committee" was made from your office through your personal secretary. Even though we were to meet in Congressman Fowler's office, I can see how that might have been a tad intimidating to someone wanting to give testimony about staff if they had a relative in the institution.

                                 Sincerely yours,

                                 Arlene G. Peck

P.S. Are you aware of the very positive results and programs that are in the prison and a direct result of my Wednesday evening guests? For example, the ongoing salesmen's club, taught by Mr. Seigle at no charge and the Astrology class taught by Mrs. Bunsten, also free, that the men seemed to enjoy very much. It is a shame that Father Ohndall decided to cancel it.

cc: Congressman Levitas, Congressman Fowler, Senator Talmadge, Senator Nunn, Rabbi Shlomo Bluming, Norman Carlson

Sir, Mrs Arlene Peck has - for some years - provided the Jewish prisoner with a two hour relief (each week) from the horror and hell of these great cell houses. Many men from many faiths attend these meetings and find that these two hours-by far-outweigh the hundred and sixty-six left in the week.

Sir, I respectfully ask of you; is it just and right that a lower echelon member of a bureaucracy should demand a servile and obsequious passivism from those with whom he (the bureaucrat) condescends to <u>tolerate</u> dialogue?

Honorable Senator Nunn, Mrs. Peck is a zealous advocate of prison reform - reform within the frame-work of the great Constitution of the United States of America. Honorable Sir, I submit that Mrs. Peck is being deprived of her rights to pursue this worthy and just cause. I submit that she is the victim of the eflated ego of lower echelon bureaucrats who trimble under the role of thier self-imposed low profile.

Honorable Sir, I submit that Mrs. Peck is the victim of men who have abdicated their responsible positions (positions which demand solutions to grave social problems), but remain on the government payroll; I submit to you, Honorable Senator Nunn, that these bureaucrats fear any personality who may have the boldness to confront and confound a system that provides payrolls for its members, but looses the product for which the payroll was appropriated.

Sir, all that I have written is not intended to indicate that Mrs. Peck has-in any way- interposed her will or personal convictions into the orderly administration of this prison; but I do emphasize that she has given her time and love to a group of men who, if they are ever to be productive citizens in a highly competitive society, need her, her love, and the knowledge of love that she imparts.

Honorable Senator Nunn, as the president of Temple Yaakov, and as president of the Wednesday evening Jewish Cultural Discussion Group, I humbly ask for your help in this matter. Arlene Peck has - at the behest of neandorthal emotions on the part of this bureaucracy - become 'persona non grata'. I, and my men, believe you to be a just and discerning man of the people; therefore, we believe you can bring Arlene Peck back to us. Sir, my boys need Mrs. Peck.

Respectfully and Sincerely Yours,

Jacob Stern Nance

Jacob Stern Nance
President-Temple Yaakov
Shalom

Appendix II

The Articles

Hanberry Hearing Delayed Again

By Gail Epstein
Constitution Staff Writer

A preliminary hearing in Atlanta Municipal Court for U.S. Penitentiary Warden Jack Hanberry, who is charged with shoplifting, was postponed a second time Tuesday, until Oct. 27, at the request of his attorney.

Also Tuesday, a federal prison official confirmed that Hanberry has been suspended with pay until an internal investigation of the incident with which he is charged is completed.

Hanberry was arrested Sept. 27 after a security guard in a southeast Atlanta supermarket allegedly saw the warden take a hairbrush from its package and place it in his pocket.

Gary McCune, regional director of the Federal Bureau of Prisons, confirmed that Hanberry was placed on "non-duty status with pay" on Oct. 2 and said Associate Warden Pete Carlson is now acting warden.

"Hanberry has not been to the prison since Oct. 2," McCune said, adding that the Bureau of Prisons began its investigation Sept. 28, the same day that Hanberry's hearing first was delayed.

"The present action is not disciplinary action," McCune said. "It's common practice where there's been allegations of wrongdoing."

McCune said the Office of Professional Responsibility of the U.S. Attorney General's Office is conducting the investigation.

After his first scheduled court appearance was delayed, Hanberry told reporters the charges resulted from "a ghastly and bizarre mistake." A friend said Hanberry had told him the mistake arose when he compared the brush offered by the store to one he had purchased in another store.

"I have no doubt that after all the facts are out," he said, "I will be exonerated."

Prison
It's a nice place to visit, but...

by Arlene Peck

For the past four years I have been chairperson of the Atlanta Bureau of Jewish Education Discussion Group at the U.S. Federal Penitentiary, Atlanta. Throughout the years there have been many wonderful concerned Atlantans who have become a part of this program. Their first reaction was typical when I would ask them to attend one of our Wednesday evenings. "What! Jewish prisoners? There couldn't be." "Jewish inmates in a Maximum Security Prison? I don't believe it!"

These new participants might have gone into the place with misgivings or curiosity but, after they spent an evening with the group, most requested to have their names put on my list for return visits. Once they saw the need for a Jewish educational program "in a place like that" and the void that the visits from the Jewish community filled, they learned the real meaning of "mitzva."

The Atlanta Bureau of Jewish Education believes that a man can be a Jack the Ripper, but there are certain rights that he is entitled to and among those are religion and the right to practice, discuss, question and learn! The need during this time of incarceration seems to be greater, and by a program such as this, it has been fulfilled.

Rabbi Shlomo Bluming of the Atlanta Chabad Center is the Jewish chaplain and ably conducts services on Sunday mornings for the men. And, although proselytizing and converting aren't our bag, it has evolved that Sundays are for saving the soul and Wednesday evenings for stimulating the mind.

Arlene Peck (center) visits Atlanta Federal Penitentiary with Entebee hijack victims Janet and Ezra Almog.

Although an average of sixty men attend the weekly sessions, only twenty to twenty-five of the men in the institution of approximately twenty-five hundred are Jewish. Most of the others joined the group out of curiosity, stayed and then returned. For many of these men it was their first encounter with Jews and it has been wonderful to see that these evenings have been ones of good "vibes." Their interest in our Jewish culture has been great and important questions have been answered. It is difficult for anti-Semitism to arise when differences are discussed and education is stressed.

Last year, Andy Andraovitz, who at the time was a ringmaster on WRNG radio, and I spent several days touring the local state prisons. We were interested in finding out how many Jewish inmates were in them and if a program such as this was needed on the state level. We visited the women's prison, geriatric, (yes, there really is one), and juvenile institutions, and were delighted to learn that none of these had one Jewish inmate. We did find a Jewish warden with an Italian name at one of the prisons.

So, it did reaffirm my feelings that it's not very Jewish to be in jail, but for those that are there, the Atlanta Bureau of Jewish Education's program serves a definite need. These men need a link with the outside Jewish community. Thanks to the many people who year in and year out have graciously given their time to go into the prison with me this need has been filled.

Friday, March 3, 1978　The Atlanta Journal　3-C

KIDNAPPER WILLIAM WILLIAMS 'CONVERTED'
Prison Seminars Changed His Views

REG MURPHY CASE
Kidnapper Claims Outlook Changed

By RON TAYLOR

William A.H. Williams, convicted kidnapper of former Atlanta Constitution editor Reg Murphy, apparently has undergone a conversion inside the U.S. Penitentiary here.

In a letter, Williams, known as an avowed anti-Semite, says he no longer hates Jews and now attends a weekly seminar sponsored by the Atlanta Bureau of Jewish Education.

The letter was sent to Leon H. Spotts, executive director of the bureau. Mrs. Arlene Peck, who operates the bureau's prison seminars, confirmed Williams sent the letter.

Williams writes that "I was a devout and confirmed anti-Semite and as such my views and opinions of the Jewish 'problem' were similar in nature to those espoused by Hitler."

However, he adds, "at this particular point in my life I can honestly say that I am deeply ashamed of my formerly held views against the Jewish people."

Williams, who is serving a 40-year sentence for extorting $700,000 from Atlanta Newspapers as ransom in the kidnapping of Murphy, now publisher of the San Francisco Examiner, writes that he joined the discussion group "out of sheer boredom and not without cynicism."

But, he says, "my feelings were slowly changed and before long I found myself looking forward to those meetings with much hope and anticipation."

He says Mrs. Peck is "directly responsible for changing my former views. Without her present policy of open-house discussions I would still be an anti-Semite."

Mrs. Peck has been operating the program, held every Wednesday night inside the walls, for about five years. She says Williams, a high school drop-out, is now taking college courses at the prison.

A Lilburn, Ga., sheetrock contractor, Williams was first convicted in 1974. But that 40-year sentence was overturned on appeal. He was convicted in a second trial in 1976 in Key West, Fla., after attorneys got a change of venue from Atlanta, and was sentenced then to 40 years.

The Southern Israelite

The Weekly Newspaper For Southern Jewry
Our 54th Year

VOL. LIV — Atlanta, Georgia, Friday, March 31, 1978 — NO. 13

Jewish group leaders barred
Prison program in jeopardy?

by Vida Goldgar

Others are trying to get out of prison. Arlene Peck is trying to get in. Or back in, to be more accurate.

Barred "indefinitely" earlier this month from attending the regular Wednesday night Jewish discussion group she has led for the past five years for inmates at the U.S. Penitentiary in Atlanta, Mrs. Peck has enlisted widespread support in and out of the Jewish community (and in and out of the penitentiary) in her efforts to get reinstated. The discussion group is sponsored by the Bureau of Jewish Education.

The controversy erupted early this month when Mrs. Peck invited State Sen. Julian Bond, his aide, and an off-duty television news reporter to join her and other regular volunteers for the Wednesday night discussion. Penitentiary officials refused admission to Bond, his aide and the reporter, claiming Mrs. Peck had violated regulations by not giving written notice in advance that Bond was coming. The reason given was that Bond posed a security risk.

Admitting that she had not submitted the names in writing, Mrs. Peck insists that she received verbal permission by telephone, a procedure she says she often followed in the past.

A prison spokesman, William Noonan, executive assistant to warden Jack Hanberry, disagrees. Noonan told The Southern Israelite Mrs. Peck called when neither of the regular chaplains was available and gave the message to an assistant chaplain who was not authorized to grant permission. Mrs. Peck denies this.

Noonan's explanation of the refusal to admit Sen. Bond was that because Bond is a celebrity, word of his presence would circulate among prisoners not part of the regular Jewish Discussion Group who would want to crowd into the small area. This situation could be "potentially explosive in a prison setting," Noonan said, and would require extra security "not available on such short notice."

Claiming discrimination, both against Bond and the Jewish Discussion Group, Mrs. Peck objected strongly at the time to the prison's refusal to admit Bond and the others. A memo from the duty officer, quoted by Noonan, says he emphatically told Mrs. Peck she and the regular visitors could come in without Bond, his aide and the reporter (who was present as a private citizen but was felt by officials to be a minor security risk as well). This alternative was unacceptable to the group and they left.

Leon Spotts, director of the sponsoring Bureau of Jewish Education, received word from the penitentiary the next day that Mrs. Peck had been barred indefinitely, along with Andy Androvich and Timi Silver, both regular volunteers who were present at the confrontation.

Androvich this week said he telephoned assistant warden Dick Witkowski after the incident. According to Androvich,

See Prison, Page 26.

Continued from page 1

Witkowski told him: "Let sleeping dogs lie. Sleeping dogs have a great tendency to forget, but if you keep irritating the dog, the dog will keep snapping."

Arlene Peck apparently has no intention of "letting sleeping dogs lie." She, Andreovich and others allege that the action by the prison officials is "arbitrary, unfair, and an attempt to kill the program."

This issue has become something of a *cause celebre*, prompting newspaper and television coverage, inquiries by Congressman Wyche Fowler, and talk of a lawsuit by the prisoners themselves.

Spotts, who also asked prison officials to reconsider, said in a telephone interview, "They felt from their standpoint there had been a significant violation of their procedure and they could not allow Mrs. Peck to continue."

Noonan told *The Southern Israelite* that Warden Hanberry, answering a direct question about the suspension, said he "might be willing, at some later date, to reconsider, but with no guarantees."

Hanberry wanted it made clear that he and other officials have no quarrel with the program itself, pointing out that if that were the case, they always have the option to discontinue it. "We allow almost any program as long as it is of a positive nature, with good connections in the outside community, as this (the Jewish group, (certainly is, and we can fit it into the schedule."

"Why, then," Mrs. Peck asked during an interview with *The Southern Israelite*, "is this the only program that was required, even before the Bond incident, to get written permission for guests?" Noonan says this is not true but an activist in at least one other group which visits the prison on a regular basis confirms that she had often taken guests into the prison without written clearance. Now that has been changed.

Strangely, just a few days after she had been barred from the Prison, Mrs. Peck was invited to accompany an NAACP group to one of the meetings they hold there, without having her name submitted in writing or otherwise. She was not denied admission. Noonan says this was because the staff sponsor for that program though unaware of her suspension, recognized her and didn't want to cause her embarrassment. Mrs. Peck disagrees.

While many of those involved agree there is a "personality conflict" between Mrs. Peck and penitentiary officials (Dr. Spotts admits there were previous complaints about her from the prison), it is also a concensus that she is the "backbone" of the very successful program.

Mrs. Peck apparently pursues her goals in a somewhat unorthodox, possibly controversial, manner. She is outspoken and determined. But she appears dedicated to the program and intends to continue helping behind the scenes as other volunteers troop out to the gray stone complex on McDonough Blvd. on Wednesday evening, doing their best to carry on. Whether the program will continue without its long-time leader remains a question in many minds. But Arlene Peck hasn't stopped fighting.

THE ATLANTA CONSTITUTION

For 109 Years the South's Standard Newspaper

James M. Cox, Chairman 1950-1957 — James M. Cox Jr. Chairman 1957-1974

Jack Tarver	Tom Wood	Hal Gulliver	Edward Sears
Publisher	President	Editor	Managing Editor

PAGE 4-A, TUESDAY, MAY 16, 1978

Jack Anderson
A Horrible Look Inside The Big A

WASHINGTON — Like the Germans who pretended not to know what was happening in Adolf Hitler's concentration camps, many Americans would also prefer to close their eyes to conditions in the nation's teeming, tumultuous prisons.

We have smuggled reporters, therefore, into some of America's most forbidding prisons to bring out the story. First, Terry Repak managed to slip into the maximum security Clinton Correctional Facility in rural New York. Then Hal Berston spent a few days in the tense, cramped barracks of Mississippi's Parchman prison camp.

Now we have sent Jack Mitchell into one of the worst of the federal prisons. With the help of inside contacts, we slipped inside the Atlanta penitentiary, a great, gray-green concrete compound that the inmates call the "Big A." Nine inmates have been murdered there in 16 months. Mitchell tried to find out why.

All three of our reporters found prison conditions intolerable. The Constitution guarantees that prisoners will not be subjected to cruel and unusual punishment. Yet they are in daily danger of being raped, abused, beaten and murdered. The guards, who are supposed to protect the prisoners from abuse, sometimes contribute to it. Thus in many U.S. prisons, a sentence becomes cruel and unusual punishment.

Inside the Big A, Mitchell met with a dozen inmates, without the knowledge or consent of prison officials. He heard ugly tales of human rights violations in Jimmy Carter's own backyard. One inmate after another, whispering in hushed tones, related a host of abuses. As one inmate phrased it, the Big A is the "toilet bowl of society."

Sexual pressure is so intense, for example, that many inmates are forced to pay other prisoners for protection against the sexual advances of "daddies" on the prowl for new partners. There are many brutal rapes.

Inmates who have appealed for protection said they are advised to procure homemade weapons. Most prisoners conceal shivs or blunt clubs, which have become essential for simple survival. An inmate never knows when one of the borderline psychopaths in the prison population will turn on him without warning or provocation.

Within the massive green walls, more than 2,200 sullen inmates are crowded in dank, musty cellblocks. The harassment and tension lead to frequent fights, which sometimes end in fatalities.

Inmates who are unpopular with prison officials allegedly are subjected to psychological torture. Their visiting rights, personal phone calls or parole hearings may be withheld or delayed. One inmate, whose mother was critically ill, was told cruelly that he could appear either at the woman's deathbed or her funeral. But the prison paperwork was dragged out and the inmate reached his mother's bedside scant moments before her death.

All the inmates complained about the medical care, which they said was amateurish. One physician, who has just been removed from surgical duties, was known among the prisoners by the derisive nickname "Dr. Shaky." Prison medical records were smuggled out to us as evidence that several inmates had received improper or haphazard medical treatment.

Without exception, the inmates who were interviewed complained about arbitrary furlough policies. Of the 35,000 federal furloughs last year, relatively few were granted to Atlanta inmates. "Why should a big-name crook like (former attorney general) John Mitchell be out of prison on a medical furlough and not me?" groused one prisoner. He claimed his knee needed an operation that couldn't be performed inside the prison.

Both black and white inmates agreed there is little racial animosity inside the walls. Black organizations seem to have constant access to the prison, perhaps because more than 40 percent of the inmates are black. But a Jewish discussion group, led by prison activist Arlene Peck, has run into repeated resistance from officials.

It has been suggested that a society can be judged by its prisons. By that moral yardstick, American society is sick to the soul.

Footnote: The complaints about conditions inside the Atlanta pen, of course, came from inmates with axes to grind. But inmates, interviewed separately, told the same basic stories. We have also spoken to prison social workers and lawyers, who confirmed the complaints of the prisoners.

Warden Jack Hanberry explained in a lengthy interview that his staff is "overtaxed and overworked." He denied that his subordinates harass inmates or that the tension is worsening inside his prison. He conceded that he has heard complaints about lax medical care but said a new system of daily medical appointments should improve the situation.

'Polish Princess' Mobbed By 200 Mad Prisoners

Despite all the attention that has been focused on the Atlanta Penitentiary in the last few weeks, not much real information has come out of there. Statistics about overcrowding and murders paint the outline, but it's in the day to day events that the real spirit of the place emerges.

One such event was the annual horse show on April 2. And what it showed is the hatred some of the inmates have for a few of the men at top.

According to an insider, as the horse show got underway assistant warden Dick Witkowski, nicknamed the "Polish Princess" by the inmates, collared a man and accused him of being drunk. He called in two guards and told them to take the inmate back to his cell.

The inmate didn't care for that and jumped Witkowski.

Before the guards could move in Witkowski and the inmate had been surrounded by some 200 other prisoners who were eager to see the assistant warden taken down a notch. Witkowski had been on the wrong side of some unpopular actions lately, among them his interference with a successful Jewish discussion group (NRI 3/31). Even on his best days Witkowski is not too popular, and April 2 was not one of his best days.

It took only a few minutes for the guards to get through the mob of inmates, but by that time Witkowski had already been roughed up. The prisoner the assistant warden had pointed to as drunk was dragged off to his cell along with some inmates who had allegedly joined in the attack. Prison officials have been mum about the encounter, claiming that until they decide whether or not to put out a press release on it they can reveal no information.

Going to Jail

Arlene Peck would like to get into prison. In particular, she would like to get into the Atlanta penitentiary. But because of a conflict outside the gates earlier this month the five year leader of a Jewish discussion group among inmates has been barred from the institution.

The problem arose when Peck tried to get state Senator Julian Bond into one of her Wednesday night discussion groups to talk about the N.A.A.C.P's reaction to the Bakke "reverse discrimination" case now before the Supreme Court. Prison policy requires that names of people wanting to enter be submitted in writing to prison officials two weeks in advance. Peck admits that she had not sent in Bond's name, but claims that in the past she had been able to get oral approval for guests up to a week beforehand. That's what she did with Bond, calling three times to make certain he and a tape recorder Peck planned to carry would be allowed. Still, when she, Bond, WAGA-5 reporter Barbara Nevins (attending as a private citizen), Timi Silver and Tom Houck arrived they were told Bond would not be let in. Cited as a reason was the lack of two week's written notice and insufficient security to protect the state senator.

Within a few days after Bond was turned away, Peck says she was contacted and told she wouldn't be allowed back into the prison, guests or no guests. Though the Bond incident was given as the reason, Peck is certain prison officials were bothered by the success of her discussion group. Weekly attendance had risen to 60, though only 20 to 25 of the inmates are Jewish. People familiar with the program agree Peck was the main reason it worked, and that there was little love lost between her and the prison administration.

Since her banning Peck has contacted Congressman Wyche Fowler to see if he can't work out a way for her to return. Bond complained to Fowler after he was denied entrance, and Fowler followed through by complaining to warden Jack Hanberry. Leon Spotts, executive director of the Jewish Education Bureau, asked the prison if Peck couldn't go in to continue her discussion program and was turned down. If she is unable to get get back in after peaceful discussion, Peck has indicated she may take the prison to court. For now her discussion group is being continued by helpers, but nobody is certain how long it can stay successful without her presence.

Prisoners Had Plans To Escape From Bus

By Tyrone D. Terry
Constitution Staff Writer

Prisoners bused from the Atlanta Penitentiary last April planned to escape during their trip to the U.S. prison in Lewisburg, Pa. by freeing themselves from handcuffs with home-made keys, a federal Bureau of Prisons official said Monday.

The 60 prisoners were part of a group of 92 inmates transferred from the Atlanta prison to federal facilities throughout the nation in an effort to stem murders and other acts of violence at the Atlanta pen.

But a spokesman for the American Civil Liberties Union (ACLU) charged that guards at the Lewisburg federal prison made the handcuffed and chained inmates march between two lines of guards, then beat the prisoners with pickaxe handles.

"They hit these men in the head, neck and back and many of the prisoners were in handcuffs, waist chains and leg irons," said Roberta Messalle, legislative liaison officer for the ACLU's National Prison Project.

The Justice Department is investigating complaints of brutality made by 35 inmates in affidavits given to the ACLU. A Justice Department spokesman said the FBI will be asked to investigate the complaints if there are any "unresolved" questions.

Michael Aun, a Bureau of Prisons spokesman, argued Monday that there wasn't "a shred of evidence" that guards had beaten the prisoners.

"They (guards) used no more force than was necessary," Aun claimed. That "force" amounted to pushing some of the inmates off the bus and into the prison after they refused to go voluntarily, Aun said.

"They were actually getting out of their handcuffs; they had home-made keys," he said.

When asked why the inmates had not escaped before they reached the prison and how many had managed to free themselves, Aun said he "can't go any further" in commenting on the case.

Meanwhile, Arlene Peck, an Atlanta prison reform activist, charged Monday that the secret Atlanta federal inmate being questioned by U.S. Sen. Sam Nunn and his Permanent Subcommittee on Investigations was ignored by U.S. Rep. Wyche Fowler, who had ordered an investigation of problems at the facility last March.

"This guy (secret inmate) was dying to give information to Fowler and he couldn't take it so he went to Nunn," said Peck, who plans to write a book about her five years of discussions with inmates at the murder-plagued prison.

Rep. Fowler had talked to Peck and directed her to committee investigators, said Betsy Weltner, the congressman's press aid.

ron hudspeth

In Dark Of Night, Beware Of 'The Duke'

Short shots around town:

A security company guard was cruising through a northwest Atlanta apartment complex the other night when he noticed a couple in intimate embrace in the parking lot.

Here was his report: "Foan! a couple undressed in an automobile in the parking lot. Ordered them out of the car, gave them a good lecture about that sort of thing and sent them on their way."

A report well handled. And why not? The security guard's name was John Wayne.

★ ★ ★

Spotted in the front yard of a wooden-frame home not far from downtown: a 30-foot flagpole sporting a Confederate flag. Nearby is a white sign reading: "If you don't vote for Stoner, you're a goner."

Loonies still live among us.

★ ★ ★

Remember the woman whose Volkswagen was sat on by an elephant while she visited the circus at the Omni a few months ago?

If so, you'll love this one.

A man visited the high-rise Peachtree Street apartment of a couple he knew only slightly. The trio planned to go out to dinner, but the visitor arrived a bit early.

"Fix yourself a drink and give us a couple minutes to finish getting dressed," said the husband of the house.

About that time, in bounced Fido with a ball in his mouth. "He won't hurt you," said the husband, "he's just playful. He wants you to throw his ball for him."

The husband disappears to the bedroom and soon the visitor is engrossed in a game of pitch and chase with Fido.

Bounce, bounce, bounce and, whamo, the ball is in Fido's mouth and Fido tears back to the visitor to play again.

The visitor makes himself another drink and the game continues with each throw getting harder and harder.

Soon, Fido is scrambling out on the balcony to grab the ball, and then, suddenly, a toss bounces over the balcony wall. Right behind it is Fido, who sails eagerly over the wall and out of the 21st-story apartment.

Shortly, the couple appear in the living room, while the horrified visitor is attempting to hide his shock.

"Are we ready?" says the husband.

"Where's Fido?" says the wife.

★ ★ ★

name of two strippers at a Memorial Day celebration for inmates at the Atlanta Federal Penitentiary is hardly anything new.

"Last year, Miss Nude America was there just as her title advertising," says my source.

Talk about a captive audience.

★ ★ ★

Is DeKalb County full of lonely people?

Well, only the lonely people really know, but if there are many, then 48-year-old Rachel Segev, who moved here from Israel recently, will be in the chips.

Rachel has opened DeKalb County's first dating service. "It took me forever to get a business license," she said. "It is fortunate my references were good."

Rachel's dating service is a bit different. She claims to be the area's "first matchmaker."

If you're single and want one, Rachel will attempt to match you up with a marriage partner. She advertises her business as a "service for marriage-oriented people seeking long-term relationships."

Rachel says she'll do extensive counseling with each of her clients.

But is there really a market, Rachel?

"Sure," she says. "Actually, there are a lot of people who simply can't bring themselves to say the magic words, 'I want to get married.'"

★ ★ ★

I hope this dastardly practice hasn't reached Atlanta, but as soon as I mention it, I fear someone will call and confirm its existence locally.

Seems the Indianapolis firm that first thought up pay locks for public toilets is now marketing a coin-operated timing valve to be attached to gas station air pumps.

For 25 cents, it will give consumers four minutes of formerly free air.

No more free air? One can only guess what's next.

About the Author

Arlene Peck is now an internationally syndicated columnist and television talk show hostess. Her celebrity interview television show: Wow! It's Arlene Peck is rated among the top ten shows on West Coast cable network. Arlene is now a weekly commentator on: "Shalom TV," the National Jewish channel. The show can be seen nationally on Comcast and Time Warner. Arlene serves as an expert on the Middle East for radio station KABC and is in high demand as a speaker in other forums. She is the queen of political incorrectness in a world awash in lies and double-talk that often passes for journalism today.

A woman who has always heard the drum of a different drummer, Arlene is a native of Atlanta, Georgia. She began college at the University of Alabama and concluded her studies at Columbia University, where she majored in Real Estate and Business Law. She currently lives in Marina Del Rey, California.

While still living in Atlanta, Arlene was one of the original twenty five members of the committee that began the Martin Luther King parade. That event is huge today.

During the early years she thought she was "pot-roast;" then came the discovery that she was actually "chateaubriand." Arlene Peck founded and was president of many Jewish organizations in that city: ORT, Friends of Technion, and Hadassah, to name a few. Along the way, she became the first female vice president of a synagogue in that city. One thing led to another and for a period of over six years she was the only woman to ever lead a discussion group at the Atlanta Federal Penitentiary.

In 1976, she traveled to Russia and was detained by the KGB for smuggling prayer books and Jewish stars into the synagogues there. Because Arlene was traveling with the Los Angeles Press Club and the Russians at that time were looking for good press coverage, she was shortly released. That led to her keeping a diary of her experiences which led to a column. Syndication followed.

In June of 1982 she spent five weeks in Israel as a journalist. She was there when the first Lebanese-Israeli war broke out and filed dozens of first hand reports of the war from Beirut and Israel. Arlene was also in Lebanon during Operation Accountability in 1993.

Arlene travels extensively worldwide. This international syndicated columnist and television talk show host has lived in Israel and socialized with many of its luminaries. Arlene is usually seen reporting on such diverse topics as political events, travel insights, openings, and must see spots. If there is a place to see and be seen, she'll write about it. Her audience is international. Arlene's weekly syndicated column is read by millions, her television show seen by millions, and she is a popular speaker.

Arlene Peck is listed in the 100 most influential Jewish women, (http://www.worldjewishnewsagency.com) and featured in magazines, such as Lifestyles, where Arlene was featured as: "Politically Incorrect and Loving it." She was dubbed as USA's brightest, most delightful and tragic-comic columnist and TV host (see *http://europeanjournal.net/most_and_the_less.htm*).

She has also written two other books, been mentioned in six others, and, on the cover of four. In November 2007, Arlene was the guest honoree at the America Truth Forum symposium: "Understanding the Threat of Radical Islamist Terrorism."

For more about this woman, check her out at www.arlenepeck.com. Or click her name on Yahoo.